Reading Hinduism

Brij Mohan Sagar

Originals

Delhi-110052

First Published 2012

ISBN 13: 978-81-8454-123-6
ISBN 10: 81-8454-123-6

Published By
Originals
A-6, Second Floor, Nimri Commercial Centre,
Ashok Vihar Phase-4, Delhi - 110 052 (India)
Tel.: +91 11 2730 2453 Fax: 011 4706 1936
website: www.Lppindia.com
e-mail: info@Lppindia.com

Printed At
D K Fine Art Press P Ltd.
Delhi-110052

PRINTED IN INDIA

Dedicated to My Son
Tojo Sagar
Who Died at Sea in 1990

Preface

We have produced a system of education in India in which students can pass through the primary class to the doctoral studies without ever studying a Hindu scripture. In this way we uproot them from their ancient tradition. This has been done in the name of secularism in order to please all religious groups, especially those who are opposed to Hindus.

Obviously it is a policy of cultivating ignorance of what makes India what it is, and of drying it up at its very roots, a continuation of the British imperial policies. As a result, a system of education was created in which generations of Indians have grown up who are called Hindus, but who do not know why they are called Hindus. They may copy some rituals done by their parents or neighbors. But that is about all. They have the name but not its substance. People who were not Hindus created their history. They destroyed their ways of living, their temples and idols, their ideals and social institutions. This tradition continues even today.

Many Hindus internalized the abuse inflicted on them by those who conquered their lands, from large areas of which they were wiped out. Many of them seem to dislike themselves and would like to be somebody else. This is considered to be an index of their modernity. They think of India as a name without a meaning. But it need not be so. India is an ancient civilization with a wisdom that can still be useful. There is no need to create a state that is alien and destructive of Hindu society.

I decided to learn about that ancient wisdom, and hopefully present a rational and comprehensive understanding of the ancient past.

I depended on a number of books listed in the bibliography. I express my gratitude to their authors for keeping the ancient traditions alive. Since I was writing a general book for voluntary pleasure reading, I did not clutter it with bibliographical references. I looked for significant ancient ideas that kept repeating through human experience, trying to understand them in contemporary idiom, and to share my understanding with others in the hope that they would find it useful.

Simplifying such a vast subject as Hinduism, the oldest spiritual tradition of the world and a possible alternative to the modern way of living of western consumerism in about four hundred pages was a difficult task and the choice of topics was sometimes arbitrary. I kept my focus largely on the main, high tradition.

I express my gratitude to all the RISHIS, GURUS and scholars who created, nourished and enlarged the spiritual heritage of India.

Perhaps a few words about me are in order. I was born in 1936 at AMRITSAR, PUNJAB, where I spent my childhood. Later I did BA (Honors), MA, and PhD in English, and retired in 1996 after working as Professor and Dean of Studies in English, and Director of the LUCKNOW Campus of the Central Institute of English and Foreign Languages, now called EFL University, HYDERABAD.

Later I did a book on SHEIKH FARID, which was published by GURU NANAK DEV University, and a book on RAVI DAS, which was published by PANJAB University.

I now offer my understanding of Hinduism to people in general in the hope that they will benefit from it.

Brij Mohan Sagar

1218, DLF Phase IV, Gurgaon-122009, INDIA

Telephone: 0124- 2386734

Contents

yourself for positive social action, in which you remain undisturbed and overflowing with your higher life, whatever your condition, in which you remain absorbed in the skills of doing actions, giving your best to social action, forgetting your personal rewards, relying on divine powers to take care of your genuine needs, aware of your being one and alone, and so on.

It narrates episodes of the story of SRI KRISHNA to bring out their contemporary significance, engagement in public and political affairs rather than escape from them, and a quality of mind, without which they become a form of personal aggrandizement.

YOGA is life of action that enters the world through high moral values and rules of living for the initiated, and physical and breathing exercises for a healthy body and relaxed mind, and withdraws from the world through control of the senses and their mind, choosing an ideal suited to ones inherited nature, and devotion to it with such concentration as to release unknown sources of energy that provide rare mystical experience of the one without a second, making living joyful.

Man is his awareness that witnesses the objective, subjective and subtle realities he experiences while he is awake, dreaming, or asleep. Cultivating awareness in some ways suggested here connects him directly to the source of cosmic energy.

It provides a rapid panoramic view of Hinduism, its ideals, aspirations and efforts, with a new understanding of the human mind and its expressions through a variety of resolves and techniques.

Chapter I

Thank You

Hindus have composed numerous scriptures over thousands of years in different parts of India for different groups of people in different contexts and for different purposes. This is a continuing process. These scriptures have guided people in peace and war.

People have different natures, capabilities, occupations, age groups, duties and aims. They need different guidelines to grow up spiritually from their initial condition in which they find themselves to their experience of divine reality in its awe-inspiring diversity and its fundamental unity.

One scripture for everyone or one final scripture till the end of time can never help anyone, except through the use of force, terror, fear, temptation and manipulation, leaving the spirit untouched or even crushed. One scripture for everyone requires destruction or conversion of those who disagree or have a different nature and experience of the divine.

Ideally everyone should have his own scripture for his spiritual guidance to suit his nature and his initial position, his circumstances and experience. As BUDDHA said: Be your own light.

Hindu scriptures are ancient. MAX MULLER calculated that the earliest Hindu scripture called RIG VEDA could not have been composed earlier than 1200 BCE. This declaration determined the later dates of all other Hindu scriptures and historical events.

THOMAS BABBINGTON MACAULAY (1800-1859) was Education Secretary of the British Imperial Government Of India. In 1836 A.D, he said that if his plans of education were implemented there would not be a single idolater left among the respectable classes in Bengal in thirty years. He employed FRIEDRICH MAX MULLER, a German Christian scholar of VEDAS to achieve his objectives. MAX MULLER used SAYANA, a Sanskrit commentator on the rituals in VEDAS to translate them. He concluded that Hinduism is dying or dead. He wrote to his wife that VEDA is the root of Hindu religion and to show them the root is the only way of uprooting all that has sprung from it in the last three thousand years.

Western scholars created the idea that there was an ARYAN race that invaded India around 1500 B.C. and destroyed the existing DRAVIDIAN civilization there. Then the ARYAN race forgot all about the wonderful towns they had just destroyed and started living in little huts in villages and composed the VEDAS, which these scholars found to be crude primitive poems of no value composed by illiterate nomads praying to unknown gods for the satisfaction of this or that desire.

This ARYAN invasion theory was created in the archetypal pattern of invasion, destruction, loot and ownership visualized in the Bible as in Deuteronomy (7.1,2), which says that when you overpower and defeat a people, you must kill them and loot them.

Sanskrit literature shows no memory of an ARYAN race invading India. According to a Sanskrit lexicon of 500 AD, the word ARYA means of a noble family, of gentle behavior, cultured, good-natured, of righteous conduct. It does not refer to any race. As a form of address, it shows respect for the person addressed and refinement of the person who speaks.

According to MANU SMRITI (X 43-45), all people are either ARYAN or NON-ARYAN. They are ARYANS if they do sacred rites and follow sages. Otherwise they gradually sink to the level of servants.

GAUTAM BUDDHA called his path ARYA path, the way to being noble. He shows no memory of any ARYANS invading India. He did not create any new separate religion antagonistic to the religion of his ancestors. Criticizing the inherited tradition and providing new insights into the spiritual experience was a fundamental function of a great spiritual leader. It was his normal and expected duty. Sometimes it even led to his being called BHAGVAN or DEVA. SRI KRISHNA too criticizes the VEDAS in the GITA. He criticizes the worship of nature and devotion to the senses, and rebels against INDRA DEVA, but gives a value to it in a hierarchy of lower and higher nature. INDRA got so angry that he rained for seven days and seven nights. But then he cooled down, controlled his anger and saw the light and honored KRISHNA with his own name, calling him GOVINDA, meaning INDRA of the earth, his cow of plenty. The Sanskrit for cow also means the earth and the rays of the sun, which give light, heat and life. It bathed KRISHNA with her milk of nourishment. This was a concrete narrative of tradition and innovation.

In XIX century A.D, Europeans took ARYA to mean a race of conquerors from a nowhere land. At least twenty different regions have been proposed as the place of origin of these people. BHAGVAN SINGH in The VEDIC HARAPPANS lists these regions as Arctic region, Baltic region, Danube basin, Central European Steppes including the Carpathian plains, Siberia, Ukrainian Steppes, lower Volga area, southern Russia, TURKMENIA, North-Western KIRGHIZ steppes, PAMIRS, Asia Minor, BACTRIA or SOGDIANA, great plateau of Central Asia, and SAPTA SINDHU area. The Indian subcontinent as a whole is never mentioned as one of the likely places of their origin.

The hypothesis of an ARYAN invasion of India was created to explain similarities between some words of Sanskrit, Greek and Latin. A simpler explanation would have been transmission of culture through trade.

SIR H. M. ELLIOT AND JOHN DOWSON'S The History Of India as told by Muslim historians who accompanied Muslim invaders describes how they delighted in the destruction of Hindu KAFARS and their temples and the immense quantities of gold and a large variety of precious stones that they looted. From where did this wealth come if not from trading with distant countries?

PUSHKAR BHATNAGAR, in his DATING THE ERA OF LORD RAM, says that SRI RAM of VALMIKI'S RAMAYANA was born on January 10, 5114 B.C. He calculates this date from the position of stars at the time of RAM'S birth and two solar eclipses and one lunar eclipse mentioned in VALMIKI'S RAMAYAN. He uses a computer program used in modern Astronomy.

RAJARAM and FRAWLEY list evidence from Astronomy. According to them, TAITTIRIYA SANHITA (6.5.3) places PLEIADES ASTERISM at winter solstice, which dates it to 8500 B.C. RIG VEDA (1.117.22, 1.116.12) says that winter solstice begins in ARIES, which dates it to 6500 B.C. They mention Professor A. SEIDENBERG, who in his Origin of Mathematics, says that the mathematics of Old Babylonia (1700 B.C.) and the mathematics of Egyptian Middle Kingdom (2050-1800 B.C.) derives from the mathematics of SULVASUTRAS, which are a part of rules for constructing altars of different shapes and sizes for different types of sacrifices for different communities and purposes. Indus valley towns, which show remains of sacrificial altars, require knowledge of mathematics as given in SULVASUTRAS for their planning and construction. It is unreasonable to say that some illiterate nomads first destroyed numerous towns and then settled down in village huts to compose the mathematics that underlies the towns they had just destroyed.

SHRIKANT TALAGERI in THE ARYAN INVASION THEORY AND INDIAN NATIONALISM presents astronomical evidence to show that the earliest RIGVEDA hymns were composed in the fifth millennium B.C. A solar eclipse mentioned in RV (V.40.5-9) is dated to July 26, 3928 B.C.

STEPHEN KNAPP in his "Death of the Aryan Invasion Theory" argues for a final burial of this theory. So do GEORG FEUERSTEIN, SIBHASH KAK & DAVID FRAWLEY in their IN SEARCH OF THE CRADDLE OF CIVILIZATION.

VEDAS took centuries to compose. Numerous people dedicated their lives to spiritual experience, experimenting with their bodies and minds and varied techniques of reaching their aim, failing or succeeding, and thinking out its individual and social implications and aims. There is a depth of living spiritual experience in their compositions full of symbols that are deeper than mere lexical words or even ideas.

Hindu scriptures consist of four VEDAS, RIG, SAM, YAJUR, AND ATHARVA, which include MANTRAS, BRAHMANAS and UPANISHADS. Then there are SUTRAS and DARSHANS; PURANS that include RAMAYANA and MAHABHARATA; TANTRAS that include SHAKTI PUJA in numerous forms; compositions of SIDDHAS, ACHARYAS, NATHS, SANTS and GURUS.

According to SHRI PANDIT JAIDEVJI SHARMA'S RIG VED SANHITA VOL I, RIG VEDA had 24 versions. YAJUR VEDA had 101 versions. SAM VEDA had 1000 versions. ATHARVA VEDA had 9 versions. There were numerous UPANISHADS and PURANS. Many of these scriptures and versions were lost. They were passed on orally from the GURU to the disciple for generations. And if some of them died without passing it on, their scripture ended there. Some of these traditions are alive in some parts of the country even today. Some of these scriptures rose into prominence, while others fell into disuse.

All scriptures everywhere are historically shaped. But what they say is outside time. New scriptures can be composed even today. Every human being has a right to compose his own scripture, his own declaration of truth as he experiences it. Once he experiences his divinity, then what he says becomes a scripture.

No Hindu could have followed all the Hindu scriptures. Those who were born earlier could not have followed the scriptures composed later. Hindus of one region did not know all the scriptures composed in distant parts of the country. They largely followed their family and neighborhood traditions. Their gurus traveled far and wide, as did their traders and pilgrims.

Many of these scriptures took a long time to compose. One could hardly have followed them in their entirety during the time they were being composed, compiled, experimented with, added to, altered or deleted, and variously interpreted by different RISHIS and their families, including their students, who followed their own selections and versions that suited and expressed their experience, which they interpreted, created or inherited. Many of these scriptures share many ideas even though they express diverse modes of being and living. Disagreement and debate is a normal feature of Hindu religious discourse. But it does not lead to killing the opponent. BUDDHA opposed many well-established ideas as did KRISHNA, and both lived to a ripe old age. Nor did they assert a uniquely separate religion, differentiating themselves from others as opposing adversaries, claiming victories, because their basic thinking was reconciliatory, not adversarial. They might even quarrel for a time, but then someone of them would reconcile and they would settle down. Sometimes doubt and debate became an occasion for contest and celebration, part of a ceremony or festival. Great scholars would sit opposite each other reinterpreting their inherited tradition in a new context and many others would sit around them to enjoy the give and take of argument and interpretation. This was often done in the presence of a king, as in the case of RAJA JANAKA, or some affluent merchants. Sometimes BRAHAMANS and SHUDRAS sat opposite each other around a fire, and one praised DEVAS, and the other questioned their very existence. Dialogue could happen even on a battlefield as in the case of BHAGVADGITA. ADI SHANKARACHARYA debated with MANDAN MISHRA at KASHI on Vedantic versus ritualistic interpretation of the Vedas. And imagine who was the judge. MANDAN MISHRA'S scholarly wife. And she declared ADI SHANKARACHARYA the victor. As late as the second half of XIX century A.D., DAYANANDA debated with three hundred pundits in the presence of MAHARAJA of KASHI before he published his SATYARTHPRAKASHA that started the movement called ARYA SAMAJ.

Some common ideas in the scriptures may be stated here briefly.

We are individuals with a body that has life, mind, joy, and an unknown immortal self. We follow customs and moral values like commands and prohibitions. We act to earn our livelihood, wealth and power and enjoy ourselves in various ways. But sometimes we get tired of enjoyments and earning money and start reflecting on our life. Are we really individuals except in the superficial sense of appearances, our height and weight for example, whereas deep down in sorrow and in joy every one is like every one else, the same? What is this sameness in diversity?

We experience the universe produced by motion. We are expressions of this universe, not in opposition to it. We are like the waves that express the sea. Is every one a food to every one else, big fish eating small fish? Is there a cycle of energy that keeps moving on, always remaining the same?

The individuals and the universe have a common source. Absolute reality sustains and supports the reality of phenomena that we experience. The wise call it by many names like the supreme self of the universe. Its nature is existence, consciousness and joy. The projective power of this absolute reality is named ISHVARA and ISHVARI. The divine power has both male and female qualities. As creator, it is called BRAHMA and SARASVATI. As preserver, it is called VISHNU and LAKSHMI. As destroyer, it is called SHIVA and KALI. When these and many more powers are seen together, it is called MAHADEVA and MAHADEVI, or MAHESHVARA and MAHESHVARI. What is projected is nature. Its elements and forces, MAHABHUTAS and DEVAS, are interrelated. Their organic interrelationship is called PURUSHA. They together make the body of PARAM ATMA, the supreme self.

Nature creates cosmic intelligence. It helps and guides every being. It works through the law of actions one expression of which is cause and effect. There are many other expressions as well, like the ideal and the path leading towards it. It operates at physical, moral, and spiritual levels. Action includes transformation, rebirth and incarnation. One being changes into another being. This change includes birth and death. To find spiritual freedom from this bondage of action and resulting actions, one has to offer one's actions and their basis in feelings and mind to the cosmic powers from where they have emerged and of which they are an expression. This incorporates death into living.

To experience spiritual freedom, rituals were created. Rituals change with time and place. They never remain constant. One can object to this or that ritual, but one has to create new rituals, as one cannot do without them, as they contribute to the creation of order in life, like our stock responses. Rituals must lead to spiritual growth and freedom from nature in a particular place and time. If they do not lead to spiritual growth and freedom from nature, they have to be given up often gradually and replaced by a new set of rituals

There are numerous truths that underlie such broad ideas. The divine power acts in many ways. These ways have names and forms. They are beings in which the divine is present. The divine is their inner controller, the power that regulates them. It is the inherent truth, the universal law. It is the unchanging support, the refuge and the mother of the changing universe.

This changing universe is conscious, divine and holy. It is one integrated whole. So is the individual self. Individuals have infinite opportunities to attain perfection. They have to manifest their innate divine nature to gain spiritual freedom. Every one is divine and the goal of life is spiritual freedom. There are many paths that lead to divinity. One should take the path best suited to him. All these paths include moral values and practical methods.

Normally Hindus went to a neighborhood Guru or their family Guru. They invited him to their house. The guru instructed them according to whatever selections, versions, and interpretations of scriptures he had acquired and tested on the basis of his own experience of dealing with life and its problems, crises and conflicts, while engaged in his own spiritual growth from a morally neutral life full of pleasure and suffering and identified with the body and its mind to a good, noble, admirable and joyful life identified with higher, deeper and vaster ideals and forces that create this marvelous universe.

Hindus have never attached final authority to any particular scripture, though they stand by the scripture they and their family follow. The final authority always rests with the spiritual reality that exists in the universe, which they seek to experience, and for which various names, ideas and methods are used. They experience this spiritual reality through UPASANA, which means being mentally near their chosen cosmic power or DEVA.

Western civilization, does not accept the idea of DEVAS, though it accepts the idea of being. Hindus however tell an incredible story of their experience.

Some years ago PASCHIM DEVA came to India. More abstractly the wise call him westernization and even modernization. He helped a princess get well. Her father was so pleased that he granted him his wish, which was a plot of land, one kilometer wide and six kilometers long in the region of MUKAMBIKA DEVI that he could use for building store houses. The king said, yes, though he was amazed at the greed of PASCHIM DEVA, trying to acquire land in his kingdom, because if a medical doctor is greedy he will either delay curing a disease or cure one disease and create another. But he did not record his surprise and so his subjective feeling never became history, though speculations of modern historians on broken pieces of old pots and pans do become history nevertheless.

Now PASCHIM DEVA built big storehouses on his land, and he acquired more lands for his storehouses in the regions of CHENNAI DEVI and KALI DEVI GHAT. His great problem was that he had nothing much to store. He had come from a cold and windy place, where nothing worthwhile ever grew, not even a blade of thought. He had looted his thought from the Greeks after abusing them as pagans and destroying their temples and supporting social institutions for a thousand years. And then he called Greek thought his very own and talked of Renaissance though truly he had no ancient learning of his own to renew. He had looted his religion from JERUSALAM though he kept modifying it in the shape of his own aggressive urges and tendencies instead of controlling his aggression in the light of BUDDHA'S compassion that had spread to that area. Luckily for him his religion was equally aggressive requiring its followers to go out and loot other lands and he did so in Americas, Australia, Canada, Africa and Asia. He had looted his empire building from the pagans of Rome, even though he kept abusing pagans all the time. He looted his wealth from everywhere. He lived on stale flesh. So he wanted to hide its smells with spices and came to India for purchasing them. He had however learnt to fight and kill others. So he helped one king kill another and got a fee for his help. Then he helped one king kill another and got an honorarium for his help. Then he helped one king kill another and became a partner in kingship. He assumed the kingly duties himself and gave security, food and sex to the other kings, who twirled their moustaches, patted their bellies and belched, living in borrowed security, and kept calling themselves kings and emperors though they had lost political power, the royal duty of protecting their people and their ways of living.

PASCHIM DEVA kept making promises to kings, which read one way meant one thing but read in another way meant a different thing. He called it the culture of words and diplomacy, though he had never cultured his aggressive urges and instincts. He produced lots of words in the form of diaries and memoirs and notes on files and saying different things in the same words and the same things in different words. He overwhelmed them all with his words and aggression and became the most powerful DEVA in the world.

When he heard this incredible story, he called the black man and thundered: This is not history.

The Hindu squeaked: Sir, if this is not history, what else is history?

PASCHIM DEVA screwed his forehead, expended his energy, and proclaimed: History is objective, with evidence and proofs, promoting one's own interest.

Now all the RISHIS of India who had assembled there to receive the proclamation of MAHADEVA clapped their hands in thunderous applause and gave him a standing ovation in praise of his profound declaration. Then they got into their VIMANS and flew into the lands of PASCHIM DEVA, where he had kept his wealth taken away from many communities through diplomacy and war. Some went with their bodies only, and some went with their minds only, and some went with both their bodies and minds. There he had stored his wealth taken by force and fraud, known by many names like diplomacy, imperialism, capitalism and globalization.

The Hindu, left behind, said: Sir now I understand. If you shake me by the hand, then my hand is history because you can touch it. But if I dream at night or think of my interest, it is not history, not objective and tangible enough, not provable, and not in your interest anyway. You are the king of kings and therefore what you say is truth. Might is right. Your history is my history and your interest is my interest, and my history is nobody's history because my memory and way of looking is nobody's memory and way of looking, of nobody's interest. And the story of Hindu living and experience ended forever, though the idea of DEVA like the formless reality present in many forms remained.

Some ways of experiencing spiritual reality are UPASANA, sitting near, UPAVASA, living near, or VRATA, fasting and so rising above the demands of the body, while making a vow or resolve and sticking to it; PUJA, or worshipping a deity that over flows the mind, and so externalizing one's inner ideal, TAPASYA, self-discipline through penance and intensity of effort in the spiritual struggle and remaining the same whatever the conditions, VAIRAGYA, detachment and renunciation that happens when we are entirely absorbed in a great idol or ideal and have no time or energy left for anything else; GURU, spiritual teacher who guides our mind to change our feelings, attitudes and actions and so our tradition and history on the basis of his actual spiritual experience and evolution after having been brought up in a tradition for many years; DIKSHA, formal initiation and declaration of a commitment through a prayer and MANTRA or sacred formulas while focusing the mind on their visuals; TIRTH YATRA, pilgrimage to places of inspiration, and YOGA that includes numerous exercises and disciplines of the body and mind, the senses and moral values that help in getting freedom from suffering and living a nobler and morally elevated life.

How to live well is an eternal problem. In the presence of suffering, it is an even greater problem.

Suffering is a common experience of life. One form of suffering is death, especially of the one we love deeply. Some deaths do not move us at all. Some deaths move us not because we love the person who has died but because we are adversely affected in some way by this death. But some deaths inflict a terrible suffering that burns us through and through and we are changed profoundly in many ways and a part of us just dries up and dies with that death. Another form of death of which we remain ignorant is the death that we die when we do not live according to our own nature, but live according to somebody else's nature. We do not express our true nature but express somebody else's nature necessarily inadequately and superficially. We live as the circumstances, neighbors or fashions dictate. We live as dominant people with their army and police, their administration, achievements, propaganda and advertising shape us. We live as we are compelled or manipulated to live. This too is a form of death, though we remain ignorant of this death, and never mourn at it, but rather enjoy it and suffer the stress and distortion and futility inside us.

There are other forms of suffering too, like the disease that does not leave us, even after the best possible medical treatment available has been tried for years. "Learn to live with it," says the doctor. Disease then is not merely a matter of a particular illness, and going to a doctor or a hospital, a diagnostic center or a druggist. Disease then becomes the very core of one's being, the criterion of judging people and situations, what to eat or not to eat, when to sleep or not to sleep, whether to go out or not, how sensitive you are to sound, to touch, to smell, to environment, whether or not to meet people and how they affect you, whether they should or should not do certain things, and so on. We naturally start living our disease in a hundred ways. Disease becomes a part of our moral being. We may even start enjoying our disease, without necessarily being aware of it. We may even realize that suffering and enjoyment are deeply related, and we cannot have one without the other. We may not want to get well in that case, though we may not be aware of this ambiguity.

Another form of suffering is old age, the decay of the body and mind. It makes the body helpless and dependent and lonely. Senses start weakening. They may stop doing their work. Things get renounced even if we do not want to renounce them, like having to give up sugar and salt, or the use of teeth, ears and eyes. Even a little effort becomes a big effort. One starts experiencing the utter futility of having lived at all. One may then start reflecting on one's experience of life, of what one has lived through, as in a dream, thinking about its meaning and nature, the best way of living that was not chosen, about our source and purpose and possibilities, though it would be rather late. How to grow old wisely may become an important problem. Grow old, we must, we have no choice. But we may or may not grow old wisely and here we have a choice. Or we may start coloring our hair and doing up our faces in numerous ways to look and act younger and so foolishly reject our growing old and ourselves.

Many are the forms of personal suffering. But there are forms of social suffering too, as when we undergo financial loss, especially through the immorality of some cleverer or stronger people, who may even have been our friends or relatives or even our rulers who have taken a vow to protect us and represent us through work for our benefit. We may see injustice being done to us, to our children and other relatives and friends, though the contents of injustice keep changing over time and space. We may see love that changes or suddenly turns out to be a form of habit or greed or even hatred or merely a selfish use of another, and we feel let down, degraded and deceived, in our family and community. We may suffer different forms of robbery and conflict and insensitivity of the law. We may become a victim of power in a war or a riot, or a clash of powerful personalities when arrogant kings and princes plunder and loot us, taking away our life and honor, wealth and resources, and enslaving us, while producing morally high sounding words of national security and law and order and raising revenues and defending and spreading religion or ideology and declaring that they are royal and noble because they can do such terrible things to us. We may be taxed heavily, both legally and illegally, like taking away from our produce by force as well as through bribes and inflation and depreciation and raising prices that squeeze us. A large part of such collections may be intended entirely for their personal comfort, luxury and security, though hidden behind morally high sounding, rational and impressive language. They may talk of democracy, equality and justice and stash away their beloved monies into nameless bank accounts in foreign countries and build up huge private properties that last their families for seven generations, knowing full well that accumulation of capital and power does not recognize or promote equality. People are inherently unequal in so far as they are identified with their bodies and minds, and not with their selves. One may be the greatest or the lowest in society, but their self is the same, feeling joy and sorrow.

There are still wider forms of suffering as in natural disasters like earthquakes, floods, volcanoes and forest fires, drying up of rivers or their changing their courses, or building dams. There is historical suffering too, like the destruction of Hindus and their temples and associated social institutions during the destructive ages of Islamic invaders.

Scriptures may help us in understanding and dealing with life and its suffering and enjoyment and in learning how to live a noble life dedicated to morally and spiritually higher forces of life. There can be no suffering in hell because suffering is of the body and its mind, and they are lost on death. But they can be lost even when we are alive if we are detached from them.

Many such scriptures were produced in ancient India. A greater India included some surrounding areas and was called MAHABHARATA. A great epic of this name was composed in its honor.

The land of MAHABHARATA extended from AFGANISTAN in the west across modern PANJAB, HARYANA, UTTAR PRADESH, BIHAR, VIDEH and ANGA in the east, and from HIMALAYAS in the north to river NARBADA and beyond it to the seas in the south.

India or BHARATVARSHA was considered to be a cultural unity, though it had many kingdoms frequently at war with each other. Victory in battle often resulted in replacing the king of the defeated country by another person of the same country. RISHIS did not approve of wiping out local dynasties, their cultures and people.

The Sanskrit word SINDHU means both river and ocean. The sound H is a variant of the sound S, and SINDHU can be pronounced HINDHU. SAPTA SINDHU referred to North Western India, largely the plains of River SINDHU and its tributaries. It included Rivers Indus and SARASVATI along with the five Punjab Rivers. River SINDHU begins its long course beyond the HIMALAYAS. It flows north and then turns southwest to enter the plains. Its tributaries are JHELUM, CHENAB, RAVI, SATLUJ that kept changing its course, and BEAS. River SARASWATI flowed from SHIVALAK Hills, SIRMOUR, BILASPUR, KURUKSHETRA, KAITHAL and SIRSA onwards to KUCHH, SAURASHTRA.

BRAHMAVRATA was the KURUKSHETRA region, called MANUSHA, near KAITHAL and THANESAR. It was also called ILYASPADA, now HARYANA. Three DEVIS, BHARTI, ILA, and SARASVATI were worshipped here.

ARYAVARTA, called MADHYADESH, now UTTRA PRADESH, was largely the plains of Rivers GANGA and YAMUNA, and their fringes. Sometimes it even extended up to the northern mountains, HINDU KUSH and SULAIMAN Mountains to the North West and HIMALAYAS to the North and North East. BIHAR was known as KIKATAS. Trading caravans and herds of cattle and horses went across the various passes like KHYBER, BOLAN, and GOMAL. KARAKORUM Highway passed through GILGIT, CHITRAL, and HUNZA, known as the silk route. TAXILA, and later PESHAWAR, and KABUL developed around the Khyber Pass. AFGANISTAN was referred to as the land of GANDHAR, where the SOMA plants grew, and the people were fond of music. SOMA plant also grew in North West Punjab, and in KASHMIR.

ARAVALLI Hills separate the sands of RAJASTHAN from the GANGA plains, passing through HARYANA, RAJASTHAN to GUJARAT. River BRAHMAPUTRA flows East across TIBET and after a long distance takes a U turn and enters the plains in the North East. The peninsula extended up to the seas. It influenced the island of SRI LANKA.

The kingdom of BHARATAS spread from river PURUSHNI (RAVI) in the west, where BHARATAS mixed with ANU tribes, to river GANGA in the east up to KASHI, where BHARATAS mixed with IKSHVAKUS. Their civi lization was spread over seven rivers SINDHU, ASIKINI (CHENAB), PURUSHNI (RAVI), SARASWATI (GHAGGAR), YAMUNA, GANGA, and SARAYU. Rivers SHUTUDRI (SATLUJ) and VIPAS (BEAS) flowed into the river SARASWATI (GAGGAR in the upper reaches, and HAKRA flowing parallel to the present day SATLUJ and the lower INDUS) that entered the sea at the RANN of KACHCHH. This river gradually dried up around 1900 B.C. This was the area of the Great Disappearance mentioned in MANUSMRITI.

MAHARSHI MANU says that the land between the rivers SARASVATI and DRSHADVATI is the holy land of BRAHMAVRATA. DHARMA has been handed down here from one generation to the next for centuries. Next to it is the land of KURUS, MATSYAS, PANCHALAS, and SURASENAKAS. It is the land of RISHIS. He says that we should learn our individual and family values and traditions from our family guru or a guru of this region. The land from HIMALAYAS in the north to the VINDHYA Mountains in the south, and from the great disappearance in the east to PRAYAGA in the west is the middle country. The land from the eastern to the western seas is fit for sacrifices.

Cultural unity was ritually created through prayers and ceremonies. In the ABHISHEK ceremony of RAJASUYA YAJNA, the king was crowned and other kings and leaders of all castes brought water from numerous rivers and streams of BHARATVARSHA and sprinkled it on the crown, which consisted of a branch of UDUMBARA tree fixed to a large ring of gold fit for the king, placed ceremoniously on his head, symbolizing immortality. Many centuries later ADI SHANKARACHARYA proclaimed this cultural unity of BHARATA by setting up four monasteries in four directions, BADRINATH, DWARKA, RAMESHWARAM, and PURI in the North, West, South and East of India.

Rivers were seen as powerful living beings that shaped and influenced human lives. Objects of nature were not merely objects of nature, as they are today. They were the constituents of one's being and destiny. The food that we eat with our mouth and nose and eyes and ears and skin becomes our body and its mind. So we should take care. What is outside in nature is inside our body and mind too. River SARASWATI was central to SAPTA SINDHU and came to be worshipped as SARASWATI DEVI, the spirit of clear flowing waters that produced the HINDU culture and civilization.

Rivers were so productive of crops and ideas that a profound reverence for waters developed as they created many centers of wealth in the form of towns and large cities as well as the sciences that supported them.

The first towns of this civilization that were excavated in the twentieth century were MOHENJODARO at the lower river SINDHU and HARRAPPA, 350 miles away, at the river RAVI. Much older towns than these were excavated later on like MEHRGARH, which had rectangular houses in clusters of mud bricks with 4 to 6 rooms each, dated 6500 B.C and spread over many acres, at the foot of BOLAN PASS in BALOCHISTHAN in PAKISTAN, and RAKHIGARHI in HARYANA.

RIG VEDA (VI.27.5) mentions HARIYUPIYA, which SAYAN who came centuries later interpreted as a city of golden sacrificial posts, a VEDIC city. Fire sacrificial altars have been found in KALIBANGAN, near SARASVATI River, LOTHAL, south of AHMEDABAD, and BANAWALI.

RIG VEDA (VII. 95.1-2) says SARASVATI flows from the mountains to the ocean, showing wealth and world's abundance, yielding milk and GHEE for RAJA NAHUSHA.

MOHENJO-DARO has a tank 39 by 29 feet, used for rituals like ablutions in tanks near temples today. Towns had storage rooms and workrooms for artisans like potters, bread makers, basket makers and stonemasons. These were large, fortified cities with well-planned big houses that had sanitary arrangements like underground drainage systems, public and private baths. The roads and streets were straight with lights opening on to them. There were citadels, communal granaries, warehouses and dockyards. They indicate considerable use of crafts. Male and female figurines could be idols of mother goddess and a male god similar to SHIVA in a YOGA posture and surrounded by animals, probably PASHUPATI. LINGA and YONI too have been found. The construction of such towns implied knowledge of weights and measures, materials and transportation, and accounts, buildings, architecture and town planning, mathematics, geometry, astronomy, administration and governance, moral values, religion and philosophy and support of guilds of craftsmen. Their mathematics, called SULVA SUTRAS, was an application of mathematics associated with SHRAUT SUTRAS used for building altars of different shapes and sizes for performing public sacrifices of different kinds, for different people and places. Around these bigger cities and smaller towns there were villages with practical knowledge, skills and handicrafts, as well as dense forests. This civilization spread over 8,40,000 square miles and lasted many centuries.

The main tribes of people who lived here were PURUS, TURVASHAS, IKSHVAKUS, YADUS, ANU and DRUHU tribes.

PURUS belonged to a BHARATA family. One of their lines were KURU kings who ruled from Rivers SARASVATI to GANGA, from SATLUJ to MATHURA, under the dynasty of SURSENAS, and from ROHTAK to PANCHALA, including ROHILKHAND, THANESAR, DELHI, and UPPER GANGA DOAB. PANDUS were an offshoot of KURUS. One of their kings was PARIKSHAT, ARJUNA'S grandson, who held court in TAKSHILA that became famous for its university.

PURUS of GANGA YAMUNA conflicted with ANU and DRUHYU tribes of WEST PANJAB and AFGANISTAN. BHARATAS and IKSHVAKUS of the north conflicted with TURVASHAS and YADHUS of the south and central India. The latter came to be called RAKSHAS and YAKSHAS because of differences in their moral codes and styles of living. These conflicts often emerged from imposing limits of moral and spiritual laws on materialistic and expansionist urges.

RIG VEDA mentions maritime and agricultural activities. It frequently mentions earning and accumulating wealth through trade. ATHARVA VEDA says that DEVA worshippers increase their wealth through investing wealth. The manual of rituals of RIG VEDA is AITREYA. This part of the VEDA contains a discussion on the nature of kingship and the establishment and sustenance of nations and empires. It describes ceremonies like ASHVAMEDHA YAJNA relating to CHAKARVARTI kings, whose symbol was the wheel, and RAJASUYA YAJNA, or ritualistic celebrations of political victories of emperors and their coronation.

Sometimes in some places people elected kings, but mostly kings were hereditary. Sometimes in some places aristocrats exercised royal power, and affluent merchants became RAJAS, as they employed armed men to protect their caravans and so built up armies and exercised royal power.

BHAGVAN SINGH in VEDIC HARAPPANS points out that RIG VEDA uses the dual noun RAJANAU or two kings in the same place, and words like RAJAKAS, RAJANYAS mean local lords. It says that of all kings on River SARASVATI, CHITRA alone is the real king; others are kings only in name. Indian RAJAS did not display their power by hunting wild beasts or trampling their enemies. Many of them were RAJAS of trade and commerce. Sometimes they made large gifts of cows, horses, chariots, gold, and clothes as a form of investment in education to RISHIS, who supported not only their own extended families but also their students and guests, treated as members of their family. Their residence became ASHRAM, a place of rest and freedom from labor attained through support of these gifts, available for exploring higher thought in various disciplines of knowledge. These ASHRAMS were the centers of education of those days. When RAMA and BUDDHA left their homes, they moved from one to the other ASHRAM, discussing problems and learning from RISHIS, who were concerned with spirituality as well as with many other subjects. Large ASHRAMS became GURU KULS or universities. Schools and universities grew up around the houses of learned people.

Kings led their people to war in defense of their communities. Protection of life and property was their sacred duty. A king was not the owner of land. Nor did he make laws. He only protected the laws and customs already in existence. People paid him a tribute for protection of their life and property as a form of investment in their security and welfare. Committees of people and aristocrats advised him. After discussions on political and other affairs, they had meals together, vegetarian and non-vegetarian. They drank SURA, liquor made of corn and barley, and SOMA, the sweet juice of SOMA plant fermented with milk and made intoxicating. It was offered to DEVAS.

Enjoying life was never a sin in BHARATVARSHA. In fact actions done in pursuit of KAMA, desires and pleasures, and ARTHA, power, wealth and prosperity, were a part of DHARMA, as they supported the life of the householder, who supported all other stages of life in society, like students, retired persons and those who are very old. When pleasures became bitter, the inward life began. And inward life did not begin for every one. Actions bring forward their consequences, which sometimes could be painful. Therefore limits had to be imposed on the actions of acquiring money and power, satisfying desires and having pleasures. These limits were imposed by DHARMA. Entering life and enjoying it, as well as withdrawing from life and reflecting on it constitute a cycle of life. Both are desirable, says SHIVA.

People emphasized ethics, self-restraint, non-violence, benevolence and charity. They cultivated material prosperity without its display. They aimed at harmonious living with nature in association with animals, plants, water bodies, mountains, seasonal changes and other people, even enemies. They consumed as little as necessary, wasting nothing, saving and giving charity to the worthy and the needy. Minimum necessary consumption and charity were considered to be great values.

There were numerous occupations in that society, like cultivators and hunters, fishermen, cowherds, goatherds, leather workers, weavers, tailors, dyers, embroiderers, carpenters, blacksmiths, ship builders, goldsmiths, miners, merchants, physicians and priests, philosophers and mathematicians, as well as sailors, soldiers, horse and elephant trainers, and royal courtiers, who fought wars and used bows and arrows, axes and circular discs, swords and knives, even ethics of war, which sometimes led to their own destruction, and built fortified towns the accidental remains of which are admired today.

The basic unit of society was the family, not the individual, as society is created only when two individuals unite, and relatives and neighbors provide nourishment, security and culture. Several families joined by real or imagined kindred made a clan. Several clans joined by a remote ancestor made a tribe or caste. Several tribes and communities made a kingdom, seen as a living organic being, different groups of which acted as limbs of one body for common welfare.

People doing similar work that emerged from their nature and showed certain broad qualities made a VARNA, which became an abstract organizing principle of social life. Social work was predominantly intellectual, martial, materially productive, or service. These theoretical divisions of society were only four, but practical divisions in society were numerous. They all expressed the same spirit called PURUSHA, and were organically related like the limbs of one body, expected to work for their common welfare, though with passage of time this unity got lost, especially when foreign rulers started dividing people rather than uniting them.

JATI or caste was a relationship of blood, based on birth. It was a principle of social order as communities of people related to each other by the strong ties of marriage, blood and family was the foundation of society. This relationship of blood is a natural relationship. It cannot be abolished even if we legalize divorce in the name of freedom, compelled by our bodies and their juices, fashions and daily news and absence of any tradition of daily reflection and meditation on our experience of life. Family ties are strong especially in small societies staying at one place for generations. They become weak in large societies where blood relationships beyond the nuclear family are ignored or forgotten as unprofitable.

The caste system protected the rights of the extended family and larger groups based on real or imagined blood relationships. MANU did not include occupation groups in the caste system, which was done much later.

The caste system is now condemned as society has become individualistic and the family is breaking up. Individualism breaks family bonds and commercializes them. The son may have to pay his parents for board and lodge after a certain age, and grandparents may have to be paid money for taking care of their grandchildren. How much do I love you? Let me count my pulse rate or your money, or the number of times a week I have sex with you. That is called freedom and modernity.

The essential principle of the VARNA system for social organization was that one should act according to one's flow of nature. Everyone has a nature that flows into his feelings and dreams, urges and actions. And this nature is pre-moral, having both good and evil tendencies. We need to express these in pursuit of noble ideals, nourishing the good and weakening the evil inherent in them.

When we do not act according to our nature, self-regulating it in pursuit of noble ideals, as when we follow fashions or neighbors or media, we theoretically go outside the VARNA system by not allowing our divinely given nature to find expression, which may cause illness and obstructions in the free flow of our energy.

We accept the divine power when we express our nature given to us initially by invisible powers. It is the cause, the source of our actions, though not their purpose. And if we do this with awareness of their origin, continuity, and dissolution in pursuit of high ideals in our mind and heart, we will find that the evil tendencies inherent in our nature start weakening and dropping off for want of our mental support, and the good tendencies inherent in our nature start getting nourishment from our attention and interest, as we aim to realize noble ideals.

We should do what our nature directs us to do, manifest our nature in our feelings, dreams, attitudes and actions, while observing ourselves while doing so, keeping high ideals in our mind and heart, reducing evil and nourishing nobler life. If we watch our motives, urges, actions and their consequences, we would evolve spiritually, and rise above evil and suffering.

Focusing our mind on this self-transformation was UPASANA of our ISHTHA DEVA, sitting mentally near our chosen noble ideal.

Craftsmen did UPASANA of the one who crafted the universe and its innumerable beings, their wonderful forms and designs, shapes and colors, out of his mind. They gradually learnt to see forms in whatever they saw. Just look around observantly. What is it that has no form? That which has no form like pleasure and pain or high ideals before they are enacted in life, we cannot see with our physical eyes, though we can experience it. They were devoted to seeing and feeling forms of nature, like plants and animals and human beings and their lives. This devotion and love for form, its beauty, harmony and evocative powers, was their form of worship of the divine formless power present in all forms. Many YOGIC and dance postures were a development of these observations of form.

No work is low when we see our ideal in it. Any work could be made noble through appropriate UPASANA and a door of entry into the divine spiritual experience. But in practice in a society especially after loss of political freedom to foreign invaders and the consequent destruction of countless intellectual, martial and practical leaders in numerous towns and villages, one after the other, and loot and rape and plunder and enslavement of hundreds of thousands of others and their sale into slavery, and their withdrawal into a forest or gypsy life, and the consequent loss of many avenues of varied and higher level of social duty and responsibility, action and profit, freedom and creativity, caste became static, a manner of survival, because the JIHAD was not against the state alone, but against society as well, destruction of their temples and social institutions, value systems and minds.

JATI came to mean, "Do what your father did." It was an attempt at self-protection in a demoralized society. This destruction of Hindus has never been adequately described, calculated and graphically displayed. So it does not register in the social mind except as attitudes and images created by forgotten experiences. Some Hindus now say that this destruction of Hindus never happened at all. Foreign invaders came in for our own good. They destroyed us in order to help us, to do us good and remove the evils of Hindu society and we should thank them for our destruction and reform. This view is expressed in "The Historical Role of Islam", in M.N. Roy's "Selected Works", Vol. IV. He gives no evidence that anti-caste feelings helped Islam grow in India, but communist historians keep repeating this view. Some Hindus say that India was invaded for its wealth and for no religious reason whatsoever, and invaders and the historians who accompanied them told lies when they talked of destroying KAFARS. Such denials and evasions are symptoms of a traumatized mind.

The caste system in earlier times was a way of accommodating social diversities and natural human inequalities in a manner that was created by the people themselves through customs, as it was based on blood relationships in small communities, which was why it lasted so long. If people had resented it at that time, they would not have created it in the first place and it could not have lasted that long.

RISHIS were people dedicated to a higher life. They were highly prized like the lights in darkness, like the constellation of stars in the northern sky, the center of the universe around which all the heavenly lights move in dark spaces, the plough of the earth leading us upwards towards the north. They are like the elements of nature, our source of the material world. They are the progenitors of mankind, who saw forces and elements of nature, who saw good and bad people and many kinds of demons, animals and plants, giving them names and forms. They are the eyes, the ears, the nostrils and the mouth, the very motions of life in the dead body, the breaths that show the presence of life and regulate it. They are the mind born sons of BRAHMA who saw visions and hymns teaching us what should be and how to live. They are the ascetics, leading austere lives, consuming the minimum, bearing heat and cold but remaining the same, unchanged in all seasons and circumstances, engaged in self-discipline. They are the founders of lineages and families trace their descent from them. Some of them are VISHVAMITRA, JAMADAGNI, BHARADVAJA, GOTAMA, ATRI, VASISHTHA with his wife RISHI ARUNDHATI, KASHYAPA, AGASTYA, BRIGHU, ANGIRAS, MARICHI and many more.

Many RISHIS became kings and kings became RISHIS. RAJA JANAK was both king and RISHI. He was RAJRSIHI. VISHWAMITRA was RAJA of KANYAKUBAJA, who renounced his kingship on seeing its hollowness. He saw an invisible universe present inside the visible universe and composed the famous prayer of Hindus, the GAYATRI MANTRA that expresses their commitment to meditate on the source of light and life present in all beings. He became a BRAHMRISHI. VASHISHTH was a VAISHYA who had a full awareness of his nature. He composed a new form of YOGA to experience the unity of all being. It came to be known by his name. He created numerous hymns and wealth for himself and others. He became a BRAHMRISHI and political advisor to RAJA DASHRAT. He created RAJPUTS, warriors who displayed awesome deeds of valor. Many RISHIS, like ATHARVANS, emerged from among the common people. They were called JANRISHIS. Ordinary people who followed a particular RISHI often adopted his name as their own surname, expressing their ideological commitment to that RISHI. Many castes were formed in this way. They felt as if they were related by blood, children of the same guru.

The influence of RISHIS spread far and wide as they tried to bring activities seeking wealth, power and pleasure under the control of morality and restraint. They even created a morality that must be observed while fighting a war and winning a victory. Making money and seeking pleasure and power was not considered sinful. It was crossing the limits of morality and justice while seeking money, power and pleasure that was sinful and evil, hurtful to leading a noble life, even though it was enjoyable to the people seeking them.

There was a time before the RIG VEDA when waters came down from the heavens, the ice melted and the land was flooded. A man caught a fish for his survival. The fish cried, " Do not kill me. Protect me and I will protect you." The man let go his grip on his possession, and the fish asked him to build a raft to cross the floods that come in the world, and this he did. When the time of heavenly anger came, the fish guided him to the safety of the HIMALAYAS to a place that came to be called MANUSAROVER. Here he created fire and light, and SOMA RASA, fermented juice of sweet herbs. Here began the Rivers SINDHU, SARASWATI, and SARAYU. Some scholars think that this was Mount KAILASH, where SHIVA meditated in icy stillness. Here YAJNA, YOGA, and TANTRA were created. MANSAROVAR is a place of pilgrimage for Hindus.

Hindus worship the fire that transforms one into purer, subtler and higher ways of seeing and being. This is the first MANTRA of RIG VEDA. It requires a firm resolve, UPAVASA, living near, to be always kept alive in mind and manifested in feeling, thought and action.

To say that Hindus worship fire that is lit with a matchstick is like saying that when people salute their national flag, they worship a piece of cloth of a certain shape and color, size and design, stuck to a pole of wood or metal and put out to dry on special occasions even when the cloth is not wet, on seeing which people hit their foreheads with their hands in shame, and sometimes show their slap of hatred to worshippers of other national flags and sometimes show their slap to the mother earth that supports them, but which they want to exploit and conquer. Nations have even created manuals of worship called the government acts concerning the national flag, which meticulously lay down the rules and regulations that govern the making of the national flag, inspiring life into it, and the honor or dishonor shown to it, and lay down hellish punishments for those who dishonor this piece of cloth. This is a fairly objective description of what is seen from the outside as worship of the national flag, but it shows no understanding of anything non-material implicit in reverence for the national flag, obviously a symbol, an idol, a LINGA or a phallic organ of the national spirit and manliness today. Even idol breakers worship this idol.

The worship of the national flag started in various countries some years ago. It is likely to die out in another few centuries when one world government gets created through the use of force and violence, manipulation and globalization, since the governing classes of the world have forgotten the first vow of man, which is to control their own bodies and minds, desires and urges before they can legitimately exercise control over others and direct their lives. This vow initiates action on various disciplines of control of one's body and mind and their urges, resulting in transformation of perceptions and attitudes of seeing and being that were developed through meditations on various objects and their appreciation that were available thousands of years ago and tested through centuries of experience.

Manu and his children and followers lived in the HIMALAYAS and the plains adjacent to them, the confluence of Rivers SARASVATI and DRISHADVATI. This region was later called KURUKSHETRA.

KURUKSHETRA was the land of KURUS, where BHARTA kings were anointed, the land where RISHIS had ASHRAMS and did YAJNA and YOGA, disciplines of the mind and body, of seeing and being. It became a place of pilgrimage. Many saints and gurus built their ASHRAMS there.

MANU had a son NAHUSHA, who had a son YAYATI, who had sons TURVASHA and YADHU from wife DEVAYANI, daughter of RISHI BRIGHU, and sons ANU, DRUHYU and PURU from wife SHARMISHTHA, daughter of king VRISHAPARVAN. They were progenitors of the VEDIC people and civilization, the union of RAJAS and RISHIS, of power and wisdom.

BRIGHUS were RISHIS of ASURA king VRISHAPARVAN. Their first RISHI was SHUKRA. They had spiritual, occult as well as scientific knowledge. The heavenly sculptor and craftsman were BRIGHUS, as was MAYA who taught astronomy and architecture. They had knowledge of body and mind, of longevity and rejuvenation, and were masters of AYURVEDA, the science of living, as well as JYOTISH, which at that time meant the study of stars or lights, which was necessary for accurate calculation of time for rituals and ceremonies and for sailing across the seas for trade. They were sons of VARUNA, the lord of the seas, having ships going across to different lands. Their center of power was GUJARAT, and their city was BRIGHU KACHCHH. They were related to YADHUS, who had a militant temperament and were ever fighting and so were called ASURAS.

ANGIRASES were the oldest RISHI family, companions of MANU, who looked after rituals and actions done for personal and social growth. They presided over forest schools, concerned with knowledge available at that time as well as sacrifices and ritual actions of concrete thought and perception. Such actions and their significance were discussed, sequenced, refined and formulated, discarded and developed and explained for spiritual growth, which was the final test of their acceptance or rejection. To reject a ritual and its doctrine was as important as to formulate it. Here developed numerous doctrines like those of PASHUPATI mode of worship, sacrificing the animal inside and outside man for the sake of husband, the controller inside and outside man. And what is the difference between inside and outside? Is the sun really outside us, especially when we are drinking its rays, its days and nights, its seasons, its change of fruits and vegetation and herbs, and digesting this drink through growing old with wisdom, maturing and making its heat our own warmth? Discrete separate identities were questioned. Were they real? Were they true? What is the boundary of our body and mind, including their food and drink and breathing and ideas? Continuities were seen, appreciated and admired. Along with seeing objects, the space between objects must also be seen, says SHIVA.

Free and open debate, speech in search of truth, acceptance and rejection of ideas were a part of the search for DHARMA. That is why so many different scriptures could be created and no one was killed on the ground that he belonged to a different religion. The forest schools were places of free concrete thinking and experiment. They encouraged devotion to subtle forces, which were not seen and yet were felt to be real and even concrete. In fact anything that is worthwhile and valuable is invisible, say mathematics, or moral values, or joy and sorrow. Visibility can be deceptive, like acting, or like love that masks hatred or is commercial or equates it with chemicals in the body.

The first ANGIRAS RISHI was BRIHASPATI. He was the guru of MAHARAJA INDRA, the lord of heavenly prosperity, power and pleasures and good things of life and what lies beyond them. BRIHASPATI is an ideal guru for many a family man to follow, as he saw common sense and wisdom, useful in one's devotion to family and enjoyment of life. His school came to be known as CHARVAK.

ANGIRAS discovered the use of fire and transformations in life. His family produced eminent MAHARSHIS like GAUTAMA, KANVA, ATRI, VAMADEVA, and BHARDWAJA. They were called gods on earth as they demonstrated in their lives what it means to be divine. MAHARSHI GAUTAMA created logic and fair ways of seeing and reasoning in his NYAYA DARSHAN. MAHARSHI KANVA explicated the spiritual significance of concrete rituals like YAJNAS. Spiritual rituals are not external actions that are objectively seen with the physical eyes, as in the case of worshipping the spirit of the nation. They are inward struggles and states of mind. MAHARSHI ATRI explicated the royal and political meanings of concrete rituals that were done along with political actions like getting tributes from other kings or organizing sports to find the best sportsmen for recruitment to the service of the king. Political rituals and ceremonies too have corresponding inward states of mind. He produced and fashioned

CHAKRAVARTI KINGS or emperors, teaching them royal duties and rights, responsibilities and privileges, like CHANAKYA did many centuries later. RISHIS were thinkers, visionaries, artists, scientists, and administrators, developing social orders, imposing moral and spiritual control on body and mind and social urges. Many of them like MAHARSHI PATANJALI are still influential.

DEVAS and ASURAS, with their ANGIRAS and BRIGHU RISHIS fought with each other at the time of RAJA YAYATI. DEVAS lived in the KURUKSHETRA region of SARASVATI and DRISHADVATI. ASURAS lived around the lower SARASVATI and RANN of KACHCHH. Many of them migrated to foreign lands.

The king followed the tradition of choosing an able successor. When MAHARAJA BHARATA did not have a successor as great as required, his guru MAHARSHI BHARDWAJA took over power and ruled the country. RISHIS were not impractical visionaries, but could take on practical affairs when necessary and give them up when necessary. RAJA SAGAR disinherited his son as unfit to rule and made his grandson his heir, who became a great ruler. PARSHURAMA was a BRAHMIN who was also an eminent warrior. He defeated many royal families and became immortal.

VEDAS require collaboration between spiritual experience and political power. The power of action is necessary to manifest the power of spiritual wisdom. Their collaboration sustains the individual and the society. The goal of life is freedom. One gets freedom through realization of one's true self. This process results in discarding what is not one's true self. Thereby one rises to a nobler level of living. One has to subject the pursuit of desire and prosperity to the discipline and limits of moral goodness and justice. One becomes free from demands of the non-self. One acts out one's nobler nature, eliminating the evil tendencies, and realizes one's highest self.

This ideal of freedom creates a social order in which an individual's higher nature finds free expression. It teaches self-discipline and sublimation of gross urges, rising higher than them, symbolised by Agni or fire. It promotes minimum consumption and wide dispersal of wealth rather than its accumulation and concentration. It dissuades political leaders from reigning too long by promoting ret irement. How can a political leader serve his society.for fifty or sixty years of his life? Does he not have his own family to serve, especially when he is unable to control his narrow selfish urges? Politics grounded in falsehood, making false accusations against perceived enemies and always talking of grievances and dissatisfactions and making highly exaggerated claims about one's own importance, and utter incompetence of the rivals, all in the name of serving society, can only create evil and suffering.

VEDA means knowledge, seen as sacred because knowledge underlies, constitutes and supports what appears to be reality to our senses. It is this knowledge that sciences struggle to grasp, but only through the senses and only through the scientific method, making many assumptions, like reality can be tested only in this way and in no other way, which may not be true.

VEDAS as individual literary works, is sacred knowledge that grew up over centuries and was orally handed down from generation to generation, tested against experience of life. Some of it is in the form of formulas that bring order to chaotic minds, and some in the form of hymns, prayers, charms, symbols, as well as observations on life and contemporary environment. They are called collections. Some of it is in the form of speculations about the meanings of hymns, their application to life, stories concerning the origin of rituals and their secret meanings. Included in them are works that contain philosophical speculations on the nature of the universe and man and their relation and the art and skills of living.

RISHIS saw VEDAS. Their names often refer to their families and followers over many generations rather than to individuals. They created another class of literature called UPVEDA, like AYUR VEDA, or the knowledge of living and herbs, DHANUR VEDA, or the knowledge of warfare, GANDHARVA VEDA, or the knowledge of music and dance, ARTHA SHASTRA, or knowledge of wealth and power, and VASTU SHASTRA, or knowledge of building and architecture.

The first VEDA is RIG VEDA. It has 10 books, which have a total of 1028 hymns, consisting of 10,552 verses, composed by more than 400 RISHIS.

RISHIS did penance and meditation. They performed YAJNA ceremonies and helped kings win battles and in governing their kingdom. They saw visions that they expounded to others and built up schools of thought. They spoke only truth, as they knew it. Many of them married and raised families that carried their names over generations. AGASTYA married LOPAMUDRA, who was an independent RISHI. GAUTAM married AHALYA. VASHISHTHA married ARUNDHATI. ATRI married ANUSUYA who discoursed on female DHARMA to SITA, when SHRI RAMA spent some time with MAHARSHI ATRI on his way south. JAMADAGNI married RENUKA. KASHYAPA married ADITI. CHYAVANA married SUKANYA.

The homes of RISHIS became ASHRAMS, centers of learning where travelers on the spiritual and educational path could find support and rest. Some of these institutions became large like GURUKULS, which required skills of administration and accounts. VISHWAMITRA renounced the kingship of KANYAKUBAJA or KANAUJ that he had inherited from his father GADHI. He built his ASHRAM on the banks of river KAUSHIKI held in reverence in East BIHAR and later on at lake PUSHKAR in RAJASTHAN, where he did UPASANA of BRAHMA. GAUTAM had an ASHRAM in MITHILA and later he retired to the HIMALAYAS. BHARDWAJA had an ASHRAM at the confluence of GANGA and YAMUNA, ATRI at CHITRAKOOT in PRAYAG, AGASTYA at the source of GODAVARI, KANVA on the banks of river MALINI, and UPAMANYU on a peak of the HIMALAYAS. NARADA was a traveling RISHI. They studied VEDAS or all that was known at that time. They acquired and imparted knowledge of many different kinds, and did rituals for the benefit of others. They visited holy places, the sources of their inspiration. Wherever we are inspired, that is our holy place.

RISHIS taught many subjects, not just spirituality. BHARDWAJA taught DHANURVEDA, the science of warfare in a school of martial arts for royal princes, and AYURVEDA to the king of KASHI. PARSHURAM taught DHANURVEDA to BHISHAM PATAMA. They acted as family priests of kings and prosperous, affluent merchants, of people whose material needs were well satisfied and who faced spiritual conflicts. They did sacrifices for them to fulfill their desires. One normally progressed on the spiritual path after meeting the physical and economic needs of the family, even though it was his duty to do spiritual rituals. VISHWAMITRA, JANAK, RAMA, and KRISHNA were kings. BUDDHA was a prince, so was MAHAVIRA. Hindu religion was not opium of the masses, or creation of an orphan fighting wars in order to become rich, or a poor man bringing down the rich and the powerful people to occupy their place, but the creation of kings and princes, of a materially satisfied nature in the thick of battle and worldly affairs.

Not all RISHIS believed in the divine. MAHARSHI BRIHASPATI formulated the school of thought that rejected scriptures and required cultivation of desires and the senses. Later on, TANTRAS used the senses and their pleasures for internal spiritual growth, even though the path of the senses was dangerous and sometimes led to immorality and depravity.

Not all RISHIS believed in BRAHMA, one absolute unchanging creative order seen as the source of the universe. Some did not believe even in ISHWAR, divine power seen as becoming the universe, remaining in it for some time and then dissolving it to be reborn again. MAHARSHI KAPILA founded the SANKHYA school of thought, based on evolution from the invisible to the visible nature, which rejected the notion that there is only one god. Instead he argued for two fundamental realities, the subjective self and the objective nature. He and his followers formulated a universal manner of living to eliminate suffering, and devoted themselves to counting, separating, analyzing, making discrete the continuous flow of evolution of nature and its flow in our body and mind.

RISHIS perceived the principle of life inherent in all beings. They saw the dynamics and order of nature and tried to live in harmony with it. They loved and valued what they saw as well as the seer, both the body with its mind and the self. They were scientists, mathematicians and doctors, mystics and pleasure lovers and ascetics, who cared for matter and society and for what happened when the two ceased.

We thank all those who were devoted to truth, the hunters and the settled, the nomads and the tillers of the soil, the villagers, the townsmen, the dwellers of forests and the cities, sometimes living in pre-fabricated houses, meticulously planned, wonderful seats of power and governance, encouraging arts and sciences. We are what we are because they were what they were, and so our life is thanks to them, as we pay them our debt by trying to know and remember them. We thank all those who feasted and fasted, the makers and the breakers of vows and rules, doing body and mind and spiritual exercises, still current today after millennia with many variations.

Some saw divine energy concretely as a woman, calling it DEVI, and sacrificing human beings to be dedicated to her for their whole life and sacrificing animals to her for communal feasting. We are still continuing with this form of devotion in our wars and suicide bombs and capital punishment, sacrificing human beings to please the invisible divine power of righteousness and justice, to achieve our desires, which are often petty, concerned with making profits, as we have changed our perceptions of her in many ways.

Some saw the source of power in the self control of the YOGI sitting comfortably for a long time on his throne, ever creative in his mind, even though surrounded by animals like tigers, buffaloes, rhinoceros, and deer supporting his seat, carved in stones accidentally left behind in MOHENJODARO and HARAPPA.

Some saw the divine power visually as abstract shapes, like the swastika and the wheel, cylindrical stones and LINGAS, markers of the invisible forces, though today we see it mostly in the shape of the national flag, as a LINGA of national pride, or in the form of a company logo, the loyalty to a tribal group created to make profits rightly or wrongly many times the input, sucking the blood of consumers in a thousand ways while talking deceptively of serving society.

Some saw the divine power as beings dwelling in trees and animals and in elements of nature and vegetation, like land and water, fire and air and space, concretely visualizing vaguely felt and experienced forces.

Some kept long hair, wore black turbans and deerskins, beads in ears, gems around necks, and sandals under feet. They had no caste. They did no agriculture or trade, though they experimented with herbs. They were unmarried, but not celibate. Red eyed, intoxicated, they were possessed, keeping strange vows and fasts, doing unbelievable experiments with their bodies and minds and creating the techniques of knowing, experiencing and being the real, often ending up in blind alleys of degrading sexuality.

Some guarded the divine secret truths of the sacred body and mind, uniting man and woman in one body and mind, intoxicated with sexual practices.

Some sat in SAMADHI, creating YOGAS of many forms, experiencing a consciousness that did not change, controlling their senses and releasing their spirit, as if out of their body, free of the linkages with their body and mind and society, playing with supra normal phenomena, which they saw as quite normal and natural if seeing and being are changed in certain ways.

Some were ascetics, who wore saffron clothes, avoided cooked food, spoke only truth, created ideals of isolation and inner quiet, reliance on human effort, focus on man, forgetting god and his grace. Never killing an animal, they did severe penance, experimenting with human possibilities.

Some saw, revealed, composed, edited, recited, and expounded sacred formulas, performing sacrifices, living virtuous lives devoted to families, wearing deerskins and barks of trees thousands of years ago.

Some built ASHRAMS, some lived in the open. Some abandoned their wives, children, and property; others married, adopted children and owned property. Some founded kingdoms; others gave them up of their own free will.

Some taught that nature is essentially the creative principle, the evolutionary change. The universe evolves out of the primal sound made by the vibrations of existence that are heard as AUM, as mystic formulas, and visualized in the abstract forms. They visualized these designs and recited these formulas with concentration on the shapes and sounds of nature, transforming and schematizing their manifest forms, trying to experience its very seed and so transcending the form.

Some taught that nature is conscious and when it becomes man, it becomes self-conscious. But some said that it was not so, and so they disagreed and debated in large halls in the presence of kings and affluent commoners. These were festivals, cause for celebration. They did not kill or convert for the sake of ideology and religion, but provoked discussion, agreement or disagreement. Even in the rituals of sacrifice, sometimes, BRAHMANS, who believed in an inherent order in the universe, and SHUDRAS, who believed only in the body and its needs and nature, sat opposite each other praising and condemning BRAHMA alternately and ritualistically.

Some say that man is a complex of the elements of nature, organized and enlivened, with organs of knowledge and action, with a mind, a consciousness, an ego and an unknown being. Some say that man is a field of formless forces, not a body and mind with a separately out-lined form, not an individual at all. Only the formless forces exist. The rest is only a practical, useful illusion created by the perceiving organs, like the illusion of numbering years or naming days, or seeing that there is a sky and that its color is blue. Some say that when body and mind ceases, consciousness ceases, but before this there is life and identity. Some say that when body and mind ceases, consciousness passes on to another life and identity. Some say that nature gives and takes everything and so is supreme. Some say that man is consciousness as long as he lives. He becomes aware of the outside world and the inside world. He feels pleasure and pain, acquires knowledge and does actions. He is a body and mind complex, a field in which many forces operate constantly. The core of this field normally remains unknown, the center of his being. To know and experience this unknown center and to live according to its nature is the vow of SANATANA DHARMA.

Chapter II

Forms of Existence

Whatever form of existence we see, whatever we experience is power of the one who creates the universe and lives in it as its lord and regulator, its inner controller. We may see beings with different forms and functions, qualities and characteristics. All these are forms of the divine power, the same invisible force that we experience in different beings.

This divine power is intelligent and conscious, playful and joyful. It limits itself in numerous ways to constitute beings and things that have forms and functions, qualities, purposes and uses. These beings when seen as forms of divine power are DEVAS. They constitute us and give us that which we take and experience. They are numerous. When we do not see them as forms of divine power, they are merely beings and things and nothing more. To learn to see the divine power that takes the form of everything that we see and experience including our self is spiritual growth.

DEVAS are the earth, the sky and space. They are the air and winds and clouds, and water falling down, and numerous rivers and the one sea. They are the stars in the mornings and the evenings and in clusters and the moon and the sun and the time. They are the beauty that fascinates and the terror that destroys, the birth and death and different states of mind.

DEVAS are not ideas that were thought out. They are living powers that are present, felt and worshipped with devotion, and recollections of past experiences. Their stories are narrated for entertainment and instruction of people gathered in their homes or under trees to pass their time wisely and to lead children to sleep, and for self-direction.

It is wrong to translate DEVAS as gods. They are born and they shine. They give and remain for some time. They change and dissolve and reconstitute again. This cycle like a wheel repeats through eternity.

How many DEVAS are there, sir?

There are no DEVAS.

Yes that is true, if you see yourself as your body and mind alone independently of any other power. But are you independent and autonomous, sir? You can see your body, but can you see your mind, sir? Your body has organs in it that work on their own without consulting you. Do they work with your permission, sir? Are you your organs and their organization? Think again, sir.

There are innumerable DEVAS, say 33 KOTIS, or 33,00,00,000 DEVAS.

Yes, that is true, if you see each being, each radiant form of the ultimate power, through love and devotion as one that is unique, unlike anyone else, incomparable. Each tree is different from every other tree, with a form, marking a history with birth and death, if you know how to see it. Love makes what you love into a unique being, alive with a personality of its own, and entirely different from everything else. Then you love with utter devotion what you see and experience. Love never puts the beloved into a class, as thinking does. And yet each unique being may share something with another. So think again, sir.

There are 33 KOTIS or classes of DEVAS.

Yes, that is true, if you see these shining forms of light and life in classes that you create.

MAHARSHI YAJNAVALKYA says that there are eight VASU DEVAS, namely fire, earth, air, sky, sun, moon, stars, and heaven, eleven RUDRA DEVAS, namely ten senses and one mind, so that when they stop doing their duty, the relatives start crying, twelve ADITYA DEVAS, the changing months of the year, one INDRA of thunder and rains, and one PRAJAPATI who sacrificed himself to become the universe, making self-sacrifice the basic duty of man. There are many such classes of beings. But are these the only classes possible? Think again, sir.

There are 3 DEVAS.

Yes, that is true, if you see them as a few forms and functions of the divine power subsuming many other forms and functions as their transformations. They are the earth, the sky and the beyond. Think again, sir.

There are one and a half DEVAS.

Yes, that is true, if you see life with its consciousness and motion as one, and all that it produces in the form of the universe, as half. It is the formless one and the formed half. But think again, sir.

There is one and only one DEVA, without a second, seen in many ways. It is beyond reason, mind and speech, beyond the senses, without divisions, differences, and limitations, the nameless one, whole and full, making the second impossible.

Yes, that is true, if you see mystically, sacrificing yourself into the other, seeing yourself in the other, seeing one whole, transcending all divisions and separations. Till you do that, you cannot see the sameness in all, and be whole. Then you cease to be you. You cannot have any experience of one DEVA, and still worship or talk of the other as an adversary, an enemy.

Learn the skills of seeing, sir. Your skills of seeing decide what you see. Learn to see. Worship SURYA DEVA, the source of light that enables you to see.

Learn to see many things in the same thing.

Learn to see the same thing in many things.

Learn to see and accept and appreciate what you are, and what you see.

Learn to see that what you see is what you are.

Learn to see that what you are is what you see.

This is the mystery and the integrity of your seeing and being.

We do not begin with one DEVA, the formless, nameless one. We end with it. We begin with the chaos and diversity of our experience, the numerous beings that we see and the numerous states of mind and life and body that we are.

We begin with love, with the concrete and the unique. If we do not begin with love, devotion and trust, we cannot begin at all. We cannot even be born. If we do not love, we do not see the unique in others and ourselves. Then we become abstract, a number in a calculation. Then we manipulate and are manipulated. So many thousands killed in a war. So many thousands cheated on the stock exchange. That is our power and our greatness, when we do not see and do not love and trust.

We should give full attention to what we see, feel and touch and sense with all our senses. We should see and appreciate the unique. Unless we see that each form is different, we do not see at all. We see only partly, half-heartedly and inattentively. Our seeing similarity and sameness does not destroy the unique diversity of form. Seeing uniqueness is the art of seeing.

Then we learn to analyze, if we are intellectually inclined. Then we see gradations and abstract them into classes. We see our classes merging into each other. These classes and categories are what we construct with the divine force of our human mind. We should learn to see our mental constructions as our mental constructions. They are our creations. We should see their beauty, their uniqueness and their usefulness.

Then we learn to see our doings, see them coming, staying and going away. Then we see actions happening mostly independently of us, and actions bringing in more actions.

We should detach our self from what we see, detach our self from the one who sees it. Then only seeing remains. We should experience this freedom from our limitations.

All this comes through accepting what we are. We should not hate and reject our self, competing with the other, or even with our earlier performance. We should see our self with love and full attention and so rise higher.

DEVAS are living and conscious powers. Some powers are higher than man, just as some living beings are lower than man, like animals, plants, and minerals. All forms of reality are alive and conscious. But it is their own kind of life and consciousness. It is not our kind of human life and consciousness.

Begin with ISHTHA DEVA. Everyone has his guardian, the source and cause of his actions and feelings. It is his nature, his flow of energy. It is the normal flow of his feelings, ideas, dreams, hopes, attitudes, urges and actions. If we learn to meditate and reflect on our nature and its actions quietly everyday, we may learn to see our nature more and more clearly. We may not like what we see. It may have too much wickedness, too much irrelevance and dispersal of energy. We may learn to nourish our virtue through devotion to high ideals, learn to see ourselves more concretely, externalizing our nature. Not all people flow in the same way. But some flows are similar in many ways.

We may become aware of our KUL DEVA. Everyone has a tradition his family has been following customarily. The spirit of his family and its tradition lives through him. A family does not consist of husband, wife, and their children alone. These relationships go much beyond them, even if they are not recognized. These relationships would normally include grandparents, uncles and aunts and their children, though they reach out to the limits of memory. This extended family has been doing actions, good or bad, constituting custom and tradition that continue for years. These traditions change more or less with time. These are the forms of KUL DEVA. It may be given a name and a form, an idol and a mode of remembrance, worship and devotion. Some people adopt their KUL DEVA as their ISHTHA DEVA, as they are deeply identified with the tradition of their family. They follow their family and community custom.

We may become aware of our GRAM DEVA too. Everyone absorbs the spirit of the place of his birth and nurture. It nurtures a person into a form, gives him a shape. It is not just the person who lives in a place. The place also lives in him, in his heart and mind. Without it, the roots dry up, and the diversity and love of life is adversely affected. The place of birth has a spirit that is now being destroyed through standardization and modernization in the name of progress. But this progress destroys the rich diversity of experience. We visualize the land we were born and brought up in, and attached to, our house or farm and street and village or town, region and country, its past and present and dreams of future. We give it a name and a form.

We may become aware of our NAG DEVA too. Everyone has a poison that he has to drink, retain and overcome and learn to live with. There is a weakness, inferiority, obstruction or a flaw in every one of us, howsoever great we may be. It is given to us to overcome it and be stronger than what we begin with.

A Hindu is expected to do UPASANA of some of these DEVAS. They are the lights that shine, give and pervade the world. UPASANA means near seat. It means sitting near them, keeping them in the mind, becoming aware of them. It means reflecting on the self and on these formative forces. This reflection is the study of oneself. We cannot depend on another to study our self. It is the initial form of meditation or concentration, which one should do in the morning and evening, create a vision or an image of it and offer it some water and flowers. This is a symbolic language. It is an offering of what sustains his life and what blossoms from it. His sustenance and its produce is an offering to his spirit. His feelings, ideas, dreams, images, attitudes, urges and actions express his UPASANA, what he is close to in his mind or what he is devoted to. As he makes progress, the nature of his meditation changes.

ISHWAR is a name for the power that lives in diverse forms of existence. Whatever are the most powerful phenomena in nature and culture, whatever overwhelms us with its greatness, its sheer marvel, not as expressed in words but in actual impact, making us dumb and speechless, whatever abolishes our small, petty ego, and absorbs us in all this vastness, howsoever temporarily and so shapes us, whatever is the mystery greater than us, that is the wonderful form in which ISHWAR is meeting us.

ISHWAR is wonderful, unique, incomparable, all-inclusive, and sovereign. He has been known through many names. These are words that the wise use to express their experiences of the wonderful. Most traditions give a thousand names of the divine.

ISHWAR is the supreme, cosmic being. He is present in the universe and outside it. He is present in what we do and outside it. He is that with which the seeker devoted to it tries to identify with. When he is experienced, nothing else remains in consciousness.

He is also called SARVESHWAR, the lord of all beings that we reach, whatever the path we take. We may do actions that express our nature. We may reach perfection in seeing and doing and its heavenly rewards. We may praise and glorify what we love in awe and admiration. We may be devoted to it, utterly absorbed in it. We may struggle and exert in knowing the final truth. We may even reach it. The end is the same, whatever the path we take. He is the truth we struggle to know. He is the lord that controls us. He is the perfection we act to achieve. He is the presence everywhere that we train to see. He is the heart and the center of every thing. He is the organic cosmic being, who relates everything to everything else. He is alive and conscious.

BRAHMA is the one who responds to prayers, when they are sincere, when they emerge from our genuine needs, when we are helpless, without pride or ego and when we are not manipulating for an already thought out purpose. He is lord of prayers. He helps in unforeseen ways through coincidence or dreams. Pray to him for protection, for success, and for ordering the chaos in our living.

He created RISHI ANGIRAS, who found the use of herbs and their sap for our sustenance and good health. He saw actions and their consequences, which are also actions.

He is GANAPATI, the lord of the people when they act together.

He is GANESHA, the one who gives success to men's endeavors and of their sacrifices and prayers. He is sacred and pure. He is the presence in assemblies of holy effort. He is the law and order that governs the universe.

He is BRAHASPATI, the priest of DEVAS. He intercedes for men. He is the channel between man and the forces that affect him.

He is VACHASPATI, the lord of the sacred word that creates order out of chaos. The word is the daughter that BRAHMA produced out of his mind. He combined the word with order for creation.

He rides a cow, which is VISHVARUPA, the form of the world. It is the blue tipped flame of the sacrificial fire. He created plants that flower and those that do not. He created medicinal herbs. When ASURAS wounded DEVAS in the war, he brought them back to life. He is the healer.

DEVAS refused to accept the supremacy of INDRA, the lord of rains and prosperity, and of pleasures of the senses. BRAHMA intervened and showed them the need for a sovereign to create prosperity. You cannot have welfare and security without a king. They all agreed. He is the adviser of DEVAS.

SAVITR is SURYA DEVA. He is the sun that enlightens, abolishing darkness and ignorance, danger and sin. He reveals the truth, unconcerned with our joy and sorrow.

He is our self, riding a golden chariot that takes us to work and to rest. He does not rise and does not set. He is ever the same.

He is the eye that watches what we do. He is the power that enters us, linking us all into one family of the sun.

He enters the north and the south and changes our seasons. He changes our seeing, the color of our life. He enters fruits and vegetables, herbs and plants. He enters animals and man and their ways of living. He is the very sap and warmth of our life. He is the beginning and end of time.

Pray to him as he enters AGNI in the evening and see with your eyes how darkness surrounds you. Pray to him as AGNI enters him in the morning and see with your eyes how light surrounds you. Open yourself to nature in the morning and the evening and do SURYA NAMASHKAR like a yogi, stretching your body with the right postures. He enters deep into everything and makes it.

He is the knowledge present everywhere, worthy of reverence. He removes sickness and suffering. He is the source of blessings and life. He teaches us to see.

Meditate daily on what enlightens, what removes darkness, ignorance, and suffering, and recite the GAYATRI MANTRA.

AGNI is guardian of the world, one of its constituents. He lives in the mouth of the cosmic being. He changes everything. He is the priest who carries our message to the higher powers. He is a friend of man, mediating between him and the higher forces. He is the ideal priest, who guides one to prosperity at home. He accepts all offerings, including the body when it dies.

He has many forms, everywhere the same and yet different. He is RUDRA, the fierce, who became SHIVA, the benevolent. He is MITRA at dawn, SAVITR while passing through the sky, and VARUNA in the evening. He warms the heavens as INDRA. He is always young and very old. He is present in all, heavens and earth and waters, the sun and the home and the hearth. He lives in wood and in plants, and deep in the earth. He comes down on earth with rain and lives in water.

He is the lord of the house. He burns down all growth on land and helps people to settle down on it. He is present in all beings right in their hearts and all their parts. He is present in the stomach and genitals, in the throat and the eyes, the source of their energy. All sacrifices end in him. He knows all as he consumes all.

He purifies, holy and unmixed with anything else, worthy of praise.

He is terrible, vast and illimitable. He is present everywhere. He moves upwards and from east to west. He moves with speed, burning and changing things, effective in action. He melts some and hardens others. He creates and digests all foods and sacrifices. He gives health and death.

He keeps families together, sustaining love and sharing food. He brings communities together and brings down higher powers to accept their offerings. He creates intensity of effort, giving knowledge, grasping everything. He gives light and heat in darkness and cold.

Many families worship fire. They focus their minds on its qualities and values. They try to acquire them and be like him.

Be like a fire that takes you upwards and burns up what takes you downwards. Be like a fire that destroys the enemy forts with power and strength.

Offer your fire to your ancestors, your customs and tradition. Offer your fire to your DEVAS and high ideals. Protect yourself with fire that devours all experience to reach the truth.

DEVAS shine and give us things. We pay our debt and give them back through sacrifice. They give us rains and plants and fruits and seed and life. We give them our feelings and urges, speech and praise, devotion and the results of our actions, their fragrance and fruits. We light the fire and offer them milk and water. We are part of this inter-active play of divine powers. May we be aware of it!

DEVARAJA INDRA is the lord of heavens, of the senses and their pleasures and what is beyond the senses. He drank lakes of liquor. Half of him was heaven and earth, and plenty was left of his girth for the beyond.

He is the ruler of the world, mighty, powerful and invincible. He can go wherever he likes, and digest anything he takes fancy to. He does wonderful actions. He is above everything, the greatest seer in the body. He has a thousand eyes and he sees everything. He pours down showers of what we desire. He brings down waters to the dry and dusty lands, satisfying desires, giving blessings, the brother of winds and life. He gives the gift of wealth, full of charity.

He was born to a mother through a cut on her side. He was born like a bull full of unlimited strength.

He was born to seven mothers, worshipped as DEVIS. His mothers are Rivers SINDHU, ASIKINI. PARUSHINI, SARASVATI, YAMUNA, GANGA, and SARAYU.

A demon in the form of a wet nurse came to devour him, but he killed her.

His wife is powerful INDRANI worshipped by those who fight.

He kills monsters with his thunderbolt. He makes weapons of those who meditate and control themselves. He is a noble warrior, full of power and vigor. He is a great warrior, who liberates the world from its enemy, putting them to flight.

He fought a hundred battles and conquered a hundred cities of the enemy RAJA SHAMBHARA. He gave wealth to RAJA DIVODAS and RISHI BHARDWAJA. He fought the enemy in HARIYUPIYA. He protected RAJA SUDAS when followers of RISHI VASHISHTHA appealed to him for help. He heard their appeals and rescued RAJA SUDAS from the siege. He helped him cross the river PARUSHINI, now called RAVI. He told RAJA PURU to sacrifice to him alone. In return he promised to give him his friendship, protection and generosity. He shared his wealth with RAJA VASU of the CHEDIS, now BUNDELKHAND. He gave him the royal insignia. He killed his enemy SHIPRU of the magical powers and gave his wealth to his own devotees. When PANNIS stole his cows, his dog smelled them out and he brought them home. He brings spoils of war, wealth and cows to his followers. He helps us in battle to win the spoils. He hurls his thunderbolt on the enemy. He destroys cities of enemies and overcomes obstacles. He is the mighty man with well-set jaws, angry and wrathful, full of valor. He is the hero of mighty deeds that arouse our awe and reverence, an ideal of warriors.

The tribes who dwell in India worship him. He is famous, praised by all who are devoted to him. He rides a chariot driven by seven horses, all of different colors. He makes a bow in the sky. He released the waters held up in dams and quenched the thirst of the fields. He released the waters of seven rivers, cutting paths in mountains for their flow.

He said to PRAJAPATI, the creator: I shall be as great as you.

PRAJAPATI said: Who am I?

INDRA retorted: Just what you said. You are KA. (Who?)

He is the master everywhere. He fought with DEVAS to establish his sovereignty and reigned supreme for some time. So he was punished and excluded from all sacrifices. All alone he killed the enemy, the coiled up serpent that blocks the flow of waters and brings drought and gloom to the world. So he was called MAHENDRA, INDRA the great.

He retrieves the stolen cattle and wealth. He defends his devotees. He makes friends with those who worship monkeys and are devoted to animals.

His companions are howling winds that make the homeless cry. They make us fearless and grant us victory over enemies.

He restores sight to the blind and legs to the lame. He removes sorrows as he fills the earth with food through rains, and gives blessings and wealth.

INDRA brings rain and water, crops and prosperity. Like an elephant he sprinkles water through his trunk. He fills the earth with food and life. Then the sun truly rises and the light truly shines and offerings of sacrifice can be made. He prefers the life of prosperous householders to the life of renunciation.

He helps outcastes. He works against castes and social customs and high norms. Why be moral? He says. Be active, earn wealth and learn to enjoy it, he says. Be not bound with too many restrictions, he says. Do what you will and have the power to enforce your will, he says.

INDRA is our higher self, beyond good and evil, beyond all social customs and values, seen by the wise, utterly natural. He often does what the wise forbid, as we now do in our dreams. Deep down in our minds we are neither moral nor human. Deep down we all are rooted in him.

INDRA is a great philanderer, seducing women. He gains his ends, whatever the means he uses. No one is safe with him. He even suffers as a consequence of his actions. Then he does penance for his actions. But after the penance, he does those actions again.

He killed TVASHTAR in a far away land and brought SOMA home. He likes to drink ravenously and enjoys revelry.

He is the force of life. Life is in the good. Life is in the bad. He does all actions as he desires.

He is the lord of rituals of a hundred sacrifices. He honors those who sacrifice.

He is the patron of music and dance and festivals of senses and pleasures. Music and songs reach him like rivers reach the sea. He lives in mountains, sending down rivers and cutting their paths. His favorite River SARASVATI has ASHRAMS of RISHIS on its banks.

He taught AYURVEDA to DHANVANTRI, the physician. He created the thunderbolt and weapons. He improves upon weapons to fight as he acts effectively.

He is the sun, the maker of cosmic deeds. He set the earth in the sky and fixed the mountains. He changed the course of a river. He controlled the moon, days and nights and seasons with numbers. He made a path for the sun in the sky and made the stars that shine.

INDRA is offered roasted barley and meat with liquor. The ox and bull and buffalo are slaughtered in his honor. He was the eagle that brought SOMA down from heavenly mountains. He drinks liquor and eats meat and bread.

Celebrate the festival INDRA MAHOTSAVA in his honor. Celebrate the arrival of rains after a hot and dusty season. Begin this celebration on the full moon day of the month of rains. The northwesterly winds bring down showers on hot and parched lands. Celebrate for twenty-eight days. Offer yourself meat and bread with liquor and music and dance. Enjoy yourself. Raise a stick of bamboo in his honor and hang a yellow pennant on it. A bamboo stick with a yellow pennant is his royal insignia. It is the rod that supports the world. The world moves on the rod of power. Resolve to enjoy nature in all its variety, and feel its changing colors and seasons. Remember that you yourself are nature, its most wonderful expression.

SOMA is the lord of joy and immortality. He pours himself into DEVAS and men.

He came down from the lands of GHANDARVAS, who cherish him. He came down from the higher lands of River SINDHU. He came down from the lands of KASHYAPA'S MIRA. He is hidden deep in the herbs that grow on earth. He waits for the sap to be released for the rapture of men.

He is lord of the moon and king of the vegetable world. He is the wine that passes from earth to heaven in the ritual of sacrifice. Men elect him to be their king.

He is the lord of kings. He is the lord of the learned ones. Ordinary kings rule ordinary people. SOMA rules the powerful and the learned.

Drink SOMA for health, to find release from sin and evil dreams. Drink its juice, ferment it strong and learn to enjoy life.

Sacrifice in his honor on the full moon of after the rains.

KAMA DEVA is the lord of love, desire and passion, the quiver on the lips and in the hands. He is the son of NARAYANA, the man dissolved and carried forwards, and LAKSHMI DEVI, the ideal of beauty, wealth and leisure.

He is a column of fire that burns the world. He moves the world, changes and creates it. He is the pain in the heart, the arrow of flowers. He is the seed in the mind, a great disturber. The bride invokes him, bathed and dressed in smiles and jests.

SHIVA consumed KAMA through his third eye of wisdom, but rubbed his ashes all over his body. KAMA resides in every cell of the body and mind, in all the senses, in smells and sights and forms and tastes and sounds and touch and especially in the procreative organ, the temple of love. No one can do without him and continue and feel secure.

VISHVAKARMA is a form of BRAHMA, the chief architect and engineer of all individual forms of the same substance called power and energy. He is present everywhere in everything with hands to make forms and face to witness the making of forms. He creates new designs, weapons and missiles and machines and buildings and materials and clothes and foods and drinks. He made VISHNU'S CHAKRA, SHIVA'S TRISHUL, and KARTIKEY'S spear, and many more weapons out of sun's energy.

Craftsmen worship him on SANKRANTI of the month of BHADRABHAD (August-September) as they resolve to see form in everything that they see. Instruments used for earning livelihood are made neat and clean and beautified as one thinks of improving them and creating new forms.

See the form, the design when you see a thing. See the spaces in things and between things.

VARUNA is the lord of the sky. Dressed in a golden dress like the sun, he shines in the morning as the king of DEVAS. He rules all the lands as king. He is imperial, royal and glorious. He is the sovereign on the horse, the supreme warrior. The horse belongs to him and he belongs to the horse. The horse is a part of him. The horse and he are one. He travels to help people. He inspires awe and humility. He is strong and speedy. He has a powerful stomach that digests everything.

Worship VARUNA when you consecrate kings. Then RAJAS make a sacred vow to protect and serve their people. Anyone who protects and serves the people is a RAJA. He is lord of the land and the sea. He keeps people on the righteous path with a rod. He blesses them with their welfare.

He is the seer with a vision and knowledge full of wisdom. He has knowledge of herbs and of cattle and wealth. He helps in illness and prosperity.

He knows the truth and falsehood of men. He has a thousand spies like the stars at night and fireflies in the trees. He knows the secrets of men. His knowledge of secrets is the noose around their necks. He ties them up in knots. When two persons talk, VARUNA is present as the third.

He carries a sling and a disc and a club and a loop. He throws them around the neck of people he wants to destroy. He punishes the transgressor and those who do not keep their promises. He sees their malice and punishes a liar and punishes adultery. He afflicts the guilty with disease, abnormality, deformity and premature decay. He binds all in the sacred order. He makes and guards the law of nature.

He is the night that swallows birds and beasts. He knows the path of birds and of ships. When the ship is lost, he sends out birds to find the land. He knows the paths of rivers, as he travels. He knows the paths of the sun and the moon and days. He counts and calculates. He taught BRIGHU the knowledge of calculating the paths of rivers and seas, the paths of the sun and the moon, the past and the future. He knows the paths we cannot see.

He enforces laws, the wise governor. He is DHARMA, the order that sustains the world. Do not flout DHARMA and invite his wrath. Be like him and strive for righteousness. His path is straight, regular and fixed. He conquered both the good and the wicked people. He is the law that punishes the wicked and rewards the good.

He is the lord of seas and lakes and of waters. His son is PUSHKAR, ever present on his right side. He lives in water in DWARKA, a town of precious stones in the western seas. He guards the west. He lost to KRISHNA in a fight.

He sits on a fish, a chariot driven by seven swans. He rides on a crocodile. He is the lord of the deformed and the ugly, the pot-bellied. His head is bald, his teeth protrude, and his eyes are red. He is the father of apes and snakes. He is surrounded by danger and death. He is dark and malevolent. Offer him what is hot and spicy.

KUBER is the lord of wealth. Wealth is alive and moving and changing places. Wealth needs a virtuous controller to stay at one place. Wealth is best used in charity for the welfare of all.

He is the lord of treasures hidden in the earth and across the seas. He is the lord of miners and the rich and distant traders. He lives in effort and intense action. He is a companion of SHIVA and self-discipline.

Offer flowers and water with reverence to the lord of wealth. Sit near him in your mind.

YAMA is the lord of death. He controls all, but is controlled by HARI, his guru, as he depends on life but life does not depend on him. Fate appointed him to distinguish between good and bad actions. He is the lord of justice. He appears as life to the virtuous and as death to the wicked. He lives in the south in the house of discipline. He is the lord of punishment that brings reform and purity of the wicked.

On DEEPAVALI, you close your old account and open a new one. You balance your income and expenditure. A day before this closure, offer flowers and water with reverence to YAMA RAJA, the lord of death. Give a part of your income in charity and discharge your debts to your life that is gone.

CHITTRA GUPTA keeps accounts of good and bad actions. He records in your subtle body all your actions and feelings, motives and urges, intentions and aspirations, dreams and images. Nothing that you feel or do is ever lost. The records pass on from one birth to the next. They are born with you as your tendencies to action. They take shape in your life, its length and quality. Take care of what comes into your mind. Control your mind and lead it towards the best in you. That is the offering you make to him. He is the patron DEVA the ideal of all accountants.

ARYAMA keeps the spirits of ancestors at peace. He accepts all offerings to the dead, to your custom and tradition that they created. He accepts all offerings to the beyond that you make in faith and ignorance. He is the friend, the ancestor of all. He is worshipped for protection of the family traditions and customs.

Worship him by keeping alive what your ancestors cultivated and admired as their best, their highest.

PUSHA is the blind lord of beasts. He is physical strength, animal pleasures and behavior, pure and simple. When he rises, only he matters. Keep him cool and satisfied.

ASHVANI KUMARS are the lords of health and long life. They are the divine ideal of doctors. They traveled on horses giving medicine to the needy whatever the status and wealth of the patients. They composed a treatise on AYURVEDA, now lost.

CHANDRA goes around the earth. He is the lord of mind, peace and contemplation. He helps us reflect on our life as we re-live our experiences in the moonlight. We can go to him for reflection and re-living our life, or we can go to SURYA for living our life spontaneously. He is the lord of the rise and fall of waters in the seas and the body. He helps medicinal herbs and changes their potencies. Bathe in moonlight and relax when the days are hot. Moonlit night is the time for pleasure and for contemplation. Soak in his virtues and qualities. He is the brother of LAKSHMI, DEVI of wealth, pleasure and leisure. CHANDERVANSHI KSHATRIYAS worship him, as they are devoted to pleasures and contemplation.

MARUTS are forms of air. Airs have many forms. They are harsh and soft, dark and light, wet and dry, soothing and stinging, silent and noisy. There are the fierce winds that howl in the open lands and make you cry. There are the airs that are worshipped for health and status.

GANESHA is the son of SHIVA and PARVATI.

He is DEVA of MULADHARA CHAKRA, the basic cycle of energy on which other cycles of energy are based. He is worshipped before any other DEVA is worshipped. He is auspicious. He overcomes obstacles.

Once he was at the gate of his mother's chamber when father wanted to enter. He stopped him and father cut off his head without any feelings. Mother mourned. Father put an elephant's head of unforgettable memory on him.

He records instantly and never forgets. He uses a mouse that cuts and separates things to pieces as his vehicle.

His symbol is SWASTIKA, which is a plus sign in which the vertical line is turned right at the top and left at the bottom, and the horizontal line is turned up on the left and down on the right, with a dot placed in each of the four open squares so made. It is an auspicious sign of being settled in one's own self, the cyclical nature of the eternal truth of the endless rising, falling and rising again. One invokes it in prayer for long life and success in accomplishing the enterprise one is about to start.

Another symbol is GANESH CHAKRA, which is two intersecting triangles, one on top of another and penetrating to make a hexagon inside a circle with eight petals coming out of its circumference, radiating energy. This figure is enclosed in a square, on the middle of each side of which a rectangle with concave sides juts out.

VISHNU is NARAYANA, who moves on waters of the dissolved universe. After the universe dissolves, he brings it out in all its beautiful forms. His symbol is water on which he stands or reclines. He rests on the snake of infinity. It has seven heads of dissolved elements.

VISHNU reclines on time. He rides on eagle. He has four arms, and carries a U on his forehead. He carries a conch shell to announce his victory over demons. He carries the right seeing rotating wheel, brilliant like the sun. He uses it against the enemies of the divine order. He carries a golden mace that shows his royal power over men and DEVAS. He carries a lotus flower to show his purity and detachment. He lives in a paradise made of immortal gold and precious stones. He lives in wealth that is good and life giving.

During the age of truth, the divine order did not need to be protected. So he did not incarnate then. Later, he took birth as fish to protect MANU. He warned him about the coming flood. The fish tied a rope to MANU'S ship. She prevented it from smashing against the Himalaya Mountains. He saved knowledge from the floods.

Next, he was born as a tortoise. He retrieved the divine treasures lost in the flood. He recovered the nectar of immortality, the dissolved elements and knowledge of changing forms. DEVAS and demons churned the cosmic ocean, standing on the tortoise, and winding the snake of infinity around the central mountain. This fight between DEVAS and demons is eternal and necessary for progress to disturb the peace of nature and to make things for the world to continue. Such fighting is good, and churning of the ocean produced many things. The fight produced poison, which only SHIVA could swallow, and the cow of plenty, mother of all that is needed, and wine, and LAKSHMI DEVI of beauty, pleasure and wealth that VISHNU married, and CHANDRA that adorned SHIVA'S hair like the mind about to disappear, and precious stone as wealth that VISHNU took, and the heavenly nymph, the ancestor of all heavenly dancers, and the tree that fulfils every desire that INDRA planted in his garden for his wife. It produced the winged elephant that flew in the air that INDRA took for his mount, and the powerful bow, which was later given to RAMA, and DHANVANTRI, the physician of DEVAS.

Next VISHNU was born as a boar to save the earth from a demon that had dragged the earth to the depths of the dissolved cosmic ocean. He brought it out on his tusks to set right the cosmic equilibrium.

Next he was born as man-lion to destroy the demon who could not be destroyed by god or man or beast, neither in the day nor at night, neither in his house nor outside it, and who tortured his own son, forcing him to be devoted to his father as the supreme power instead of life, as he had become a devotee of VISHNU.

Next he was born as dwarf, who was no dwarf. Listen to his story.

PRAHALAD was a prince of demons who turned to the worship of VISHNU who sustains life. His grandson RAJA BALI did ASHVAMEDHA YAJNA to conquer the world. VISHNU appeared to him in the form of a dwarf. Many think that man is only a dwarf. They do not know that the divine is present in him. RAJA BALI granted him as much land as he could cover in three steps. VISHNU assumed his divine form. With one step he covered the earth. With the second step he covered the air. With the third step he went beyond what could be seen and experienced. RAJA BALI learnt the lesson that he did not own the world, though he was powerful.

Next VISHNU was born as PARSHURAMA. He came to strengthen the power of the wise against the power of warriors, who are drunk with power and struggle to control all beings. He killed numerous warriors many times. He taught that morality and knowledge must always control brutal power. He fulfilled his mission, after which he lost to his own power in devotion to RAMA and became human.

VISHNU was born as RAMA and then as KRISHNA and then as BUDDHA. He is yet to be born as KALKI.

VISHNU is the protector of embryos, of life in origin, granting birth. His head is the sun, giving light and heat, and day and wealth. He lives on the seas and in life and in man as he changes. He lives in the individual and in society. He wields the right seeing wheel that rolls, cycles and circles and returns. It kills all that comes in its way.

To do UPASÀNA of VISHNU, feel reverence and devotion for life.

Sit close to him in your mind by doing the duty that emerges from your nature. Express the flow of your nature according to your age and circumstances. Lead your morally neutral divine nature to the best in you, the highest it is capable of, away from the evil present in you by doing actions that bring people together.

Do not copy another's nature or impose your own nature on others.

Be aware of your flow of nature. Ignorance of it is a form of suicide.

Do your duty emerging from the best in you skillfully in the best way in a detached manner, as an offering of your fruit to the divine present in all. Offer its results for the welfare of all in place of your narrow selfish interest.

Be the same to all, friends or foes.

VISHNU has a thousand names. Visualize him in his numerous names and forms. Reflect on some of them that appeal to you.

VISHNU is the power that pervades all. That power is PARAMATMA, the self of all.

He is PURUSHA, who relates all as limbs of the same one living conscious being.

He is SAKSHI, who witnesses everything, sees all happenings, as in self-reflection.

He is SHIVA, the auspicious, who is unaffected by the compulsions of nature.

He is SATYA, the truth that does not change.

He is ISHVARA, the divine power present in all that exists.

He is ANTARYAMI, the inner controller and regulator of all beings.

He is SVAYAMBHU, who manifests himself on its own, without a cause.

He is ADITYA, the golden presence in the sun.

He is VIDHATA, who creates results of actions, producing fruits and effects.

He is VISHVAKARMA, who creates all forms in the universe.

He is MANU, the one who thinks and reflects.

He is PRAJAPATI, the creator of all living beings.

He is VASU, in whom all beings live and who lives in all beings.

He is RUDRA, who makes all beings cry on their dissolution.

He is VEDA, the knowledge that forms and regulates all beings.

He is KAVI, the poet who sees everything, all beings, past present and future.

He is BHOJANAM and BHOKTA, the food and its enjoyer, nature and its observer.

He is VISHVAYONI, the source of the universe.

He is YAMA, who regulates and disciplines all, remaining within them.

He is MAHAMAYA, the illusion he creates.

He is NARAYANA, the residence of all beings on their self-dissolution.

He is PRABHU, the sovereign who surpasses all.

He is ISHTHA DEVA, dear to all as their nature.

He is ADI DEVA, the source of all powers.

He is PARAMESHVARA the supreme power.

He is DEVA, the power that shines in all and gives what they do.

He is DHARMA, the support of all beings, their nature, the best in them.

He is YAJNA, who sacrifices himself to become and know all.

He is JIVA, who knows the individual body and its life.

He is KAPILACHARYA, who formulated SANKHYA, knowledge of nature and the pure self.

He is BHAGVAN, who knows the origin, growth, decay, attachment, freedom and limitations of the world, the sequence of actions, known to all as their self, riding on fate, detached from everything.

He is NIRVANA, where suffering ceases.

He is HARI, who destroys suffering, the sequence of birth and death.

He is BRAHMA, who creates the order of everything.

He is VISHVAMURTI, whose idol and symbol is the universe.

He is SHUNYA, empty, without attributes.

He is ACHINTYA, beyond thought and senses.

He is ANU, the subtlest being, smallest of the small.

He is NIRGUNA, without the qualities of nature.

He is ASHRAM, where beings rest.

He is DHANURVEDA, the knowledge of warfare.

He is DANDA, the rod of punishment by rules, inflicting punishment as YAMA.

He is DAMA, self-discipline.

He is RAVI, SURYA, SAVITA, or the sun that gives light and heat, life and creation, reveals knowledge and removes ignorance.

He is never defeated, and never obstructed.

He is the self-radiant light.

His will is always good, ever wonderful and blissful.

He is without beginning, the essence of all beings, without decay or destruction.

He is the residence of all forms of wealth, like power, morality and beauty.

He is support of the universe, ever giving, and expert in all actions.

He is master of the senses, purifying everything.

He is auspicious life, the lord of lords, established in his own nature.

He is the same towards all beings, austere and simple.

He inflicts suffering on evil men.

He is with four arms, four army divisions, four Varnas and social functions.

He keeps everything in its subtle form.

He is wisdom, heroic action, strength and skill.

He is two-winged, made up of opposite pairs like light and dark, pleasure and pain.

He exists and does not exist. He changes and does not change.

He is the final teacher of all truth that scriptures try to approximate more or less.

He excels at everything.

He is the medicine that cures.

He is without smell, without the qualities our senses create, incomparable.

He is that which brings all together, like earth, water, air, sky and fire.

He is the immortal golden womb of the world.

His knowledge brings the highest good.

He is time that limits everything and the eternity present in each moment.

He accomplishes everything efficiently, effectively.

He is peace, where beings remain after dissolution.

He is without the limits of space, time, and cause.

He has no form and has all forms.

He cannot be described.

He unites all worlds.

Meditate on a few of these ideas regularly. Internalize them and express them in your feelings, attitudes, and actions. Try to create an idol, an image, design, or drawing of some of these.

All art is symbolic, a human construction that reminds one of something else. There can be no realistic art. In itself, words are only sounds, and drawing is only dots and dashes. Make your own visuals and symbols, but experience their meanings.

Creation and Human Values

MAHARSHI PRAJAPATI reflects on creation

In the beginning, all that we see and experience did not exist. Nor can we truly say that it did not exist at all. What we see is reality and this reality cannot come out of what does not exist. Nor can this reality cease to exist when it dies. That which comes to exist also exists before its birth in its cause as a possible effect, making its birth and death only an appearance, a set of conditions.

In the beginning was neither existence, nor non-existence. Neither was there being, nor non-being, neither something, nor nothing. Neither was there all this mighty energy, nor space, nor time to spread out. There was no life or what is beyond life. There was no death, nor deathlessness, no night, no day.

In the beginning, when time and motion were not born, what covered all this? Concealed or hid it? What seminal fluid was there, dense and deep, incomprehensible?

There was the One that projected all that could ever exist, alone, without a breath. Nothing else was there. It was darkness profound, unexpressed, formless fluid of all. A subtle form of seed it was, invisible, containing all that can be.

That One emerged through its own fire and heat, intense, unbearable. Awareness of what it was came to be. It saw itself. That One was present everywhere like desire born of mind in the beginning. That was the original seed of all bursting into the universe.

They who know see energy all around, truth expressed that binds and brings all together. These rays of Truth and its Energy, the flow of seeds, the force of the universe of mighty competence, self-supporting internally, through their nature, rushed far above, below and beyond.

Who knows that Truth? Who can speak of it? From where was all this born? This motion of many forms was born of what and why? Even DEVAS that became the universe and us came to exist after That One. Then who knows the Truth from which came all these that we see in all directions? This motion that takes many forms was born of what cause, for what purpose? What supports it? Or does not support it?

That Master Seed Of All, the Highest, is present in all. That One is the Truth, even if we do not know it, nor do DEVAS that it created.

Most translations render the last verse as "Even gods do not know it", which makes the poem absurd. Nor do they insert interpretative clauses in the modern idiom, which makes the poem archaic.

DEVAS are expressions of one Supreme Being. They are the ones that take forms and come into existence. These forms stay for a short or a long time. They dissolve their forms to reconstitute again in some other form. They are the ones that shine, the ones that give, the ones that constitute beings. They are the earth and water, rain and air and fire, the sun and the moon, the space and time, intelligence, mind and ego outside and inside us. They all have numerous forms and personal stories.

DEVAS are countless. In the ancient land of HARYANA, BHARTI, the divine motherland that nourishes us, ILA, the divine language that expresses us, and SARASVATI, the flow of divine knowledge that constitutes us seen by RISHI'S on the banks of this river were popular DEVAS. We are still devoted to them

Any form of existence can be seen as independent of other forms. Or we can see them as expressions of the ultimate divine power as limited by the conditions required by that particular form, which is what the ancients did.

DEVAS are themselves creatures of the one without a name. The nameless cannot be worshipped because when we experience the one without a name, we cease to be us in that oneness and there is no other. Then who can worship whom?

Worship of one God is a contradiction in terms, because worship requires two, the one who worships and the one who is worshipped, and so it denies oneness.

When we experience oneness, worship and meditation cease. We worship only expressions of the nameless one.

That One looked at itself intently and saw that it was the self of all. Self-awareness came into being. It was alone. There was nothing else to look at. So it became intensely aware of itself. Its intensity released a mighty blaze of energy that projected DEVAS, forces that make the universe. That projection was its first sacrifice, called YAJNA. It projected and saw itself as the other, the universe.

We see what we are. We see our sensations, our ideas and constructions. We see our self. That is the sacrifice constantly repeated everywhere. The universe is projected and renewed every moment. That renewal is its birth and death. We are That One, the release of its energy. We are the sequence of actions, release of consequences, repeated renewals, births and deaths, an expression of that power.

That One, alone and self-sufficient, was full and whole. There was no lack, no reason to create, no aim to achieve. Its intensity released energy, fire and light. It was knowledge that manifests in actions immediately. It flows out in all directions. Intense fervor is the fire and the concentration, called TAPA. It is the focused energy through which order and truth, desire and action, emerge in all conditions. It is the cosmic energy that takes on numerous forms.

That which is born of motion is the universe. It stands on its own, turning its back on its source. It falls into disorder and decay. Therefore That One enters it, lives in it and regulates it. That was DANA, a giving of oneself.

Through intense fervor it creates desire, cycles that are constantly repeated. That One has many names.

That One is called PASHUPATI, the Lord of animals, including human animals. It requires sacrifice of animals, the animal in us for the sake of the husband, the order and the inner controller.

That one is called PRAJAPATI, the Lord of the people, of citizens and society, who creates the social order, harmony and well being, which is like the order of the universe.

We should learn to control ourselves and be one with the order in nature and society.

YAJNA, TAPA, and DANA are the basic values in VEDAS, and have been commented upon and elaborated in numerous ways, as given below.

In the beginning was YAJNA, the sacrifice. It was fervor and intensity, desire and fire, light and wisdom becoming a vast intelligence that projected all that is, has been, and ever shall be. We should sacrifice our nature, and project it into action through our desire and will, penance and austerity, to become our action, to create of our self what we are capable of being.

In the beginning was YAJNA, the pure action. The doer, the action, the instrument, the manner, the purpose of doing action and for whom it is done, were all absorbed in one single act rising above space and time, intense and creative. This action is its own agent and result, process and material, like a child's play. We should do pure actions, absorbed in the skills of doing the action, seeing only actions happening all around, without you or me or anything else, absorbed in the sequence of actions and skills, creating our world.

A YAJNA is an act of ritual worship done with devotion and concentration. It lifts up the mind from worldly concerns towards That One, the only reality. This inner uplift is the aim of all worship. Outward actions express it and symbols emerge from it. We should do ritual actions that lift us up higher than where we are. If they do not raise us up to a higher level of living and awareness, we should stop doing them as they lose their value and replace them with actions more suited to us.

YAJNA is the action that renews the world every moment. It is like the seed sacrificing itself to become the tree. It is like the moment sacrificing itself to become the next moment. It is one's nature expressing itself in attitudes and urges, feelings and actions, experiencing and becoming events and objects of the world. What happens is what people feel and think according to their natures.

A YAJNA is what we offer to the sacred fire. It is what we sacrifice to sustain the universe that we know. It is our aspiration to face the power that has taken our form. It projects our intelligence and mind on to the world. It takes the form of our ideas and feelings, judgments and choices, actions we do. It links the act with its results, relates us to the world. It changes forms but is ever the same. Nothing can become if, in some subtle way, it does not already exist. What comes to be has already been, as is occasionally revealed in premonitions. The process of acting out the universe is a process of expressing what is present as potentiality. Changing forms emerge from the seed of all possible forms. We normally see changing forms, one form of fire changing into another form of fire. The universe is a process of acting out the initial energy. Be a part of this process. We should display the sacred in our being. We aspire to see the formless fire that exists in all varied forms of fire, in all different conditions and limitations, in the sun and in the plants, in wood and in water, in body and in mind. This formless power of That One does not depend on nature or man or their interaction.

Sacrifice, Self-Discipline and Charity

A YAJNA is an offering to the fire, the ritual of the sacrifice of men, animals and things.

In this ritual, men and beasts were tied to the crotch of a post, a tree with two arms rising upwards in supplication that later became SHIVA'S TRISHUL, and the sacred fire was carried around them with recitation of MANTRAS three times from left to right and then men were set free, dedicated to the eternal for ever and adopted by the priests or the householder hosting the ritual, and animals, if edible, were eaten in a community feast. In their place clarified butter was offered to the fire.

It was a form of renunciation, a dedication of one's life to the divine. A modern version of this ritual is enacted when a man wanting to renounce the world and found qualified for it is first drowned in River GANGA as if he were dead and then brought out as if reborn, dedicated forever to the Supreme Being.

Some people condemn YAJNA as human sacrifice. Today men are sacrificed in wars, or in riots, or as suicide bombs, or through revenge and honor murders, or through legal capital punishment to propitiate the DEVA of justice or some other religious or political DEVA held to be dear even by those who take bribes, tell lies, make false accusations against their opponents, true or imaginary, and inflict injustice on the weak and the ignorant, taking away their lands and resources in the form of taxes, business deals or conquests.

Today animals are sacrificed in hunting or for decoration, hanging trophies on the walls or in non-vegetarian food and in worship of the body through beauty creams with prayer and aspiration to make the body beautiful as if the divine body were inherently ugly and the Supreme Being were an ugly creator of ugly bodies.

Today many of those who condemn human and animal sacrifice eat non-vegetarian food and vote for war, both sides of war desiring to sacrifice a large number of human beings for a cause they think is just or profitable. They assume that the war can decide what is right. But we can win a war and yet be wrong.

Today precious natural resources, including one's own health and the health of the earth and environment, are sacrificed in intense devotion to the formation and accumulation of wealth in worship of LAKSHMI DEVI and then not knowing what to do with this wealth except to have more food, more sex, more bathrooms, more bed and sitting rooms and more words, and sounds or what they call the culture of words and diplomacy that does not cultivate the animal in man but nourishes it and of course more development and creation of rootless needs through advertising and the media in order to continue this unending cycle, as desire is never satisfied through its satisfaction.

All these sacrifices have their own verbal formulas and ritual actions.

When we turn inwards, we start sacrificing what we hold as our dear possessions and the most precious animal in us, like our appetites and senses, body and mind. We learn to see our own self as the same as the self of others, the same joys and sorrows. We learn to see powerful forces of nature, of history and ideals, working themselves out in our lives. They bring us together for a short time into being and then they take us apart into non-being. They enlarge our narrow individual self into the unlimited universal self. It frees us from the boundaries of our limited body and mind and its society. We withdraw our mind from the senses and direct it to a higher and vaster reality. We learn to see our self as different from its body and mind.

If we do not perform action as YAJNA, as a form of dedication to the divine power, then we cook our own rice, doing actions only for our body and its mind. We satisfy our desires for acquiring money and power and status. Then we head towards suffering and sin and unending desires. We are reduced, belittled, made hollow and small. At the end of it all, we see our life as meaningless to be flushed away through death.

When we do actions as YAJNA, as actions for the divine power present in all, we please the forces that constitute us. They bless us with reflection and meditation, devotion and goodness and service, as we learn to limit and control our actions done for pleasure and prosperity. Such actions liberate us.

There are many forms of YAJNA.

PITRI YAJNA requires sacrificing our life and time to nourish our ancestors, parents and grand parents and to take care of our children and grand children. We nourish the good in the traditions of our family and society, as they nourished us with food and ideas, feelings and actions. We are not independent of the forces that produced us. We are their continuation. We received something precious from them. We should enrich it and return it. We should study the tradition of our family, community and history and sustain what is good in it and enrich it and eliminate what is undesirable and painful in it. This is our song of praise for our ancestors, our offering of oblation to them for their maintenance.

NARA YAJNA requires sacrificing our life and time to nourish fellow human beings in the family and the region, in the devotion to livelihood, and in the larger organization of society around the learned people and their temples that provided free social services. We take care of the less fortunate, the poor, the hungry and the handicapped, helping them with free food and medicine, and give charity to the deserving, the worthy and the honorable. We choose an institution for regular charity for public welfare, becoming constructive and helpful in our attitudes, praising the divine presence in all.

RISHI YAJNA requires keeping alive the work of RISHIS who saw visions and created our culture and civilization. We study their creation, their achievements and protect them, trying to live accordingly. We need to learn about their manner of living and their methods of work and seek their blessings in our mind and so keep them alive.

BHUTA YAJNA requires sacrificing our life and time for beings less evolved than us, like plants and animals, like human beings identified with their bodies and senses and their pleasures, and like supernatural beings stuck to their subtle bodies.

We may not believe in supernatural beings. We may think that what science cannot see does not exist. But one day we may have an experience that will transform us, and it will be beyond reason, repetition and scientific verification or explanation.

We should pray to super nature from which nature emerges and into which it goes back, but our prayer must emerge from our deep mind, not from our superficial desires. Super nature is not unnatural. It is the invisible source of the visible nature, beyond expression.

Kings performed ASHVAMEDHA YAJNA, along with heroic narratives of praise, inviting tributes and gifts from neighboring kings, resulting in wars in case they refused. They conquered the kingdoms around them in search of wealth and resources around them.

We can do ASHVAMEDHA YAJNA by concentrating our disparate states of mind into one-pointed mind, and centralizing our tendencies to action in pursuit of the CHAKRAVARTI ideal.

We should sacrifice the horse on which we ride and journey through life. The various limbs and organs of this horse are the day and night, the rising and the setting sun, the waxing and the waning moon, the changing seasons and desires, the changing fruits and vegetables they produce, the rivers and sands, mountains and plains, rain, lightning and thunder, as explained in BRIHAD ARANYAKA UPANISHAD.

We should sacrifice our time and nature on which we travel in life. We should focus our mind in meditation, rising above nature and time. If we do not sacrifice our horse, we continue our journey forever. But if we sacrifice it, rise above it, the ravages of time and space on our body and mind will start disappearing, as will impressions and effects of our past actions. We will acquire a spiritual glow beyond the capacity of food, exercise and medicine.

Kings performed RAJASUYA YAJNA that lasted a year, and expressed the highest wisdom through public discource and actions. Leaders of all castes brought jars of water from different rivers and streams and mixed it with water from River SARASVATI, and water from a whirlpool, a pond, a well and some dew for sprinkling on the crown during the coronation ceremony and so exerting a symbolic effort at political unity of different tribes and communities on this vast land. For twelve days the king visited the houses of leaders of all communities, high and low, for feasting and bonhomie. Only the most powerful kings could do this YAJNA.

Kings also performed DHANUR YAJNA, in which devotion to weapons was expressed, and chiefs of towns and villages paid their tribute and taxes and people showed their strength and skills in sports and games, including wrestling and taming elephants, and the best among them were recruited to the king's service that included fighting and keeping law and order and other duties of the kingdom.

BRAHMA YAJNA requires sacrifice of life and time for the forces that make the universe and us, and their creative order. We meditate on what constitutes the universe and us, and what the universe and we cannot live without, and express our understanding through feelings and actions. We dedicate the flow of our life to forces higher and larger than us and identify ourselves with them. We do actions dedicated to the highest self and pay our debt to the past, the present, and the future, to the lower and higher beings.

My maternal uncle performed a YAJNA as a thanks-giving ceremony on the birth of his son. All residents of his village and of some neighboring villages were invited to the ceremony. While the priests sat around a fire reciting MANTRAS along with some elders, crowds assembled around open air cooking of vegetarian and non-vegetarian food along with country liquor. Hinduism includes the tradition not only of non-violence and Yoga, but also of INDRA with his horse and thunderbolt, the ideal of those who fight. And who can fight better than the villager in defense of his land and community? This tradition has been downgraded historically, and needs to be given due importance.

We need to remember that divine incarnations carried weapons for warfare, which were used when necessary.

Our sacrifice and dedication of life to a noble ideal, the divine self present in us is accompanied by TAPA, the intensity of our effort.

TAPA is a way of establishing ourselves in our own nature. It identifies us with our self and detaches us from the non-self. In this way renunciation of what is not our true self is implicit in TAPA. We are so absorbed in working out our nature that other things do not matter.

TAPA nurtures many forms of virtue, like endurance in the face of heat or cold, pleasure and pain, and difficulties. We learn to see larger forces working through us, and acquire virtues like patience, self-control, renunciation, compassion, forgiveness, humility, fortitude, maintaining peace in adversity and in the face of abuse and cruelty, trials and tribulations. It creates energy, radiance, truthfulness, and perseverance in doing one's duty. Speech becomes non-offensive, truthful, pleasant, and beneficial. One starts practicing purity, simplicity, chastity, and non-violence. One remains mentally close to the larger forces of nature and ideals of tradition, and self-realized gurus who know these forces. One integrates one's lower nature like search for pleasure, power and security, with a high purpose in devotion to our higher and nobler nature.

Intensity of effort will vary according to one's nature, whether truth, energy, or ignorance predominates. It may lead to self-less thinking, firm faith in the supreme, doing one's duty according to one's nature, and giving to the body and mind only what is their due for efficient maintenance and no more.

TAPA may be done for fame and personal benefits. It may take the form of fasts, rituals, and penance and self-torture like remaining hungry, standing in cold water or near fire, etc. It may inflict injury and violence on the body in ignorance and delusion to harm another or to take revenge. We should avoid such actions.

While searching for one's true self through intense effort, we start giving DANA, or gifts to the right persons at the right time.

We should give gifts like food, clothes, or wealth to priests and learned people, to our guru, father, mother, relatives, sick or handicapped persons or the unemployed. We should give our wealth, time, effort, abilities and competence to others to help them. We should give what the other needs like money, employment, skills, and practical guidance, joining a breaking family, reviving friendships, reconciliation with a son or spouse, or digging wells, supplying water, setting up free inns and rest houses for travelers. We should not hoard wealth, but distribute and circulate it.

DANA is giving gifts as duty that emerges from our nature, the right thing to do, to a worthy and honorable person, in a proper place and time, without expecting any returns and changing it into a trade. It elevates us and justifies our living, relating us to others. It varies according to one's nature. It leads us to sharing our wealth in humility, with love and faith, acknowledging the rights of others in our earnings.

MAHARAJA ASHOKA gave away his entire wealth in charity, except the state treasury, which was in the custody of his ministers. Many years later MAHARAJA HARSHA repeated this festival of DANA in the same way. No one is too poor to give. Poverty is a belief created in us by those who took away our wealth in the past and will not hesitate to take away our wealth in the future in different ways, though giving them high-sounding but deceptive names, like building an empire then and building a global economy now of which they can be rulers.

We do not earn our wealth all by our self. Many contribute to it. Our family, parents, relatives and ancestors, our society and its institutions, our teachers and creators of our culture and civilization have contributed to our earning and wealth. How do we repay the debt we owe them? Where is their share? Where is our gratitude, our voluntary share paid out of love and gratitude because of our awareness of their contribution? That awareness shows our spiritual growth, and it is missing.

We should not talk of taxes. The taxes that we pay are compulsory under the threat of violence to be inflicted on our person and property by law supported by the police and the army in case we do not pay. Taxes are our labor taken away from us by the powerful through the threat or use of force. A large part of the taxes gathered in the name of security and service, in the name of the state are spent by the powerful on their own personal security and comforts and pleasures, though it is done discretely and mostly invisibly and with high-sounding moral justifications. Public money is nobody's money especially when the rulers are selfish and unscrupulous. And a lot of taxes are misused and wasted but always with proper justifications.

Sometimes gifts are given while expecting returns and benefits like health and long life, going to heaven, or some blessings or increase in possessions, or expecting the other to give us a bigger gift in return. If we give one kilogram of sweets in charity, we expect twenty kilograms of sweets in return, or is it a thousand kilograms now? The rates keep going up or down, as in stock exchange. Charity has become a form of commercial activity with some people, like giving charity and service for conversion in order to increase the number of members in our church.

Sometimes gifts are given thoughtlessly to wrong persons at the wrong time and place, without reverence or respect in order to degrade, insult and ridicule the recipient and to give pride to the donor. We should avoid such charity.

Devis

The word DEVA refers to forms of existence like earth and water, fire, air and space, the sun and the moon, the powers of wealth and wisdom, beauty and love, life and death, and so on. These forms can be seen as independent, having no relation to any divine power. But the ancient mind saw these forms concretely as expressions of divine power. Some of them were seen as feminine or DEVIS for reasons of linguistic gender or their customary psychological association with women.

DEVI says: I am present in all the worlds like the earth. I am present in all life that makes the ignorant cry in fear of death. I am present in months and time and all the beings that shine. I sustain the waters and rain, fire and rays of the sun. I sustain the ruler who protects all and destroys their enemies. I sustain the sun and the earth that nourish. I offer food of many kinds as charity, the best of sacrifices. He who sees the eternal truth listens to me as he breathes this life. He sees his actions and their consequences. He sees himself as actions happening. So he is detached from actions as he sees them.

The ignorant too worship me, staying near the guru, trying to acquire knowledge. You see me according to your capacity. I teach you truth worthy of trust. I teach you the truth that the learned see, the truth on which they meditate.

I make people who rule destroyers of their enemies. I make people see visions of order and truth. I make people good in intelligence, in speech and in force. I make those too who hate truth and order. I stretch the bow and make the violent cry. I bring people together on what pleases them on the earth and in the sky.

I create the sun that nourishes them. I live in space and in the waters, in all the worlds as their cause. I am like them as I sustain them. I am present in the air and in all beings. I am beyond space in this vast universe. I manifest myself on my own.

To do UPASANA of DEVI, or to sit near her, feel reverence and devotion for her. Reflect on her thousand names and visualize them in your life. Make idols, drawings, or geometric, schematic designs of her power present in the universe.

She is MAHAVIDYA, the highest wisdom and supreme consciousness.

She is JAGANMATA, mother of the universe as its cause, reason and support.

She is MAHESHVARI, the power that creates mind and will in every heart.

She is MAHAKALI, the power of time that creates and destroys and re-creates.

She is MAHALAKSHMI, the power of wealth, moral values and relationships

She is MAHASARASVATI, the power of speech, knowledge and arts.

She is SHIVASHAKTI, the power of SHIVA, objectless consciousness.

She is VISHNUMAYA, the illusion of form that hides the sameness of reality.

She is PARVATI, auspicious intelligence that knows its self.

She is CHANDIKA, the angry mother who destroys enemies of her child.

She is VEDAMATA, mother of true knowledge.

She is VAISHNAVI, the power of VISHNU that sustains life.

She is NARAYANI, the support and goal of man.

She is TARA, the power of self-expression that helps all swim across time.

She is KALIKA, who absorbs time, like blackness that absorbs colors.

She is OMKAR, the constant unheard sound of vibration that creates the universe, the form that the formless takes.

She is CHETNA, the power of consciousness.

She is SATI, the chaste companion of SHIVA.

She is the power of Rivers SINDHU, GANGA, YAMUNA, BRAHMPUTRA, SARASVATI, GODAVARI, KAVERI, and all other clear flowing rivers.

She is the sacred place of pilgrimage, like MANUSAROVAR, KURUKSHETRA, KASHI, MATHURA, AYODHYA, KANCHI, DWARAKA, and UJJAYANI.

She is BHAGVATI, the power of supremacy, righteousness, fame, prosperity, wisdom, and discrimination of the eternal from the ephemeral.

She is CHANDI, the power that destroys darkness and ignorance.

She is GAURI, the brilliance of excellence.

She is MULAPRAKRTI, the power that becomes visible nature.

She is KAMAKHYA, compassion that fulfils all desires.

She is GAYATRI, aspiration for knowledge and immortality.

She is SANDHYA, when the night enters day and the day enters night.

She is SAVITRI, the power that creates and heals the universe, including society.

She is INDRANI, the power that destroys opposition to the cosmic law.

She is BHAIRAVI, the power that removes fear of the enemy.

She is the MANTRA that initiates one into spiritual life.

She is JATI, the essential nature of a species.

She is TRIMURTI, the combined power of SARASVATI, LAKSHMI, and KALI.

She is the moonlight that changes hatred into love.

She is the beauty and affection of a woman in love.

She is the fire that rises in the earth, the fire that rises in the spinal chord.

She is the will to create, the power of life.

She is the sap of plants, the power of creation.

She is the maiden aspiring to mature, the fragrance of golden flowers.

She is peace, perfection, and forgiveness, the energy beyond the qualities of nature.

She is the cow that satisfies all desires, the knowledge and sacrifices that liberate.

She is nectar and bliss and fortitude, the earth, and the great mother.

She is the wine that heightens awareness, the power expressed in sound.

She is truth without support, the brilliance of all lights.

She is the sleep of full awareness, the wisdom of intuition.

She is the formless power that manifests all forms.

She is an unaffected lotus that grows in mud.

She is the power of music, liberating through wisdom.

She is the wealth of fulfillment that comes through self-realization.

She is the power of justice, the power of action.

She is the power of faith that leads to the divine.

She is the one that blossoms differently at different places.

She is the power that moves the body.

She is the desire for what you already have inside you.

She is like the limited number of letters of the alphabet that combine to express all learning, like the limited number of arts, like vocal and instrumental music, dance and drama, drawing and painting that express all states of mind.

She is the moment of grace, the power of grace that helps achieve the aims of life.

She is the power of senses and the speed of mind.

She is the power of self realization expressed through actions.

She is the arrow of flowers that carry love and excite the senses.

She is the power of land, water, fire, air, space, moon, sun, and stars.

She is the infinite power that always wins, the power of knowing the self.

She is the power that cools anger in the heart, good temper, and subtle consciousness.

She is knowledge, completeness, consciousness, freedom, power, and infinity.

She is will, knowledge and action, fire, moon and sun.

She is penance, the medicinal herb, and the healer.

She is the imperishable seed, four basic colors and varnas.

She is the unborn, uncaused, whole, and immeasurable, beyond the senses.

She is the source and support of the world.

She is the power of the seven notes of music.

She is the act of worship and death.

She is supernormal powers and the unheard sound of vibrating creation.

She is the power that enjoys and assimilates food into energy.

She is the power of concentrated awareness that destroys restless activity.

She is the power that protects wealth, the power of writing and authority.

She is wakefulness, dream, deep sleep, and that from which they emerge.

She is the power that makes the impossible possible.

She is the eldest and the greatest.

She is the power of pleasure and pain, the power that nourishes and destroys.

She is the power of love and the spirit of service.

Meditate and reflect on a few of these powers. Internalize them and express them in your feelings, attitudes and actions. Visualize them, making their sketches, idols, pictures, designs and descriptions for concentrating on.

We cannot manipulate them or tell lies to them. We can benefit from them if we love them and keep them in mind. We cannot be selfish, superficial, or casual.

Once upon a time, BRAHMA blessed a demon known as DURGAMMA. He had taken control of all knowledge and power, and deprived others of it. He controlled food and waters. He caused drought on earth for many years. Knowledge is dangerous without compassion and regard for others. Possession is dangerous without sharing it with others. So many creatures suffered greatly.

DEVAS prayed to DEVI to save the world. She came riding a tiger and destroyed DURGAMMA and filled the waters of the earth. She restored knowledge and power to the right people who know how to deal with it. Everybody cannot have power and knowledge and use it well. Power and knowledge lie in their use. One has to be qualified morally and also in gaining and using forms of knowledge and power. DEVI came to be known as DURGA. She is the savior in battles. While fighting, soldiers call on her with the war cry: JAI DURGA!

Once upon a time, MAHAVISHNU assumed the form of a child. He floated on a leaf when the world dissolved into its constituent waters. He started wondering who he was, who had created him, and how he should act, and what his duty is. He heard a voice, "I am all that is. There is nothing else than me." VISHNU wondered who spoke it.

DEVI appeared before him. Along with her were numerous powers with different names. They were peace, perfection, divine wisdom, intuition, beneficence, effulgence, supreme light, water lily in moonlight, charm, beautiful woman, lotus eyes, wine, the erotic, intelligence, determination, reputation, fame, understanding, memory, faith and attention, intellect, taste, the beyond, thirst, deep sleep in which doubts and suffering disappear, the sleep of YOGA, compassion, motion, delight, pleasure and satisfaction, growth and progress, forgiveness, fortitude a nd forbearance, trust, modesty, and indolence.

See these powers one by one for a long time, and visualize their numerous forms. Reflect on them and internalize them. See them acting out in your life.

DEVI said: what is there to wonder at? Whenever there is projection, existence and dissolution of the universe, you come again and again with DEVI SHAKTI, your divine power. You are without attributes, now visible to you in numerous forms. From your navel, your center, the place of truth and existence will be born BRAHMA full of the energy of action who will create the universe through his intensity of effort like fire. From the center of his eyebrows, his vision, will be born RUDRA who destroys the universe to recreate it, when its time comes. You will nourish it.

She appeared to VISHNU as DURGA, LAKSHMI, SARASVATI, SAVITRI, RADHA, TARA and many other forms.

DURGA DEVI has been worshipped in India since time immemorial. She is a DEVI with sixty-four forms and arts of doing.

As PARVATI, she knows herself. She is the mother of GANESH, the initiating energy, and wife of SHIVA, ever auspicious.

She upholds DHARMA, the truth, destroys evil and suffering and makes us noble.

She is known as KALI, the black time that controls destruction and destroys all to recreate it.

She is KAPALI, the wearer of skulls that time produces.

She takes wine, flesh, and animal sacrifice. War is her ritual of sacrifice. Human lives are sacrificed for a cause seen as just and high. Human lives are sacrificed through the punishment of death.

Perform her rituals with skill, efficiency and detachment. Bow to DURGA and imagine success. See her with ten arms each with a different weapon and eyes focused on the enemy to be destroyed.

LAKSHMI DEVI is the power of wealth and moral values and rich relationships. She is beauty, compassion, welfare, peace, and goodness. She serves the power of life.

I adore you MOTHER LAKSHMI, beautiful like the moonlight. You are full of joy and nourishment. I think of you every day and call on you to live with me in my family. You are present in my heart, my life, and in my body. You are present in my food and in my family and children. You are present in my cows and cattle, horses and chariots, my friends and followers. You are present in the shine of gold and silver, in garlands and ornaments. You are present in all beings, in all values of life that make life adorable. You bring fame and envy and unknown prosperity. You are SHRI, the companion of VISHNU, the power of life that sustains the universe. You are RADHA of KRISHNA, the celebration of life in all its forms, like music and dance and working for others.

As my mind sits near you every day, my heart and life unfolds. My invisible nature and life take shape, as I follow you every day in my feelings, thoughts and actions. I earn money, responsibility, and status within the limits of DHARMA, goodness and compassion. May the form of life I make for my self every day have beauty and worth, love and devotion! Nourish me Mother and nourish my dreams and aspirations, as I work and struggle to realize them. Fulfill my desires and show grace to me. May I be lucky, as I train myself to see value in all beings, in all things! I shall help their value to emerge and flower.

SARASVATI DEVI is the power of speech and learning, knowledge, wisdom and the arts. She is the power of music and poetry, reason, logic and understanding. She creates and gives shape to order.

She plays on VEENA, creating forms of music and harmony. She liberates through wisdom. We sit close to her in our mind with love.

She was born in HIMALAYAS, the beauty of nature. She gave birth to VEDAS and RISHIS and taught scholars who lived by her side and made centers of pilgrimage, and many other expressions of awe and wonder. She went deep underground as a river in HARYANA and RAJASTHAN, and deep into the Hindu mind.

I adore you Mother SARASWATI, as I open up my senses and mind to nature and reflect on what lies beyond it, and experience what exists beyond reason and mind. I listen to you with attention and full awareness.

You nourish my life and mind. Help me to know and to do what is right. Help me make unheard of music in my life that shows my nature and wisdom in my feelings and actions. Help me understand confusion and conflict. Help me to rise higher to peace and harmony.

SAVITRI DEVI is the wisdom of organizing society and healing its wounds according to the nature of people and the single-mindedness of their effort in self-expression and self-direction in the light of their freely chosen divine ideal and evolution towards oneness and peace, dissolving egos and resolving conflicts.

She gave birth to TANTRA techniques that are used to change the lower nature into higher levels of awareness and being.

She is the science that reveals the powers of nature.

She is JAPA, the chanting of holy names while remembering the divine presence in all forms.

She is MANTRA, the ancient way of clearing the mind of unnecessary things and directing it towards noble ideals.

She is TAPASYA, the intensity of effort and self-discipline, the essence of truth and existence.

May I have a clearer awareness of the order in society and love and power to make it healthy and happy!

KALI DEVI is time in its concrete forms, the change that does not stop, as it is eternal. She is the power of things to grow, decay and die to be reborn. Through repeated births and deaths, she leads to eternity. She is the substance of our experience, our life working through our bodies, feelings and consciousness. She is the source of our birth and growth, decay and death, and rebirth. She drinks human blood to sustain continuity of life. As we sacrifice food into our mouth, she transforms it into life and spirit. She is the life that lives in death and the death that lives in life. She is love that stays in life and death. She is death to the ignorant. She is discrimination of the eternal from the transient to the wise. We should be conscious of the presence of death in life and the presence of life in death.

KALI DEVI is Mother Nature's expression of time in things. She is fierce and destructive with blood trickling from her mouth. She wears a girdle of skulls, like letters of the alphabet and states of mind. She has a sword in her right hand and a severed head in her left hand. She writes through time, dark and black, past and future, dissolution in space. She is naked, clothed in space, active and restless with disheveled hair. She offers us fearlessness and grace, the eternal night of peace and joy, rooted in SHIVA, its source, beyond action and motivation. She is his power and his grace, always auspicious.

KALI says: Be not attached to events in the past. They are forms of time. In this way master time that is eternal. Have no idea of the future. In this way master death that is present in each moment.

We worship KALI by rising above events as forms of time into eternity. We die daily to our likes and dislikes, loves and hates, ambitions and anxieties, worries and thoughts. We offer them all into the fire of awareness. We offer them all to that which is beyond time and beyond our senses. We offer them all to SVAHA, the beyond. We meditate on the transience of all that we experience and know.

TARA DEVI is the power of speech that accomplishes goals. She is the creative speech on which we swim across the ocean of ignorance and fear. She saves us from drowning in individual, social, and natural suffering. She guides us along the creative path, beyond difficulties. She is prosperity of the righteous and poverty of the wicked. She is intelligence of the prudent, faith of the good, and modesty of the highborn. She protects the order in the universe. She is the sun that gives light and heat, knowledge and life. Her symbol is AUM.

We worship TARA, the power of the lord of wisdom. She lives in the tongue of fire, in the taste of the aesthetic mind. She lives in the roots of thoughts in silence. She helps the nectar of ecstasy to flow. She gives birth to intelligence, increases our knowledge, destroying to create, and takes us to light.

SUNDRI DEVI is the power of beauty. To worship SUNDRI, we follow the path of beauty and delight in the world of nature and of men and women.

Beauty is born of order, structure, texture, harmony, and such other causes. We focus on form, the source of beauty. It leads us to the beyond.

Beauty of form is KAMLA. Beauty is not in the form, nor apart from it. Beauty lies in seeing. It is seen somewhere, anywhere. Any form can look beautiful. Any form can look ugly. We need to learn to see beauty everywhere, to purify our self for this seeing. We learn to see the universe in our self. Then we are free of time and space, distance and self-importance. We see the eternal presence. Then the mind stops. We enter SAMADHI. Form leads us to the formless. Illusion leads us to reality. Every form is an opening to reality.

Beauty of the supreme self is present in the gross and the subtle worlds, present in wakefulness, dream, and deep sleep. Wakefulness lives in the eye, dream in the mind, and deep sleep in the heart. She transcends them in the awareness that is common to these three.

Beauty of play is LALITA, the one who plays. The universe is a play of the divine mother for the delight of consciousness. When we see the universe as a play of her forces, we are detached and happy. What are we in the presence of the suns and the stars?

Beauty of the supreme ruler of the universe is RAJ RAJESHWARI. Beauty governs the universe. There is beauty in its order, in its symmetry, in its harmony. Their power is wonderful, full of beauty, blissful and playful, full of innocence and youth. It is the power of understanding and appreciating, of being aware of truth. We learn to see manifestations of divine power as a play.

We search for her and do something beautiful in our life. She commands us through love, not authority. We open our heart to beauty and love and give up the desire to control things.

BHUVANESHVARI is the power of space, where light is born. She is the mother of suns, the mother of light and consciousness. She makes space outside and inside us. She creates many kinds of spaces. She creates infinity in our hearts, where she lives. Space is peace and rest. Space is void, where forms come and go.

She creates forms in space. She begins, enlightens, matures and completes them. She creates directions. When we see objects, we should learn to see the spaces between them, not the objects alone, one isolated from the other.

Creating space in the mind releases us from stress and tension, as in meditation.

We should worship her by acquiring a broad vision, free of narrow opinions and beliefs. We should do actions that remove narrow limits and meditate on continuity, space and infinity and be at peace.

Space is divine. We should be like space, detached. We should be empty, motiveless and open to truth, like space. We can experience this when we do PRANAYAMA, focusing our mind on life, going in and changing us and going out.

BHAIRAVI is like a mother who destroys what threatens her child. She destroys our demons and blocks our negative urges.

She is our high aspiration that gives up our lower attachments. We control our senses and wandering thoughts. She destroys obstacles to the noble aims of living.

She is worshipped through turning our senses away from their objects. We should meditate on the inner light and sound, becoming silent in our mind.

CHHINNAMASTA is the headless power, the consciousness beyond thought. She is the power of non-mind.

Our head is a part of our body. Our body changes, so our mind changes. A juice produces a thought. We should see this and be free of thought and have objectless awareness. She liberates us from the body. She is like lightning, the dissolution of ego. She lives in the third eye, the power of divine vision.

We should find out how we see things and focus our awareness on seeing. We should not be identified with any object.

DHUMVATI is grandmother. She is the eldest guide and advisor. She is sleep and loss of memory, illusion and dullness, without will or motivation. She is the original darkness, chaos and ignorance. She is made up of smoke. She prevents our seeing the one behind the many.

She reveals the potential and shows what is going to be. What is going to be has already been.

GANGA MAI came down from heavens into the hair locks of SHIVA, the auspicious. He let go the waters of the mountains, across the vast plains into the sea.

Mother GANGA is incomparable, joyful, pure, deathless, virtuous, fulfilling, creating wealth, reason, intelligence, fame and love. She is wonderful, full of musical sounds.

We should hear the sounds of rivers, the sounds in air. We should learn to see their limpid flow, their changing shine, and receive impressions of their immense variety.

GANGA is tranquil, like the moon, loving, festive and full of grace. She is life and medicine, giver of long life and health.

She flows constantly like AUM, praised by YOGIS.

She gave birth to numerous ASHRAMS, thousands of thinkers, and artists, like MAHARSHI KAPILA who shaped us and who lived in GANGA SAGAR, where GANGA joins the seas.

She gave birth to wonderful cities like HARIDWAR, PRYAG, KASHI, and PATALIPUTRA.

She receives tributes from Rivers YAMUNA, GANDAK, SON, and KOSHI before joining BRAHMAPUTRA, and spread out into the seas.

She is now polluted, made filthy by thoughtless man who must learn to keep Ganga clean.

She is desirable, worthy of reverence and homage and sacrifice.

She is worthy of worship and reflection, chanting and gratitude.

She is reached through meditation, the flow of constant sound and purity, righteousness and devotion.

Mahadeva

We know the great DEVA in a thousand ways.

He is anger that BRAHMA felt when his mind born children refused to procreate.

He was RUDRA, who cried when he was born. He was half male and half female, and his right and left arms had different strengths. He gave birth to terrible forms that made people cry. He made eleven RUDRAS. These are forms of nature and the empty sky. But some knew them as ten senses and one mind.

Some see him as genitals. Some see him as man and nature that create what we experience.

He is called SHIVA and BHOLE NATH, SURYA, SAVITA and VISHNU, without beginning or end, or limits, or death, or grief.

He is the effective will, the source of all existence that has been or shall be, perishable and imperishable, one and many, the basis and refuge and self of all beings.

He is time and space and victory, a thousand hands, a thousand feet, a thousand heads, the power that creates everywhere.

See the power of nature in trees and forests, in mountains and snowy peaks, in empty deserts and deep oceans of water and space. Learn to see the mystery of the universe.

He is the lord of beasts, of the beast in man and of the animals around him.

He wears poisonous snakes that come with ambrosia, the sleeping energy that rises up like fire full of the knowledge of herbs and immortality, ever young and healthy.

He is the spirit of communities of people, of forces for their welfare, the spirit that lives in them when they act together.

He is the lord of terrible beings full of anger and destruction, the terror of death.

He is the weapon that destroys for the good of all, the battle-axe that killed the enemy.

He carries a TRISHUL, the symbol of the tree of life with its two arms that were raised upwards in supplication. The man or the animal to be sacrificed was tied to the arms of the tree of life during the ceremony of the ritual of sacrifice. The sacred fire was moved around him three times left to right with the recitation of MANTRAS, like our going round the temples three times today. The man or animal offered as sacrifice to the divine power was set free and dedicated to MAHA DEVA forever and adopted by the priests or their host for life, except when the animal was edible. If permitted by custom, it was eaten in a feast.

He is the lord of the howling winds, of floods and epidemics, the cry of life.

He is the lord of medicine, cure of diseases and fears, terrible and benevolent, the source of suffering and relief.

He gives birth through death. The seed dies and the plant is born. A moment dies and the next moment is born.

He is the creative urge, unseen by human eyes.

He is the desire that procreates, the power in nature.

He is LINGA, the column of fire that appeared to BRAHMA and VISHNU who could not see the formless without a name, as the formless has no form and therefore cannot be seen, and they could not reach its two ends, as it has no ends. He is an idol of the formless, that which makes the universe. He is the source of all that is or can be.

He is MAHA YOGI, the concentrated self, wearing the mind as ornament like the moon about to disappear, giving out energy and life of many kinds.

His energy is his power, always auspicious and holy, whatever may happen.

His power is pure sovereign knowledge alone. His power creates illusion for man, appearing as existence, giving experience of time, the will that creates and destroys. His power appears as knowledge acting out in phenomena, names and forms. It creates attachment to the experience of objects that gives pain and pleasure. It creates detachment, withdrawal from objects of nature.

We visualize MAHA DEVA in our mind, sitting near him, as our ancestors did for millennia in times gone by.

SHIVA SAYS

All happenings are necessary. One thing causes another. That is destiny.

Enjoyment of phenomena is as necessary as withdrawal from it, whether you like it or not.

Knowledge alone is eternal. Knowledge is without beginning or end. Knowledge is without subject or object. That which appears as subject is knowledge. That which appears as object is knowledge. There is no reality other than knowledge.

What we see is created by our senses and their mind, our instruments of seeing. When they cease, knowledge alone remains.

Know it through the discipline of YOGA that leads to experience of truth. It leads away from falsehood that the senses and their mind create.

Some seekers praise truth, created by the senses and their mind.

Some praise asceticism, starving the senses of their food, leading to their purification and awareness without an object.

Some praise sacrifice in fire and tradition, the worship of ancestors and customs.

Some praise equality, sincerity, charity, and moral values.

Some praise actions done for a purpose, actions for achieving objectives.

Some praise detachment from actions and their results.

Some praise repeating sacred formulas, meditating on them, acquiring occult powers.

Some praise going on pilgrimages for rejuvenation of their spiritual life.

Some create images in stones or words and worship them.

Each of these ideals has many forms.

Many such ways to freedom from falsehood are advocated.

All this is very confusing.

Praises that are heard from others, gurus or scriptures, are borrowed praises. The experience of others howsoever great is not your experience. They cannot be you and you cannot be them.

Such seekers do good and bad actions. They wander in the cycle of change, of birth and death, by necessity. They are stuck to forms.

Some say that only that is true that is perceived by the senses. There is no heaven or hell for them.

Some say that only consciousness exists and matter is only a form of consciousness.

Some say that there are two essences, nature and the self.

Some say that there is ISHWAR, the one who creates the universe and lives in his creation and regulates it.

Some say that there is no ISHWAR. No one created the universe. No one lives in it. It regulates itself. It is without beginning or end.

They all give strong arguments and quote scriptures. They do not base their views on any personal experience of their own. Their ideas are borrowed ideas, not their own experiences.

Learn to have and express your own experience of life. ATMA must be experienced, seen and heard directly. YOGA is the method that teaches how to have this experience.

Knowledge enjoins actions, good or bad. Actions must be done and enjoyed while living in this beautiful world. Actions bring merit or sin, heaven or hell, pleasure or pain of different kinds. They produce a chain of consequences, happiness or suffering. You experience the results of your actions in this life. If you do not, you require rebirth in order to experience them in a future life.

If there is no rebirth, then some of the actions you do have no consequences for you. If your actions have no consequences for you, then there is chaos. But there is no chaos, though you may not see the order.

Actions have consequences, which must be experienced. Actions are done for results. If the results are not desired for oneself but offered to the divine presence in all, one is freed of the effects of actions. The effects of actions will come, but you will not be touched. This is detachment from the fruits of your actions. Detachment is a preliminary qualification for becoming a yogi.

Do all your actions skillfully with full awareness but do not expect to be rewarded. Reward is not in your control.

Leave the choice of good and bad actions aside. Focus your mind on knowledge and skills of doing, the foundation of reality.

I am that which creates, preserves and absorbs the universe.

I am the source of change and the wisdom that creates virtue and vice.

I am the spirit. Nothing other than the spirit exists or can exist.

All individual beings reflect me, like the one sun reflected in many cups of water.

Many forms appear in one mind in a dream. The mind is one, but its forms in its dream or wakefulness are many. PARAM ATMA is one but its forms are varied realities in the universe. These realities change into one another.

The universe emerges from consciousness. From ISHWAR to matter, it is one existence. It is consciousness and bliss, without a second to compete with it. It pervades all, the light that illumines all, unlimited by time or space.

The universe that we know is created by our senses. They do their duty and create the sensations they are capable of creating. These senses are only ten and separate from one another. These senses are limited in their range and capacity. These limits may be enlarged with instruments and aids, but the limits remain. They and their mind shape their knowledge. The mind changes the impressions it receives. The mind forgets, combines, evaluates, and so distorts. It is influenced by memory or tradition, impressions it received in this and earlier lives. The mind and its senses color the universe that we come to know. Therefore the universe that we come to know through our senses and mind is our own creation, false and imperfect.

Reality is reached through YOGA, when you go beyond the mind. Then the illusion of a varied and differentiated universe created by the senses and mind disappears. Then ignorance and sorrow disappear. Then reality is one, though many words are used to express it.

That one reality is unity that exists always. It is consciousness, overflowing existence and bliss. The diversity that we experience does not exist always. This diversity is known as DEVAS. They are limited forms that one reality assumes. They are its creations. They are born and they die

After giving up all that is false, the YOGI sees ATMA in himself. He forgets the universe in deep meditation. Then dropping his limitations, he identifies himself with that one reality. That reality is the self of the universe.

MAYA is its power of creation and delusion, when we do not see the one present in the many. It is the source of diversity in the universe.

One reality assumes limitations and differentiates itself into different beings. The YOGI frees himself from these divisions. He tries to see the one seed of knowledge, without anything else mixed in it. That is his search for purity, the formless unity that underlies the living diversity.

That seed of knowledge relates everything to everything else, the lord and master controller of the universe. It willed to project the universe, which emerged from that seed of knowledge. The universe pre-existed its emergence. It existed in a subtle form in the seed, from where it emerged.

BRAHMA who keeps expanding and space emerged. Then came air, fire, water and earth in their subtle forms, one different from the other. In various combinations, they produced the gross elements that we can sense. Sound, touch, taste, form, and smell were their characteristics for our senses. Organs of perception, eyes, nose, tongue, skin, and ears perceived these qualities.

One thing causes another to happen. Every thing emerges from consciousness and returns to it.

My energy goes out, scattering and transforming itself. It has all potentiality of whatever can happen and of power and happiness. It has three constituents, truth, energy, and inertia, in different proportions. It gives birth to the power that creates the universe and lives in it, and to life itself, and to the wealth that nourishes life, and to the order inherent in the universe, and to the wisdom that sees the order in the universe, and to the power that destroys obstructions. All matter and forms are born of my energy. They dissolve back into my energy. All forms are limited and have qualities.

Many things arise in words only. There is nothing in reality that corresponds to them. Learn to distinguish words from reality. Understand illusion through doubt and reasoning. Resolve the universe back into that which alone exists.

My energy comes back through concentration and absorption.

The body and mind comes from parents. It is the temple of suffering and enjoyment. Knowledge is present in this combination of gross and subtle elements. It is the individual embodied self. The chain of actions and their effects regulates its destiny. One is born to experience the results of past actions. When these are exhausted, the individual comes back into the universal self.

In the body and mind exists the center of the universe. Islands and rivers, seas, mountains, fields and lords of the fields surround it.

In the body and mind are seers and sages, stars and planets, pilgrims and shrines with their presiding deities, the beings that rule their reality. Each part has its own functioning spirit and being.

In the body and mind are the sun and moon, the agents of creation and destruction, and the great elements of nature. They are subtle and invisible.

All beings and realities in the body and mind do their assigned functions and do their own duties.

The body and mind and the universe mirror each other. What exists in the universe exists in the body and mind as well. It is the same essential reality. As is the universe, so is the individual, and vice versa. The individual limited self is essentially the same as the universal, unlimited self.

On top of the spinal cord is a moon, facing downwards, whose subtle rays give life. They pass through different channels. One ray of nectar passes through a channel to nourish the body. One ray of joy enters the middle of the spinal cord to create the moon. The power of the lord of creation and destruction moves through these invisible channels, and gives freedom. In the body are numerous channels. But only one channel is chief, the way to immortality.

At the bottom is a triangular YONI. It is KUNDALINI DEVI, like a creeper of electricity. It is the serpent coiled three times as sleep, dream, and wakefulness, and a half time that is common to the three standing up like a hood on top of the LINGA.

It is the ever-active creative force of the world. It is the DEVI of expression of the divine nature given to us that the speech cannot express. In the center burns the fire with rays that digest all foods that are taken in through all the senses of perception and action. This fire increases life, gives strength and nourishment, energizes the body, destroys diseases, and gives health.

The body has many parts, of different names and forms. Pervading the body is the individual self that is conscious, aware. The self is enclosed in bliss, nature of joy. Bliss is enclosed in a network of intelligence. Intelligence is enclosed in the mind, thinking, feeling, sensing, receiving, ordering, changing and organizing. The mind is enclosed in the energy of life, which manifests as motion in the body in different ways. Life is enclosed in the subtle body that resides in the physical material body. The physical material body that we see is the surface. Inside it is an invisible network of truth, each layer with its own laws. In this way, the self is chained to the body. It is full of heat, desires and actions, an urge to express. It experiences their consequences and gathers qualities. It becomes an agent. It is not separate from its actions. It is actions that become further actions.

Experience of pleasure and pain comes through actions and their consequences. An excess of virtuous actions in the past life leads to a happy present life, with good things of life to enjoy, without any trouble. Otherwise man suffers.

As were his actions, so is his life, happy or miserable. As were the desires and their consequences, deeds and misdeeds, so is the birth and life, death and rebirth, delusion and suffering.

Desires disappear through knowledge. Desires become objects through actions.

Man thinks of the universe as the objective universe. The objective world absorbs you because you become your objective world. This is MAYA, the untruth in which man lives, the untruth that hides the truth. Freedom from this untruth is MOKSHA, the highest aim of life. This freedom happens when the unreality of the objective universe is seen. This objective world is seen to be a creation of your own senses and their mind. They create your objective world. When you see this, your desires, cravings and longings are reduced. Then the universal reality is experienced in detachment and no mind.

Deep investigation destroys false knowledge. Till we experience the one that objectifies as the universe, all things appear real, separate and many.

This body is acquired through actions. When it is used to experience the reality of the universe, bearing its burden is fruitful. Not otherwise.

They who follow pleasures and their senses go astray from the path to freedom. They enter falsehood as a consequence of their actions.

They who follow YOGA should do all their duties that emerge from their nature skillfully according to their status in society and age in life. They should not be concerned with the fruits of their duties, over which their control is only partial. They should offer them to the divine presence in all beings.

On this path, practice YAMA, five moral principles or absolute vows that have to be kept to have spiritual experience and to be socially good and noble.

Practice non-violence in speech, thought, and action. Avoid injuring or hurting others. Accept life and its diversity. Your enemies will start disappearing. You may not see enemies at all.

Be truthful in speech, thought and action. Always search for truth and express it, whatever your situation or consequence. What you wish for deeply and spontaneously will start coming true.

Take only what is morally and legally yours. You can cheat others but not yourself, not the divine presence in you, or evolve on the divine path even if you worship for a thousand years. If you live in this way, your minimum genuine needs will always be divinely met.

Follow the path to divine consciousness with such a focused mind of devotion that you do not go on to the path of physical pleasures. Your sexual energy will start becoming your spiritual energy.

Let go of things other than what your body and mind truly need to live and do their duty efficiently. You may start seeing the past and the future.

Constant practice of these five moral principles in practical daily living over a period of time will start producing supernatural powers that are present in you. These powers come through divine grace, not through your effort. But you have to persist in your practice and qualify, remembering that you cannot cheat the divine.

Practice NIYAMA, five rules that initiate you in this discipline and enable you to evolve spiritually as an individual and reduce your tendencies to outward action.

Remain clean externally in your body and internally in your mind. Take bath regularly. Be happy when others are happy. Share their sorrow. Follow AYURVEDA and YOGA, the natural paths to physical and mental health.

Remain contented. Avoid unnecessary desires. Be grateful for what you have. Peace and wisdom will start coming to you. Controlling your senses will become easier.

Be intense and self-disciplined in your objective of experiencing your self. Learn to slow down your body. Try fasting, reducing intake through your senses. Learn to distinguish the higher from the lower mind. Learn to reflect on your experience of living, to discriminate cause and effect, the ideal and the steps towards it, the high and the low, the significant and the trivial.

Study your scriptures and your self. Chant MANTRAS. Meditate on divine powers, one at a time. Try to visualize them. Draw their images and models. Remain focused on each divine power for many days. This is UPASANA, sitting close to the divine qualities and powers in your mind.

Surrender the body and mind to ISHWAR, the being of all powers present in the universe. You may enter SAMADHI.

Reality in the universe is organic, alive, conscious and free. Focus your mind on it. Eat healthy sweet foods. Drink buttermilk or cow's thin milk in small quantities. Eat only when hungry. Do not eat otherwise. Speak the truth in kind and pleasant words. Otherwise do not speak. Practice the virtues of patience, constancy, forgiveness, modesty, purity and austerity. Serve your guru, your spiritual guide. Do all your duties with a detached mind.

When a person sees only his self in everything, he gives up religious rituals and ceremonies. Religious rituals and ceremonies are only an initial guide, never a final destination. Finally one is entirely alone, focused and whole.

There are many forms of life, some major, some minor. There are different functions, like breathing, speaking, beating of the pulse, digesting and movements, passing of urine and stools and activation of genitals. Life flows in the entire body, controlling digestion and assimilation, the motion of the limbs, the senses and the brain and the reflex actions. Regulate your life in all its forms.

Learn the right postures of the body for absorbing life in the body and mind and balancing its flow. See the forms of objects, plants and animals with love and devotion. Learn to copy them to still and silence your body and mind joyfully in a relaxed manner. They are your body and mind postures, your ASANAS.

There are eighty-four well-known postures of the body. Out of these you will choose the ones that suit you. You will learn to be in a posture in which you can stay still comfortably for a long time.

The YOGI will pass through many stages while practicing different postures of the body and concentrating on different centers and sources of energy in his subtle body.

Do PRANAYAMA and learn to regulate your breathing properly. You do not breathe in air. You breathe in life. What you do not need, you return. You do not eat food. You eat life. What you do not use, you return. Learn to use, activate, increase and absorb the flow of your life. Remove obstructions in the flow of life in your body and mind. Purify your body and mind of illness and obstructions, making it calm and energetic.

A living guru gives knowledge of it based on his experience. Learn from him through devotion. But without his personal experience of the unity of being and its expression in actions, he is not a guru. And you have to have your own experience, not his.

From perfection in PRANAYAMA comes decrease in sleep and excretions, freedom from disease, sorrow or affliction. One can even have freedom from hunger and thirst, if mother of the universe, the power that creates and sustains it, shows its grace.

Practice YOGA with self-control and perseverance. Have faith in your knowledge and the guru. Trust that your effort will succeed and bring fruit. Restrain your senses and eat moderately. Learn what to eat and drink, when and how much.

Experience that all beings are the same. They are forms of the same power. Your feelings and ideas, your attitudes and actions are not particularly yours. They are present in others too. See yourself in others and others in yourself. Expand yourself to include all.

Retire to a quiet, pleasant place. Assume a comfortable posture, and stay relaxed.

Feel reverence for your guru, and the basic energy of all energies, the order of the universe and its source.

You are engaging your body and mind in a way that you do not know. Do you think you know your body and its mind? You aspire towards the unknown. So you need blessings of the higher powers.

If you think you do not need their blessings, then you will stay where you are. At the most you will achieve what your actions alone are capable of achieving.

Press your right nostril with the right thumb. Inspire air through the left nostril slowly and fully. Keep the air inside you as long as comfortable. Press your left nostril with the right index finger. Breathe out air slowly through the right nostril. Keep the air out as long as comfortable. Inspire air through the right nostril, keeping the left pressed. Retain it as long as comfortable. Expire through the left nostril. Repeat, and so regulate the motions of your life.

Practice twenty retentions of breath in a detached and focused mind. Focus your mind on your breathing alone and on nothing else and so extinguish time and space. Do it at sunrise and at sunset initially. Later practice it at mid-day as well. If you can be aware even while your body is asleep, then practice it at mid-night too.

When practiced daily for three months, channels in the subtle body are purified. Illnesses will start disappearing. On further practice, one feels light and energetic as if one were floating in the air. Then, a no-thought consciousness happens. Obstacles in the path of YOGA are removed. The YOGI enters the first stage of his discipline. He will then acquire a proper appetite and assimilation. He will be full of strength and courage, cheerfulness and enthusiasm, and handsomeness. He will give up bitter, fried, acidic, salty foods. He will give up excessive sex, eating, fasting, resting, walking, and talking. Many benefits will follow.

Be devoted to the living conscious life present in the universe. Everything is related to everything else like the limbs of a vast cosmic being. Imagine everything to be alive with a life of its own. Listen to spiritual music. Gradually through intensive practice, you may acquire paranormal powers.

There are seven revolving centers of energy in the subtle body that underlie and control the gross physical body. Concentrate on these centers for a long time, one by one. Focus attention on the source of your energy. Your energy does not come from food alone. Awareness of it strengthens you.

These centers appear to yogis to have forms that look to them like petals of flowers, like letters of the alphabet of SANSKRIT. They are the building blocks of his universe of self-expression. From a few letters of the alphabet the entire universe of language and culture is built up. So from a few centers of energy the entire universe of existence is built up. Each center of energy affects an element of nature, an organ of sensation and action, the vitality of life and a function of the mind.

When we focus our mind on energy, we find it to be real and conscious, an ever-evolving transformation, full of warmth, by the side of a cold, inactive consciousness. Consciousness is seen in the form of a lotus with a thousand petals. It is like the sun with a thousand rays. It sits at the top in the head, while energy is active at the bottom.

The first center of this active energy is MOOLADHAR. It is the root, the basis of energy, between the anus and the genitals. It affects the earth element, excretion and sex, the pleasures of ejaculation, sensuous and physical pleasures. It affects animal propensities like fear, anger, anxiety, excitement, aggression, self-centeredness, and ignorance. It affects instincts, life and death, and evolution to higher beings. Its energy affects the bones and governs the organs of action. Its energy in the mind is ego or I-am-the-doer principle that moves downwards, to the excretory genital system. Its symbol is seen as deep crimson red, represented as a square. When this center is opened, the solid earth matter ceases to appear solid and real. Solidity becomes an illusion. There is nothing solid in the universe. The body and mind become light. One reduces eating, drinking and excretions. When it is opened, one controls elimination and reproduction, negative thoughts and emotions. Learning becomes easy.

The second center of energy is SVADHISHTHAN at the root of genitals. It affects the water element, abiding in the self, in the reproductive system. Its energy affects fat, body fluids, and organs of action and taste. Its energy in the mind is the emotional principle working through the senses. When you sense, you also feel. Its energy moves inwards. It is represented as the crescent moon, seen as dark blue. When it is opened, the liquid element ceases to be real. There is nothing liquid in the universe. One masters action, the principle of purification. Passions like lust, anger, and greed are eliminated. The body and mind become flexible and adaptable.

The third center is MANIPUR at the root of the navel. Meditate on this region of fire, the digestive system. It reveals a golden light like the fire element, radiating sparks of light. Its energy relates to muscles. It rules the organs of sight and movement, reasoning and upward urges. It is represented as a downward pointing triangle. Its color is blue. When opened, one sees light and motion as unreal. There is no light or motion. The body and mind become radiant. The skin and eyes become lustrous.

The fourth center is ANAHAT, the air element, located in the heart. It controls the vibrations of reality. Its energy affects blood, the organs of touch and grasping, the skin and hands. It rules all life, the circulatory system, love, compassion, and sensibility to arts, beauty, creativity, refinement, culture, humanitarian attitudes and higher emotions. Its color is deep red. It is represented as a six-pointed smoke colored star. When it is opened, one sees all gases as unreal. One sees one air element behind all gases in space. One sees all form-giving actions as the cosmic function of doing things. The limits of the body and mind start disappearing in the mind.

The fifth center is VISHUDDH, the purifying cycle of energy located in the throat. Its energy affects the organs of hearing and speaking, the respiratory system, the site of the individual ATMA, the source of inspiration, and the vital force. It rejuvenates the body, dissolving contradictions. A dark blue circle represents it. When it is opened, it frees us of the idea that space is real. One sees the cosmic being instead of space. Everything is seen as related to everything else. One masters speech and hearing, the nature of expression and the movement of energy. The body and mind lose their limits and their impurities for which it secretes AMRIT or nectar in the throat that rejuvenates the body and mind. A feeling of the infinite void arises. Supernatural powers start emerging.

A drop of AMRIT dropped down the throat of PRAHLAD JANI, who then remained without food or drink for seventy years. He was kept under observation of Defense Institute of Physiology and Allied Sciences at Ahmedabad, Gujarat, for 15 days in 2010 AD.

The sixth center is AJNA, behind and between the two eyebrows. It is the third eye of SHIVA, the intuition, unrelated to any element or organ. The mind, intellect and I-am-the-doer principle are located in it. The impressions of the past actions are located in it. All the principal channels of life converge towards it. It is the command center. Always start with focusing your mind on this center of energy, as it regulates the energy of all other centers.

From here the energy moves upwards towards the seventh center, the lotus with a thousand petals, on top of the brain, where it unites with MAHA DEVA.

First learn to breathe and silence your mind. Focus your attention on your center of energy behind and between your eyebrows. After mastering it, focus your attention on MOOLADHAR. Learn to visualize grand images of love and compassion and supreme intelligence. Learn to imagine your subtle body. It is like a flame of fire rising up along your spinal column from one center of your energy to the next, up and down. Practice this regularly every day.

The practice of YOGA is obstructed by pleasures of life. Religious rituals and intellectual theories also obstruct it. What is required is practice with devotion. Different devotees practice different YOGAS to different degrees. Devotion to symbols and visualizing what they stand for purifies the mind.

Look steadily into the clear unclouded sky, and see your self. Learn to see that you make the sky that you see. Now try to see the sky. The sky is not there.

Try to see your feelings, or your shadow in the sky. Gradually strange powers will start appearing to you according to your nature and capability.

Gaze at an object on the earth for a long time. Then shift your gaze to the sky and try to see the object there.

Learn to focus your attention on different parts of your body till those parts disappear from your consciousness. Try to see your subtle body.

Focus your attention on your needs like hunger, thirst, till those needs disappear.

Focus your attention on your feelings till your feelings disappear.

Fix your attention on an object, first on its presence and then on its absence.

Fix your attention on each center of your energy one by one for a long time.

Have no hope in your mind. Have no society in your mind either. You are alone.

Try to imagine that you are dead. Fix your attention on non-existence.

Learn to feel that you are consciousness alone.

Practice contemplation.

Practice one or two of these techniques for as long as comfortable.

Make a pilgrimage to one or more of the temples of SHIVA.

Chapter III

Actions Alone

The world is called JAGAT or born of motion. The world is seen as a produce of an unending sequence, a network of actions. The world, its minerals, plants and animals, and human, moral and spiritual life are forms of action, rooted in physical, moral and spiritual laws. These laws constitute an organic being that lives inside the universe and gives rise to actions. It is a creative order, the inner controller. These laws operate. Their fruits or consequences are actions. When they are violated, the violations are actions. Our happiness and sorrow, the length and quality of our life that emerges from our actions are actions too. Actions express these sequences and networks, these laws.

We use different words for actions that show our different ways of seeing them. We talk of the source of nature and what comes from this source, the seed and its fruits, the cause and its effects. We see actions and reactions, ends and means, actions and their fruits, intended and unintended, near and distant consequences. Whatever the words we use, we refer to actions and their chains in all directions. Even the words we use are actions. KARMA refers to actions, known through many names.

When we see a tree, we see only actions. When we see an animal, we see only actions. When we see our body and mind, we see only actions. Our seeing is an action too. These actions happen over more or less time. The time may be less than the twinkling of an eye or more than many life times. These actions may or may not be seen by the mind with its physical eyes and within the limitations of the human body and its mind. When they are not seen, they seem to be non-action. But they are actions nevertheless.

Our sense of action is falsely limited to a humanly sensible duration. Duration in reality extends beyond the limits of the human capacity to sense, beyond its lower and upper limits. This ignorance of action, beyond the limits of our sensing, is the power of delusion that exists in the very nature of things.

We have acquired the habit of thinking of clock time. This habit is useful for the civilization we have created. Otherwise we would not have acquired and nourished this habit. But nature has its own ways of revealing time, like the changing moon and seasons and plants, and the changing of pole star. Time has many forms. Time is a form of action.

Action may be voluntary or involuntary. Human morality is concerned largely with deliberate action. Action may be right or wrong in relation to a human aim, leading to good or evil for human beings. But human aim is not the only aim in existence. There are other aims as well. Action may be external or internal, visible or invisible. Action may give us knowledge of truth or falsehood, happiness or unhappiness.

Action is the law of life. It is an expression of the divine power. It includes the good, the evil, and the morally indifferent. They all are actions. Its one expression is cause and effect, instincts and urges finding expression in thoughts and actions. Another expression is using the will to achieve a purpose, rising above nature and its cause and effect and compulsions and limits to a nobler life, forgetting that we are hungry when we are thoroughly absorbed in our purpose and work, or sacrificing for a public cause, or earning prosperity to satisfy desires within the limits of goodness, or finding freedom.

GITA says that actions emerge from the nature and capacities of the gross body and its life and mind, the subtle ego with its past experience and present effects, instruments and materials and methods used, the strength and intensity of effort applied, and fate or destiny, divine intervention or chance. Each is equally important. Fate is only one element. Other elements can dominate and rise above it.

Whether we like it or not, everything aims at dying or moving towards its own decomposition. Everything aims towards freedom from what it is. We prefer to remain ignorant of this motion, because its awareness alters our actions in a manner that we do not like.

Right actions for man are DHARMA. They sustain our existence and truth, consciousness and life. They sustain our joy and eliminate our suffering. They make us noble, enabling us to lead a moral and meaningful life. They enable us to be pure, to be more of what we are and to be less of what we are not. They help us experience our self, or become what we are capable of becoming. They are divine, the best we can be. They express the reality given to us by nature at our birth. We may help or hinder expression of our nature and its transformation towards noble ideals, and enjoy or suffer accordingly. We must find out what we are and what we are not through our actions.

We must become our actions, entirely absorbed in the sequence of their skills. Then we lose our ego, forget ourselves in this vast sea of actions. Then we are devoted to them. Then our action and duty becomes a divine play. Whatever we do should be done in this way, fully absorbed in the skills of doing the action and leaving all else to the higher forces to take care of. We must gather our food and earn our money in this way. We must keep our house in order in this way and create a body of DHARMA, transcending nature, nourishing the good and eliminating the evil. Then we are not bound to expectations of results of our actions, our little benefits. Then we are detached, observant, unconcerned, taking care of things as they come and letting them go. We do what we must do. We have no choice. We are our actions and in heaven.

If we are not entirely absorbed in our actions, we remain separate from them. We think of them as a means of satisfying our desires for more money and power, more food, more houses with more bedrooms and bathrooms, more sex and more spouses and children, more books and more music or paintings, the culture of languages. We think of nobility as power and wealth. We try to govern others without cultivating and governing ourselves. Then we remain bound to our expectations of results of actions, bound to suffering. Then we are tied to the wheel of change, the sequence of actions, going up and down.

Our lives reveal what kind of actions we are doing. They reveal our experience of the divine. We may have suppressed or expressed our nature. We may not have expressed the best in our nature. We may have never known our nature. We may have even deformed our nature. We may have even disliked our nature, like a woman wanting to be a man, or an old man trying to be a young man. We may have followed others, leaders, neighbors or fashion, rather than our nature. We may have cultivated desires that do not reflect our nature. We may have cultivated our lower rather than higher nature, our evil rather than our goodness. We may have remained entirely fixed on our stomach, anus and genitals, and never known anything higher like the heart, the throat, the forehead, and the top of the head. Our lives indicate our spiritual experience.

We must learn what we should do, what our duty is and what our duty is not. We must learn what to do in a state of conflict between our duties. Duty does not enslave us to morality, as we are already slaves to our likes and dislikes, our loves and hatreds, our instincts and appetites. Duty gives us the freedom to be the best of what we already are deep down within us, where there is no choice, our own inherited nature, and to shape it freely like an artist on the path of the ideal we carefully choose. It makes us responsible to the best in ourselves, to our higher nature, and to the society in which we live and grow up, and which contributes to our growth. Duty is a command to hold, preserve and sustain the world. Duty changes over time and place and circumstances. Duty requires our understanding our nature, expressing the best in it, uplifting it. Duty requires understanding the time and place in which we have to act.

Non-violence is a law of DHARMA for the spiritually evolved. It covers numerous actions of love and compassion. It accepts the other and helps constructively. It includes forgiveness, peace and kindness. But there is also the duty of self-defense. We live in a world of people who may not be spiritually evolved. We may have to fight and become violent and even kill others when such a need arises. We maintain an army and police in order to defend ourselves, our families and properties, tribes and country against those who are brutal and greedy and deceptive. We may have to hunt for food or train for martial duty. Such conflicts of duty exist in the nature of things.

Truth is a law of DHARMA. Truth is that which exists, which never ceases to exist, which is not affected by time. There is no religion higher than truth. In ancient days, when a student was about to leave his teacher, after completing his course of studies in the GURUKUL, the family of the guru, the teacher blessed him by saying, "Find and speak the truth and live righteously." Truth and righteous living are fundamental duties, the final and highest instruction.

The law of truth requires actions like integrating mind, speech and action, keeping promises, as they underlie all treatise, contracts, and social interaction. But speaking the truth may help the enemy or lead to the murder of innocent people. Welfare of others may be more important than speaking the truth. Such conflicts of duty exist in the nature of things.

Non-stealing, or taking only what is morally and legally ours is a law of DHARMA. It requires contentment with what we earn, with what we have. And yet in a state of deprivation, food may have to be stolen to avoid death. To keep alive may be more important than not stealing.

Controlling the senses and organs of the body and disciplining its mind is a law of DHARMA. It is a form of austerity. Desire, anger, and greed are three gates of hell. Since they are destructive they must be controlled. But they are necessary too in certain situations. One has to desire to remain alive and healthy. Desire creates society. One has to be angry at injustice and immorality and not submit to insult. Anger destroys evils in society. One has to be greedy for knowledge and freedom. Greed develops society and makes it more comfortable, complex and sophisticated. But these urges must remain within the limits of DHARMA.

RISHIS have praised high value aspects of DHARMA like self-sacrifice, intensity of effort, austerity and self discipline, giving charity, not hoarding or accumulating wealth, giving food and medical aid and education to the needy, the poor, the hungry, the handicapped, making a donation, an offering to the learned, the honorable, the worthy, and establishing relationships with them.

We need to justify our life, making it meaningful, orderly, searching for the creative truth that underlies nature and society.

We need to accept the other through non-violence, love, forgiveness and compassion, extending the range of sympathy, while keeping the same, contented, undisturbed, detached mind in all situations.

We need to be devoted to our higher nature that is focused on the divine, centered in the heart and mind, feelings and thought, throat and eyes or skills of self-expression and seeing, not to be led astray by unrestricted demands of the body and society.

We need to listen to spiritual discourses, reading and trusting them and studying our own self, observing it, especially its hidden and secret motives.

We need to learn to see the auspicious everywhere, and feel the wonder of vast immensity and beauty, singing praises of the divine present in all beings and so appreciating and serving them.

We need to do rituals and symbolic actions that express deep thoughts in order to internalize feelings and attitudes, doing actions for public welfare like digging wells and tanks, planting trees, leaving it to the divine powers to take care of our genuine needs.

We need to learn to discriminate the real from the unreal, and let go of things and ideas, learning to remain silent and alone that we are, and so be pure.

Actions become rituals, ceremonies and festivals, right and wrong conduct.

They should lead to enlightenment, experience of the thought they symbolize, and so help in our spiritual evolution. If they do not, they must be changed, dropped or modified. Therefore we must do ritual actions with understanding. If we do not understand ritual actions, we cannot judge, modify or discard them. We get stuck to them, regardless of their effect on us.

Reflection on actions is as important as breathing is for living. We do our own breathing. Nobody else does it for us. But we may be breathing wrongly and may have to rectify it through PRANAYAMA, which means life control. Similarly we do our own reflection on our own actions. Nobody else can do it for us. But we may be reflecting wrongly, inadequately, with prejudices, partially. We are the best to know our secret motivations, half understood urges. We can be dishonest with ourselves just as with others, but not with our inner controller. We must learn to observe our actions as they emerge, remain, and pass away, in a detached manner, as if they were not our own. This is the initial form of meditation.

We need to listen to authoritative words that express truth that comes of experience of wise people and listen to scriptures. But we must understand them. We must relate them to our nature to express the best in us. Otherwise we can ignore them as meaningless chatter.

We should be devoted to our mother and father, teacher, family and GURUKUL or school of education that constitutes the family of our guru. We should be devoted to our vocation and earn our livelihood, and support order, society and state. We should express our devotion through gifts and donations. But they may have to be criticized if they do a wrong action. Therefore we should be devoted to only their good actions and follow and spread them.

If we do not do right actions, we suffer. But this suffering is not eternal. It lasts only for some time. A moment of sin cannot result in an eternity of suffering. That would be injustice. Eternal hell of suffering is an unjust idea. But consequences of actions must happen. And consequences are actions that come, stay and go away. They may bring joy or suffering. This is a fact, not an idea.

Actions produce consequences, which we must experience. If we do not experience consequences of our actions, then there is no order in the world. Then the world is chaos.

Can chaos create this wonderful world of order in all its immense diversity? Do we desire chaos? Do we create chaos? Chaos is only ignorance of the order that exists, which we must find. There is regularity, growth and decay, harmony and disharmony, birth and death. There is a creative order that we see partly, dimly, and aspire to see fully and clearly.

If we do not experience consequences of our actions in this life, we must experience them in another life. REBIRTH is a logical necessity for actions to have consequences, for order to exist. Some people have memories of an earlier birth. Rebirth happens till we realize truth. We can always improve over many lives. Our life continues till we flower into the divine. Till we reach that stage we shall have to lead some kind of life.

On death our body dissolves into the forces that make it. But our life is shaped or misshaped by the actions that it has been doing. It gets into another appropriate body. It creates the body it needs just as it creates the body from childhood to old age. The body is not a machine. The body is a creative sequence of actions. Actions happen over more or less time.

The capacities of various organs accompany life in its rebirth. The effects of learning and impressions of actions go along with life. These impressions and effects are our inborn tendencies to action. These impressions and effects happen when we do actions of living. They may happen accidentally, as they do in most lives, when we receive chaotic impressions from the media, colleagues and neighbors. Or we may make an effort to direct, regulate and control them.

Some control is exercised through formal education. The actions of disciplined living and focused social interactions too exercise some control. Some impressions are deliberately created through spiritual exercises and rituals. We reflect on our experience of living in our memory, daily thinking and meditation. We know that our actions have vast, known and unknown consequences. Therefore whatever we do, we should be careful and fully aware of our doings.

Some important moments of influence on us when awareness is needed are conception and birth, entering society and formal education, physical maturing and puberty, leaving formal education and entering marriage, earning livelihood and housekeeping, social and professional maturing, supporting different sections of society and social institutions, spiritual cultivation and dealing with problems and conflicts, disease, decay and death. We need to do appropriate actions, rituals and ceremonies for these occasions.

We may reject one set of rituals and adopt another, but there is a human need to have some rituals and ceremonies. Many rituals and ceremonies were created in the past. Some dropped out and some were continued, modified and embellished.

When a child was born we dabbed its lips with honey and clarified butter and prayed that he may grow up to be sweet and wise like honey that removes illnesses and live long and be strong and intelligent like a learned man, or a strong fighter or a prosperous trader, or skillful in service and in doing rituals that lead him to his aims in life and be full of history and legends, actions and meditations.

Our rituals have meanings. To act out rituals without enacting their meanings in our lives is like saluting the national flag and taking bribes and commissions in awarding public contracts. We make a public commitment through our prayerful anthem and the ritual of saluting the national flag that we shall sacrifice for the national spirit, but do we have appropriate ideas and actions that we must follow for the ritual and prayer to be truthful? Prayers are actions. They require us to act appropriately to realize them and leave the results to divine grace.

Admission to a GURUKUL was a big ritual. The teacher gave the seeker of education a new garment to wear. That was his second birth. The teacher asked him to remember the power that produced the cotton and spun it and wove the threads into cloth and colored it saffron and fashioned the new garment. May the same power give you strength and life to weave your thread of life and make your cloth appropriate for a student! RISHI BRIHASPATI gave this cloth to INDRA DEVA. He gives it to you now and links you to your ancient past. May you do rituals and actions that help you reach your aims, increase your wealth and use it for public welfare and protect your friends and mankind and be like a DEVA, strong and full of light and splendor! The teacher offered him the sacred thread of self-sacrifice and self-control. It admitted him to a cultured, sacred and holy life. He offered him a girdle, requiring chastity, austerity and vigor. He asked him to do PRANAYAMA to control and regulate his life. It regulated his breathing and stabilized his mind so that it remained the same in all circumstances, joyful or sorrowful. He offered him a staff, disciplining him into the social order. The teacher entrusted his pupil to the protection of DEVAS, to the powers of light and warmth, excellence and strength, ancestors and customs, law and tradition. He taught him SAVITRI MANTRA in the GAYATRI meter as his prayer for light and knowledge. He asked him to kindle his fire for enlightenment and immortality. He sprinkled water on him thrice, saying BHUR, BHUVAH, SVAHA, as an offering and dedication to the earth, the air, and the beyond, all that there is or can be. May INDRA, ADITYA and all the divine powers guide you to prosperity and public welfare, knowledge and authority! Do your duty and tend your fire and do not waste your time. The pupil took a bath and left his home for his school, his Guru's family.

After completion of his education another ceremony was performed, in which the student tied a turban that showed his respectability, wore an ornament, held an umbrella, put on new clothes and sandals and took a bamboo stick in the style of a well-dressed man. The teacher blessed him: May you always search for truth and live righteously! Do your actions skillfully while utterly absorbed in them, leaving it to the divine powers to look after your genuine needs and welfare. Earn profits that are auspicious and legitimate, within the limits of moral goodness, never becoming immoral for earning money or power. All accounts must carry the legend: AUM SHUBH LABH, certifying that the account truthfully shows that the profit is auspicious, morally good, in the eyes of God. So it debarred illegal and unscrupulous practices, setting up a high ideal of accountancy and business behavior that made India so rich that it tempted invaders.

On completing his studies he starts earning his livelihood and marries. In the marriage ritual, the bride and the groom held hands, promising to protect each other, praying for children and prosperity. This is the ceremony of holding hands. Then they stood on a slab of stone and promised to be strong and steadfast. This is the ceremony of being steadfast like a rock. Then a fire was lighted. The groom offered a handful of parched grain into the cupped hands of the bride. She scattered the grain behind her. The groom promised to provide her prosperity and welfare, which she was to spread among relatives and friends. Then they went around the lighted fire seven times, praying to AGNI and SURYA, who create life and live inside everyone, for strength, vitality, prosperity, happiness, cattle or nourishment, for good seasons, both physical and emotional, and mutual friendship, children and devotion throughout their lives. This is the ceremony of going around the fire. Then they took seven steps together, repeating their seven prayers. Then they looked at the pole star and resolved to be firm like him in their vows and live for a hundred years, flourishing and having children.

Married life is central to any society and full of sacrifices. A ritual the ancients performed in married life everyday was offering to fire. The sun enters the household fire in the evening and the household fire enters the sun in the morning. The sun enters day and night, the seasons and plants. The sun enters our body and mind, and the warmth of our hearts. We offer this food to fire to reach him as we do actions for the warmth in all and pay our debt to the powers that constitute us.

The sun and fire, meet at dawn and in the evening, the times of prayers. At dawn one stood before the sun, showing reverence to the him, doing SURYA NAMASHKAR, saluting it with a set of twelve YOGIC exercises for healthy living, along with PRANAYAMA, to still the mind and offer the water of life to the sun, dedicating the day to skillful actions as duty in the hope of enlightenment, repeating SAVITRI MANTRA in the GAYATRI meter that publicly commits one to meditation on the source of fire and heat and light, life and creation, praying for enlightenment. moral elevation and removal of ignorance, suffering and evil. In the evening as one lighted the fire, one covered the head out of reverence and did NAMASHKAR to it, dissolving the ego into the daily cycle of actions, as one let go and relaxed in love and contemplation.

Even if we dislike rituals and give them up, we create new ones, and replace one set of rituals with another set of rituals. These days we go for a walk in a park in the morning and evening. This is a lighter but incomplete physical exercise amidst cultivated nature.

Rituals should reduce suffering like illness, and raise our living to a higher moral level, and discipline and focus our mind. If they do not do that, they should be modified, given up and substituted. For this we need to reflect on our experience of life and see the effects of rituals.

Some actions are done every day, like bathing and prayers, reflection and meditation.

Some actions are done occasionally, like celebrating a festival or resolving a conflict, or for satisfying particular desires like freedom from illness, or for acquiring abundance, property or children.

Some actions are objectionable and prohibited, like theft and murder.

All actions change according to time and place and society and emerge from our nature as modified through our nurture and reflection on great ideals, which we have internalized.

Some actions follow the forces of nature, like the actions of plants, animals and heavenly bodies. Such actions change one name and form into another name and form, while the power in them remains the same. This same power is present both in the universe and in man. It organically relates diverse actions into a creative order. This order does not occupy space and is invisible and timeless. It can take on any form. One is to be always devoted to this truth, and be absorbed in devotion to it, as a form of worship.

Some actions are our duties and social functions. They separate different kinds of lives. Actions may emerge from intelligence. They may be devoted to education, medicine, the study of heavenly lights, sciences and the formulation of law. Actions may emerge from physical strength, devoted to fighting, defense, executing the law, maintaining social order and engaging in public enterprises. Actions may create wealth through the produce of land and cattle, their trade, exchange and manufacture. Actions may serve others through sale of labor for livelihood.

To some extent these duties and functions separate one class of people from another. To some extent they overlap, as these tendencies are mixed in different proportions.

These classes are only four, seen as the limbs of a living, organic being. Each supports the other. Without the one the other suffers. They work for what brings them together, for their mutual benefit. This enables one to be fully absorbed in the skills of doing actions and to leave it to the divine power to take care of genuine needs. They are the organizing principles of society. But actual duties and social functions are mixed and numerous.

These duties are different expressions of the same self. To some extent they emerge from one's nature, body and mind at birth. To some extent they are acquired through family nurture and education, culture and one's own effort and application. To some extent they depend on whether we are free or wounded, overpowered and enslaved.

We learn to reflect on our experience of life, and to recognize the truth of our nature and its constituents and qualities, and manifest them in actions directed towards our chosen ideals. We learn to see the source of our suffering and remove it. We learn to nourish our moral goodness to elevate our being and living. Otherwise we are rejecting our initial gift that is our divine natural inheritance.

Duties Organize Society

Hindu society was organized on a complex of principles and institutions. Society is composed of social groups, like the family, the occupation group, the educational institution, the administrative unit, not of isolated, unrelated individuals.

The individual is not born till a man and a woman unite, nourish and protect it, nurture and help it flower. The individual cannot realize his highest potential till he imbibes moral values, technical and educational skills, cultural and material traditions of the family, the community and the locality. Whereas spiritual growth begins with the individual, the individual begins with the family and grows up in it.

The family performs two distinguishing functions. One is procreation and its related work of nourishment, health care, security and nurture of the individual. The second is inheritance of material wealth, forms of behavior, skills and customs, remembered as family traditions that showed high moral values that came to be called KUL DEVAS.

The family may be seen as small, husband, wife, and children, which is the norm today. Thc family may also be seen as large, including grandparents, uncles, aunts, cousins, and even more distant but remembered relatives. They were called KUL.

A few individuals may also experience the family as all-inclusive, including guests, visitors, colleagues, neighbors, animals and plants. The larger the family experienced the richer was one's emotional life and depth of experience. Ultimately all beings were seen to be related as a family.

The family and the individual had their own unknown, undiscovered, unique flow of nature present in their body and mind, instincts and urges, feelings and attitudes, impressions of experiences of this and earlier lives, images, dreams and desires that produce actions in particular individuals and groups. This flow of inherited, unknown, divine nature reveals constituents and qualities, broadly classified into three groups, SATTVA, RAJAS, and TAMAS.

SATTVA referred to constituents of nature that had qualities like truth, intelligence, knowledge, understanding, goodness, sympathy, compassion, love, harmony, reconciliation, renunciation, equilibrium, peace, happiness, enlightenment and so on. They were the constituents and qualities that led one upwards.

RAJAS referred to constituents of nature that had qualities like desire, effort, struggle, creativity, destruction, power, fight, victory, failure, achievement, attachment, clinging to possessions, disappointment and so on. They were the constituents and qualities that needed guidance and direction as they could lead one upwards or downwards, for which DEVAS were contemplated for guidance.

TAMAS referred to constituents of nature that had qualities like ignorance, darkness, obscurity, lack of awareness, inertia, routine, mechanical response and so on. They were the constituents and qualities that led one downwards.

Countless mixtures in different proportions of these constituents and qualities produced particular, unique individuals and groups that were seldom repeated. Their expression in actions produced VARNA, the color of their actions emerging from the inherited flow of their nature and its direction.

JATI was a network of relationships created by marriage and birth, bonds of families descending from the same real or imagined ancestor. It referred to the factual experience of strong bonding of individuals brought up as members of families sharing a common descent or lineage.

Sometimes people dedicated themselves to a particular RISHI or GURU and so changed their JATI, as they developed new strong emotional relationships. Many people called themselves BHARDWAJ or VASISHTHA in admiration of the RISHI they followed. Movement up or down in a hierarchy of knowledge and power happened in this way through intensity of application of the chosen ideal to the inherited seed.

There were numerous occupational brotherhoods that decided the conditions of their work, improving their skills and quality of work as well as social and economic returns through dedication to their work and cultivation of skills over many generations. They too developed strong emotional relationships with each other, and later on came to be called JATI.

Another basic unit of society was the place of one's birth, village or town. We are born at a place and grow up in it, but the place too is born in us and grows up in us in various ways. The memory of the place of birth and nurture grows up in the human mind along with its little traditions, habits of actions, values and ideals that came to be called GRAM DEVA that came to be concretely visualized in the form of an idol. Sometimes these idols were joined to create new forms.

The place had its resources the use of which created its political economy, its production, distribution, consumption and ordering of wealth that satisfied immediate needs. One form of these relationships later came to be called the JAJMANI system. The strong and powerful land owning and affluent groups used the services of landless people and in return satisfied their basic needs through their customary share in the production, and they acquired status as members of the family. These days the landed groups are criticized and the landless groups are praised, but the landless groups too aim to acquire land and deprive others of it so that inequality and hierarchy between the two remains true, though its form keeps changing over years.

RISHIS created numerous forms of organizing of political economy, like earning livelihood through expression of one's nature, while directing it to noble ideals to satisfy minimum genuine needs in the interest of all beings. Profits were to be declared auspicious through truthful keeping of accounts and fortnightly check on prices, weights and measures, followed by just punishment to corrupt officials and businessmen, as recorded in MANU SMRITI. While interest could be legitimately earned within limits, doubling the principal amount on one borrowing was considered null and void, even if agreed to between two parties. While local economy was promoted, long distance trade too was undertaken over land and across the seas. Large public works were undertaken for redistribution of wealth. The focus largely was on knowledge as skills of doing actions and quality of living. Consumption was restricted to minimum necessary for efficient maintenance of the body and mind, though there were affluent families as well. Even water was to be consumed only when one is wise, as the spirit of the trees taught the PANDVA brothers. Wasteful expenditure was avoided and savings were offered as charity to worthy people who created and nourished the culture in which the people participated. Generally society was seen as a conscious living being in which everyone was related to everyone else.

Another institution was called GRAM or NAGAR PANCHAYAT of village or town. It was a group of five old and wise people chosen through consensus to administer the place and resolve conflicts and lay down the custom based on remembered precedents. Basically it was an administrative unit that performed the functions of local government, municipal and judicial, as well as revenue collection and local expenditure. Conflicts were sought to be resolved through negotiation and consensus, in search of truth with the help of local wise people. Conflict resolution was seen as an expression of their wisdom. There were no lawyers determined to win a legal battle even at the cost of truth.

They had the institution of SABHA, where they all met for entertainment and relaxation as well as exchange of useful information. Power rose upwards, keeping the people free, full of their enterprise and prosperity of men of practical experience instead of trickling downwards through misshaping laws quickly created to siphon off the wealth of unknown citizens held in contempt as abstract numbers of votes.

PANCHAYATS have now been so treated that they hardly have any municipal, financial, judicial and self-created powers, or scientific, educational and cultural inputs from contemporary RISHIS and their GURUKULS. It is a result of the deliberate policy of uprooting all that was born of the ancient ways of living. At present the basic unit of administration are various forms of district authority that represent only a remote central authority or some memory of western civilization, as learnt from formal textbooks, or a borrowed constitution, or even their own selves. They exercise power over gatherings of wiser people, but are not chosen by them for their wisdom.

Sometimes PANCHAYATS of numerous villages or towns combined into a MAHAPANCHAYAT to discuss larger problems that concerned them. They formulated the customary law. The central authority like the RAJA was expected to protect the custom, not to interfere with it, though he could make administrative laws for efficient governance.

They had the institution of SAMITI, a gathering of learned people who provided expert guidance on problems as they arose.

Another unit of society was ASHRAM, the residence of RISHIS, the learned people of all castes and classes who devoted themselves to truth. They cultivated many sciences and arts and skills, and gave free education to those who had competence or qualification for acquiring knowledge, skills and duties. Their devotees, affluent merchants and the king supported them with large gifts, as a form of investment in education and culture.

Another institution was DANASHALA, the house of charity that gave wealth to worthy causes like ASHRAMS and public works. Large ASHRAMS became GURUKULS, or educational institutions. They were concerned with teaching all kinds of subjects including knowledge of war that included the training of soldiers as well as elephants, horses, camels and dogs for the purpose of war, though they tried to reduce the cruelty of war with the help of ethics, which sometimes went to their own disadvantage at the hands of unethical invaders. They also taught many other subjects like medicine and music, astronomy and architecture.

There were temples called DEV MANDARS for meditation and reflection on the powers of nature. They had residences of learned people, schools, libraries and rest houses. They provided free food and medicine to the needy, and different forms of entertainment, like music, dance and drama, and even drum beats to create laughter. Comedy and romance were considered high forms of art. A common form of art was enacting episodes from ancient stories and exposition of their themes and implications. This created an idea of history that was different from the modern idea of objective history, which largely served the interests of conquerors, but not of the common people.

Any event has different meanings for different participants in it. Those meanings constitute the tradition and history of those people, and it is for them to decide what is relevant and beneficial to them.

Leaders of different communities met in temples for discussion of social problems in the light of ancient wisdom and arrive at common decisions.

The people who withdrew from society in one sense and re-entered it in another sense were called SANYASI. They traveled on foot from place to place and stayed with people or under trees or in village temples and inns, giving lectures on goodness, moral values and legends, explaining skills of living, and giving medical aid and information available at that time, and helping resolve local conflicts. Renunciation meant a larger and non-selfish engagement with the people through dedication to their interests. In today's idiom, their contribution to society would be called non-formal adult education, but it was without certification for getting jobs under governments that concentrate all power into their own hands under the unreal notion of sovereignty. All power is limited in different ways, and there is inequality of power among states.

YATRA or pilgrimage to chosen places of inspiration was a common practice. Related to it were travels of Gurus in search of truth and of merchants in search of wealth. It was a search for truth that underlies change and search for wealth that is both objective in the form of material wealth and subjective in the form of good health, high moral values, and satisfying relationships with other beings.

People engaged in actions, good, evil or indifferent, and in varied occupations in pursuit of their livelihood to achieve the aims and purpose of life as well as to do ritual actions enabling them to live in harmony with the real and the eternal.

Many of them did actions inspired by desire for pleasures of the senses, took liquor with roasted barley and meat and celebrated life as it came to them. But some of them rose above pleasures of the senses and followed moral ideals of actions done without expectations of any personal benefits, and actions done while remaining absorbed in the skills of doing them and leaving it to the divine power to provide for their genuine material needs, and actions done to bring people together for their common welfare instead of separating them into mutually conflicting, hostile adversaries, and actions done in the interest of all beings including animals and plants.

The aims of life were found to be four: 1. actions emerging from one's nature that sustain life, imposing limits on them that make them good and valuable, crossing which they become bad, evil or meaningless, 2. earning livelihood, and providing for satisfaction of genuine needs, acquiring objective and visible material prosperity, wealth, power and status, as well as subjective and invisible feelings of being well and great, related to others, happy and satisfied, 3. actions leading to pleasures of eating, drinking and laughter, wearing clothes, ornaments and fragrances, sexual urges, procreation, and living together and raising a family, talking and listening, literature, music, dance and drama, painting, and sculpture and the general satisfaction of needs and desires for comforts, and 4. actions leading to freedom from subservience to the body, its needs and compulsions and suffering, and constant demands of society. These four aims, righteousness, wealth, pleasure, and freedom, were important in human life in this very order of priority. They were called PURUSHARTHA, actions done for the cosmic being that lives in the world and relates every being to every other being.

These aims were to be realized at the individual and group levels. The highest authority of the group was called RAJA. He could be the chief of a small tribe living in a village or two, or he could be the chief of numerous villages and towns. The highest was

CHAKRAVARTI RAJA, who received voluntary tribute from numerous villages and towns for services rendered.

It was not considered right to occupy another king's land and take away his resources. Tribute from another king was enough acceptance of the supremacy of power of the CHAKRAVARTI RAJA, and the independence and pride of a people was not to be crushed. This was an effort to reconcile central authority with regional independence, which often proved difficult.

BHARATVARSHA had numerous kingdoms, some big and some small. They thought of war as an expression of personal strength and bravery, largely defensive, fought for self-protection rather than for aggressive conquest and acquisition of other lands. In the hour of need, they called on other landlords to assemble with their followers, but lacked unity of plan and command, and appropriate weapons, strategy and training for a larger war where no holds were barred. As a consequence, Hindus never set up a military empire outside their boundaries, and generally fought defensive wars.

The king had friends, committees and assemblies of advisors and ministers and their large families to help him run his kingdom according to the customary law, which he could interpret but not change. Some of the customs sought to create cultural unity in this vast land known as BHARATVARSHA. For example, in the coronation ceremony, leaders of different castes, villages and towns brought waters from distant rivers and streams together to sprinkle on the crown along with recitation of MANTRAS. People carried GANGA water to distant homes as part of ritual ceremonies, which united them culturally.

The king shared food and bonhomie with leaders of all castes, including craftsmen, on all important life ceremonies. SRI RAMA stayed in the houses of leaders of all castes during his educational tours in childhood.

Though there was a hierarchy of order among groups of people, based on wisdom, strength, wealth and labor, they could rise high or fall low, depending on their inherited seed and the intensity of their effort in its expression.

Hindu society was strengthened and made self-conscious often by members of the lower castes, like VALMIKI, a hunter who became a poet and wrote the RAMAYANA, and VEDVYAS, son of a fisherwoman, who became learned and composed MAHABHARTA. CHANDRAGUPTA MAURYA, who succeeded in creating a vast empire, was a villager of unknown parentage. They influenced actions and their importance and value in society. They showed that the path to a higher status lay through the intensity of their effort, wisely directed.

But today Hindu society is taken to mean only the caste system in its present form, and all other ideals and institutions that shape their society are ignored. Caste is reduced to mean doing what father did, and hurtful social gradations of permanent high and low status without permission to intermarry or inter-dine, and people who are so low as to be untouchable. This sense needs to be corrected through seeing the truth and falsehood present in it.

Everyone is born of parents, who were born to their parents, and so on. Everyone has brothers, sisters, uncles, aunts, cousins, children and grandchildren. Everyone is related to everyone else through known blood relationships, or through unknown because forgotten blood relationships, or through unknown but imagined and emotionally felt relationships, like the relationships between students and teachers or between students of the same teacher or between people working in the same profession, occupation, service, or craft, or people living at the same time and locality, like neighbors who have lived near each other in the same village for generations, and those who have faced the same joys and sorrows together for a long time as a community.

Family members generally engaged in occupations in the same craft, producing similar things or services, or doing related functions. Even today some families remain mostly in politics or in law or in business or in medicine or in engineering or in agriculture or in services, or in particular crafts.

Sometimes one changed occupations as well. For example, affluent traders engaged armies of servants to protect their wealth and when that power became considerable they became kings. Sometimes some affluent kings saw the hollowness of wealth and power and started reflecting on life, its meaning and purpose, and became wise, like RAJA VISHWAMITRA who became a MAHARISHI, or Prince GAUTAMA who became BUDDHA, which means the enlightened one. Sometimes a learned man became a warrior like PARSHURAM, son of RISHI JAMADAGNI who started killing warriors because his mother had gone astray with one of them. Some people combined power with wisdom like RAJA JANAK.

Relationships of husband, wife, son, daughter, father and mother are created through marriage combining blood and based on mutual love and helpfulness. They are generally accepted, though sometimes today even these are rejected, resulting in single parent family. But their rejection does not mean their non-existence. One can divorce a wife or a husband, but the blood mixed in children cannot be unmixed. Relationships with grandparents, uncles, aunts, and cousins are not warm these days. But even if they are rejected, they exist. Rejecting them is cultivation of ignorance and falsehood, part of an effort to shrink into narrow calculating selfishness for creating objective wealth and emotional poverty.

Ancient recognition of marriage and mixing of blood and expression of love was fuller and wider. Marriage was not thought of only as a sexual union of man and woman for procreation, though this was true, because animals procreate too, but the human animal has a DEVA riding it, guiding and directing it, and so marriage was thought of as a sacred union between two sets of families. Each member of the two sets of families had a named relationship with the boy and the girl who married. Family relationships included grandparents, uncles and aunts and their children and grandchildren, and they went back far in time, leaving behind impressions and memories that affected actions and relationships.

Family relationships included even earlier ancestors one had never met, or one had merely heard about or even entirely imagined, as well as their descendants. Family relationships included helpers and supporting staff. A servant was never merely a paid servant but an uncle or aunt with rights and obligations. Today servants are reduced to employees low paid or high paid with rights and duties but no love or feelings of belonging to a family.

Inequality was accepted as a fact of natural physical life and given a place in society. Are human beings equal when they are identified with their bodies and minds? Human beings who cultivate selfish interests can never act on the principle of equality. Even those who talk of equality brilliantly act on inequality secretly.

When a President, Prime Minister, or political leader says that he loves the common people and feels one with them, give him the wages of a commoner and stop his security, comforts and the invisible inflows of wealth, and see what happens, what he thinks and does about his being a common man. All his life, he has struggled to rise above being a common man, and therefore his declaration is a denial of his truth. The game being played today is to talk of equality and to act on inequality. Loud talk of equality effectively reasoned out invites admiration from the poor, the weak and the ignorant and gets their votes, submission and labor, but silent acts of inequality help build up personal wealth and power of the few, build up their properties and empires that last many generations.

JATI was a large network of strongly felt family relationships, extending in time and space, often forgotten but believed to exist. Members of the same JATI were called JATI brothers or sisters and had rights and duties and responsibilities associated with a brother or sister even to the extent of laying down one's life in their honor.

But JATI has been rejected these days just as large family has been reduced to one parent family at some places. People travel much more widely and meet many more people and work in more distant places than they did earlier, and they pick up short duration relationships that they easily discard as used goods or books or friends like marriages by the hour in one night stay hotels. Earlier they did not travel far from the places of their birth and gradually absorbed and created its spirit. They met fewer people and knew them and their parents and grandparents and had long lasting strong relationships. Now scientific thinking is so abstract, reductive and mathematical that it tends to blank out emotional, imagistic and holistic thought. After all, what is love if not sex, increased blood pressure and pulse rate, or chemistry, as they say now in the media, where truth is to be stated in ten seconds in the interest of commercial breaks? And who places his severed head on the palm of his hand before entering the street of the beloved? And one can always go to the next shop for love. We have produced a morality of science, usefulness and profit to the individual in the immediate present. Even educationists calculate cost benefit ratios and feel great about it. It is no more an act of charity to the duly qualified. If we have the money and power, we can even buy education and culture. But can we really?

One can now decide what to do or not to do, what to value or not to value, what relationships to recognize or not to recognize on the basis entirely of self-interest, often called freedom. But what freedom can we have if we are slaves to our personal interests, our biological chemicals, urges and appetites? There is even a mathematical model or calculus of self-interest, which can predict what we will do, in spite of our freedom, if we are a caste devoted and entirely dedicated to the principle of rationality?

The rationality of science can never see the purpose and meaning of life, and it can have no moral choice based on ideals. Luckily for man not everyone is or can be rational and rational to an equal extent, which makes living so human.

Besides, we may not know our self-interest in the long run. We all may want to live long, but lose our body functions. And we may not know our self. This knowledge of our self may be wrong sometimes. It may even be a form of self-deception, an illusion, merely following another like our neighbor or colleague, newspaper, fashions, actors or sportsmen.

The importance attached to JATI depends on the importance attached to relationships created by marriage and family and to their wide or narrow limits. Many relationships are rejected, as memory in a culture based on printing is short and relationships are spread over a wide area one visits in search of money or pleasure, like ancient hunters and food gatherers. Memories in an oral culture in a limited area were much longer and more vivid. There were even specialists in remembrance of family lineage at pilgrim centers near rivers, where people went to immerse ashes of the dead and recorded their lineage. Many of these pilgrim centers and family memory specialists were destroyed and debased by foreign invaders. Taxes were imposed on pilgrims, which had to be paid in humiliation to rulers who thought of themselves as great because they could kill and inflict such inhuman punishments.

Many people today record the history of their family or community. Many such histories today are merely intellectual pastime. They do not excite blood, invoking strong feelings, duties and responsibilities. If they did, that would be JATI.

People differ in many ways, though they are the same in many other ways. They have their own nature, inborn tendencies to action in them. Some people are more or less understanding and receptive than some others. Some people are more or less aggressive and dominating than some others. Some people are more or less law abiding and scrupulous than some others. Some people are more or less creative and experimental than some others. Experts can give long lists of differences and similarities in individual natures by birth. These natural differences and similarities are a factual reality. They constitute the diversity of life and produce inequality.

One is bound to express one's nature. It is one's fundamental duty to express one's own divinely given flow of inherited nature. One's right to life is meaningless if it leads to the death of one's own nature. If one tries to suppress one's nature, it expresses itself in some other distorted way anyway. It may even create suffering in life.

Some of these inherited tendencies and resulting actions are desirable while some others are not. The divine nature is morally neutral from the human and social point of view. It may be morally good, evil or neutral. The divine power is equally present in all conflicting human and non-human beings, and in the good as well as in the wicked.

Therefore we have to observe our nature and be aware of its expression in dreams, urges and actions, and see it as an observer of oneself. This is one form of meditation, and it results in detachment and in a clearer awareness of what we are, and it changes and transforms us, as seeing ourselves enables us to rise above our nature and lead it in the direction of our chosen idol or ideal that we worship or dedicate ourselves to.

We learn to see our own wickedness and its evil effects on others and on ourselves and to restrain the evil and express the good present in our nature. We try to express our highest potential of goodness, the best in us, as a way of accepting and expressing our devotion to the divine power present in us. This leads to spiritual evolution.

If the natural urges are not expressed and observed, directed and guided, the flow of one's energy is obstructed and debased. That causes illnesses of various types, social and individual, physical and mental. So there is an in-built requirement to express the best in one's nature at the cost of punishment for defiance. YOGA devised numerous physical, mental and spiritual exercises for eliminating these obstructions to the flow of one's invisible energy and to ennoble it. It is a form of devotion to the supreme and search for the highest truth in one's self.

We express our nature in actions that came to be specialized and cultivated by families. BRAHMANS were those people who were concerned with knowledge and teaching, contemplation and worship. They influenced laws through custom without always having political power to enforce them. They were concerned with medicine and stars in the sky and the changing seasons of nature and human life. KASHATRIYAS were those people who were concerned with security and defense against external and internal enemies and with public works. They controlled administration and justice and enforced obedience to the prevailing customs of the people. VAISHYAS were those people who were concerned with creating wealth, making and selling goods, agriculture, cattle, trade and banking. SHUDRAS were those people who provided their labor to others in return for their livelihood. These four orders in theory organized thousands of family and occupation groups. Society was organized as a hierarchy of knowledge, power, production and exchange, and service in this very order of importance.

Upward and downward movements of individuals and groups happened on the basis of their actions. MAHARSHI MANU says that castes go up or down in society depending on the inherited seed and the inner heat, which means inherited nature, and the intensity of its free and well directed expression. But with passage of time, groups came to depend entirely on birth, and upward mobility ceased along with the loss of political freedom.

Social thought gave a place and value to different natures and actions. These actions were harmonized into cooperative groups. They all were required to work for common welfare, for what brings people together in the interest of all beings. These orders were required to relate to each other like the limbs of one vast cosmic being. Such were the theoretical constructs.

Hindu social organization decayed over time and was largely destroyed through foreign invasions. In response to this decay and destruction, caste became rigid, exclusive and self-protecting, and blood relationships shrank. But caste protected itself as well as numerous other tribes and communities like Jews, PARSIS, Syrian Christians, and helped them retain their group identity. It gave a place and value to every group, assuring it life and independence and escape from political destruction of exclusive and destructive religions. It created numerous centers of social power instead of one. Even if one was destroyed, there were others to protect Hindu society.

Castes developed into hierarchies, as some were sought after and others were disliked. They developed their own rules and regulations, their own ways of working or not working, in the interest of their efficiency and production. They aimed at wealth and hid their trade secrets. This helped the country grow rich. It collected thousands of kilograms of gold and precious stones through foreign trade. These were looted as recorded by contemporary Muslim historians, who accompanied invaders, as compiled in SIR H. M. ELLIOT and JOHN DOWSON'S THE HISTORY OF INDIA. What was the social organization that produced the wealth that was looted? How much was this wealth, the sheer grand total, the benefit of this organization and its principles?

Even today many institutions have the power to frame their own customary law in view of the special product or service they produce. There are national associations of lawmakers, teachers, engineers, doctors, traders, accountants, builders, farmers and so on? But are they concerned with the ideal of being so absorbed in the skills of doing their work that they leave it to the divine power to take care of their consumption needs?Are they concerned with the quality of their product, its improvement, auspicious profits, fair prices and wealth along with public welfare?

Do lawmakers agree to speak the truth and not to make false accusations deliberately against their perceived enemies or raise false grievances and differences of this or that community to get their votes?

An ancient view was that we had to be working in a field for a few generations before we become experts in that field emotionally and instinctively. Skillfulness is yoga, says SRI KRISHNA, as one is entirely absorbed in the skills of doing action, resulting in forgetfulness of one's ego and personal benefits.

Power was held by the skillful in different departments of life, and popularity was an incidental fruit of skillful productive and protective actions, not a criterion for election to the office.

Invaders obviously looted wealth and killed or converted people, imposing constant warfare on them, town after town, destroying the social systems that created that huge wealth. The present poverty and social distortions is a consequence of that loot carried on for centuries, as the rulers have not protected or represented the people for a long time or tried to keep them united.

Loss of political freedom had many effects. Upward mobility became impossible except through religious conversion and cultural destruction. Castes became rigid, high or low, and developed numerous prohibitions and taboos to protect people, as the people were unable to defend themselves against superior military might.

Dr. B.R.AMBEDKAR in his incisive lecture on Annihilation of Caste thinks that Hindu society does not exist and that Hindu religion should be abolished. His idea of religion obviously means that it can be abolished, like a sentence that can be deleted and replaced by another sentence, as in religious conversion or law, while SANATAN DHARMA claims to be finding spiritual truths that cannot be abolished, whatever you might do. One such truth is the fact of natural human inequality, when man is identified with his body and mind, which is also called human diversity, and another equally important truth is the human need to make natural inequality less harsh, less painful, and more acceptable.

Western talk of human equality and actions that further human inequality is a form of double-speak, which has always been a useful tool of empire building and of accumulation of wealth and power called imperialism, capitalism and globalization. The conqueror is not equal to the conquered, nor is the rich equal to the poor, nor is the creative equal to the non-creative, nor is the one who dominates the world equal to the one that is dominated. The idea of sovereignty seeks to make the factual inequality of nations less harsh and more acceptable, facilitating actions that result in further inequality. Even if talk of equality is reduced to a mere equality of opportunity, it ignores the fact that unequal people cannot use equal opportunity equally well. Neither intense competition in all walks of life even in sports, games and entertainment, nor the educational system based on examinations and grading, nor the defense, industrial or commercial hierarchy of organization recognizes or promotes equality.

DR. B.R. AMBEDKAR says: Men do not become a society by living in physical proximity, or through similarity of customs, habits, beliefs and thoughts. They become a society when they have things, which they share and possess in common. They have similar festivals, but this has not united them. Caste came to express the pride and selfishness of BRAHMANS, who felt superior. They had the status and moral authority to enforce their views.

He ignores the loss of freedom, power, and status of BRAHMANS. They were thought to be the source of KUFR or anti-Islam for a thousand years and made into objects of hatred, condemnation and destruction, an idiom of thought and language that still persists in social comments.

He says that caste came to divide and demoralize Hindus. They did not feel the need of a common community. They are a collection of castes, but there is no federation of castes. Each caste is conscious of its existence as separate from other castes. It is anti-social, as they do not feel one. Even sub-castes think of themselves as separate from other sub-castes. Caste survival is their aim. They unite only when there is a Hindu-Muslim riot. On all other occasions castes separate themselves from each other. They think of themselves as superior to others. Caste consciousness keeps past feuds alive.

Social unity however is a complex matter, and never an undifferentiated oneness and equality. The first unity is always at the level of self-expression and family.

Are we united with our own nature? Do we express what we are? Or do we obstruct our nature for one reason or the other? Do we direct ourselves to express the best in our nature and our tradition or do we remain without self-direction, copying and imitating our present and former rulers, or even the wicked people, expressing in our lives their worst? Are we united with our children and grandchildren, parents and grandparents and our large network of relationships, working for their benefit? The question of VARNA arises in theory only when we express our nature. Otherwise it does not arise at all. Then the color of our actions will be a false color, not a public declaration of the divine truth present in us.

In practice however along with destruction of the best of men in numerous wars, resulting in loss of political freedom and upward mobility, destruction of temples and universities along with their associated social functions, resulting in cultural sterility, everything got decided by birth and made inward looking, as befits a slave nation. Our temples got smaller and lost their grandeur and social functions, and marriages got to be performed secretly at night.

The next unity is created through our nurture, education and culture. Are we united with the place we grew up in, or are we united with the places from were our invaders came? Are we creating the same Islamic or western place wherever we go hunting for money, power or pleasure? Are we trying to create the same town, the same village, the same hotel and the same mode of entertainment everywhere? Is it this that we mean by unity? Are we aware of the consequences of standardization on nature and the human mind? Are we saying that the earth needs only one animal and all other animals are to be eliminated as sub-standard, be they wild animals about to become extinct, or Non-Christians, heathens and pagans, or KAFARS, Non-Muslims, worshippers of idols and devils, or Non-Westerners like Asians, Africans, or Latin Americans?

Are we united with our childhood friends and schoolteachers? Do we feel any moral obligation towards them? Or did we merely use them as a ladder in our upward social mobility honored as progress, and then forgot about them, like the used cars?

Do we participate in local festivals and buy things that benefit the local economy, creating a unity with our immediate surroundings rather than the distant Western capitals or Mecca?

Are we united with our ancient past, building on it like we build our adult life and old age on our childhood? Can we have a borrowed modernity without becoming sterile? Or do we reject our cultural past as we reject our childhood past?

Is it possible to imagine a modern professor of medicine, or astronomy, or engineering or philosophy working in a first rate university of India today, saying to himself at age 50 that enough is enough, and changing his clothes and moving from village to village and sharing his knowledge, wisdom and experience with the common people, resolving their problems and conflicts, and helping them enjoy life within their limited resources? The modern gurus seen on the TV have no inputs from RISHIS of contemporary GURUKULS, and so they lack future direction and keep repeating what was said centuries ago, without even interpreting it afresh.

The next unity is created through our occupations and modes of earning our livelihood. There are numerous professional, occupational brotherhoods, and modern forms of the caste system, in which political, martial, industrial, and commercial powers somehow remain within the same families for generations. Are we devoted to the work we do, trying to be the best of men in the skills required, or are we doing less than our best, using power and status inefficiently, pretending to be serving the people? Does our heart lie in our skills used for the benefit of all or elsewhere like the money earned and stacked abroad, or power abused? Do we have interests we cannot live without, or do we have temporary interest in this or that job that brings more money? Such questions apply as much to the king, his ministers, advisors and officials as to ordinary craftsmen, producers and labor.

Social unity is a network of many diverse unities of self-expression, families, small localities or villages, communities, regions and all regions. The overall unity is nurtured by the ruling, governing classes. These governing classes have been destroying this unity for over a thousand years. India has been a region of constant warfare for centuries. Their kings and governors destroyed, killed, looted, converted, enslaved, raped, debased and humiliated hundreds of thousands of people of all castes over many centuries, facts which are politely ignored and forgotten, without regrets or sense of shame or apology. What we see around us is not the best possible flowering of the ancient ideas.

SITA RAM GOEL in his HINDU TEMPLES, WHAT HAPPENED TO THEM, VOL.II gives a detailed list with supporting evidence of numerous temples that were destroyed in the name of Islam. Much else was destroyed: congregations of devotees who met in these temples, meditated and thought of idols and ideals, discussing problems including social unity, common welfare and interest, entertaining themselves, as well as schools of learning, social institutions providing charity, free food and medicine to the needy. It is a miracle that Hindus survived. They survived because of their caste system and layers within layers of their social organization. Their society was deformed and demonized, but they kept up their resistance in different regions, like SIKHS at one place, RAJPUTS at another, and MARATHAS at still another.

Dr. KOENRAAD ELST in his book "DECOLONIZING THE HINDU MIND" cites K. S. LAL who quotes a 1345 A.D. inscription of the REDDY dynasty of ANDHRA, which says that when KSHATRIYA defenders were destroyed, the duty of defending BRAHMANS (learned people) and cows (cattle and wealth) fell to SHUDRAS, born of VISHNU'S feet. Their first king VEMA defeated the MUSLIMS, restored the land grants of BRAHMANS, and ruled the territories earlier ruled by KSHATRIYAS. They used wealth to sponsor men of learning (BRAHMANS).

Another inscription of 1368 A.D. of SINGAYA NAYAKA says that the fourth caste was born of VISHNU'S feet along with GANGA as they both purify the three worlds. They are attentive to their duties, devoid of passion, without wickedness, and help KSHATRIYAS. Another inscription says that his relative KAPAYA-

NAYAKA rescued the ANDHRA country from the ravages of the MOHAMMEDANS.

SHUDRAS defended the country against Muslims, upheld BRAHMAN culture, and felt pride in being born of VISHNU'S feet. REDDYS rose fighting against the Muslims. JATS rose fighting against the MUGHALS. JATS and MEDS helped BRAHMANS and KSHATRIYA rulers of SINDH against Arab invaders. JATS and KHOKHARS joined SHAHIYA kings of PANJAB against MAHMUD of GAZNI, and one of them stabbed the foreign invader to death. Some peasant communities took shelter in forests to escape payment of JIZZYA in humiliating conditions and punitive Muslim military expeditions. When GOND Queen RANI DURGAVATI was defeated, her people became a low tribe in a forest. Some women of her tribe enact their traumatic experience by marching a few kilometers with sticks and bows and arrows in their hands. Many proud RAJPUTS took to the road and became gypsies. Some withdrew into mountains like NEPAL. Some went deep into deserts like the descendants of RAJA JAI CHANDRA RATHOR of KANAUJ, who refused to become Muslims.

Caste was not the only principle of social organization. It should be deleted, if it can be deleted, as so many people dislike it. But it can take on new names and forms. It is significant that secular political leaders who loudly condemn the caste system from public platforms engage in intensive caste calculations as part of the secular electoral process. The secular political system seems to be promoting the caste system deceptively. And caste exists in Muslim and Christian religions as well.

Chapter IV

High Tradition

MAHARSHI VALMIKI was a contemporary of SRI RAMA. He composed an epic that narrates his story. The story was passed on orally for many generations before it was recorded. In this process many changes and spices were added, like making forest men VANNA NARA into monkeys VANARA. Numerous episodes like the burning of SRI LANKA by HANUMAN, or RAMA banishing SITA or slaying SHAMBUKA or BALI, or RAMA and SITA marrying at the ages 13 and 6 rather than 24 and 18 and staying at AYODHIA for 12 years rather than one year before exile, are later additions according to P.L. BHARGAVA'S "Retrieval of Histoty from Puranic Myths".

Many devotees of SRI RAMA composed their own understanding of the story. SWAMI RAMANANDA in his ADHYATAMA RAMAYANA deified SRI RAMA and gave allegorical meanings to the story. RAMACHARITMANAS of SANT TULSI DAS is a scripture of devotion recited non-stop by groups of people in some places.

The story of SRI RAMA has inspired Hindus for centuries. They have created new meanings in the context of their own local culture. Many devotees of different castes and at different levels of understanding have recited, recreated and enacted this story to suit their minds every year. Many devotees have tried to emulate the ideals SRI RAMA and lived by them in their own lives. Some RAJPUT kings emulated him on the battlefield, fighting ethically.

One should first do PRANAYAMA for a few minutes, focusing the mind on breathing alone, thereby forgetting all else. Then one should read the text with a single mind full of devotion. After reading the text, one should meditate on one's own nature, customs and tradition and resolve to dedicate one's life to the best in the tradition. In this way one should engage in PITRI PUJA, the worship of ancestors and express the highest moral values of one's tradition and so transform one's nature. SRI RAMA was MARYADA PURSHOTAMA, the best man of tradition.

According to an ancient tradition, SRI RAMA was the 39th king in his line that descended from RAJA IKSHVAKU, the founder of solar dynasty and a son of MAHARSHI MANU who composed a treatise on the law that governs man. PUNDITS specializing in recording lineage maintained genealogical records in those days in places of pilgrimage, like HARIDWAR.

SRI RAMA exempiified such admirable moral values in his life that his people called him MAHATMA, the great soul. They believed him to be an incarnation of VISHNU, the one who sustains life, as he expressed the power that nourishes life in the world.

SRI RAMA had control of his senses and mind, which was focused, detached and chaste. He knew his essential nature and the essence of scriptures. He knew what is right, and spoke the truth. He had a good memory and was skillful in many subjects. He knew the science of warfare. He killed his enemies and was effectively powerful and famous. He worked for public welfare. He was compassionate or angry as the situation required. He was wise and effective in speech and behavior. He followed moral values that sustain us in the ups and downs of life. He maintained ancient traditions and customary laws. So he was called the ideal man of tradition.

People in their struggle of life create customs that suit them. They know best what is to be done in their situation. They need freedom to create their own customs. Otherwise foreign customs are imposed on them and their own customs become fossils. Customs are created slowly, allowing time to the mind to adjust to changes. Customs sustain life. They make tradition by which men live. In the name of revolutionary change, we destroy tradition. But genuine long lasting revolution rises from tradition and lapses back into it. Even those thinkers who talk against tradition would like to create their own tradition. Otherwise they have no right to be GURUS.

Custom is the first basis of law. Every society and group evolves and follows its own customs. In those days the duty of the king was to protect and maintain custom. People in their daily interactions with each other made customary laws as it suited them and changed customs as circumstances changed. Common people rather than the king had the legislative power.

Some of RAMA'S ancestors were BRAHMA, the creator, MARICHI, the powerful winds of change, MAHARSHI KASHYAPA, the philosopher, SURYA DEVA, the sun that gives light and heat, reveals knowledge, life, and creation, MAHARSHI MANU, who compiled and codified the customary law that governs man, IKSHVAKU, the king who founded the solar dynasty, and powerful kings like MANDHATA, SATYAVRAT, HARISH CHANDRA, who gave away his all in charity, SAGAR, who tried to establish an empire and sacrificed his sons, facing the wrath of DHARMA, and BHAGIRATH, who in repentance brought down the waters of GANGA from the heavenly mountains to dry lands, RAJA SUDAS and DASHARATHA, who fought the enemy on ten fronts with the help of his warrior queen, obliging him to make a wild promise for which his son had to pay a heavy price.

There is a need for everyone to keep a record of his ancestors and family, especially of important events and moral values that guided them. If families keep a truthful record of events and their experience of life, and pass on this record from generation to generation with every generation making additions of high value work done,. it will become a great history of the people in future. This will be the history of man, not a history of the killers of man. This recording of visiting families was done in important places of pilgrimage in the past.

Once upon a time, RAVANA was the king of SRI LANKA. He became extremely powerful. So he started behaving lawlessly. He disregarded DHARMA and imposed his own will on others. Power without the control of custom and law results in terrorizing the powerless. Power promotes its own interest and works against others. People and animals were killed for the fun of it. Political power was gained for personal comfort and wealth, not for the welfare of the people. Good people were ignored or punished. So mother earth was full of pain. Do not think that the earth does not feel the pain of our excesses. Her kind of pain however may be different from the human kind of pain. She is like a cow that nourishes us. She appealed to INDRA DEVA in heaven. He along with BRAHMA and SHIVA appealed to VISHNU who sustains life. He said: Mother earth and good people must always be protected. So I shall incarnate as man, as a son of DASHRATHA, of ten chariots, ten senses of perception and action, the king of AYODHYA, of peace and no war. You all take birth on earth along with me to protect mother earth, and to help good people do their work well.

RAJA DASHARATHA of the SURYA dynasty ruled the state of KOSHAL from AYODHYA as his capital in the modern state of UTTRA PRADESH. MAHARSHI MANU had set up AYODHYA many generations earlier. It had grown up to be a large town in the shape of an octagon with a wide moat on all its sides. It had royal palaces and public offices in the center with eight wide roads radiating out in opposite directions. The roads had trees and flowers on both the sides. Adjoining the roads were gardens and fields. At their back were large mansions of high officials and affluent traders. At their back were smaller roads and streets and lanes with houses of different sizes. Shops in different BAZARS specialized in different things with workers in different skills. People picked up occupations and handicrafts from their parents and grandparents and became skillful experts, devoting themselves fully to their occupations. The town had horses, chariots, elephants, camels, cattle and their supporting and maintenance staff and skills.

The guru of RAJA DASHRATHA was MAHARSHI VASHISHTHA. A council of eight ministers advised the king. They were experts on different subjects and morally good, belonging to old and loyal families and personally reliable and great warriors. They governed the country, protecting it from enemies and leading it on the path of prosperity and welfare of the people.

RAJA DASHARATHA had a wife KAUSHALYA. Years passed and he had no son. Then he married KAIKEYI, daughter of the

RAJA of KEKAYA, in WESTERN PUNJAB. But she too gave him no heir. So he took a third wife SUMITRA, daughter of the RAJA of KASHI. But it did not help.

Once RAJA DASHARATHA went hunting deep into the forest. As he was resting on the bank of river SARYU in darkness, he heard the sound of an animal drinking water. He shot an arrow in that direction in the dark. On reaching the spot, he found that he had wounded a young boy, who said that he was fetching water for his blind, aged parents, who were resting nearby. He requested the king to take water to them.

DASHARATHA took the pot of water to them and told them the unfortunate story. The parents wept and cursed him that he would die of separation from his son. They gave up their life.

DASHARATHA returned to AYODHYA and confided this curse to his guru. He advised him to pray and perform the rituals for having sons. The RAJA did so and was blessed by a divine presence.

In due course of time, RANI KAUSHALYA gave birth to a son. It happened on 10 January 5114 B.C. between 12.15 and 1 P.M. according to PUSHKAR BHATNAGAR'S DATING THE ERA OF LORD RAM. He has calculated dates of birth on the basis of the position of stars at the birth of RAMA and three eclipses mentioned in VALMIKI'S RAMAYANA with the help of software named PLANETARIUM GOLD used in modern astronomy.

The son was named RAMA in memory of the Supreme Being who pervades the universe. RANI KAIKEYI gave birth to a son the next day in the morning. He was named BHARATA. RANI SUMITRA gave birth to twins a day later at noon. They were named LAKSHMANA and SHATRUGANA.

Traditionally the birth of RAMA is celebrated on the day of RAM NAOMI in the month of CHAITRA, which falls in April. His devotees fast and resolve to follow the values by which RAMA lived. The story of RAMA is narrated or recited. At midday a coconut is broken and the birth of RAMA is announced. Sweets are distributed.

The sons grew up in AYODHYA. They were trained in different sciences and arts known in those days.

In his youth, RAJA DASHRATHA used to be called NEMI. He was a friend of RAJA INDRA. When a barbarian attacked this king, NEMI went to defend his friend. He was attacked from ten different points. NEMI was so skillful in defending different directions that he defeated the barbarian. Therefore he was called DASHRATHA. During this battle, his wife KAIKEYI helped him. Women used to fight in wars along with their husbands in those days. Because of her help the husband succeeded. Therefore RAJA DASHRATH granted two boons to his wife. She said she would ask for their fulfillment later.

MAHARSHI VISHWAMITRA was a friend of the world. He had composed the famous prayer to SAVITUR in GAYATRI meter. It prays for a change of life from darkness to light, ignorance to knowledge, from being identified with the mortal body and its mind to being identified with the immortal spirit through meditation. Pious Hindus recite this GAYATRI MANTRA every day in the morning and evening.

VISHWAMITRA was once conducting a YAJNA ritual near modern PATNA in BIHAR for the happiness and friendship of all beings on earth. Naturally some people did not like it, as they wanted to use others for their own benefit, accumulating gold and wealth only for themselves and not sharing it with others. They kept obstructing his actions and rituals. So he decided to take the help of prince RAMA to get rid of these obstructions. He approached RAJA DASHRATHA with this request.

The RAJA did not like to separate from his young son. He took advice from his guru, MAHARSHI VASISHTHA. The guru said that when a learned spiritual guide asks for help he should be helped.

RAMA hesitated. He said: I have just returned from extensive educational travels. I have met many people, lived with them, and seen their ways of living and doing things. I have learnt much about the land and the people. But I do not know why I should be doing what I am doing. Why should I engage in public life? Why must I be a king and do my duty of protecting people and engage in public causes and welfare and keep them satisfied? Why should I not simply enjoy life? All are born to die. So why not enjoy while you live? Why should I do rituals and actions, the royal duty of protecting people and their ways of living? How can I help in a public cause when I am so unclear about my duty and myself? I am not at peace with myself. How can I help? Why should I help?

GURU VASISHTHA smiled to see RAMA questioning himself at the maturing age of 12. He decided to share his experience of YOGA with him. Later it came to be called YOGA VASISHTHA and MAHARSHI VALMIKI composed another voluminous text on this subject. He said: RAMA, in order to achieve great results in life it is necessary to put in appropriate great effort. MAHARSHI VISHVAMITRA is doing this.

The human mind is full of tendencies and dispositions to action. They are also called memories, images, impressions of experiences in this life and earlier lives, natural urges in the body inherited from parents and ancestors. One is compelled to enact these tendencies and dispositions to action. This compulsion to enact them is our bondage to our body and nature. Therefore we do not know freedom, though we talk of freedom. We claim that we are free to do this or that, but actually we are slaves to our dispositions to enact them. We cannot act freely. Freedom from this bondage to the body and its mind has to be acquired and cultivated through effort. This is MOKSHA, freedom to feel, act and think, the highest ideal of man.

These tendencies in the mind may be good, evil or mixed. If they are good, one easily reaches the immortal. Otherwise one has to struggle and apply great effort to do what is good. In any case, good, evil or mixed, one is bound to enact them. But one can be free of them. How? One can empty the mind of them through cultivation of silence and contentment. One can also cultivate rational enquiry and company of the wiser people. Then one can become free, liberated, enlightened and know the truth of life and reality.

When you ask who you are, you are separating yourself from the world. What you see is the world, you and me and others and things. You think you are separate and different from what you see. So you ask who you are. This is dividing your experience in two parts. There is one part that sees and one part that is seen. This action of division always results in conflict, ignorance and illusion.

This illusion exists in the nature of things. When this illusion exists you ask the question and never get the answer. When this illusion ceases you know the answer and never ask the question. You become free.

You are not separate from what you see. You are the world that you see and create. You see the sky. You are creating it. You taste sweetness. You are creating it. You create your sensations with your senses. Different senses would create different worlds. Senses different from the ones you have would have created a different world from the one you experience. You create the world you experience. This whole world that perishes is your creation. It exists in reality that does not perish. All beings are reduced to the reality that became them. Then that reality alone exists. It is nameless, formless, non-manifest, neither light, nor darkness. It has been variously named.

Through rational enquiry into our own mind, it appears as the self of the individual. We have actually to do this enquiry ourselves, not merely hear about it from others. Then the world becomes constant change and transmigration, or delusive appearance of one and the same divine power everywhere, or our engagement with this delusion and ignorance of the reality underlying it, and our bondage and attachment to this appearance.

Take a simple illustration. Bangle is a form of gold. Any gold that you see is gold with form. Gold is reality with form. The universe is reality with form. The form perishes. The reality remains. That reality is intelligence, knowledge that is enacted in every thing in the universe. It spreads out in many directions. It takes many forms. It changes by place and time.

When thoughts cease, you are your self. When the universe ceases, stillness remains. That is the great self that takes many forms. That is the sun that takes numerous forms of light. That is you. That is the solar dynasty.

They who travel on the path of knowledge reflect on the self. They experience freedom even when they are alive. They are not affected by their tendencies and dispositions to action. They rise above them. They are neither elated nor depressed. They are detached from the objects of the senses and withdrawn from them. Then they can see them. They act as right and proper in all circumstances. They do their duty in their best way without expectations of results that are not entirely in their power. They are aware even in sleep. They are pure like space. They do not fear, nor do they frighten others. They study scriptures and reflect on them and their self.

The Supreme Being is seen in the twinkling of the eye. Then the inner self and the outer creation are suddenly united as one. That is the supreme experience of oneness. When you experience this oneness, differences cease. You are not separate from what you see. You are not divided from the other. You are what you see, what you feel and think and do. You become integrated.

You are responsible for what happens, for what you do. You make your world. This is the fourth state of consciousness. It underlies the three states of wakefulness, dream and deep sleep. These three states are rooted in the same one consciousness. They are its play. The dreamer and the dream are one. The dancer and the dance are one. That is NATARAJA, SHIVA dancing.

Till you become pure, you worship a separate form of God. There is one who worships and one who is worshipped. When you become pure, separate forms disappear. This is done through UPASANA, or sitting near in the mind. Only truth that is consciousness remains. Then you do not rest or sleep. Then you delight in the world. Then you truly act. Then your action is free. Through doing your action, your duty, you see who you are. You should always do your duty skillfully with full devotion, entirely absorbed in it.

RAMA felt blessed. He touched the feet of his guru and showed his reverence to all present. He got up to do his royal duty. The two young boys RAMA and LAKSHMANA went along with MAHARSHI VISHWAMITRA into the unknown forests.

VISHWAMITRA was a king who was working to become a learned RISHI. He aimed at combining physical power with spiritual wisdom, an ancient ideal. He thought a king should be a BRAHMRISHI. He should understand the nature of the formless reality as it takes the form of various forces and powers that emerge from it. But in the process of acquiring spiritual power he had ceased being a king. So he was seeking help from the princes of AYODHYA.

They passed through many villages and spent many nights on the banks of rivers and streams. They slept on mats of reeds under the starry skies, remaining alert to defend themselves in the wilderness. The RISHI taught them the secrets of strength and weakness, the arts and skills of warfare and the use of medicinal herbs and how to deal with injuries and hunger and thirst and the lie of the land on the field of battle. They hunted animals for food and lived on wild fruits.

As they traveled through unknown forests, VISHWAMITRA narrated many ancient stories. He narrated how KAMA DEVA, the lord of love who lives in all human beings, one day shot an arrow of flowers at MAHADEVA, the great yogi, who had come out of his ASHRAM in the company of howling and frightening winds. MAHADEVA was surprised at himself, at the presence of love. He looked intently at KAMA DEVA with a focused mind. Under that look of critical and concentrated observation, love burnt into ashes. With a smile, SHIVA smeared his entire body with ashes, as love is present in every pore of it.

A fight took place between the princes and those who were obstructing them. RAMA defeated the barbarians. VISHWAMITRA completed his ritual actions and made vows of friendship to all beings.

Then he took RAMA and LAKSHMANA to the marriage ceremony of SITA. She was the daughter of RAJA JANAK in MITHILA in BIHAR. On the way he taught them stories and skills of living and dealing with the problems of life.

They went to an ASHRAM, where MAHARSHI GAUTAMA, a devotee of rationality, had once lived. He had formulated the science of logic and a way of seeing reality with the help of fair reasoning, which is now known as the discipline of logic.

Once upon a time, INDRA DEVA, the lord of rains and prosperity, pleasurable senses and good things of life, seduced the wife of MAHARSHI GAUTAMA by assuming his form and appearing to be like him. The senses deceive and he played with her, when the husband had gone out to bathe in the cold river so early in the morning. When MAHARSHI GAUTAMA came back, he got angry at this immoral behavior and his wife became a stone. She was to remain a stone till VISHNU, the source of life, touched her again. When SRI RAMA touched the stone, it became alive. The RISHI'S wife AHALYA rose up into the air, as light as a DEVI.

In time, VISHWAMITRA along with RAMA and LAKSHMANA reached the palace of RAJA JANAKA in MITHILA in BIHAR.

In the ceremony of selecting a suitable boy for his daughter, RAJA JANAKA had asked the invited princes to shoot an arrow with SHIVA'S bow. The bow was heavy and inflexible. The aim was to find out the prince who was strong and powerful, the best fighter. Only RAMA was able to do so. He was selected to be SITA'S husband. Her cousins were to be married to RAMA'S brothers.

RAJA JANAKA invited RAJA DASHRATHA to MITHILA, where the marriage ceremonies were performed. He gave away wealth in charity. The town was decorated and made joyful with music and songs, dance and drama. Many RISHIS and RAJAS took part in the main ceremony. A fire was lighted according to ancient rites. Boys and girls to be married were dressed up in fine clothes. They sat by the fire facing each other.

RAJA JANAKA stood up with some water in his hand. He recited MANTRAS to the fire present before them and in the sun and in the earth and in the air and in water and in plants and in fruits and in vegetables and in the human body and mind and in his resolve as he offered SITA in marriage to RAMA. He poured that water into the cupped hand of RAMA and handed over the hand of SITA in marriage to him. RAMA held her hand and went around the fire clockwise. They took seven rounds of the fire, one round each for food, strength, prosperity, comfort, children, enjoyment of changing seasons of nature and life, finally each asking the other to be a friend and unite for having sons who would live long. Then they took seven steps together repeating these vows.

At age 13, RAMA married SITA who was six years of age at that time. Her three young cousins too were married to RAMA'S brothers.

There are many kinds of marriage in the world. There is hardly a conceivable form of man woman relationship that has not been enacted into marriage at some place or the other, some time or the other. It is ignorance to think that the idea of marriage that we like and approve is the only idea of marriage that can be allowed to exist. Sex is not the only reason why people marry, even though marriage results in procreation. Sex becomes routine and meaningless too quickly. The girl child is married so that she may grow up in the groom's house. She may absorb the ways of living of the family of the groom. This may hopefully lead to peace in married life rather than mutual quarrels. The idea of child marriage like its opposite idea of adult marriage may or may not lead to peace at home. But that did not stop people in ancient times from acting on the possibility of having peace at home. It does not stop adult marriages either, even though many adult marriages end in divorce and many more end up in constant mutual bickering that damages each other's mind and self-respect. Is peace at home less important than sexual activity?

They celebrated the marriage ceremonies there for some time. Then RAJA DASHRATHA returned to AYODHYA.

They reached the ASHRAM of RISHI BHARGAVA. This ASHRAM was devoted to the study of stars and mathematical calculations.

MAHARSHI BRIGHU had founded it. He is remembered today for his BRIGHU SANHITA. It is a book of astrological predictions. Astronomy and astrology in those days was one science. At their base was mathematical calculation. Objects of nature were studied from the perspective of man. Every object was seen as related to man. The very act of seeing changed it and made it a part of man.

A learned man who had the glow of a warrior suddenly appeared before them. He was PARSHURAM BHARGAVA. He was full of anger at RAMA, because he had broken the bow of SHIVA, his guru. He challenged RAMA to shoot another arrow with PARSHURAMA'S bow. RAMA easily bent the bow and asked him where the target was. PARSHURAMA mockingly told him to shoot at his self-discipline because he was completely identified with it. But self-discipline is the force of life and it belongs to VISHNU. The power shifted to RAMA at once. PARSHURAMA felt ashamed at his loss of self-control. He went back to his ASHRAM. If you cannot control yourself, you cannot control power.

For 12 years RAMA and SITA lived happily together with their parents, making no story. Happiness has no history. They accumulated many things at home that they did not really need. SITA also picked up the ways of living in her new family.

RAJA DASHRATHA wanted to consecrate RAMA as the crown prince on his 25th birthday. He said: RAMA, You are a wise man. But on the evening of your consecration, I must say a few words to you.

You must keep your desires and anger under strict control. No one has a right to rule others if he is unable to rule himself. When people speak to you in the court, compare their public speech with the secret information about them, which you get from your spies and then arrive at just decisions. Public speech is not to be fully trusted. It must be checked against actions and reliable secret information. Objectives and motives are seldom revealed. Always engage in increasing wealth and weapons in your kingdom. Kingdoms stand on wealth and weapons. Keep your people, ministers and army chiefs happy. It is the important men who keep the kingdom safe. Nourish the land and its people that give you so much wealth. Follow the highest ideals of kingship. Without high ideals, life is empty and meaningless. Keep awake and fast this night to firm up these vows.

People were happily looking forward to the ceremony. A maid watched from the balcony elaborate preparations going on in the large courtyard below. She felt pangs of jealousy. She incited RANI KAIKEYI to feel like a stepmother towards RAMA. After all he was only a stepson. He would make her and her son into his servants. She must ask for fulfillment of the boons granted to her by her foolish husband. She must make her son the heir to the throne and exile RAMA for fourteen years.

When the king came in, the queen reminded him of his promise to her. She asked that BHARATA be made the crown prince and RAMA be exiled for fourteen years. DASHRATHA was shocked. He fainted.

When RAMA came to know of it, he put on the clothes of a forester without any protest. He decided to walk away to a forest for fourteen years after appropriate farewells.

RAMA was 25 and SITA was 18 years old. He asked SITA to stay back in the comfort of the palace, but she refused. She must share both the joys and the sorrows of her husband. He asked LAKSHMANA to stay back, but he refused. He must accompany his elder brother to help him in his need. They followed RAMA in the clothes of foresters. The other brother stayed back to help the parents. RAMA and SITA gave all their household things in charity. Why keep things in the house when you are not going to use them? The people felt miserable at the turn of events.

SITA, RAMA, and LAKSHMANA crossed the River GANGA with the help of the chief of fishermen, who himself rowed the boat. On their way further south, they spent some time with MAHARSHI VALMIKI in his ASHRAM.

VALMIKI was a hunter who had become a learned poet. He was so intently absorbed in listening to all the details of their life that he could foresee the rest. He was a true poet. From seeing the past clearly he built a picture of the future that was outside time and must happen.

They reached the ASHRAM of RISHI BHARDWAJA, who suggested that they settle down at CHITTRAKOOT, which is now a place of pilgrimage, located in BANDA District of UTTAR PRADESH on the border of MADHYA PRADESH, near Mountain KAMADGIRI, on the bank of River PAYASWANI.

Some time earlier RISHI BHARDWAJ had met RISHI YAJNAVALKYA during the ritual baths of KUMBHA MELA at PRYAGA. He had asked: Sir, when prince RAMA is the son of RAJA DASHRATHA and RANI KAUSHALYA, how come people are devoted to him as the creator of the universe?

RISHI YAJNAVALKYA replied: Sir, whatever you worship, whatsoever it might be, be it a stone, or a plant, or an animal, or a human being, or a super human force, it will always be your creation, your idea, a created being. What you call a fact is your creation, your thinking and feeling. Your knowing it makes it your creation. While knowing it you change it and create it. What man worships is his creation. His creation at the deepest level of worship is the creation of his world too.

Worship has many degrees and forms. There is no one form of worship or the only true way of worship. Worship can be pretentious or superficial, deepest or highest, the one that unites or the one that separates, and so on. In the highest form of worship, you experience everything as one integrated whole. In that one whole, you cease to be. The individual self and the self of the universe become one. That is the experience of unity, the experience of one God, the oneness of reality, one without a second, not the one of a series. You cannot have experience of one God and think of yourself as a worshipper, as a separate individual or community and think of another individual or community as your enemy. In that experience of oneness, sir, who is the friend and who is the enemy, who is the creator and who is the created?

Some people are interested in social action. They rate moral goodness very high, as high as the divine. But goodness is only a human way of seeing. There are non-human worlds too and there is diversity of human nature as well.

Is goodness of the master the same as the goodness of the servant? Is the goodness of an old man the same as the goodness of a young child? Is goodness the same in all occupations, unrelated to the work they do, their duty, and what they make? Yet in spite of this variety, there is some common goodness too.

If you do not rate moral goodness high, then you engage in action for personal benefit. Even your social action becomes a form of action for personal benefit. Then what you call your social action is a form of ignorance of social action. It is a form of give and take, of commerce, not just giving, not just divine.

If you express moral goodness through values like sacrifice, truth, non-violence, compassion, tradition, justice, in all actions of your life, you become divine. Those who value moral goodness as divine will call you DEVA or MAHATMA. Then you will be worshipped. Then you will live a life that others want to emulate, to live by. Then you will create their universe. This has happened to RAMA. It can happen to others. There are many expressions of the same divine power. There can never be only one expression of the infinite divine. The path of moral goodness has its own difficulties. But it is the clearest path to becoming divine.

DASHRATHA could not bear separation from his son. He died six days later, unable to bear the loss.

His ministers were RISHIS MARKANDEY, MUDGAL, VAMDEVA, KASHYAP, KATYAN, GAUTAMA and GURU VASHISHTHA. They held a meeting, and said to one another: Sir, a kingdom without a king invites disorder. Enemies take over the kingdom. Prosperity and wealth disappear. Relationships disintegrate. No one protects people from those who loot and destroy.

No one builds PANCHAYATS or forms of local government for gathering revenue and spending it to improve living and resolve conflicts.

Courts of justice cease to function. No one decides on allegations and counter allegations between businessmen.

No one builds DHARAMSHALAS or free inns for travelers. Roads get infested with robbers. Traders do not travel far with their goods. They are looted on the way.

No one builds temples for contemplating different forms of high ideals and moral values. Without morality, life becomes empty and destructive. Young girls with beautiful clothes and ornaments cannot move about freely in the gardens. Lustful men harass them.

No one builds YAJNASHALAS for celebrating great vows and firm resolves. No great action can be undertaken without a firm resolve.

No one organizes festivals, dramas, dances, and art exhibitions to help wealth to change hands. Entertainment helps in changing the flow of wealth from those who have abundance to those who have little or none.

Men of pleasure and their attractive companions do not go out in fast moving vehicles. Rich people do not feel safe.

Traders, cattle raisers and agriculturists have sleepless nights.

People are not be able to get what they need, or protect what the have.

Learned people are not be able to talk freely or spread their ideas.

Anti-social people have a free time.

Even ministers are not able to function well as they only reflect the king's power.

The king sustains the kingdom. RAJA DASHRATHA is dead. RAMA and LAKSHMANA are in exile. BHARATA has gone on a holiday to his maternal grandfather in PANJAB. Something must be done quickly to protect the kingdom.

GURU VASHISHTHA said: RAJA DASHRATHA declared BHARATA as the crown prince. So he must be brought back to rule. We shall send five messengers on different routes to bring him back. Meanwhile I shall take all decisions after consulting you all.

BHARATA had gone to visit his maternal grandfather, the king of KAKAYA, the land between Rivers CHANDRABHAGA (CHENAB) and VITASTA (JHELUM) and was staying in their capital RAJAGRIHA. Different messengers by different routes were sent to bring him back. When he returned and met his mother he was greatly upset at what had happened. He immediately left for the forest to bring his brother RAMA back to the palace.

The two met at CHITRAKOOT Mountain. RAMA wept on hearing of father's death, but refused to return to AYODHYA. As his elder brother trained to be the next king, RAMA gave his younger brother some advice.

He said: Remember the family tradition. You may lose your life, but not break your promise. Promise is the basis of all contracts and treatise.

Always follow moral goodness, keeping your urges within the limits of morality.

Acquire knowledge and learn about the nature of order in reality.

Follow VASISHTH ACHARYA, our family guru. Follow our family priest, who does rituals and knows many subjects and never finds faults, a rare quality.

Respect the forces of nature and the power of ancestors and tradition.

Respect women, gurus and old people. Honor medical doctors and learned people.

Study weapons and their use. Collect money and weapons and men with skills.

Have advisors who are fearless and expert in different subjects. They should be self-controlled and of noble families. They should know the other's mind through observing their external actions.

Keep secrets and study solutions of problems. Do the work that requires minimum resources and produces maximum results.

Employ people of noble families who have been working for you for generations. They should be good inside and outside and not take bribes. Test their worth before appointing them.

Do not be harsh or impose high taxes. Take taxes from subordinate kings. Destroy those who threaten your kingdom. Pay your soldiers well and on time.

Your ambassadors should be of your own country, not of another. They should be learned, efficient, and effective. They should do only what they are told.

Use spies for collecting information. Keep your eyes on your enemy kings, their ministers, priests, heir apparent, generals, gate keepers, jailors, finance secretaries, those who spend public finances, those who are in charge of towns, builders, religious leaders, chairmen of assemblies, judges, keepers of forts and boundaries and those who live in forests. Get this information from three different sets of spies for comparison and check. Do not underestimate your enemy. Attend to dissatisfied servants of enemy kings. Tempt them.

Do not follow those who seek pleasures and who do not work for the benefit of others.

Have many horses, chariots and elephants and keep them well trained. Prepare your defenses and protect your capital. Develop your fields and cattle and trade. Your fields should not depend on rains alone. Take water to them through channels. Look after mines and establish your rights on them. Establish people on wastelands. Destroy criminals and show no compassion to thieves.

Build bridges. Build forts near water, on mountains, in deserts, in wilderness and in forests. Keep them well filled with wealth, weapons, water, medicines, soldiers and workmen.

Increase your income and decrease your expenditure. See that money goes into the right hands. Desire, wealth and righteousness should not hurt each other, as each is important. Enjoy each of them at the right time.

Always discus state affairs with three or four advisors and ministers, both separately and collectively. Once decided, act quickly. Never attack all your enemies at once. Attack them when necessary and wait for the right time. Enter into treatise with enemy kings when necessary.

Do not sing or dance, drink or gamble, or sleep during the day. Do not talk against others or move about aimlessly. Attend to fires, floods, diseases, epidemics and famines.

Give others what they want but always follow your royal interest.

GURU VASISHTHA said: RAMA, it is the custom of IKSHAVAKU dynasty that the eldest son inherits the kingdom. You should follow the custom and protect DHARMA.

RAMA said: Sir, it is also the custom to keep your promise. Otherwise how can relationships, contracts and treatise be honored?

JABBALI, the chief of BRAHMANS said: RAMA, you are creating problems where none exist. You are born alone. You die alone. Then who is related to whom? RAJA DASHRATHA is dead and nothing to you now. You are nothing to him now. You are suffering for nothing. We stay with our family and wealth like we stay in a village inn and then we vanish. There is no world other than this. Kingdom has come your way. Grab it and enjoy yourself. Follow immediate gain. They who abandon prosperity for the sake of living in a forest merely choose to suffer. Why choose suffering?

There is nothing in DHARMA. It is only a word. Do you think the food a BRAHMAN eats in the SHRADA ceremony reaches the dead? Do you think an animal killed in the YAJNA ceremony reaches heaven? Do you think a MANTRA whispered in a child's ear leads him to enlightenment? Do you think some water offered to the sun reaches the sun? Do you think living in a forest will make you noble? Religious rituals are exercises created to make man less selfish, more liberal. There is nothing more in them. But if you think you must keep your father's promise, you know well that it was a promise without any content. He made it as a thank you after a crisis on a battlefield where the queen had helped him. Did the king intend to disinherit you? Does not an action include its intention and its consequence? Does a king have a right to make a commitment without knowing its content? If he does so, is not he exceeding his authority? If he exceeds his authority, must the heir stand by it? Must he do so, whatever the content put into it by an enemy? Do you have a right to discomfort your wife and brother? Do you have a right to injure the kingdom?

RAMA said: Dear Sir, there is something called tradition. Actions are done according to custom in a family or a dynasty. Even if you start afresh with no tradition, you will raise your family on high moral values and create its tradition. And you will live by those family traditions. You are the chief of BRAHMANS associated with our family. Tell me how your ancestors advised us in the past. How much different can you be from your past? Does not the past live in you? Are you denying your parentage for the sake of protecting your kingdom? Are you being selfish?

BHARATA touched RAMA'S feet to show his reverence for him. They all returned to AYODHYA. They brought back RAMA'S sandals as a symbol of his authority. BHARATA did not enter the palace. He built an ASHRAM nearby at NANDIGRAM, where he started living like a hermit. He placed RAMA'S sandals on the throne and ruled over the country in his name.

From CHITRAKOOT, RAMA along with his brother and wife went deeper into the forest towards DANDAKARANYA.

On the way, they visited the ASHRAM of MAHARSHI ATRI, who had composed an exposition of various rituals and commandments associated with RIG VEDA. He showed that rituals have deep meanings. If you forget those meanings and do not devote yourself to them by acting accordingly, you need not do the rituals. Rituals are done as a reminder to one to experience and act out those meanings in one's life.

MAHARISHI ATRI welcomed them with proper ceremonies. His wife ANASUYA, who was a RISHI in her cwn right, gave SITA a pair of earrings, a couple of silk dresses, and a paste for the body to keep it young and radiant. She also gave her a profound discourse on PATIVRATA DHARMA or wife's loyalty to her husband that makes her life full of high values like love and meaning, while going from one man to another reduces her to the level of animals.

From there they went still further south into the forest and faced numerous difficulties.

They visited RISHI SARABHANGA'S ASHRAM in the KUMUD forest. The RISHI was so overwhelmed on seeing them that he lost his speech and his mind disappeared. He suddenly saw his eyes and ears working independently of him. He saw his breathing working independently of him. He saw his mind and heart and belly working independently of him. He saw his body working independently of him. He saw his actions happening independently of him, without any beginning or end and he disappeared in these actions. In that twinkling of an eye, he died, so to say, and was reborn anew. He knew the divine now.

They traveled further on and met many RISHIS engaged in study, physical and spiritual exercises of various kinds. They heard about barbarians who rejected self-restraint as a way of life and who did whatever came into their minds, as they pleased.

They visited the ASHRAM of RISHI SUTIKSHIN. He welcomed them with forest fruits and said: Sir, I am always identified with my body and mind, with my wife, children and relatives. I am identified with my large ASHRAM. I have to manage its many students and their gurus and keep detailed accounts of its income and expenditure and balance the accounts and see that all dealings are morally good and auspicious and beneficial to all. Yet I am devoted to you, your presence in all beings, in my heart and mind while I do all these worldly activities. I always keep you in my mind whatever I do. You are the unknown being that lives in the forest of the heart, in the center of our being. You are hidden behind our ignorance. You are the source, the life and death of me. I see you present in all forms of the universe. You are seen by the pure in heart. Please accept my devotion to you.

They went on to MRKANDU forest, and visited the ASHRAM of MAHARSHI AGASTYA, who had spread DHARMA across the seas. He saw the divine in RAMA and welcomed them with fruits and flowers.

He said: Before creation you alone existed. Your power is MAYA. It has no independent existence. It expresses itself as nature, which keeps us ignorant of you. Nature is always active, one action leading to many other actions. These actions create the universe that we experience. They attach us to its numerous forms and changes. They become the great elements like space, air, fire, water, and earth. They become the great forces like the senses and the mind. They become the great principles, like the principle that I think I am the doer of various things, good, bad or indifferent. All these actions are in the seed of the universe. They are the LINGA, the sign that marks all the possibilities of the world.

You are the creator, the preserver, and the destroyer. They see you who are even minded and detached. They see you who control their senses and give up evil and selfish actions. They see you who are devoted to you. They practice YOGA and its moral values and rules. They act spontaneously according to their nature, fully aware. They nourish their strengths and eliminate their weaknesses. You have come into the world to relieve the earth of its wickedness. You have come to help good people.

Here RAMA took the vow to kill RAVANA and other RAKSHAS. He vowed to secure the land for RISHIS to develop a different form of living, of fire and moral intensity in order to continue their pursuit of the nature of order and reality.

RISHI AGASTYA presented a VAISHNAVA bow, a BRAHMA arrow and SHIVA quiver to RAMA. He combined different forms of power in one weapon. RAMA accepted the weapon and requested that these powers be delivered to him at the time of his need, wherever he might be, as he would use power only when necessary.

AGAYSTYA gave RAMA a divine weapon for protection, which RAMA tied around SITA'S neck.

Then they went on to DANDAK forest, where they met JATAYU, the king of birds. They renewed their old friendship with birds and agreed to help each other. Do not kill birds for your pleasure because they help you in many ways. Men, animals, plants and minerals are inter-dependent. For man to ignore other species is harmful ignorance.

Then they went to the south bank of river GODAVARI. They saw a cluster of five PEEPLE trees, called PANCHVATI. It was in the modern NASIK district of MAHARASHTRA. They built a hut in their center. PEEPLE trees are worshipped because they give life day and night. People can safely sleep under these trees in a forest. They lived there for many years. RISHIS of the surrounding area visited them to discus contemporary problems and find their solutions.

One day LAKSHMANA said to RAMA: Sir, what is freedom? What is the difference between knowledge and spiritual experience? What are devotion to a high ideal and renunciation of the world in its pursuit?

RAMA said: The supreme self of the universe is the object of spiritual quest. When you experience it you become free of the fear of death and birth in this universe of constant change and transmigration with birth and death as its distinguishing marks.

First understand the creations of your mind and be free of them. We think we are our body and mind, which is not true. This false identity is created by the divine power called MAYA. This power has two aspects. One is its power of projection. We see colors because we have eyes. We hear sounds because we have ears. We have five senses of perception and five senses of action. They create their own objects, which do not exist. We have one mind that receives and modifies information from them more or less in the very process of receiving it. It organizes this information in many ways and constructs further information from them. Therefore what we see and experience is what we create, what we are. If we were different from what we are we would experience the world differently. It depends on our organs, their capability and training. This is the power of projection. We are bound to this power, caught in it.

The second power of MAYA is that it hides the divine behind these projections. Reality lies behind what we sense. That reality is a parallel invisible universe. It is pure, living consciousness, not mixed with anything else. There is nothing else. The variety that we see is a delusion created by our senses. What you see and hear and remember is a delusion. Behind this delusion exists the sameness of objectless consciousness.

Our body and mind relate us to others, our wife and children and other relatives and friends and things of nature that we sense. The self, the consciousness, has no relationships. The body and mind consist of gross and subtle elements like ego, intellect, senses, mind and nature. They together make a field.

The self is independent of this field and free of happiness and sorrow. Experience of this truth is spiritual realization. It is also called enlightenment, freedom, MOKSHA.

The self of the individual and the self of the universe are the same. This realization comes through action and devotion. It is not knowledge that comes through words, reading scriptures or listening to a guru.

Do not deceive, oppress or inflict pain on others. Be straight and devoted to your spiritual teacher. Be aware, without ego. Be aware of suffering and its sources. Be a witness of what happens. Be detached and undisturbed in all circumstances. Be devoted to reality. Search for your self. Be in the company of those who are similarly engaged. Visit holy places, the sources of your inspiration. Listen to all this, meditate and fast on EKADASI, the eleventh day of the bright moon. Do ceremonious worship. Repeat the name and visualize the divine, thinking of its attributes and forms. Internalize them. Trust the divine present in you as you move from the known into the unknown.

A RAKSHUS woman was looking for love. She saw RAMA and liked him. When she proposed to marry him, he told her that he was already a married man. Then she made the same proposal to LAKSHMANA, as one man was like any other man. He gave her the same answer. She was very upset. She thought SITA was the reason why they had refused her. So she pounced upon SITA to kill her. LAKSHAMANA intervened and cut off her nose. She went crying to her brother RAVANA, the RAJA of SRI LANKA. She appealed to him to take revenge and dishonor SITA.

RAVANA sent a RAKSHUS in the form of a spotted deer to RAMA'S ASHRAM. SITA was tempted by its beauty and wanted to possess the animal. She asked RAMA to capture it. He went in pursuit of it, asking LAKSHMANA to take care of SITA. After some time, SITA heard RAMA'S voice shouting for help. She asked LAKSHMANA to go and help RAMA. He ignored her request and remained alert to the danger he was sensing. She accused him of having dark designs on her. LAKSHMANA was so deeply hurt at this false accusation of the female mind that he went out in search of RAMA.

RAVANA came there in the disguise of a SANNYASI. He asked her who she was, such a beautiful lady with round cheeks and big eyes, so brilliant and shining, and lips like rose petals, and neck like a swan's, and big breasts so tense and firm, rising up and tight, and a slim waist and a proud belly and bulging hips and thighs like the trunk of an elephant radiant through her thin robes. Who are you gorgeous in such a terrible forest? You should be in a royal palace in a big and prosperous town.

SITA smiled to hear her praise and said proudly that she was the daughter of the MAHARAJA of VIDEH, and daughter-in-law of the MAHARAJA of KAUSHAL, and wife of the crown prince SRI RAMA, exiled by his jealous stepmother. She said her husband had gone out hunting. He would be back with meat and fruits and roots. When he came back he would receive the BRAHMAN with due honor and ceremony. Till then he should wait.

RAVANA laughed to say that her husband the crown prince RAMA could not protect his beautiful wife, then how would he protect his large kingdom? He introduced himself as the

MAHARAJA of SRI LANKA. He had defeated and exiled his elder stepbrother KUBER to the cold of HIMALAYAS and taken over his town of gold. He had even raped a girl who was going to be his stepbrother's daughter in law and she was young enough to be his grand daughter. He asked SITA to marry him and be the queen of all the women he had kidnapped.

SITA was shocked and repelled. She refused him in contempt. He caught hold of her by force, carried her to his VIMANA and flew away.

JATAYU, the king of birds, saw this injustice. He tried to hit the airplane with his body in defense of SITA. But the bird hit did not work, as RAVANA cut off his wings and he fell down waiting for RAMA, and the airplane repaired itself.

When the brothers returned they found SITA missing. They went about searching for her. They reached JATAYU, who told them of SITA'S abduction by RAVANA.

RAMA and LAKSHMANA cried. They started going further south in order to reach SRI LANKA.

On the way they met SHABBRI, a female hermit in a forest. Women could become hermits and RISHIS in those days. Some of their songs are included in the VEDAS. She offered RAMA half eaten berries after tasting each one of them to see that they were sweet. RAMA was pleased at her caring love.

He blessed her, and said: Whether you are man or woman, high or low caste, young or old, of this or that famous family and name are matters that concern the body and its mind. They do not concern the spirit or the self, which is the same in all.

All can be devoted to the divine. All can love the power that creates, becomes and sustains the universe and dissolves it. Without devotion, or love for the supreme reality, there cannot be any worship, or sacrifice or charity or penance or study of scriptures or rituals or help in spiritual realization.

Learn to associate with the spiritually advanced and holy people. Learn to serve all people who are similarly engaged.

Recite the names and accounts of the divine. Appreciate, experience, and sing its glories. You can learn to praise the divine and sing its glory only if you first learn to praise all other beings and stop finding their faults, since it lives in all of them.

Hear expositions of scriptures. Be devoted to your guru. Practice virtue and be your best self.

Control your senses through ceremonial worship. Repeat and contemplate MANTRAS.

Learn to see the divine present everywhere. Cultivate detachment towards external objects. Investigate the nature of the divine. Be devoted to all this in your worship and be enlightened.

SHABBRI felt blessed. She told them that she had seen SITA being taken away by RAVANA.

They had to overcome opposition from many RAKSHUS sent by RAVANA to obstruct their path. After crossing PAMPA River, they reached the top of RISHIMUKH Mountain. They decided to take help from VANNA NARA. They were men who lived in forests, close to nature. Through wrong accent in oral transmission through the centuries and imagination of the poets who carried forward the stories, these two words became one word, VANARA meaning monkey.

There they met SUGREVE and his Prime Minister HANUMANA They narrated to them the story of SITA'S abduction.

SUGREVE told them his own story, how his elder brother BALI had expelled him from KISHKINDHA, the modern HAMPI district of KARNATAKA, which was the capital of RAJA BALI'S kingdom.

The two formed a treaty of mutual help, even though SUGREVE was doubtful of RAMA'S capacity to help. RAMA felt his doubt and decided to overcome it, because political friendships are based only on power and strength. He shot an arrow that passed through seven SAL trees and it came back to the quiver, completing its cycle of energy. Every one present marveled at it. SUGREVE showed RAMA some ornaments thrown away by a crying woman being carried away by force. RAMA recognized them as SITA'S ornaments.

Next day they went to KISHKINDHA, where SUGREVE challenged BALI to a duel.

As they were fighting, a solar eclipse occurred and RAMA shot an arrow from behind a tree that mortally wounded BALI. As RAMA appeared, BALI accused him of being immoral and violating the moral law of fighting and killing a dualist from a hidden place instead of facing him. This was against the ethics of war. RAJA BALI expected the prince of AYODHYA to fight according to the ethics of war.

SRI RAMA said: You talk of morality but you do not know what morality is. You cannot be immoral here and moral there. An elder brother is like a father and a younger brother is like a son. You have expelled your younger brother SUGREVE from your kingdom. You have lived with his wife. You have broken a family and committed incest. Therefore you have to be punished.

This land is under the control of RAJA BHARATA and royal princes are authorized to punish the wicked. I am a royal prince and so I have the right to punish you. You are like an animal searching for physical pleasures wherever you can get them, without any self-control and considerations of morality. Therefore I have hunted you from behind a tree, as royal princes do while hunting wild animals.

Our ancestor RAJA MANDHITA once inflicted a similar punishment on a criminal for a similar offence. So there is a precedent for this punishment. Our ancestor MAHARSHI MANU says that if a prince does not punish a criminal or if he punishes a criminal leniently, he himself becomes a partner in crime and he and his kingdom will have to repent of it later. He says that if a criminal accepts his punishment he becomes pure. Therefore you should accept your punishment and die in peace.

BALI accepted his punishment as just and handed over his wife and son ANGAD to his younger brother for protection and passed away. His wife TARA mourned at the loss of her husband.

RAMA said: What has happened is sad, but do not grieve. If your husband was his body as he thought he was, the body is still in front of you. So why grieve? If your husband was ATMA that could see what was right and wrong, it is now gone from his wicked body to another body that he has earned through his actions. Life does not die, though it is invisible and what you see is the moving body, which is an expression of life. If life died, it would not be life. Therefore there is no need to grieve.

During the rainy season, they took shelter in a cave. One day LAKSHAMANA asked RAMA what rituals help in spiritual experience.

RAMA said: There are many ways to having spiritual experience. You can recite a divine MANTRA and be devoted to the divine and keep your mind focused on it.

You can accept the divine as your guru and follow high moral values and traditions of your family.

Think of the divine living in your heart, feelings and reason. Think of it in forms of fire and your intensity. Think of it as an image, a picture or a stone, full of life. Think of it in the sun and elements of nature and how they pervade you everywhere. Make a symbolic design, an image or a vision of what you have chosen. Transfer your life and awareness to it. Face it with a pure and sincere mind and an austere life style. Offer flowers and fragrance and the water of life to it, your actions and feelings to it.

Bathe in the morning and keep clean outside and inside. Pray in the morning and in the evening. Offer food and charity to people.

Resolve to see reality. Recite its names and forms and meditate on them.

Meditate on your self, reflecting on your experience of living. See yourself pervading whatever you experience. Remain detached, undisturbed, and observe.

After the rains, they sent out armies in search of SITA in different directions. HANUMAN along with many others went south. They reached the land's end and were debating what to do next when they learnt from a bird that far away in the ocean was an island where RAVANA ruled. In the center of the island was his palace and nearby was a garden full of ASHOKA trees. There in a hut lived SITA. He said that once he had seen RAVANA abduct a beautiful woman of YAKSHA tribe in his PUSHPAK VIMANA. When he attacked the VIMANA, he damaged it. RAVANA had magical powers, as his airplane repaired itself.

HANUMAN went across the ocean, facing many difficulties on the way. He saw SITA sitting under an ASHOKA tree in the twilight of a lunar eclipse. RAVANA came there. He tried to flatter as well as to threaten her. But SITA did not yield. RAVANA returned disappointed.

HANUMAN came down from the tree and presented her RAMA'S ring. SITA recognized it and gave him an ornament to be carried to RAMA for his recognition.

HANUMAN went into the city to see the place. He saw RAVANA'S brother VIBHISHANA praying to VISHNU. Then he went to meet RAVANA, who tried to punish him and set him on fire. HANUMAN burnt the country with that fire and returned to RAMA. He brought information about the enemy forts, gates, army divisions and arrangements.

RAMA established a SHIVA LINGA at RAMESHWARA. He prayed to VARUNA DEVA before the war for a passage through the sea. At that time, the sea level was 10 feet lower than its present level. The land was about 2 kilometers further into the sea from its present shore. SRI LANKA was about 20 kilometers away. Small hills and islands jutted out of the sea along the way. People lived on some of them.

RAJA NAL of the Deep South was a great engineer. He built a bridge across the sea joining these lands that were jutting out. At a depth of 6 feet below water, the remains of this bridge can still be seen. The army crossed the sea. It camped in places where fresh water and fruits were available. It was divided into smaller units and plans of attack were prepared.

RAVANA called a council of war to discuss defense of the country. VIBHISHANA felt that RAMA was in the right. So he proposed peace and return of SITA. RAVANA got angry. The two brothers had a big quarrel. RAVANA exiled his brother from his kingdom. VIBHISHANA sought refuge with RAMA.

SUGREVE said to RAMA: If a man can leave his brother in adversity, whom else cannot he leave? Suppose he has been sent by RAVANA to win our confidence and kill us at the first opportunity he gets.

RAMA said: A refugee should always be protected. When RAVANA'S brother seeks refuge with us, it shows division in the enemy. His fear of RAVANA may be pretence, but his ambition to be the king cannot be pretence. He will help us to win so that he may be the king of LANKA. His ambition will protect us and we will protect him. He gave RAMA information about the defense of LANKA, its strengths and weaknesses.

A great warrior in the council of war advised RAVANA to rape SITA. RAVANA said that he had once raped a woman in the HIMALAYAS. She said she was like a daughter-in-law to him as she was in love with NALKUBER, son of his elder brother KUBER. While raping her, he became impotent with a splitting headache. He got this condition of impotency with severe headache, whenever he approached an unwilling partner. He needed help from SITA. However he felt confident that he would break SITA'S resistance through his bravery and cleverness.

RAVANA'S wife and her father tried to persuade him to return SITA to RAMA. They did not succeed in convincing him.

MALYAVAN, the maternal grandfather of RAVANA said: Taking another man's wife when she is unwilling cannot be justified. Therefore you should return SITA to RAMA and seek peace.

That king rules long who wins his enemy's heart, who changes according to times as necessary, and who keeps increasing his strength. If you keep losing friends, or if your strength is equal to your enemy's strength, you should enter into a treaty of peace with the enemy. You should never insult a king who is stronger. You should fight only when you are much stronger than the enemy.

The common people feel sympathy for RAMA. Nobody likes his wife to be taken away by another through deception and force.

But RAVANA ignored all arguments. Aggression is seldom rational. He sent his spies into RAMA'S camp to create chaos and to bring information. But they were recognized by VIBHISHANA and expelled.

The war began. RAMA attacked LANKA to the sound of martial music. As he was surveying the enemy from a mound, he saw RAVANA doing the same from an opposite mound. SUGREVE was so excited at the prospect of war that he ran towards RAVANA and the two started wrestling and boxing each other without any weapons. RAVANA was older. He got tired and withdrew. SUGREVE came back hurt. RAMA advised SUGREVE not to attack without a proper plan. Many others too had individual combats. Many people on both the sides lost their lives.

RAVANA created false images of RAMA'S severed head before SITA to weaken her will to resist him. SITA mourned at the death of RAMA. Her maid felt sympathy for SITA and contempt for RAVANA as he had used his strength against a woman. She said that RAVANA had magical power of giving false information to weaken his enemy. The war had just started after RAMA'S entry into LANKA. SITA regained her confidence.

ANGAD, son of BALI, defeated INDRAJIT, son of RAVANA, in a straight fight. But INDRAJIT disappeared magically and made RAMA and LAKSHMANA unconscious. He went to his father and reported RAMA'S death. They all drank and celebrated with dance and drama. They had acted on false information. If you give false information to others you tend to accept false information yourself.

Meanwhile GARUR, who had knowledge of herbs and long life, freed RAMA and LAKSHMANA of the poison injected into them. They regained consciousness

RAVANA sent SITA in a vehicle into the battlefield so that she herself may see that RAMA was dead. She and her maid saw that RAVANA was giving false impressions.

Many famous soldiers on both the sides were killed. HANUMAN killed so many of them. KUMBHAKARAN devastated the forces of RAMA. After many ups and downs RAMA killed him.

INDRAJIT fired his weapon BRAHMASTRA. The force of RAMA became unconscious. JAMBHVAN, a general and great AYURVAID of the Deep South, asked HANUMAN to bring SANJEEVANI herb from the HIMALAYAS. He brought a large hillock along with all its herbs. When the herb was applied they came back to consciousness.

INDRAJIT brought an image of SITA into the battlefield. He severed its head before RAMA. VIBHISHAN cautioned RAMA about INDRAJIT'S tricks.

INDRAJIT went to his temple to pray at night. LAKSHMANA challenged him in the temple and killed him after he came out of it.

RAVANA came out to fight. He made LAKSHMANA unconscious. SANJEEVANI herb brought him back to consciousness. INDRA DEVA sent a chariot for RAMA for his use against RAVANA. MAHARSHI AGAYSTYA sent him the weapon left in his custody. After a long fight RAMA killed RAVANA.

VIBHISHANA cried. My brother, asleep on the ground, so brave and learned, now your crown has fallen away. What has happened, I do not understand. You did not listen. I foresaw it all. Pride and lust combined for this ruin. You were a store of policy, strategy and artfulness. You were like the sun and the stars. Now there is darkness everywhere, burnt out ashes. The pillar of RAKSHUS race has fallen.

RAMA tried to consol him: Here lies a strong man. He should not have fallen like this, but he took the path that led to this end. He will be cremated with royal honors. He will be remembered for his strength and learning, but they are not good enough for a good life, as wisdom is needed too.

RAVANA'S wife was MANDODRI. She was a princess from MARWAR in RAJASTHAN from its capital MANDORE and had married Prince RAVANA of SRI LANKA. She had created chess as a substitute for war for her husband.

She came there mourning: I cry for you my love, younger brother of KUBER, lord of the mighty seas. He gave up his kingdom for you and went away to the HIMALAYAS. Now you have fallen. When you were angry, DEVAS trembled and RISHIS ran away. You were a giant, now fallen to a man. You were a hero, who conquered the worlds, now fallen to a forester. You could change your forms, now fallen to a man. Surely time and fate and MAHADEVA have combined to overpower you. Otherwise how could a forester kill you? You controlled your senses to overpower the world. Now your senses have overpowered you. You have lost to lust. You desired SITA and destroyed your all. I warned you but you ignored me. It was mean to steal another's woman. You were blind to do so. Now her tears have drowned you.

Many RAKSHUS women came there mourning their dead: Sad is this day. And thousands killed. They were fathers, husbands, brothers and sons. Why did this happen and for what purpose? An old and wrinkled woman felt the pang of lust. She put on the garb of beauty and proposed marriage to RAMA! What impudence she had! She should be lynched. Because of his blood relationship, RAVANA made plans that were wicked. He was brave, strong and learned. But who can take a woman against her will? Because of it we are destroyed, fourteen thousand of us. RAVANA was brave, strong and learned. But he hurt DEVAS. They sent down RAMA to set things right.

RAMA said: VIBHISHANA, comfort these women. Enmity stays only till death. Now RAVANA is my brother too. Arrange the funeral. He will have a royal cremation.

RAMA appointed VIBHISHANA the king of LANKA. When you defeat a king, you should not occupy his land, as it hurts the pride of people. You should choose a good person from that land and offer him the throne. You should bless and advise him to work for the good of the people. You may however accept gifts from the new king.

LAKSHMANA said to RAMA: Brother, LANKA is a rich, prosperous and beautiful land. Why not settle down here and be its king?

RAMA said: Because the lady next door is beautiful, does she become your mother? When you grow up in a land, the land grows up in you too. Your land reflects in you and you reflect in your land. Learn to see this unity. Go all over LANKA and the world and observe its beauty and enjoy it. But come back to AYODHYA, the land of no war, to settle there and serve it. You cannot grow up in one land and live in another and still remain of one mind for a few generations.

When RAMA met SITA, he felt some hesitation. RAMA was essentially a powerful public figure, the best of his tradition. He felt that RAVANA had dishonored him and his family by kidnapping SITA. Now he had removed the stain of dishonor by destroying RAVANA and his state. But what would the people back home say about SITA and her honor? What aspersions would they cast on her? She felt the pain and burst into fire, but AGNI DEVA protected her. RAMA was satisfied. He returned to AYODHYA with SITA and others on a fast moving PUSHPAK VIMANA.

They reached the ASHRAM of RISHI BHARDWAJA. HANUMAN went ahead to inform BHARATA about their arrival. BHARATA organized DEEPAVALI, the festival of lights to welcome SRI RAMA. This festival of DEEPAVALI is celebrated even today. People close their old accounts and start new ones, and light lamps, distribute sweets, read the story of SRI RAMA with devotion and enact some of its scenes and resolve to follow his ideals and pray for wealth, moral and material.

RAMA was crowned king in the ASHRAM of BHARATA at NANDIGRAM, near AYODHYA. He was taken out in a procession throughout the town.

He started receiving MAHARSHIS from all parts of the country. They were experts on different subjects. They had knowledge of plants, herbs, and healthy living, knowledge of mathematics and stars, knowledge of history, customs and people, knowledge of weapons, fighting, and fast moving and self-repairing vehicles, and training of elephants and horses and men, and self-reliance, knowledge of building towns and bridges across rivers and seas, and building ASHRAMS, altars and channels of water across the land, and performing music, dance and drama. RISHIS emphasized intense self-discipline and effort to achieve goals and endure difficulties till the goal is reached.

RAMA had long conversations with RISHIS. He examined family traditions, eliminating their evils and nourishing their goodness and started building clear visions of the past and the future.

He would get up early in the morning to the sound of music. After getting ready he would visit DEVA MANDAR and offer prayers and worship. He would meditate on the forces of nature and society that shape him. He would reflect on his ancestors and the high moral values they lived by. He would think of the future direction he should take.

Then he would visit the inner court where officials and those engaged in large public works joined him to discuss their problems. Then he would go to the outer court and meet high officials from provinces, to discuss their problems to find solutions, or meet chiefs of tribes, communities and guilds, and other kings. He received and gave gifts.

In the afternoon, he hunted or engaged in royal exercises. Later in the evening he along with his wife went to his private gardens. Fragrant fruit trees and flowers were beautifully laid out. Heavenly musicians and dancers entertained them. There he offered honey wine to his wife and the two relaxed.

RAMA created conditions where people could do their best within the limits of customary law. They followed the ancient path, expressing their inherited nature and finding joy in it. They lived according to their age, doing their occupational duties skillfully for the welfare of all. They lived according to moral ideals, basing their lives on truth, purity, compassion, and charity. They had found that if we live like this, a lot of avoidable suffering disappears. A lot of suffering is the result of our own actions. Avoidable political self-assertion and enmities disappear. Even nature starts helping a good man, as he keeps helping her all the time. His body and mind become youthful, free of illness and deceptions. He becomes more generous and helpful, monogamous and self-controlled. He keeps learning in life and serving the learned.

RAMA had a network of spies. They informed him about the difficulties of the people, of what they said and did, and how they got over them. One day he was brought the news that people talked ill of SITA. They said that she had lived with a stranger for a year. Now she was going to deliver a child who would rule and ruin the kingdom. What right had RAMA to pass on the kingdom to a stranger's line?

RAMA felt the pain of it, as he was essentially a public person. He ordered LAKSHMANA to take SITA to the ASHRAM of MAHARSHI VALMIKI and leave her there. MAHARSHI VALMIKI was a hunter turned poet who understood another's pain. So RAMA sent his wife to a learned SHUDRA for him to protect her and nurture her child as a royal prince. LAKSHMANA obeyed the king's order, even though he did not like it and felt the pain of it. MAHARSHI VALMIKI accepted her as his daughter. She gave birth to twin sons who were named LUV and KUSH. MAHARSHI VALMIKI brought them up as princes. He taught them the skills that kings would need.

SHATRUGAN was sent to destroy barbarians in the north. He set up the town of MADHURAPURI. Many centuries later this kingdom produced SRI KRISHNA.

BHARATA was invited by the king of KEKAYA to invade GHANDHAR. BHARATA conquered that land and set up two towns in the name of LUV and KUSH.

One day a learned man came into the court. He carried his dead son in his arms. He accused RAMA of leading the kingdom to chaos, resulting in the death of his child. RAMA promised to look into the matter.

He thought: People become so dependent on the king that if anything happens that they think is wrong and they feel pain they blame the king. Yet everything has a cause. A child is born as a result of his actions done in a past life. He must die as a result of those very actions as well. Why do not people see this? What can a king do? He has to protect the custom that people themselves create. He has to see that people express themselves within their custom and the limits of righteousness so that the king and his people are deeply inter-linked as one organism.

RAMA called for his PUSHPAK VIMANA and went on an aerial survey. He saw a man hanging upside down from a tree, engaged in self-discipline. He asked him who he was.

The man said that he was a SHUDRA by birth, doing exercises in order to be king of this land.

RAMA said: You are born with tendencies to serve others. This nature is valuable in itself. Now you are hanging upside down to learn endurance. This can make you a saint, but not a king. Neither your nature by birth, nor your culture through the actions you are doing prepares you to become what you want to become. You are neither expressing your nature, nor working appropriately for your aspiration, which must emerge from your nature and actions. In a sense you have committed suicide by rejecting yourself. With that RAMA killed him.

When his own death came, RAMA at once got up without regrets. He left the world with a smile. He entered the form of VISHNU who sustains life and the universe. The kingdom passed on to his sons, LUV and KUSH. And life continued.

Thousands of years later, foreign barbarians destroyed SRI RAMA'S birthplace in AYODHYA. But he still nourishes the Hindu mind.

Chapter V

Prayers

A prayer expresses our desires. It invokes the unknown power to help us in a moment of our helplessness when we are constantly acting to satisfy them. It is an effort to move us from what we are to what we are struggling to be.

The divine reply to our invocation comes through coincidences and dreams. But our prayer has to be genuine, an expression of a real need and action to achieve our aspiration. Otherwise there is no sense in praying. And there is no way of cheating the divine.

UPANISHADS begin and end with prayers. What are aspirations expressed in these prayers? Every prayer ends with invoking AUM, and expressing the desire for peace three times. The tradition says that one has to aspire and work for peace in a comprehensive sense for the body that includes its mind, for the surroundings that include society and nature, and for the beyond, as the religious mind is rooted in the invisible divine power beyond the senses. This would include freedom from disease in the body and mind and their efficient working. It would include harmony with nature and society and reverence for the unseen powers. For realizing these aspirations, work on practical details of individual and social life is necessary. This work is our responsibility, our agenda of a lifetime. Therefore prayer implies responsible action on our part and supplementing it through unseen powers. While we act intensely to the best of our ability, unseen cosmic powers help and guide us in the depth of our being where we are rooted in them. That response and help is grace, an experienced fact.

Here are some prayers.

AUM! That One is whole. All this is whole. All this emerges from That One. And what remains is whole. In the silence of my mind, I pray that I may hear Aum, the vibration of creative reality. I work and pray for peace! Peace in my body and mind, Peace in my environment, physical and social, Peace with the Unseen Power that makes, keeps and breaks us!

AUM! I pray and aspire to root my speech in my mind and my mind in my speech, making the one reflect the other. I think of you, who are Self-Effulgent, illumined with your own light, reveal yourself to me. Enable me to acquire Veda, knowledge in my heart and mind, as speech and mind are tools of knowledge. Help me remember all that I learn, as I resolve to spend my day and night in learning and to speak only what is true as Truth is my Law. Protect my teacher and me! In the silence of my mind I pray that I may hear Aum, the vibration of creative reality as I work and pray for peace! Peace in my body and mind, Peace in my environment, physical and social, Peace with the Unseen Power that makes, keeps and breaks us!

AUM! I pray and work to nourish and strengthen my limbs, my organs of sense and action like eyes, ears, nose, touch and speech. UPANISHADS describe the ultimate reality as BRAHMA. May I never forget it! May it never forget me! May I never be forgotten! Full of BRAHMA, I aspire to realize DHARMA, the nature that supports me, the eternal law of nature and me, described in the UPANISHADS. In the silence of my mind, may I hear AUM, the vibration of creative reality, as I work and pray for peace! Peace in my body and mind, Peace in my environment, physical and social, Peace with the unseen power that makes, keeps and breaks us!

AUM! I pray to DEVAS who constitute us! May we so change that we hear only auspicious words and see only auspicious things! May we acquire the ability to see only what is auspicious, good and helpful, what brings about the well being of all! May we engage in sacrifice, doing actions that ought to be done, not doing actions that ought not to be done. With firm limbs, we praise DEVAS and meditate on these higher forces. We see and hear only the auspicious and enjoy life that is beneficial to them and us. We acquire the skills of living and advance spiritually, making our life a prayer.

May the lord of the senses and beyond, the lord of strength, the destroyer of evil, the family teacher, may they all be auspicious and propitious and well disposed towards us and ensure our well fare! May I hear AUM, the vibration of creative reality, in the silence of my mind as I work and pray for peace! Peace in my body and mind, Peace in my environment, physical and social, Peace with the unseen power that makes, keeps and breaks us!

AUM! May SURYA DEVA bless us with heat, light and life! May VARUNA DEVA bless us with law, water and life! May VAYU DEVA bless us with air and life! May INDRA DEVA bless us with pleasures here and beyond! May ARYAMA, the ancestor of us all, custom and tradition, teach us the skills of seeing! May GURU BRAHASPATI bless us with wisdom and skills of living! May VISHNU sustain our life through destruction of evil! May they all nourish and constitute us! I feel reverence for BRAHMA, the one reality that manifests itself in so many ways. May I learn to feel reverence for life, for truth, for the law, as they protect me as I work and pray for peace! Peace in my body and mind, Peace in my environment, physical and social, Peace with the unseen power that makes, keeps and breaks us!

AUM! You are the immortal, eternal self of the universe. You know all, as you control, pervade and protect all. Nothing else is powerful enough to govern you. You project as BRAHMA! You project yourself as conscious, living and creative order that is knowledge. I seek freedom from my lower nature, to be identified with my higher nature. I take refuge in you, the self-enlightened Supreme Self of all. May your light turn me to you, my self!

AUM! May the self-enlightened rise up in me! May the pure rise up in me! May the immortal, without birth or death rise up in me! May the almighty rise up in me! May I be aware of the Supreme Being present in me!

AUM! May there be peace among DEVAS in heaven and among the stars! May there be peace on earth, among men and animals! May we not hurt each other! May we be generous to each other! May intelligence guide our life and action! May there be peace in our prayers, on our lips and in our hearts!

AUM! I first pray to the great lord of intelligence and perfection, ever-auspicious basis of all other cycles of energy. He has knowledge of herbs that cures illness and removes obstacle. He is the order that creates. I think of the power that removes obstacles to my aspirations and creates order in my life. Do help me prosper and fulfill my deep desires with wisdom, the greatest wealth.

AUM! There is peace in heavens, peace in space, peace on earth, peace in waters, peace in herbs, peace in vegetation. Peace in powers that make the world, peace in its order, peace in all beings, peace alone. May this peace come to me!

Desires and aspirations require constant action with deep devotion.

These prayers express many aspirations for which we who pray have to work in order to make our prayers genuine. But howsoever hard we may work, an unknown power helps or hinders us. The results of our actions are not entirely in our hands.

We should work for oneness of all beings and in this way become whole, full and wise. There is a vast and expanding diversity of nature including human nature and society that we experience, but underlying this diversity is the same one power of which we need to be aware.

We should work for peace in the body and mind by nourishing them, removing illness, making them strong and efficient, acquiring knowledge of herbs and skills of living that includes seeing, hearing, speaking, being only the good and the auspicious, eliminating evil, doing actions for the welfare of all beings. We should work for peace in nature and society, working for their health and order, and peace with the beyond, expressing our deepest self, bringing it into awareness, and so be self-enlightened.

We should work to honor life, truth, the nature that sustains us, the law that regulates us, the growth of our awareness of the spirit and the immortal presence in all beings and live accordingly.

We should be integrated, rooting our speech in our mind and our mind in our deepest self beyond the senses and their mind. Doing our duty, meditating on higher forces, sacrificing our nature into actions and offering them and dedicating our life to higher powers, making it into a prayer, feeling silence at the mystery, the intelligence and perfection of the universe. We have to act to realize our aspirations and overcome obstructions till we reach the one that we cannot overcome and so feel helpless and our ego disappears. That makes a genuine prayer, which receives a response.

Isha Upanishad

Yajur Veda

ISHWAR lives in all that is born of motion. Leave all to him and enjoy yourself. Be not attached and greedy, because whose is the wealth?

The universe is born of motion. I am a part of the universe, not separate from it. I should focus my attention on what makes me a part of the universe, rooted in it, born of it. If I do this, it will bring about a change in my attitudes and ideas.

This idea has to transform my thinking, feelings, attitudes and actions. Then the spirit is liberated and one lives a relaxed, long and useful life.

Change is the law of the created. It is measured by day and night, birth and death, growth and decay, change of seasons, fruits and vegetables.

The divine power lives in motion at its center, in all beings and forms, who emerge from it for a while, a fraction of a second or a few billion years, and merge back into it to reform again with variations.

Since the divine power lives in all beings, it is the true owner of wealth, the resources of nature, including man. One cannot be possessive.

One is essentially related to everyone else. What I oppose are my relatives, related to me. Learning to experience these relationships is a form of spiritual growth. This will attach me to the universe and detach me from my narrow, limited particular self. This is renunciation, resulting from one's expansion, not self-denial or self-torture.

When we learn to see spiritually, we see universal forces acting through individual forms. We enlarge ourselves, detached from our limited body and mind. Such detachment is necessary for eliminating suffering, for clearing the body and mind for the joy of living, the sheer joy of being alive.

Doing such actions, we should aspire to live a hundred years. Actions done in this way do not bind and attach us to the world. Otherwise they do.

Such actions express the flow of our nature, what we are and what we are becoming, what we admire as our goal. They express the flowering of our life, a celebration of its plenty, as we offer them to the forces of nature of which they are an expression.

Such actions done in a spirit of detachment are holy. The divine power lives in them. We feel this power working through us and offer to it our very best effort and devotion.

Such actions express its presence in us. We act on its behalf as its agent for its benefit to all beings. We do not feel attached to the world that we occupy temporarily. We will have to quit it without a warning.

Such actions reduce our suffering from the loss of what we are attached to, and clear the ground for our enjoyment of life.

Such actions create a healthy state of body and mind. Living a long and meaningful life of a hundred years or more becomes as natural and mysterious as creation of life out of what appears to be matter, or of consciousness out of what appears to be life, or the creation of our individual, particular, limited, narrow, personal and often petty experience out of this vast, impersonal grandeur of the universe through our limited five senses.

Devils live in blinding darkness. They cannot see in ignorance. They who kill their true self go to them after death.

If we ignore our true self, we die in a sense, even if we are alive. We kill or reject our true self and the true self of others.

Then we enter the dark, unenlightened world of evil. We live blindly in ignorance of our nature. We become unreal.

Then we believe that we are sovereign, that we can do no wrong, and that we are the judges of things as they are and as they should be, that our strength and reason are right independently of the true self of the universe.

Then we believe that we are the owners of life and nature, that we can do whatever we like with it, destroy it for example through suicide bombs or war or pollution or corruption and so on.

We ignore our true self when we identify ourselves with only our body and mind and its effects and relationships.

We ignore it when we do not experience the divine power that becomes the universe, living in it, changing its forms.

We ignore our true self when we are not detached from others.

The divine power does not move but is faster than the mind. The senses do not catch it, as it runs ahead of them. It is motionless but out runs all in motion. It supports all actions of nature, as it is eternally there.

The divine power lives in the universe of motion.

It does not move, because there is nowhere for it to move to, since it is everywhere.

It is swifter than the mind. Wherever the mind can reach, it is there already, since it is everywhere.

It cannot be understood by the senses, because the senses are limited, specialized, and they create what they sense.

It is the creator of the universe. So it is ahead of its creatures, prior to them, outside the reach and capacity of their understanding.

It out-runs all in motion, because when this motion comes to an end, it is still there in the motionless. Motion emerges from it and merges back into it at its end.

It supports all in motion like the sun's energy in space or the passage of time.

The divine power moves and moves not. It is far away and very near. It is outside all and inside all.

Since it moves, it is the reality of the universe in motion. So it is inside all and very near. We feel reverence for nature as its body. We experience the wonder of its mystery. We try to live in harmony with it. It is our true self, our true guru, ever ready to guide us if we but qualify ourselves and listen to it. It is compassionate to us if we appeal to it in our helplessness.

Since it moves not, it is prior to the motion of the universe, not spatially outside it. All space is inside the universe that it projects. So it is outside all and far away, beyond our senses, mind and thought.

It appears to have contradictory states and qualities. Non-contradiction is a requirement of the human reason to enable it to understand. But it is not a requirement of existence or reality. Binary oppositions like pleasure and pain are examples of it.

He who sees all beings in That One, and That One in all beings, that man does not hate anyone because of this vision.

He gives up judging others as he sees that all are essentially alike Thus he respects all beings in nature.

He who has experienced That One sees it as his self and the self of all other beings. Then what delusion of attachment and what sorrow of separation can he experience?

The same reality is there in everyone but appears differently modified in different forms. An enlightened person sees through these modifications. Such a person will be detached and free of sorrow. He will unite conflicting people and their ideologies, divergent regions and their interests rather than create conflicts. He will be compassionate.

That One is present everywhere in space. It is pure, without material forms, without injury or sin. It is the seer of time and the timeless, all-knowing ruler of the mind. It exists by itself. It has duly allotted duties to all creatures to unfold.

It is pervasive, non-discrete, and formless in space. It is pure, unmixed with anything else, there being nothing else. It has no material body, and so it is invisible. It is perfect and cannot be hurt or wounded. It is sinless and cannot go astray. It is both inside and outside time, and so it can be experienced both ways. It controls the mind, as it knows everything, as it becomes everything. It exists by itself, uncreated by anything else. It allots function to every being and so they exist by virtue of that duty. They cease to exist when that duty ends. They unfold creatively as their duty takes the form of actions. All creatures have to do their duty, according to their nature through their life span.

A spiritual seeker must find out what his flow of nature is, what his tendencies to action and feeling are. Becoming aware of his nature more clearly will help him in purifying it, doing what the best in him is, and eliminating what he is not. This is what purity means. This process of self-discovery over time releases unknown hidden energies present in him, helping him in his true evolution, identifying himself with his true self.

They who perform only rituals enter blinding darkness. They who only meditate enter greater darkness.

They who perform rituals, like worshipping a natural force, or doing actions to get their results for enjoyment in this world or the next, remain blind or ignorant of the supreme divine power.

They who worship the senses and the knowledge derived from the senses live in spiritual darkness, as they cannot know what the senses cannot know.

They who know their true self from scriptures, reflecting on it without experiencing it, worshipping the formless without undergoing a change in their attitudes and actions, they enter greater ignorance because their knowledge is not based on experience.

Scriptures and reflection are initial guides, not the final truth.

Spiritual knowledge must come through actions resulting in experience, leading to truth and innocence.

Knowledge of That One as the self gives one result, and its ignorance gives another result. Those with experience say this.

Knowledge of the divine power as the self comes through experience that results partly from our effort and partly from divine compassion. This results in a manner of living that is different from the manner of living of the ignorant.

They who combine knowledge of divine power as their self with knowledge derived from the senses and reason pass through death doing right actions.

The experiential knowledge of That One needs to be combined with knowledge derived from the senses and reason. Knowledge of nature must be combined with knowledge of the source of nature.

They who worship what is born enter darkness. They who worship what is not born enter greater darkness.

They are ignorant who worship what is born like man or ancestors or tradition or nature. Such worship may yield short-term satisfactions but they lead to suffering. They do not lead to truth.

They are even more ignorant who worship mysteries, the source of laws of nature, as they live on knowledge without any personal experience that transforms their manner of living and being.

Worshipping only what is born gives one result. Worshipping only what is not born gives another result. Those with experience say this.

What we worship is what we think of as our true self, what we act on, what we are attached and devoted to, what we admire, what motivates us. We may falsely think that we worship That One when in fact we are worshipping our profession, or money, or status, or power, or food, or sex, or family and so on. Each kind of devotion produces its own kind of result, whatever we might profess or believe.

That which is born also dies, like man or nature, tradition, belief or religion. That which is not born does not die, like the Supreme Being, or the self of all beings.

He who knows That One as what is born and what is not born passes through death identified with the unborn.

We should combine our devotion to what changes, like nature and culture, tradition and belief, by increasing our understanding of it with the devotion to what does not change, the mystery of their source, the direction of their flow, and transform our living accordingly.

The face of truth is hidden in a disc of gold. O Truth! Show yourself to me, as I am truthful.

The truth is covered by our ignorance and greed, precious to us like gold.

O You who nourish the universe! I worship you by being truthful, speaking, thinking, and feeling according to my nature directed towards noble ideals. I live truthfully in harmony with the flow of my nature. Be compassionate to me and remove my ignorance and greed. Let me experience you and identify myself with you.

If I am not truthful, I do not worship truth, even if I say I worship truth.

If I am not integrated in my feeling, thought, and speech, expression, attitude, urges and action, I do not worship truth, though I may say that I worship truth.

In order to experience That One, I have to be myself. Otherwise who will have that experience? I have to be qualified to know That One.

O SAVITUR DEVA, who nourishes! You are alone, creating, controlling, alive in the universe! Remove my ignorance, these blinding rays of illusion. Let me see that form of yours which is kindly, which gives life and nourishes, since I too am that very being which is present in you, kindly and nourishing life, O SAVITUR, desirable and worthy of worship.

O you who nourish me with life and energy and nourish all beings in nature, arousing the seed in the ground to sprout and flower!

O you who control me deciding my birth and death and aging, and control all beings in nature and fruits in many ways!

O you who make and break and own all energies present in the universe, remove the brilliance that dazzles me, the illusion that confuses me, the attractions that tempt me, the greed that distorts me, the ignorance that separates me from you and your creation.

I realize that you are present in me too, just as I am in you. Otherwise how can I come to be and live? I realize and accept this.

When I die, let my body burn to ashes and return to earth, and let my life return to universal life. AUM! Remember me, my actions offered to you.

O Power in the fire and the sun, in all nature, you know my actions and thoughts done through your energy present in them. Now lead me to the goal of my actions, thoughts and dreams. Let me experience the aim of my actions offered to you, my supreme self. You are without limits and forms. You are without sins. Remove obstacles from my path. Free me from suffering. May I be joyful, at peace, aware! May I be identified with you!

I offer this prayer to you again and again.

Kena Upanishad

Talavakra Brahmana

Sama Veda

What directs the mind towards its object? What directs breath and life to do their duty? What wills the speech that people utter? What directs the eyes and ears and other organs to do their jobs? What is the unifying force that directs all organs and limbs to do their functions?

What directs all these is the mind of mind, the life of life, the speech of speech, the eye of eye and the ear of ear. The invisible inner director initiates, controls, regulates, withdraws and stops all these functions. Knowing it, becoming identified with this immortal, people rise above nature, and so renounce the senses and their objects.

That force is so powerful and attractive that those who find it are utterly absorbed in it. As a result they lose interest in everything else, which is renunciation.

The eye does not reach that force, nor speech, nor mind. We cannot know it through the mind and its senses, nor can we teach it to others. It is different from what is known through the senses and the mind. We have heard of it from the ancients.

It is not expressed in speech. It enables the speech to function. Know it to be BRAHMA.

Senses do not perceive it. It enables the senses to perceive. Know it to be BRAHMA.

It is not what people worship as an object. BRAHMA cannot be worshipped. To worship it, it has to be different from the worshipper.

It is not comprehended by the mind. It enables the mind to comprehend objects. Know it to be BRAHMA.

Breath does not give it life. It enables breath to give life. Know it to be BRAHMA.

If you think you know it well, you have known only a little expression of it. You know it in your body and mind and in the forces of nature. Therefore think more of it.

If you think you do not know it well enough, nor can you say you do not know it at all, then you know and do not know. It is both known and unknown.

He who thinks he does not know it knows it, as he lives and works by it. He who thinks he knows it well does not know it. He knows only objects that can be known, not the subject that knows.

Since we are what it is, we know it unconsciously, as in deep sleep to some extent. Our conscious knowledge of it expressed in words is likely to be full of errors.

It is really known when it is known in each state of consciousness, when one is awake, asleep or dreaming. Then one is identified with the one that is common in these states. So one knows the immortal.

Through one's true self, one acquires strength. Through its experience, one gains immortality. Our body and mind gets its strength to work through ATMA. Once ATMA leaves, the body dies. Our awareness of ATMA enables us to identify with the immortal.

If one experiences it while one is alive, then one lives authentically in truth. If not, then one misses the point of living and life becomes meaningless.

The wise see the true self in all beings and turn away from the sensuous world.

Once upon a time DEVAS that constitute the universe fought their opponents who cause decay. BRAHMA achieved victory for them, but they thought they had won the victory themselves. They became elated and said: Ours is this life and the glory.

BRAHMA knew their pretension and appeared to them as a YAKSHA, a spirit of nature. They did not recognize it and said to AGNI DEVA: O knower of all creation, find out about this YAKSHA.

AGNI DEVA went to it. "I am AGNI, the knower of all change. Who are you?"

YAKSHA said, "What power is there in you?"

AGNI DEVA said, "I can burn everything."

YAKSHA placed a straw before AGNI and said, "Burn this."

AGNI DEVA approached the straw with all his fire, but could not burn it. He went back and reported, "I could not find out."

DEVAS asked VAYU DEVA to find out. He went to YAKSHA and said, "I am VAYU, the mover in space. Who are you?"

"What power is there in you?"

"I can blow away all this."

"Blow away this straw."

VAYU DEVA approached it with all his power, but could not blow away the straw. He returned and said, "I could not find out."

DEVAS said to INDRA DEVA, " O lord of heavenly powers and pleasures, lord of waters that give life, lord of the senses and the mind! Please find out what this venerable YAKSHA is"

INDRA DEVA approached YAKSHA who disappeared, as he could not be seen through the senses. INDRA felt helpless, as he did not know the source of his own strength, the strength of waters and pleasures, the senses and the mind.

In that very split second of helplessness and despair, INDRA DEVA saw the beautiful daughter of Himalayas. He asked her, "What is this YAKSHA?"

She said, "It was BRAHMA, the source of all your powers. He won the war between you and your opponents, but you were glorified." From that beautiful lady, INDRA learnt the truth.

DEVAS excelled others because they were near their source of strength, and INDRA was the nearest.

We learn about the ultimate being in a flash of lightning like a wink of the eye, a shift in knowing, a change in perspective, while meditating on the divine. The student is taught this with the help of stories and analogy.

BRAHMA is what the mind repeatedly moves towards and dwells on, trying to think and understand the truth within the mind's limitations. BRAHMA is adorable to all creatures as their own self, their ultimate being. Anyone who meditates on it in this way is loved and honored.

"Sir, speak to me of the secret knowledge."

"Son, I have spoken to you, but you have not understood it."

This knowledge is based on self-discipline, turning away from the senses and meditating on truth. It is known through the VEDAS. One who knows it is free of falsehood, and established in the limitless, the blissful and the highest.

Katha Upanishad

Yajur Veda

Once upon a time, the son of VAJASHRAVA did a YAJNA in which he gave away his wealth in charity. His son NACHIKETA saw that his father was giving away cows that were nearly dead. Giving worthless gifts means discarding what you do not need. It means going to hell, to a low level of living, which cannot bring happiness. Only worthwhile gifts are to be given to the deserving people at the right time and place in charity. So he asked: Father, to whom will you gift me, your dearest son? The father did not reply. But when the son persisted in knowing, the father said in anger: Go to death.

NACHIKETA thought: I must have made a mistake. So my father is angry. Otherwise what can be his objective? He said aloud:

Father, think of how our ancestors and wise people behaved. Then do the right thing. Do not regret now but honor your word. Allow me to go to YAMA, the lord of death.

NACHIKETA entered the house of death, but YAMA was not there to receive him. So he waited three days without food or water.

YAMA came and said: You have been a guest in my house for three days without food. A guest is like a DEVA. A learned guest like you should be honored like fire is honored. It changes what it touches. Therefore I shall satisfy your three wishes, one for each fast. Choose three boons and bless me.

NACHIKETA said: May my father be happy and peaceful, free of anger and sorrow, accepting me as his son, when I return. YAMA said: So be it.

NACHIKETA said: O Lord of death! In heaven there is no death or suffering, no fear of old age or sickness or hunger or thirst. In heaven is bliss. Tell me of the inner fire that changes what it touches by lighting which one may attain that heaven and become immortal.

YAMA honored him by calling it NACHIKETA AGNI, the fire hidden in the heart and mind, an intensity of effort. Just as the fire burns up the environment to produce a change, so the air goes in and out through breathing to burn the fire in the heart and mind to produce a change. He explained meditation techniques needed to lighten the fire in three stages, and create inner heat and fervor that enables one to be enlightened.

First burn out the outer environment, seeing it as an expression of your inner environment. You create the color that you see, the sound that you hear, the touch that you feel, the taste and fragrance that you enjoy. You create your sensations. You do not know your outer self. You create it. Experience this.

Then burn out your inner environment. Your inner self is not particularly yours. You search for food and sex, security, power and status, your feelings of pleasure and pain, desire, greed and anger are not particularly yours. All beings, including animals and plants have it. What you know as your inner self is present in all. Seeing it clearly, burn out your inner ego, your subjective self and feel the emptiness.

Once the objective and subjective selves have been burnt out, you experience a wonderful creativity, this vast impersonality that exists by itself playfully, and you too play your part in it, and live an active, relaxed and long life.

NACHIKETA said: Some say that man lives after death as ATMA. Some say he does not. What is the truth?

YAMA tried to dissuade NACHIKETA by offering him heavenly pleasures, and a long life of health, wealth and power. NACHIKETA refused all these and so qualified himself to receive knowledge of the ultimate reality, truth and goodness.

YAMA said: The ignorant do not see their own death. They do not see nature working in them. They think of this visible world as the only world. So they are tempted by pleasure, money and power. They lose their truc aim in life.

There is the path of goodness, duty and reason. Blessed are they who prefer it to the path of pleasure, wealth and power. It leads to wisdom.

ATMA is beyond reason and logic, beyond the good and the evil, beyond the pleasant and the unpleasant. It is to be taught only by those who have experience of it. They think, feel and act as ATMA.

Since actions begin and end, their effects also begin and end. Therefore actions cannot lead to the eternal. Rituals and ceremonies are futile. The eternal is found when we go beyond the good and the pleasant and remain detached. Then we do not judge, or choose an action. Then we act out our nature, as we must spontaneously.

The creative energy of the divine power is morally neutral. It lives in the hearts and minds of all beings, both good and bad. It lives in the dark jungle of this world. Going beyond joy and sorrow, the good and the bad, one can experience it.

NACHIKETA said: what is the divine that is experienced? Is it different from goodness and evil? Is it outside the sequence of cause and effect? Is it separate from the past, present and future, separate from all that is related to it?

YAMA said: Yogis hear that ultimate existence, the vibration of motion that creates the universe, as AUM. It is not the sound that is produced when two objects strike each other. VEDAS speak of it as the truth that is always right, that regulates the universe and society. Spiritual practices enable one to hear it in deep silence, in a path that is single-minded, in which all else including food, sex, and security gets ignored and so renounced.

AUM is the sound of the initial emerging reality, eternally resonant, heard in deep silence. Experience it, and then what comes to your mind comes true. That is the support of the universe, the ultimate refuge.

ATMA is never born. It never dies. It is neither a cause, nor an effect. It is ageless, unborn, permanent and eternal. Nothing can be added to it or taken away from it. It is whole and full.

When the body and mind die, it does not die. It cannot kill or be killed. It lives in the heart, subtle and great. It is experienced by the desire-less and the peaceful through the grace of the sustainer of all.

The divine is spread far and wide. It stays at one place, as there is no other space where it is not. It is without sound or touch or form or taste or smell or beginning or end or change or decay or manifestation. It is body-less and omnipresent. By knowing it the intelligent become free of sorrow and grief.

The divine is not known through intellect, or through repeated listening to scriptures or discourses, or through speaking to others. He whom the divine has chosen knows the divine. To him the divine reveals its nature.

If you are not serene, not free of deeply felt urges, if your mind and senses are not disciplined, you cannot know the divine, even if your intellect is sharp.

It consumes all beings when the universe dissolves and goes back into its creator. Even death that destroys all is destroyed.

They who transform the powers of their senses and action through intense meditations connect them to the immortal will. They come to know of it. They pass through such fires and sacrifices from illusion and suffering into knowledge and bliss.

If you discipline your mind and control your senses through full awareness, you reach the ultimate state. Otherwise, if you follow pleasures, you see many forms but not the ultimate reality.

ATMA is more powerful than intellect, which is more powerful than the mind, which is more powerful than the sense objects, which are more powerful than the senses. It is the self of the individual hidden in his heart. One regulates life at all these levels accordingly.

The cosmic being is the self of the universe, the ultimate abode of all. It is more powerful than the invisible creative energy or knowledge-in-action, which is more powerful than ATMA. The divine hidden within all beings as their self is invisible. Subtle eyes through its grace see it.

First withdraw the senses into the mind, then the mind into the wakeful intellect, and then the intellect into ATMA, withdrawing that into supreme self, the abode of silence. Be with the wise people who have realized it. Be free of identity with death in order to be with immortality. Share it with others at the time of death, if you are one with infinity.

The wise knows the all-pervading supreme self inside him. He experiences it in wakefulness, dream, and deep sleep. He knows the divine to be near, the provider of fruits of actions and life to all, and the ruler of all time. By its grace he senses and organs work. It was never born. It existed before nature. From it came all DEVAS, and into it they return. What is outside is inside. In reality there is no boundary, no limitation of form. It is pure, the one without a second. Knowing in this way, the wise never condemn anyone, nor do they grieve for anyone.

The body is a city of nine gates. In it lives the divine. It is pure simple consciousness, above grief and death. It is the being of the sky. It is the guest in every house, the indweller in all beings. It is the sacred fire, receiving offerings in YAJNAS. It lives in water, in all forms of life, manifested in goodness, honored by DEVAS.

Depending on actions and inclinations developed from what is heard and done, ATMA enters wombs, animal, vegetation, or mineral.

The one that projects all situations that men experience and remains awake in them while others sleep or when creation ends, that one is the eternal BRAHMA.

One fire takes many forms. So one BRAHMA reflects differently in different beings, according to their forms, functions and inclinations.

The divine within also dwells without. Though within all, it is separate from all. It is the knower of all thoughts and feelings in each moment. It is the same in all. Its light illumines all suns and moons and stars, the lightning and fires. Without it is darkness.

This universe that we see is like the PEEPAL tree. It has roots above and branches below. The deepest root is the deathless BRAHMA. It nourishes and sustains all the worlds that emerge from it. They who are identified with it are free of birth and death and transformations.

The senses, the air, water and fire, the sun, life and death do their work in fear of it. It is seen in the inner organs of action when the deep complexes in the heart are eliminated.

Mind is higher than the senses. Intellect is higher than the mind. The self is higher than the intellect. The divine power that underlies the visible universe is higher than the self. The Supreme Self is higher than the self of this divine power. It is deathless, blissful, beyond the grasp of the physical senses.

A pure heart is without desires, without past impressions and inherited tendencies to action. It can experience the Supreme Self when it meditates. Then the senses and the mind stop and the intellect makes no effort. That is the state of YOGA. Then one sees the human body and mind made of energy, not of flesh and blood. Learn YOGA to move your energy to your heart and mind, where the divine lives.

Death taught NACHIKETA the process of YOGA, freeing him of mental constructions, impurities and attachments.

There are numerous channels of energy from the heart. One goes upwards, the others go downwards. If you move upwards you become immortal, otherwise you go downwards to the cycle of birth and death.

Raise yourself to higher levels of being and living through spiritual effort.

Aitreya Upanishad

Rig Veda

In the beginning, all this that we see and experience was ATMA alone. It was conscious, alive. There was nothing else. It thought intensely and became heat and fire. It projected diverse beings, like the earth and waters below, the sky and heavens above and the beyond.

It reflected, " These are the worlds. Now I will create their protectors to stop their decay and so help them."

It picked up a cosmic being from the waters and gave it shape through the intense heat of meditation. A mouth opened from which came speech and fire. Then opened nostrils, from which came smell and air. Then opened two eyes from which came sight and light. Then opened two ears from which came hearing and directions. Then formed skin, on which grew hair, herbs and trees. Then a heart formed, from which came the mind and the moon. Then a navel formed, from which came excretion and death. Then procreative organ formed, from which came seed and water. All these were DEVAS that came into the world for a time. These powers create the world that we see and experience. They are outside man and inside him too.

ATMA made them hungry and thirsty. They said, "Find us a place where we may live and eat."

ATMA gave them the cow of plenty, which gave milk and satisfied their basic needs. But they were not satisfied. ATMA gave them a horse to travel on. It was time and nature on which we travel. But they were not satisfied. ATMA gave them man. "What a masterpiece!" they said and entered man. There live DEVAS.

Fire became speech and entered the mouth. Air became smell and entered the nostrils. Light became sight and entered the eyes. Directions became hearing and entered the ears. Herbs and trees became hair and entered the skin. Moon became the changing mind and entered the heart. Mind and heart became one center of man. Death became the breath that goes out never to come back again and entered the navel. Life had come from there. Water became semen and entered the generative organ.

Then hunger and thirst said, "Find us a place too." ATMA said, "Share the place with all DEVAS." When we make an offering to any DEVA, hunger and thirst have a share in it through our desires that demand satisfaction.

ATMA thought, "These are the senses and their powers and deities. I shall make food for them." It meditated on the waters and many forms emerged. These forms were their food. Senses live on forms.

The food tried to run away. No one likes to be eaten, but every one wants to eat.

ATMA could not catch the food with speech, or smell, or seeing, or hearing, or touching, or mind, or through sex. Otherwise these actions would have been enough to satisfy hunger and thirst. ATMA caught food through the breath that goes out never to come back again. Death alone satisfies hunger and thirst.

Death supports life. Death is not the enemy of life. If there is no death, there is no life. The seed dies and the tree is born. Death is necessary for life. We die every moment and are born every moment. This is our glory. See and feel the wonder of it.

ATMA thought, "How shall I enter? Where shall I live so that they all are of one mind, united and single?" It entered through the cleft of the skull, where it settled on the top of man. It lives in wakefulness, dream and sleep, in the eye, the mind, and the heart.

Thus born, ATMA looked around upon other beings, and wondered if it knew anyone. It saw the cosmic being that relates all diverse beings into one being, alive and pervading the universe as the one who creates it. It said in wonder, "I have seen it all." It became self-conscious. It saw itself outside itself.

That cosmic being was called IDANDRA, meaning, "I see it, experience it." What we see and experience is our self, inside us. The self inside us sees itself outside us. ATMA sees itself. Later on it came to be called INDRA, which means the one just beyond what I see, just beyond the grasp of my senses. DEVAS are known indirectly through our effort and their grace. Our effort alone is not enough. They are just beyond what we see and experience.

ATMA becomes the individual self in man. Man offers all his strength from all his limbs from all the foods he eats into a woman. ATMA takes its first birth in her. Man nourishes woman as she nourishes ATMA. She is DEVI, divine. He nourishes her and the children for continuation of the world. This nurture is the second birth of ATMA. After a man completes his work, he dies. His children continue his virtuous deeds, as they are devoted to their ancestors and their good deeds. This makes value, custom and tradition. This tradition is the third birth of ATMA. There is a birth by nature, a birth by nurture, and a birth by tradition in the high values and customs of the family and society.

What do we meditate on as our self? Which of the two is ATMA, that which senses or that which is sensed? Is ATMA that by which one sees, hears, smells, articulates, or discriminates between sweet and sour? Or is ATMA that which one sees, hears, smells, articulates, or tastes as sweet or sour?

Consciousness has many names. Some of its names are the heart, the mind, the vision, sentience, perception, power, control, direction, understanding, knowledge, memory, firmness, reflection, thinking, resolve, suffering, vitality, desire, love, and the like.

Consciousness constitutes the world. This consciousness in different forms is BRAHMA. It pervades the universe. It is INDRA, that which is seen and that which is just beyond that which is seen, the invisible source that projects it. It is PRAJAPATI, who creates diverse forms of the universe. It is all DEVAS, the forces and what they become, the powers that constitute the universe. The five great elements of nature, earth, water, air, fire, and space are this consciousness, each with its own form of consciousness, its own knowledge that we struggle to find out. This consciousness is all creatures, howsoever born, in their own form. Some of these are horses and cattle, plants and trees, those that walk and those that fly, those that move and those that do not move. They are all composed and impelled by consciousness. They are rooted in consciousness. This whole universe is alive, born of motion, guided by consciousness and supported by it. Consciousness is BRAHMA. Consciousness is this entire universe.

He who experiences this consciousness that is all, the seer and the seen, rises high on dissolution of the body. He becomes immortal.

Meditate on consciousness, the formless source. Meditate on consciousness and all the forms it takes.

Adhyatma Upanishad

In the center of the heart, there lives the unborn, eternal inner controller. It dwells in the universe, in the earth and water, in the air and space and fire. It dwells in man, in light and mind, intelligence, feelings and reason, ego and death. It dwells in nature, which is visible to the senses. It dwells in the source of nature, invisible to the senses. It is indestructible. It is the innermost self of all beings, all names and forms, all phenomena, their actions and functions. It has no limitations or restrictions. It is free, the One known by many names. It is the One that sustains the universe. It is the one that lives when everything else is dissolved and becomes formless. Your inner controller sustains you.

The body with its senses and organs is matter. The body is a form of this being. There are many other forms of this being. The feeling of I or my or mine over matter is an illusion. You are not matter and you do not own matter. Matter is an illusion with its own laws.

You can see anything and everything as of this world. Then it is matter. You can see anything and everything as expression of the divine power. Then it is not matter, but divine. Then matter is a creation of your mind and its senses. It is an illusion like the sights and sounds and tastes and pleasures that you create with your senses. There is nothing sweet or sour. Your tongue makes them so. This change in your seeing is your spiritual growth.

An intelligent person should drop this illusion. He should be devoted to the inner controlling reality. He should experience himself as the witness of his mind and its dispositions, its urges, tendencies, intentions, motives, and behaviors. He should mentally give up the feeling of possessing matter. He should change his feeling "I am this or that", "I do this or that" into "I see this happening". He should root himself in his own center through practicing YOGA. He should learn to experience his self as the self of all, the same reality present everywhere. He should not identify himself with his own body and its mind exclusively and so be controlled by their actions. He should not identify himself exclusively with his relationships and society, created by their narrow, selfish and greedy minds. Then he can give up following scriptures, composed by others. Then he can compose his own scripture.

The body is made of excretions of father and mother. It is made of flesh and blood and smells. Rise above this body and be fulfilled as the self of the universe. See your divinity, the individual self as one with the supreme self of the universe.

The space inside the pot is one with the space outside the pot. A person without ego, without feelings of being different, is able to attain to his vast self. So be without ego to be self-enlightened and blissful. See the force that works through you and has taken your form.

When one is not the doer, one cannot have desires or anxieties. Without desires, expectations, anxieties and judgments, you are free while alive. Such a free person does not neglect his duty to the self of the universe. He stops choosing and starts accepting life as it comes.

ATMA is free of divisions between the seer, the seen, and the seeing. Be rooted in it, the self that is present everywhere. This self is formless, without parts, as only a form has parts. It is pure in the sense of being unmixed with anything other than the self. There is nothing else for it to mix with. The world as different and independent of the self is untrue. See the varied world as expression of one and the same self.

This world is full of divisions, which are products of forms. There is in reality no mind, no divisions, as in deep, dreamless sleep. Therefore focus your mind on the undivided universal consciousness. This is what you are inside. Inside and outside are creations of your form. See objects as well as the spaces between them.

You lead a detached life, when you only witness sense-objects. Then you feel relaxed and transcend the ignorance that normally surrounds the self.

Understand the principle that your essence is the same as the essence of the universe. You are an expression of the universe, not different, not opposed to it. Experience this oneness of the individual embodied self and the absolute, universal self. Contemplate on its meaning in small details of your practical life. Firmly establish this meaning in your heart by living accordingly. Then drop the one that meditates and the meditation and what it meditates on. So be enlightened, living spontaneously as the self.

What is experienced is not separate from the one that experiences. That which experiences is the same as that which is experienced. You are what you see.

Infinite actions and their effects are gathered in this world without beginning. They emerge, stay and disappear. When you witness this, awareness of the nature of the pure, unmixed self grows in you. Desires dissolve. Virtue and sin are uprooted at their source. Then you have the direct experience of being the same as others.

When no desires arise, one experiences non-attachment. When non-attachment is constant, one is relaxed. When no ego or the feeling "I am the doer" arises, one experiences the ultimate. Then one sees actions happening. The self is absorbed in the supreme self. The individual self is identified with the universal self.

One does the duty that emerges from one's higher nature. Then one is spontaneously good, without ever being wicked, even in a dream. One is without I-ness for the body and its senses, without my-ness for objects. Then one becomes free while alive. Then the self of the individual is the self of the universe. One remains the same in all conditions. Then one knows the BRAHMA state of being. Then the effects of present actions cease to accumulate. The effects of past actions continue to produce results. Such a one is like the sky, present but unattached and indifferent. He is one with the self, deathless and ever young.

Past actions bring present results when we feel we are one with our body and mind. When this feeling ceases, the effects cease. This feeling is an illusion and its results are unreal. This illusion is destroyed by enlightenment. But the ignorant need a reassurance that the body and mind are true and real. Otherwise they feel lost, without a ground to stand on. They would like to fall only in death.

Actually there is nothing other than the divine self. It takes on all the forms that you see. It lives in them. It is truth, as it alone exists. It is consciousness, subtle self-awareness. It is bliss, as there is nothing else. It is immeasurable, indefinable, unchanging, omnipresent, and eternal. It is uniform, indivisible, indestructible, perfect whole, without beginning or end. It is infinite in all directions, without support. It is without action, attributes or choice. It is independent, spotless, affluent, self-evident, and pure. It is beyond mind and speech, never lost or found. It is unlike anything we know, though we experience it. Experience this and be fulfilled.

Meditate on your self, as you are, as your circumstances, relationships, customs, society, tradition, and history have made you, and as you desire to be under compulsions of your circumstances and as you can be without these compulsions.

Then, meditate on yourself as free of all this bondage, all these compulsions.

Chapter VI

The Ultimate Reality

BRAHMA is the source of what we experience, the creative order that underlies it, one without a second, without a form, that which assumes all forms, present everywhere, without qualities or attributes, imperishable, unborn, eternal, infinite, knowledge and wisdom, the one present in sleep, dream, and wakefulness, beyond thought.

We need to do its UPASANA, or be near it in the mind, internalize it.

First we should qualify ourselves to experience BRAHMA by living a life that flows from our nature, accepting the truth of our divine inheritance that comes with nature, our body and its mind, engaging in social activity, expressing high moral values in pursuit of noble ideals, following the best norms of our tradition according to our occupation, status and age, and be a good charioteer of our ten senses.

Our nature is our inborn tendencies to actions, urges and dreams, impressions of past experiences, the flow of our life. It is an expression of many higher forces that reflect one divine power. Its expression changes according to our age, whether we are a child, married, retired or old and wise, and according to our status and seniority in different occupations and ways of earning livelihood, a ruler or a servant, with or without learning, with or without power, with or without morality, and their mixtures.

We should learn to discriminate between what is lasting and eternal and what is transient and short lived, the source of nature and what issues from that source. We should see patterns repeating in our life.

We should focus our attention on our actions, their source and cause in our nature, the aims and ideals that we choose, their effects and consequences on ourselves and others, their moral values, significance and guiding principles, the higher forces working in them. In this way, we qualify ourselves to experience the truth.

We should get guidance from an experienced GURU, if we need help.

Everyone cannot experience truth. Everyone cannot understand the source of all this that we experience. Every nature has limitations of its form. Some of these limitations concern the ability to learn and to experience.

The universe has a source. The source supports it. We call it BRAHMA. You can call it by a different name. Our source is our support, like our parents, if we think we are our body and its mind. The cause is the support of its effect.

But do we think we are our body? Are we our body even if life goes away from it?

BRAHMA is the conscious self of the universe. It is what projects, sustains and dissolves the universe. It is what brings the universe together and takes it apart. It takes the form of the universe and ceases to be, while remaining outside it all the time.

It is the essence, the seed of all knowledge, of all possibility. It is knowledge acting out to expand and contract the universe as it grows and decays. It knows all, as it becomes all. It is present everywhere, as it has become everywhere. Nothing can exist in which it is not present. It is the source of all that exists or can exist.

It is the source of all scriptures. Scriptures are a valid means of knowing it. Any means of knowing it is a scripture. Its knowledge is the aim of all scriptures. It is the subject of what they say. It is the final authority that validates scriptures. Its experience is the test of all scriptures. They rise or fall and decay as they further, retard or eliminate its experience.

The truth of scriptures is not asserted through violence or conversion. A scripture is universal because its truth is universal. A scripture is not universal because all human beings on the earth are its followers. Universal truth may have only one follower and falsehood may have all human beings as its followers. Universality of a scripture is not acquired through forcing it on others, killing or destroying them, or converting them.

UPANISHADS attempt to teach us what BRAHMA is and how to experience it. Its knowledge without experiencing it is not reliable knowledge. Its experience is higher than knowledge in any scripture or any verbal formulation. This experience is the source and support of all scriptures.

Unconscious nature cannot be the source of the universe. We are conscious, as we can see, experience, think, feel, and so on. Conscious beings cannot come out of unconscious nature. Something cannot come out of nothing. Life and consciousness cannot come out of non-life and non-consciousness.

If we say that seeing, being conscious and experiencing, is not important, even then unconscious nature cannot give birth to conscious beings. Unconscious nature cannot be the self of the individual because freedom from unconscious nature is the aim of the individual, devoted to his living and conscious self. This devotion to his living and conscious self is expressed through his actions. These actions can lead to experiencing the identity of the living and conscious individual self with the living and conscious self of the universe. They do so by removing ignorance of the sameness of the two.

Consciousness is the source of the universe. UPANISHADS use the word BRAHMA for the source of the universe and the word ATMA for the source of the individual, and they say that the two are essentially the same.

The source of existence is important for existence because the source projects and supports it. The self is that which sees, experiences, thinks, feels, knows, imagines, and so on. Therefore seeing, being conscious and experiencing, is important.

The self cannot be denied because in order to deny it the denying self has to exist.

The scripture teaches the identity of the individual self with the self of the universe. The supreme self is blissful, the joy that does not end. It is the nature of joy. Bliss is possible only for the conscious self. An unconscious self cannot have joy.

The individual being merges into and rests in his self, as in sleep consciousness. One cannot say that there is no consciousness in deep sleep. One remembers having slept deeply. The self is ever awake. Only the body sleeps.

We may say that consciousness cannot be the source of the universe because it has many modifications. But BRAHMA is full, having many expressions and forms. Denying consciousness to it would make it less than full.

Something other than the self of the universe cannot be the self of the universe, as it is self-contradictory.

The self of the universe is seen to be different from the self of the individual. The individual has limitations, which the universe does not have. The mind is dedicated to the self of the universe, as it tries to find out the nature of reality through reflection and meditation.

The divine is present everywhere. So any object in the universe can be made the gate of entry into the self of the universe, provided it overwhelms us with powerful feelings of wonder. Wherever we are overwhelmed with feelings of wonder, there is an expression of the universal force for us. Experience of wonder elicits absorbing concentration. It abolishes us, our individual self, for a time with overwhelming devotion. Then everything is unlimited, wonderful and holy.

Any power is an expression of it. That is why there are numerous DEVAS. They change with time. They are born to stay alive for some time and then they change and die.

These days some fashionable DEVAS are the national flag and the company logo. Every government creates a manual of rituals that lays down rules and regulations concerning the national flag and an important company does the same for the company logo. Governments even lay down hellish punishments, which must be inflicted on those who dishonor the national flag. Companies may dismiss employees who do not follow the company logo. But quite often, outward rituals are done for personal benefit, and inner feelings of which they are an expression disappear. One can salute the national flag and yet be corrupt, inefficient and indifferent, and take bribes, and have no respect for the nation. Then one is really not saluting the national spirit, even though one keeps saluting the national flag. We may be doing rituals without the inner state of mind of which they are an expression.

Human mind requires a form on which to concentrate for devotion and worship. That is why idols are created and worshipped and people go to temples to cultivate and nourish appropriate feelings and attitudes towards those ideals. As one grows spiritually both the form for practicing meditation and the need to concentrate on it are given up. Instead, one remains spontaneously concentrated on the ideal. But most people do not grow up spiritually, though some of them die for religion.

The self of the universe is the subject that knows the universe as its object. It is the witness of the universe. It is present in the heart, the center of everything. It is inside, being everywhere. It is outside, since inside and outside are created by the limit of form. It has no form but it can assume any form. In reality there is no inside or outside. In reality there is continuity. If there is a gap in apparent continuity, that gap has a self too. In reality there is bliss and no opponent. It is the internal ruler that controls the manifested body of the individual and the universe. It cannot be unconscious nature, which is a form with limits.

One should meditate on the self of the universe. What is its nature? For meditating, it is necessary to think of its qualities and so give it a form. Without meditation one cannot be mentally close to it. But when these qualities are negated, meditation ceases.

One should try to visualize it, feel it and experience it. One can make symbols, figures and geometric designs of it. But symbols, figures, geometric designs are not the spirit. These are available only for focusing the mind and effort.

When we see from a point of view, we create a form. But BRAHMA is formless as there is no point of view, as there is every point of view. We superimpose DEVAS on it by our limited but creative seeing and experiencing. DEVAS are powers that have bodies or limited forms. These are associated with rituals and rites for worship, UPASANA or PUJA. One tries to be mentally close to them or see them out there.

The self of the universe enters the heart and mind as the self of the individual. It supports the individual. The universe rests in its self and emerges from it, supported by it as its source. Those who are free of the universe experience this self. This freedom is the aim of their life.

BRAHMA is the state of being where one does not experience anything other than it. Whatever one sees, knows or experiences is an expression, a form of the supreme reality. The world does not disappear.

It is seen as a form of the divine power; what it wills happens.

It is goodness; whatever it wills is good, auspicious.

It is glorious; whatever it wills is wonderful.

It is rich; whatever it wills enriches all.

It is knowledge; whatever it wills is knowledge in action, enacted as things and forces.

It is detached; it is not involved in what it wills.

It is superior to life; it is not the limited self of the individual.

It is beyond life and death.

We can meditate on BRAHMA in many ways. We can see BRAHMA as light. The UPANISHAD says that its light shines in the sun, in the moon and the stars, in lightning and in the household fire. It is the light of lights, the nature of light.

We can see BRAHMA as truth, the source of the gross world that we experience. It encloses itself within the intellectual, the mental, the vital and the material coverings of truth. These are the layers its of being. It is the internal controller of all layers of reality.

The universe of nature and society emerges from actions done to experience the spirit. The universe emerges from words and thoughts as they reveal objects and events. Names and forms are seen as limited beings of existence. They repeat in cycles of time.

Not all men are competent for all things, for acquiring all kinds of knowledge. BRAHMANS are those who are devoted to experiencing BRAHMA. They cannot be destructive, because destruction implies rejection of some aspects of reality, which are seen as wicked, or evil, or enemy. And if they are destructive they cannot be BRAHMANS. They cannot perform martial rituals and ceremonies like KSHATRYAS, who must fight and kill when necessary to protect what they hold dear, the land and its people, to extract tax and tribute for this purpose, to celebrate through ceremonies and ritual actions their victory over their enemies and opponents. VAISHYAS are those who work for profit, creating wealth, producing and trading what is needed. SHUDRAS are those people who serve society to keep their bodies alive. They do not engage in efforts that separate their true self from their non-self, or perform actions that seek to purify their minds of what is not their self.

Senses change what they see. Seeing becomes impure. Emotions change what they see. Seeing becomes impure. Self-interest changes what it sees. Seeing becomes impure. We have to overcome these impurities.

A BRAHMAN seeks the truth in all conditions. If we do not search for truth in all conditions, we cannot study the VEDAS. Even if we study the VEDAS, we cannot understand and experience their meaning. We cannot know the truth, when we do not think and speak the truth.

BRAHMA is life force because of its vibration and motion. It is light because it is self-effulgent in the intellect. It is space as different from names and forms of existence in space. It is truth, the same whatever the outward changing appearance. The supreme self is the resting place of the universe, heavens and earth. It is experienced through freedom from the non-self. It does not split any further. It supports all things right up to space. It is space that holds the worlds in place.

That which is not manifested is the subtle causal state. Non-manifestation does not mean non-existence. The universe is the manifestation of BRAHMA. Life and the individual self are its markers. When they dissolve, they enter BRAHMA. Unconscious nature is not independent of BRAHMA. It is his power, his MAYA. His power is not different from him.

Once RISHIS got together to discuss the cause of the universe. From what is all this born, in what are they alive and supported? What provides them joys and sorrows, and what orders their lives? Some thought it was time, or inherited nature and its actions, or destiny, or the gross elements, or all of them collectively. But then all these are dependent on consciousness, not independent. Nor is the individual self the cause because it undergoes suffering and is dependent. Consciousness alone is prior to time, outside it, and independent of all. It produces all and enters what it creates. It is the mother and source of the universe.

BRAHMA is infinite truth and knowledge. This knowledge acts itself out in different forms, forces and elements of nature. It is the material cause, the source of substance that constitutes the universe. It has the will to create, as it creates and dissolves the universe. As action, it changes forms, changing one form into another form. It is the indwelling, controlling self of all beings. It is the witness of their forms.

There cannot be many selves, the same being the self of each one. All heads, hands, legs, eyes, noses are his. All nature is his. There is no nature independent of him. A person is freed of his desires when he focuses his awareness on their source, how they emerge. If we have suffering, we should focus our attention on the source of our suffering and be aware of nothing else. Our suffering will cease. Experience of the unity of selves brings this freedom from suffering.

Yoga means constant meditation. It means reflection on the declaration: I am the self of the universe. It means seeing the sameness everywhere. I am the self of my being. I am the source of all that I experience. I am in truth the same as the self of the universe, as the self of all individuals.

BRAHMA is one, but the universe is experienced as many, as diverse. The experience of the universe has qualities like sound, taste, smell, touch and so on. These diversities are created by our diverse senses, within their own limitations and forms. They are our creations. They do not exist in what they sense. Different senses create different worlds. BRAHMA has none of these diverse qualities. It has no sound and no shape, no inside and no outside. When the universe merges back to its source, its diversity that we sense ceases. If the diversity persists there cannot be oneness.

SAMADHI is absorption in divine consciousness. The cause, the source of the universe is outside words and logic. It is beyond speech and mind. Language and reason cannot comprehend it. Arguments are never conclusive, but experience is.

Having created the universe, BRAHMA entered into it. He entered DEVAS, the numerous powers, as their limited self. One power does not become many powers just because it functions in many ways. Differences of names and forms are created through our ignorance of the limitations. It remains unchanged, beyond actions, as their source.

What it creates is its own modification. The universe and its cause are not different. The material cause and its effect are not different. The effect can exist only when the cause exists. The effect has a prior existence in the cause as its possibility. This world existed before its creation, before its projection.

In the beginning this universe was only its self, its cause and source. Creation brings about limitations, changes and variations of forms. Freed of these forms it is the same as its creator.

Limitations exist in creation. They create forms. BRAHMA is different from these limitations and the forms they create. We should search for BRAHMA and inquire into it and hear of it, reflect on it, deeply meditate on it, experience it.

BRAHMA does not need materials to project the universe. It is its own materials. It has no instrument. None is its equal or superior. Its power is supreme and of various uses. Its knowledge, power, and action are spontaneous. Its will creates without extraneous help, like forces of nature that we experience in the world. It is the universe in its diversity, but it does not have parts. If it had parts, it would decompose and not be eternal. It is without action. It is peaceful. It is faultless and taintless.

When it transcends the universe, it is called PURUSHA, or the cosmic organic being that relates everything to everything else. All are limbs of the same body. Each is valuable in its own way.

We should make a sacrifice, an offering to this being. It is co-extensive with all that is external and internal. It is without birth or death. This great, endless, infinite reality is pure intelligence. It is known through denying all identifications as not this, not this. This is our sacrifice.

One and the same mind takes the shapes of diverse beings in a dream. BRAHMA is the power that takes many forms, doing all actions. All desires, smells and tastes are his. He is present in all of them. Under his law, the sun and the moon hold their positions. He has no organ of speech. He has no longing. His desires are true. His will is inviolable. He knows all in general and in particular. He has no eyes but he sees, no ears but he hears, no vocal organs but he speaks, no mind but he senses, organizes and constructs. He has no reason, no motive to create. He is contented, lacking nothing. Creation happens as a play of his fullness as he has infinite powers.

He is the self of everything, neither partial, nor cruel. The world appears unjust. Some are happy, others are miserable. Some are both. This diversity is created by the nature of beings and their actions. As they act, so they get. Actions and their effects happen in the universe, including the human society. Actions and their fruits cause transformation and transmigration. They are without a beginning. They cause inequality and diversity. Inequality is a form of diversity, which is the law of life.

Love, hatred and delusion are three forces that create inequality and diversity, as they hide sameness. When we love a being, that being becomes more equal than all other beings. When we hate a being, that being becomes less equal than all other beings. When we are deluded about a being, that being ceases to exist for us, even if we call him equal to another.

Unconscious nature cannot cause a design in the universe. It cannot be happy or sad. It cannot be a creator. Its constituents in a state of balance cannot become active and start creating. Nor can they act spontaneously. What can activate an unconscious cause, or stop it if it is already active? What purpose can an unconscious cause have to create? The purpose of creation may be pleasure or pain or freedom from these two.

How can unconscious nature be active and conscious PURUSHA be inactive? What can relate the two, the unconscious and the conscious? The constituents of unconscious nature in balance cannot initiate action. How can unconscious nature have intelligence?

We may say that the universe arises from atoms that occupy no space. Atoms combine in twos, threes, fours and so on. The combination of atoms produces new qualities like magnitude. How can atoms occupying no space produce space on combining? Things having parts are produced from combination of parts. So the originating part must have qualities that can result in the final product. The ultimate atom must have the minutest space. Two atoms combine to produce something entirely different. From where does this difference come?

The unconscious ultimate atom cannot initiate action. Unconscious ultimate atom cannot be the cause of the universe. Without action the atoms cannot combine. If action is present in the ultimate atom, then action is eternal. There cannot be any dissolution.

If each part that composes the universe has its own originating atom having all the qualities that the final product has, then the originating atoms are not ultimate.

Non-existence cannot produce existence. It is against experience. So the universe cannot come out of nothing. PURUSHA cannot create because it is different from nature and the self of nature. It is a body of relationships between all the parts of the universe.

The supreme self is the self of all. It appears as many forms but remains one. One can sit near it by being devoted to it through contemplation. One can visit temples where other seekers are present. One can hear or read discourses on it and think and talk of it. One can appreciate and praise it.

The individual self is not born. It does not die. It does not change. Our awareness of it changes through our experience, as we learn more of it. Full awareness is liberation, enlightenment.

To say that all is known when it is known means that the universe that emerges is present in its cause. The effect is present in the cause as its possibility. Everything is derived from it.

BRAHMA is the initial cause and the final purpose. It ordains all intermediate causes, effects and purposes. Intellect and mind do not disturb this order of creation and dissolution. They emerge from it after the elements that are first created.

Birth and death are possible only when a body exists. The self is eternal, and so it is not born. The individual self does not die. It is without dimensions. It leaves the body on death. It follows a course and comes back from the next world. It is the center of being. It pervades the whole body through sentience and intelligence. The relation between the self and intelligence persists so long as the body lasts. It becomes latent in sleep and on dissolution. When we are absent-minded we do not see. Therefore we do not see with our eyes alone.

We may say that the individual self is an agent. Then only can actions be done. The self goes out of the body on its death. So it must be active. Since intelligence is active, the self must be active too. Otherwise intelligence would be more powerful than the self. But if the self is active, there cannot be freedom from action. Anything that can be acquired through action and practice is impermanent. Therefore an active self is impermanent. The self appears to be active because limiting adjuncts are superimposed on it. When everything becomes the self, there is no possibility of action or experience or enjoyment.

When there is duality, one sees another. Then there is action. The action of the self is created by ignorance. Soldiers fight to do action of the king. The action of the king is like the action of the self. Organs do the actual action.

The individual self is a reflection of the supreme self. It is one and all pervasive. The self can neither do actions nor suffer their results.

The organs are atomic, subtle and limited. Every function is an organ for the self. Eye is the cause of vision and hands of grasping. Life is not a sense organ. When the organs of perception and action go to sleep, life force keeps awake. Life force is beyond the grasp of death. Life cannot die. If life died, it would not be life.

The self is related to the body as one that experiences. When it departs, life follows it along with functions of organs of perception, action and their mind. Past actions create a dream like future body to which it is attached. Elements also go out. Water goes back into water. So do other elements. Elements that make the body go back into elements that make the universe.

After the results of actions are exhausted, the self comes back into the world along with impressions of actions, good or bad. It comes back along the same path on which it went out. One is the higher path of knowledge and meditation. The other is the lower path of actions and customs.

The self is the creator. The mind takes many shapes as in dreams. But dream creation does not have the attributes of wakeful state. In deep sleep, both these realities cease to exist. Dreamless sleep happens in the self. Wakefulness happens when the self returns from the supreme self. One remembers that the person who wakes up is the one who went to sleep.

After death, the reality of the wakeful state may be like the reality of a dream. A dream is an omen, an indication of reality and what is to happen. Powerful beings can bring you information from another time and place, as when a deeply loved one dies, or in premonition.

BRAHMA cannot be both with and without qualities. It is only formless. It is non-manifest. It is known from experience. It appears to be different during its action of manifestation. It is a symbol of the formless reality that is manifested in infinite forms.

It is neither gross, nor minute, neither short, nor long. It is without features and dimensions. It cannot be perceived or grasped. In this way, distinctions are eliminated. This is the method of elimination of qualities. All forms are perishable. The self is beyond forms, beyond cause and effect. It is the same as I. I am the same as it. Our own self is the self of all. It lives in this body, free of sins, impurity, decay, death, hunger and sorrow. Its desire is true and effective. What it wills happens immediately. It is the controller and ruler of all.

Formless reality without its manifestation cannot be worshipped. There can be no worship of one God, because worship implies two beings, the worshipper and what he worships.

ATMA after death follows one of the two ways. It depends on whether it knows BRAHMA with forms and attributes or without them. These are the path of DEVAS reached through knowledge and deep meditations, and the path of ancestors reached through actions, rituals and traditions. The self moves on the path of DEVAS through meditations on divine attributes. There are many kinds of meditations at the initial stage. Through deep meditation desires are turned back to their source. They all end up in only one meditation. Then meditation ceases.

Some say that ATMA does not exist as it depends on the body. But consciousness may not exist even when the body exists. So consciousness is independent of the body.

A symbol of the self is not the self. Identify with the self, not its symbol. The sun and the stars and the great elements are symbols, expressions of the divine self. See the self in them. Adore the divine self mentally while sitting erect and motionless.

Rituals are accompanied by meditations. Some people do rituals without any meditations. Meditate on life and air. Meditate on fire in the mind and in speech. Meditate on the mental fire and moods of all beings. Mental fires are independent of actual fires. They are thoughts lighted by the mind. Mental fires serve human needs. They are not subservient to rituals. Meditations are associated with rites and are more important than them. Any meditation can be done in place of any other meditation. The final result of all meditations is the same. Meditations on symbols yield specific results.

On experiencing BRAHMA, non-attachment to subsequent sins and destruction of previous sins happens. There is no attachment to virtue either. Virtues and vices that have not as yet borne fruit are destroyed. Those that have borne fruit in the form of this life continue. Knowledge and impressions of actions accompany the self after death of the body. Some people remember past birth partly or fully.

Sense capacities merge in the mind on death. The mind merges in life. Life merges in the self. Elements merge in greater elements. ATMA merges in PARAM ATMA.

Freedom from Suffering

MAHARSHI KAPILA was an ancestor of KURU kings. He was a son of KARDAMA PRAJAPATI and mother DEVAHUTI.

KAPILA ASHRAM is located about hundred and fifty kilometers south of KALIGHAT where River GANGA meets SAGAR, called GANGASAGAR. His devotees make an offering to his idol and memory on the full moon day of the month of KARTIK. His text has been lost, but his tradition continues in the search for MOKSHA, or freedom from suffering through detachment.

Human life is full of suffering that comes from the body and mind, from nature, human or animal, and from what is beyond nature, from which nature emerges. From suffering comes the desire to know how to eliminate suffering. To eliminate suffering one learns to distinguish what perishes from that which does not perish. This makes one fearless of death and suffering and live in spiritual freedom.

There are obvious means of eliminating suffering like medicine and religious faith.

Though all suffering is mental, some mental suffering comes from the body. For eliminating it one uses AYUR VEDA and the disciplines of YOGA. One uses knowledge of herbs as foods and medicines and the right skills of body postures and breathing, and of living, including attitudes of welcome and acceptance and withdrawal of the senses from their objects.

The body is not a machine. It is a living and conscious organism. It responds creatively to environment. Its time of response is different from the time that we normally sense. The body is a visible effect of invisible forces that are alive and conscious. It has powerful cycles of energies that must flow unobstructed. We should be conscious of these forces. They are ever auspicious. They know what they do. We should see them flowing in and out through what we eat and drink, sense and think, feel and do.

Whereas some pain is experienced and medicines stop this pain, the possibility of pain is not stopped. It exists so long as consciousness exists.

Religious faith produces moral values, directing us to do or not to do certain actions, to have or not to have certain attitudes and relationships. These directions emerge from experience in a social context and they change as society changes. Religious faith includes ritual actions and ceremonies done with understanding and devotion. They tend to internalize certain desirable impressions, urges and attitudes that enable us to see and act in certain ways. We should meditate on moral values that we act on and on the impressions that we form from our environment and the effects they leave behind and the rituals and ceremonies that we do and their meanings and how they shape us as we act on them.

Whereas medicines and religious faith help in eliminating suffering, they may not be entirely effective in every case. The relief they give may not be permanent. Suffering in some other form may come back. Medicines and religious faith are related to impurity and evil, to decay, to excess and deficiency, and to obstruction of the flow of life in the body and mind. They do not provide a final freedom from suffering.

We normally acquire wealth and prosperity for our happiness. But they do not provide happiness, and their loss causes suffering. We need to stop the possibility of experiencing suffering.

Physical needs like hunger and sex have to be satisfied repeatedly. Their satisfaction cannot be the purpose of living in this wonderful world.

SANKHYA aims to provide a lasting relief from suffering, teaching us how to live skillfully in a way that stops us from experiencing suffering, even though suffering exists in the very nature of things. It explains what is to be avoided and its cause, and the nature and means of avoiding it for experiencing spiritual freedom.

We are real and so is the world. One type of interaction between these two realities produces suffering, another type does not. We need to cultivate the type of interaction that does not produce suffering. This interaction requires that we discriminate between numerous forms of nature, their source, and the one that knows these forms of nature and their source. This discrimination emerges through daily quiet contemplation and meditation, and not through learning borrowed ideas from books, scriptures and gurus.

We should learn to remember clearly our own experience of life in all its numerous details and to reflect on it. We should observe how our experience rises, grows and decays and is forgotten. We should reflect on our experience of life and recognize the one that has the capacity to know and the many that are known through this capacity. We should learn to have nothing in our mind, making it pure, free of objects.

There is reality present in the universe. We call it PURUSHA. It is present in the human body. It is the subject, the capacity to know. It is that which knows, without being told. It is consciousness without an object of which it is the consciousness. It is a cosmic being everywhere the same, present in all beings, relating them.

PRAKRITI is all that comes to be known. It is the object that is and can be known. It is the potential of all that has been and all that can ever be created as the universe. It is the numerous forms of nature and their single source.

These are the two ultimate realities of the universe. Knowledge of these two realities is SANKHYA.

We should learn to understand nature, its actions and consequences, its source, the living consciousness present in nature. This knowledge frees one from attachment of the heart and mind to living in the world, their bondage to nature. This freedom is acquired through detached observation of living and experience that reveals the higher nature of man. It enables one to live a nobler life.

Every part of the universe has a reason why it is what it is. It has a cause that has brought it into existence. Without this cause, it could never have come into existence. It has a purpose that it works to achieve. It has a value in terms of its purpose. The purpose may be great or small. But every purpose is necessary and valuable in itself.

There is no part of nature that can come into existence without having existed earlier in some other form. The tree exists in its seed and the seed in its tree. Every effect exists in its cause. Otherwise the effect cannot come into existence. Something cannot come out of nothing. This cycle of energy exists in larger and larger cycles of energies till we reach the source of nature. We should do its UPASANA, sitting close to it in our mind.

Evolution in the world of phenomena is only a change of forms. It is a transformation of the ultimate constituent. The symbol of this evolution is fire, the transforming power of heat and intensity. Evolution happens from the invisible source of nature to the gross material nature in the presence of PURUSHA that observes this manifestation. SANKHYA aims to explain this evolution, enumerating the principles that declare the nature of the self, revealing the self through its difference from its object.

PURUSHA is free of all forms of change, unaffected by external influence. So it is free of all suffering. Suffering belongs only to nature. Man suffers because he identifies himself with nature, the body and its mind, nature and its source. If he detaches himself from nature, he detaches himself from suffering.

PURUSHA exists from the beginning. It does not act to create but its presence results in creation.

PRAKRITI or nature in its source existed along with PURUSHA before anything is produced. All objects come out of PRAKRITI and go back into it. It is the source, the root of creation. It exists without a beginning. It is primal nature or primary matter, without one object different from another, though all objects are potentially present in it. Evolution happens from the non- differentiated source of nature to differentiated objects of visible, experienced nature.

Time is marked by birth, growth, decay, and death. It is an expression of nature's will to act. Reliable knowledge of these is acquired through proofs. The accepted proofs are perception, inference and reliable authority. Other means of reliable knowledge derive from them.

Perception selects and determines particular sense objects. It is based on the senses, the mind, ego and intellect. These provide pleasure, pain and indifference to pleasure and pain. Non-perception does not mean non-existence. If we do not see something, it does not mean that it does not exist.

Inference goes beyond immediate perception through the use of reason. It provides general principles that enable experience to happen. Inference may be from cause to effect or from effect to cause or derived from previous knowledge or from some known example.

Reliable authority is verbal testimony that comes from proven experience that can be trusted. It does not contradict knowledge received from perception and inference. If it appears to do so, then the verbal testimony of reliable authority has to be re-examined or reinterpreted.

We understand things beyond the senses by means of inference. We understand things beyond inference by means of reliable authority.

Perception may not occur because of many reasons. The object may be at too much or too little distance to be perceived. One may be too inattentive to perceive the object. The sense organs may be defective. The object may be too small or too subtle to be perceived. Another object may intervene between the object and the perceiving organ. The object may be suppressed and hidden or something else may be mixed up with it. It may be indistinct and unclear and there may be other causes.

PRAKRITI as the source of nature is not perceived by the mind because mind emerges from it and so it is beyond mind. It can be understood by reason as distinct from perception. It may be experienced through the practice of YOGA that transcends the mind. It is subtle and invisible but not non-existent. It exists because its effects exist. They are the visible nature that is experienced. If effects are seen, their causes must exist. Effects may appear to be different from their causes, but are essentially similar to them. The effects of causes exist in them even before the causes operate. The effect exists in its cause as its possibility. Nature exists in its source.

That is so because of the following reasons. What does not exist cannot come into existence. That which does not exist cannot produce anything, nor can it produce everything. An effect must have an appropriate cause. A particular effect is produced only by a particular cause. Every cause cannot produce every effect. A cause can produce only that effect which it is capable of producing. A particular cause can produce only a particular effect. The nature or essence of cause is not different from the nature or essence of its effect. The cause is an effect that has not evolved yet. The effect is a cause that has evolved. There is only a change of form. Nothing new is created. Nothing new can be created. This process of changing forms is eternal, without beginning or end. Its symbol is fire. The worship of fire means its UPASANA, sitting mentally close to this changing of forms, this self-evolution.

The manifest visible nature itself has a cause. It is the productive cause of many effects. It is limited in space and time, non-pervasive and discrete. It is active and energetic and varied, having many forms. It is supported by something else. It serves as a symbol of that something else. It is a mixture composed of parts and dependent on those parts. The source of nature has opposite characteristics. It is uncaused by anything else. It is infinite in time and space. It pervades all else. It is independent, non-active, without support.

Nature as visible forms and as source of visible forms has three constituents. They are SATYA, RAJAS and TAMAS, translated as truth and existence, energy and action, limitation and restraint. They are mixed with each other in different proportions in the visible forms. They are balanced in nature as the source of visible forms. They are objective, general, non-conscious, and productive. They are the ultimate material cause of the universe. They include gross and subtle matter. Mind, ego, and intellect are subtle, invisible matter, its products.

Intellect, will, self-awareness and gross objects are produced by nature. These create pleasure, pain and indifference to these. They manifest, activate and limit one another.

Truth as existence gives pleasure and illumination. It moves upwards like fire. Energy as action produces pain and change directed outwards. It is stimulating. Limitation as restraint produces inertia and delusion. It is heavy like sleep. These constituents are present in manifest nature. Therefore they must be present in non-manifest nature too.

The non-manifest nature is the cause of specific things manifest in the world. These things are finite and so require a cause. They are similarly constituted. Their emergence implies the power of the cause.

The whole world is uniform. It functions through the interaction of these constituents in different proportions. These differences are their specific nature. These natures have diverse births, deaths, functions and faculties. Their functions occur at different times.

PURUSHA has many forms. It is the opposite of nature. It is the witness of nature. It is not the one that acts. It is free and not dependent on anything else. It is indifferent, not attached to anything. As it sees so is the world. Experiencing its reality in life frees one from suffering. It makes one noble. This experience is the aim of living.

Because it sees nature, the unconscious nature appears to be conscious and the inactive PURUSHA appears to be active. The subject changes the object seen, like we see the sky that does not exist. This is the delusion that one has to be free of. This is the source of suffering in the nature of things. These two realities are associated because nature is to be seen as free of the seer. Their association projects the manifest nature.

Nature transforms itself into great intelligence, which is knowledge in action, all that is and becomes or can become. The great intelligence, the intelligent will, has the characteristic of determining existence, deciding the truth that the senses report. It is the first principle that PURUSHA witnesses and identifies with.

From this great intelligence emerges the principle of doing. It creates an organic identity, a feeling that I am this and doing this. The self sees it and asserts itself as the doer.

From this principle of doing emerge sixteen principles. These are one mind, five capacities of sense perception, five capacities of organs of action, and five subtle imperceptible elements of sound, touch, form, taste, and smell.

Mind has the nature of both the senses of perception and the organs of action. It is inactive and active, receptive and productive. It receives, stores, alters and organizes sensations, explaining and explicating them. It is characterized by active deliberation that includes analysis, synthesis and construction of impressions. It creates memory and imagination. Therefore it is called a sense organ, INDRYA that leads to the knowledge of INDRA just beyond the senses.

The organs of perception are eye, ear, nose, tongue, and skin. The organs of action are the organs of speech, hands, feet, and the organs of generation and excretion. They leave behind subtle impressions in the mind. From these subtle imperceptible elements emerge the five gross elements, which are space, solid earth, liquid water, gaseous air, and the transforming heat of fire.

The forms of truth as existence are knowledge, virtue, non-attachment and power. Their opposites forms are ignorance, vice, attachment and powerlessness. These eight are the basic dispositions of the great intelligence, its fundamental tendencies to action and evolution. There are numerous variations and combinations within these two extremes.

The variety of external things and of organs is caused by specific limitations and changes of the constituents of nature. The function of the five sense organs is awareness of the gross elements. The functions of the five organs of action are speech, grasping, walking, excretion, and procreation. The five vital motions are the functions of life, like breathing in and out, motion downward and upward, and carrying foods in all directions to different limbs of the body. These vital motions keep the body and mind alive.

Intelligence, doing and perception function simultaneously and successively with respect to what is present in perception. With respect to what is not present in perception, the internal organs function on the basis of prior perception or memory. The internal organ functions in time, present, past and future.

The external organ, consisting of five senses of perception and five organs of action, is the field of the internal organ. It functions only in the present time.

The five senses of perception have specific and non-specific, gross and subtle objects. Speech has only sound as its object, but the remaining organs of action have all five as objects.

Intelligence, the "I do" principle, and mind comprehend every object. This internal threefold instrument is the doorkeeper. The senses of perception and organs of action are the doors.

Senses and organs, mind and "I do" are different from one another and are distinct specifications of the complex constituents of nature.

The external and internal organs coordinate with one another to provide experience. This is their sole motive to function. These organs are characterized by the functions of seizing, holding and manifesting or expressing their respective objects. They present the whole being to intelligence, illuminating it for PURUSHA. This is done because intelligence brings every enjoyment and experience to it, and discriminates it from nature.

The subtle elements are non-discrete and non-perceptible. From them emerge the five gross elements that can be perceived. The subtle body is constant and the gross body is perishable. The subtle body is unconfined, inclusive of intelligence, the "I do" principle, mind, capacities of senses and organs and five subtle elements. It does not have enjoyment. Impelled by the purpose of PURUSHA, it transmigrates. It is endowed with tendencies to action, conditions and dispositions, which associate it with causes and effects and the power of nature.

DHARMA is the innate tendency to freedom from suffering to a nobler level of being. It depends on the body and mind, which comes from parents. It moves one upwards in the scale of being, elevating it. Its opposite moves one downwards in the scale of being, deteriorating it.

Knowledge leads to the final freedom, non-attachment to the non-self. Ignorance leads to bondage to the other, attachment to the non-self. From non-attachment comes dissolution of ego in nature. The "I do" principle ceases. One becomes part of the vast field of natural forces. One starts seeing nature acting everywhere, including one's body and mind.

This is subtle creation, marked as contentment and perfection, ignorance and incapacity. Each of these is of many types. They result from suppression of different qualities, defects and injuries. Ignorance, incapacity, and complacency hinder perfections.

The subtle body is subjective. It cannot function without objective conditions, dispositions or strivings. The objective conditions cannot function without the subjective body. Therefore creation is two-fold, the subtle body and the objective conditions in which it operates.

The divine and sub-human orders are of many kinds. The human order is of one kind. This is the gross creation.

In the higher world, truth as existence predominates. In the lower world, limitation as restraint predominates. In the middle world, energy as transformation predominates. This is so from the highest being to the lowest.

PURUṢHA sees the decay and death of the gross body until the subtle body is delivered from it. Pain is inherent in this decay and death of the gross body.

Creation happens through modifications of nature for the experience of PURUSHA. Nature stops its dance after it is experienced.

Nature has constituents and acts in various ways. It reduces gross matter to subtle matter to mind, feelings and thoughts, to will and ego, to intellect and intelligence, to inertia, energy and truth.

Nature in its various forms transmigrates and is bound and released. She binds herself by herself by means of fundamental conditions and tendencies to action. She releases herself by means of truth as existence.

Consciousness does not belong to any being. What belongs to one is the "I" as in I do, I feel, I think, I am. These are objects of consciousness. Consciousness is free of objects and error. It is pure and solitary. It is not bound. It is not released. It does not migrate.

PURUSHA, as a spectator, sees nature whose activity ceases on completion of her purpose and who therefore withdraws from her forms. This is dissolution.

PURUSHA says, "I have seen her." Nature says, " I have been seen." Though they are still in proximity, no further creation happens.

After attaining this knowledge, the body still continues to live because of the force of past impressions. After nature has completed its purpose, PURUSHA leaves the body. Then it is alone and free. This is freedom.

To be free of suffering, we should practice meditation on forms of reality. There are many forms of reality. We need to focus on any one form at a time and see them one by one and visualize them in detail. We are one of its forms. We should see ourselves as a form of nature in detail. We should understand nature, its source and the self that understands nature and its source.

We should do actions that emerge from our nature suited to our age and status in life. We should do them in a detached manner with awareness of their motives and consequences. We should do them skillfully without any expectations of personal benefits and dedicate their fruits to the Supreme Being, who lives in all. We should do these actions as duty in search of the source of our reality without hurting other beings and with kindness to those who suffer.

If we disregard the divine presence in others by inflicting suffering on them, how can we have peace of mind? If we do not revere the living, if we cause suffering to them for whatever reason, how can we worship the divine present in all?

If we are self-centered, thinking of others as separate from us, to be dominated and used, we can never be at peace, even if we want to, and we can have no divine experience.

We should give gifts, honor and love to others, and control our senses of perception and action, and their product, our mind. This will set us on the path of evolution, on the spiritual path.

We should visualize the divine, its names and actions, and praise and glorify it, remembering it with devotion. We should try to internalize the name and its form and relate it to our life and act on it. This is the aim of image worship, whether the form is in stone or metal or words. This is a step in our spiritual evolution. We should be in the company of people who have similar holy inclinations.

Devotion to the cosmic being has many forms. Our form of devotion depends on our nature, on the quality of nature that dominates our life and our tradition. We should worship the divine in a manner that suits our nature and tradition, trying to concentrate on its noble aspects.

We should observe and understand our nature, reflect on it and see its fire, its evolution. We should find what we are and what we are tending to become. Our nature will evolve and be transformed through our reflection and detached attention.

Detachment from our nature means transcending it. Then we will not suffer, even though suffering will exist.

Some search for pleasure, wealth and fame. Some search for domination, revenge and exploitation. We should learn to search for freedom from nature, freedom from suffering. Freedom is from the other, from what is not our self.

We should learn to visualize our source, our past as far back as we can go and learn to be more conscious of what we are, what we do.

We should learn to reflect on our experience every day, to visualize what we feel and think and do. We should do it at dawn, in the evening and before and after sleep.

We should sit still and upright breathe slowly and deeply, focusing our consciousness on our breath. This practice releases many obstacles to our energy.

Then we should review our life, visualizing and feeling its details, remaining devoted to truth, even if we think at present that the truth is against us. In reality, truth can never be against us as it is our essence. Truth is always auspicious. It cannot cause suffering. It can only be against what is false in us.

We should learn to withdraw our senses from their objects into our heart, the center of our life and to recognize the divine presence in our own self and in every being, as we learn to recognize it in a divine image or an object.

We should learn to see the holy presence of the divine in all beings everywhere and do NAMASHKAR or bow to them, revere them.

Common Man's Wisdom

MAHARSHI BRIHASPATI is the guru of the gods on earth. He and his followers pursue pleasure and prosperity, two major aims of life. For them, there is no spirit and no spirituality. They say:

Scriptures have no authority. There is no reason why we should follow any scripture. Why should we follow anybody other than our own self? Why follow what somebody else has said or done or thought or explained or claimed as revelation or vision? We know that we make mistakes. That somebody we follow must have made mistakes too. The greater he was, the greater must have been his mistakes. Why follow his mistakes, why not our own?

Scriptures often say meaningless things. We often read them without understanding them. We sometimes do not understand them even with plenty of explanations and commentaries. Meanings are often read into scriptures by their followers who do not have the capacity to see that they are reading their own meanings in them. And if they have this capacity, they do not have the courage to admit it.

No one can fully know what really was the meaning of a scripture written long ago in an environment that no longer exists. If somebody says something to somebody else and that somebody repeats it to somebody else, and if this goes on for some time, what is finally repeated is very different from what was said initially. This experiment is proof enough that no one knows what the scriptures meant when they were first composed. How can we know what they really meant? If meanings of words can change with a few repetitions, how much can they change when scriptures are repeated over many generations? Even if scriptures are scrupulously recorded when they are first produced, even then our understanding and application of them in life will change over generations because of our changing conditions and circumstances. Why should we cultivate attitudes, relationships and judgments that were created in an entirely different environment that no longer exists?

Scriptures are sometimes ambiguous as they normally lead to divergent interpretations by different commentators, each believing that he is right and the other wrong, leading to divisions, quarrels and fights, even riots and wars. When scholars cannot agree, how can the common people agree? And why should they?

Who says that scriptures teach non-violence? All human actions requiring compliance from others use force, hidden or obvious, leaving room for manipulation, indoctrination, inducements, threats and compulsion. This is what politics is about. The basis of law and social regulation is force, which is a polite word for violence. That is why police and army exist. If advocates of non-violence truly believed in what they say, they would not have the army or the police. Then those who know that violence is right would destroy them. Violence exists in the very nature of things. It obviously exists in animals and performs a necessary function, like cleaning up the earth of dead bodies and limiting their numbers. Human animals with their desires and greed, with their falsehood and deception, with their anger and aggression are no exceptions. Violence exists in human nature. Power and violence play in all relationships, as in hierarchy and order, even if there are only two human beings, one strong and the other weak. Even self-control is a form of power that one part of the mind exercises on another part.

Scriptures are absurd sometimes. They make false claims about objective reality that are later disproved. Why cannot they be wrong about the subjective reality too? That is why we hear and read them without understanding, questioning or acting on them.

Scriptures are products of their makers despite their false claim that they come from God who is ignorant about the future and false about verifiable reality. Their moral judgments and mental attitudes may be personal to them. They are enforced through reward and punishment and organization. They suppress and destroy other minds and possibilities of human flowering. Their universality is acquired through acquiring more followers, but all believers may be wrong and no one may know the truth. They cause death and destruction to others who do not follow them.

Scriptures are sometimes contradictory. Actions praised and views expressed at one place are condemned at another. The followers sometimes go out of their way to resolve such contradictions. But they do not have the courage to give up their faith. They may even be punished and sentenced to death if they give up their faith.

Scriptures are sometimes obscene and derogatory to women. Such passages are glossed over as metaphors. They are expounded as if they had deep meanings. But they who composed obscene passages and condemned women to lechery and inferiority must have been rascals.

Scriptures are sometimes repetitive. This may have been done to increase their bulk, to look pompous and to dominate and befool the weak-minded.

Scriptures sometimes conflict with our experience. Why accept them as divine truth? Why disbelieve our own experience?

Scriptures are intended to provide an easy living to people who benefit from them, like priests, who are lazy and incompetent, parasites on society. They receive charity, gifts and freedom from taxes in return for comfortable and soothing words.

Scriptures make people see things that do not exist. Whoever has seen a god or a soul?

Composers and preachers of scriptures are fools. They talk of things they say are unknowable, incomprehensible. If you admit that you are talking about something unknowable, which therefore you do not know, you are admitting that you are a fool since you are talking about that which you do not know. If you say that God or soul cannot be known, then why do you talk about it? Fools and rascals and thieves created scriptures to deceive and cheat others for their own livelihood and for their power over people.

Rituals and magic, mumbo-jumbo and sacred formulas are repeated till the brain is dulled. Rituals are acts of buffoonery, childish play and make-believe. Ritual ceremonies, like repeating scriptures, lighting fires, making sacrifices, smearing bodies with ashes, wearing distinctive clothes or special marks, are a means of livelihood for priests. They are without manliness, without sense enough to earn their livelihood in normal, socially productive and useful ways.

If fire can take our gifts to heaven, why do not priests burn themselves to go to heaven? If a beast slain in a ritual goes to heaven, why do not priests slay themselves to go to heaven? If sacrificial ceremonies are true, then there is no need to carry provisions on a journey because relatives at home can perform the ceremony and the food will reach the distant traveler. If the dead can be fed by feeding the priests, then the flame of an extinguished lamp can also be fed with oil, as it will reach the flame that is dead.

If repeating the name of God can give us the experience of God, why not repeat the name of a food to satisfy our hunger? If repeating scriptures can give you the experience of God, why not repeat the name of your beloved to get his or her experience?

If a man can go to heaven after death, why does not he come back to console his grieving relatives?

If ATMA is the knower, it cannot be known because when it is known it ceases to be the knower. If we cannot know ATMA, how can we know that there is ATMA?

When there is only the witness and there is nothing to be witnessed, how can it be a witness of what does not exist, and how can we know that there is a witness?

If there is God to judge our actions and us, why do we not judge him as an enemy to be destroyed? Why do we not cultivate our own ability to judge ourselves? Are we not projecting our own ability to judge others to an imaginary fiction on a large scale?

There is no God, no soul, no heaven, no hell, no Day of Judgment, no goodness, no evil. There is only our body and nature that we sense and experience. Our body is a part of nature. When our body dies, everything ends for us. When we live, we create our

God and heaven and hell and Day of Judgment and standards of good and evil.

There is no life after death. The weight of the body before and after death is the same. So nothing, no soul, leaves it on death.

There is no world other than this world. Man ends in death, along with his good and bad actions. The body returns to its elements.

The murderer, the thief, the housebreaker, the plunderer, the liar commit no sin. The virtuous, the liberal, the self-controlled, abstemious, the honest earn no merit. Neither sin, nor virtue, affect life as it goes on. Living is non-moral. There is no force in moral law, as there is no heaven or hell.

We are concerned with only this world. Therefore care about this world, not some imaginary heaven or hell. Heaven is only another place and time and set of conditions in imagination. Hell is a name for grief and suffering, physical and mental pain.

Pleasure is best experienced in contrast to pain. Without the experience of pain, one cannot experience pleasure. There can be no eternal pleasure. Therefore there can be no heaven.

Pain ceases to be painful after some time. For pain to exist, pleasure is necessary. There can be no eternal pain. Therefore there can be no hell.

Man's nature is to reduce pain and increase pleasure. He knows that there cannot be total elimination of pain or total production of pleasure. Therefore be as happy when alive as possible in the circumstances.

Freedom from bondage to the body and the world is only death. While we are alive, it is self-contradictory.

Our body creates our blood and energy, urine and feces on the one side, the ideas of God and demon, goodness and evil on the other. Our body is a part of nature, which creates animals and minerals on the one side, forces and energies on the other. The body creates the mind. The bigger the use of brain, the bigger is the mind produced. Some foods and drinks and exercises help in the growth of the mind, as they do in the growth of the body.

Study plants and herbs and what helps them grow healthy. Study life. Learn about what supports and strengthens life and how to live well accordingly.

When some elements of nature happen to combine in certain proportions in certain ways, they produce the body, which in turn produces the mind. There is nothing else.

Nature is the only reality. It has four elements the solid earth, the liquid water, the gaseous air and the fire of motion that gives heat and light but is neither earth, nor water, nor air. From the transformations of these elements in different proportions arise different bodies, with more or less intelligence, which perishes when the bodies are destroyed. The elements interact to produce pleasure and pain and indifference. Combinations of these elements and motion in different proportions are called objects and living bodies, animal and human, with their sense organs that create the mind, often imagined as soul or spirit.

Properties of matter like weight can be seen in every particle of matter. But consciousness is not seen in these particles. So consciousness arises when particles of matter combine in certain ways.

Life arises from combinations of elements in particular proportions and conditions. When these combinations break, life dies. No self remains.

Events happen as they happen. It is their nature. Find out the flow of nature in you, your own flow and live accordingly.

Events exist by themselves. There are neither causes nor effects. There are neither good consequences nor bad. There is no reason or cause why the universe is as it is. There is no reason why the peacock has eye marks on its tail. Since there is no first cause, there is no second cause, no third cause, and so on. All causes are based on falsehood.

Only that exists which is seen and experienced. Inference from perception is only a guess and cannot be believed to be true till it is perceived in a case. Universal truths cannot be established by our limited perception. All universal truths, including this one, have the potential of being false.

Perception means impression of an object on our sense organs. It is restricted to the present, here and now. Reality does not extend to the past and the future or to the general.

The past is dead and gone. Everyone never perceived the past in the same way. The destroyer and the destroyed do not see the war in the same way. The powerful impose their memory on others as history. The defeated may have had a different memory, but are too powerless to protest or assert their view.

The future has many possibilities. Only one of these possibilities will be realized by an accident or human exertion. Many possibilities are never realized. All futures disappear into the past. Prediction of future is a trick to earn money.

Memory and recognition of events are always selective and biased from a point of view. Therefore they are false. They do not refer to one and the same consciousness. Different consciousnesses will have different memories and their significance. Therefore history and tradition are always biased and false and changed by strong willed persons as their desires and interests lead them.

The past is dead, and the future doubtful. Enjoy the present.

Sense perception gives us only particular truths. Comparisons made between them are acceptable. But testimony and authority require inference and are false. Moments of knowledge arise from sense organs into the mind as sense impressions. There is no knowledge in swoon or embryo, since no sense organs work there. A newborn child will create its own knowledge. Your nature is to cultivate knowledge through your body, its sense organs governed by its brain, working as mind.

The body creates consciousness. No body, no consciousness. Isolated particles of matter have no consciousness. Isolated individuals have no society and no state. When they become a body, they acquire consciousness. Dissolution of organization destroys life, the mind and its consciousness. When the body perishes, its consciousness perishes. There is nothing left to transmigrate into another body. Different bodies have different minds, just as they have organs with different capacities and qualities.

So be free as individuals, but organize to work for social welfare of the rich and the poor. Form organizations, big or small, for this purpose or that. Forming organization is forming consciousness, as indicated in its purpose and working out the practical details of its operation.

Consciousness comes and goes as in wakefulness and sleep. It changes as with drinks and drugs. It is not a constant continuity that goes on to the next world. Therefore there are no past or future births.

Consciousness is created by sense organs. When organs die, consciousness ceases. A blind man has no consciousness of color or a deaf man of sounds. If we had a different set of sense organs, we would have a different kind of consciousness and we would see and experience a different set of things. That is why different kinds of world exist in the same world. Our organs determine our consciousness as well as the objects that we see. Without sensations received through them, there is no consciousness. We should increase the capability of our sense organs. All knowledge comes from sense experience alone.

Since the body changes all the time, the body that does an action is not the body that experiences its consequences. Therefore there is no action and its consequences experienced by one and the same body.

No merits and no demerits are brought forward from a previous existence. There is no moral auditing on death, no Day of Judgment. There is no sense in practicing virtue or avoiding sin. There is no fate, no god and no devil. Religion is words. Prayer is hope of the weak. Prophets are liars. Pleasure and pain come by chance. They are mixed. They come together. But shall we stop taking rice because it comes with husk? Even detachment cannot rid us of pain, disease, or accident.

Celebrate pleasure. Dance and sing. Play and swing. Enjoy flowers and fragrance, colors and shapes. Enjoy sweets and tasty bites. Cultivate taste and your senses. Eat, drink and be merry. Learn to laugh at life, at others and yourself. Sing about the sun and the stars, the clean air, water and vegetation. Sing about crops and canals, boats and trades and the compound interest. Enjoy festivals, exhibitions and meeting people. Be free in thought and free from bondage to scriptures and priests. Have the courage to be yourself, to express your own nature. Be not a copy of somebody else's nature. Have no heroes. Do not idealize and imitate SITA, SAVITRI, or SATI. Do not idealize and imitate the murderers of people, called kings or emperors. Do not idealize and follow the manipulators of human beings, called leaders or politicians. Follow no laws except those that you make in your own interest, for your own benefit and acquire the strength and will to enforce them. Rewrite your own unreliable memory and false history in your own interest instead of following the unreliable and false history created by others in their own interest. Make your memory and history useful to you.

Satisfy your passions and desires. Have children and raise a healthy family. Love your friends and destroy your enemies.

Have no belief, follow no practice, obey no command and accept no prohibition till you have examined it in the light of your own reason and benefit, your own experience of life. Have no belief in authority or the unseen. Most authorities are unworthy, hiding behind elaborate masks, remaining silent in the name of keeping secrets, telling lies and raking in their own wealth, security and comfort, black money in bank accounts in foreign countries. Admit no authority except your own. Show no undeserved respect to anyone. If someone tries to impress you, find out his weakness and hit him there. Be not overawed by anyone. Oppose scriptures and the practice of repeating them without understanding their meaning, without doubting their truth, rejecting or accepting them. Doubt superstitions.

Desire to live healthy and long. Learn about health and longevity and apply your learning to your life. Learn about the body, human and animal, and plants, foods and medicines. Learn AYUR VEDA, knowledge of life, and YOGA, methods of living well, unconcerned with God. Promote health and long life for all. Cultivate your senses and desires. Refine and broaden them. Without desires there is no society, no organization or power. Detachment and absence of desire means defeat in war, loss of wealth and women and self-respect. Cultivate desires, make them stronger, engage in social action and organize individuals to acquire power and consciousness.

Do you think that green is only green? Go into a garden and find out. Go there during different times of the day and night. See the variety of green that the words hide. Similarly explore all that you sense. Enjoy your life whatever the circumstances. Enjoying life is a skill. Acquire it. Your life in the present is all that you have. Celebrate festivals and meet people and be one of them and then lead them to your heart's desire.

Desire to earn wealth and protect it. Learn the skills that help you earn. Save and breed your money. Protect what you save from everyone. The governments and authorities are not as good as they declare themselves to be. The governments tax heavily and waste large moneys on their own personal satisfactions, security and comforts. Examine their invisible expenditures on themselves and their hidden accounts. They make false accusations against their opponents and tell lies about their own difficulties. They have highly exaggerated grievances. The greater the confusion and ignorance they create, the greater the gains they make. They create inflation and take bribes and make people pay for their personal expenditure and give noble reasons for doing ignoble things. Stock exchange tempts ignorant commoners and wipes them clean every few years. Communists and leftists are full of envy and ill will for the rich, using high-sounding moral arguments to eliminate poverty and to condemn the rich, but aspiring to be rich themselves and live like kings. Notice how they marry off their grandchildren like old irresponsible kings.

Be friends with those who can be happy with your prosperity. Doubt and reason and acquire knowledge of nature and society. Use it for your own benefit and share a little with those who are your followers. Acquire power and learn how to use it. Impose your will on others instead of submitting to their will. Benefit others and benefit from it

Pleasure and prosperity are the two fundamental aims of living. Achieve them through knowledge and skills and devoted application. All else is hot air. Always doubt and question till you are convinced from your experience.

Chapter VII

War and Peace

MAHARSHI VEDVYAS composed an epic called MAHABHARATA, which means great India that included AFGANASTAN, SINDU valley, PANJAB, GANGA YAMUNA valley, MADHYA PRADESH, MAGADHA, VIDEH, ANGA, VANGA, ORISSA, PANDYAS, CHOLAS, and KERALA, from the HIMALAYAS to SRI LANKA, and the land between the eastern and the western seas.

The epic narrates a main story with many short stories interwoven into it. It discusses Indian philosophies and forms of worship, the aims of life, and ethics of war and peace, and governance. It describes in popular terms all that is there to India. So it is called the fifth VEDA.

Once upon a time, RAJA SOM ruled HASTINAPUR near DELHI. His son BUDHA married princess ILA. His son PURURAVAS married URVASHI and had a son AYUS, whose son NAHUSHA became so powerful and cruel that he reached heavens. There he over-threw INDRA and tried to marry his wife against her will. So the RISHIS degraded him to a snake and he fell into hell, since power had to be restrained by wisdom. His son was RAJA YAYATI. He married DEVAYANI and had two sons, YADU and TURVASU. He had a second wife, SHARMISHTHA, and three sons, DRUYU, ANU, and PURU. These five sons were the ancestors of the VEDIC tribes.

Once DEVAS and demons fought a war and DEVAS killed many demons. But their GURU SHUKRACHARYA brought them back to life with his knowledge of the rejuvenating herbs. DEVAS decided to obtain this medical knowledge and prayed to their GURU ANGIRAS BRIHASPATI for help. He sent his grandson KACHCH to RISHI SHUKARACHARYA to be his disciple and acquire his medical knowledge. RISHI SHUKRACHARYA gave his medical knowledge freely to his devoted student even though he knew that the student had come from an enemy.

The fifteenth descendant of PURU, son of YAYATI, was RAJA DUSHYANTA. He ruled a vast land surrounded by the seas in the south and mountains in the north. He ruled over some land of barbarians too, both in the south and in the north. He protected and administered the land skillfully and pleased and nourished his people, who followed righteousness and were prosperous. Social groups were based on clear-cut duties and they worked for their common welfare.

One day the king went out hunting far away from his capital HASTINAPUR. He entered wilderness by the river MALINDI. There he saw the ASHRAM of RISHI KANVA of RISHI KASHYAPA lineage whose thought had dominated the north, especially the HIMILAYAS. His place was known as KASHYAP'S MIRA, now KASHMIR.

He saw some students meditating and some others doing PUJA. He saw a lady in the dress of a hermit. He was struck with love at first sight and asked her who she was. She said she was SHAKUNTALA, the daughter of RAJA VISHWAMITRA and dancer MANEKA sent to him by RAJA INDRA to interrupt his self-discipline, as he felt jealous. She was a child of love. Her parents abandoned her, as they were not married. RISHI KANVA happened to pass by. He picked her up and brought her up as his own daughter. He was not at home.

RAJA DUSHYANTA proposed to marry her through mutual consent without any formal rites, a GANDHARVA form of marriage permitted by law to warriors. In wars and travels, proper ceremonies are often not possible. And everyone is responsible for his own welfare and has the right to decide his marriage as it affects his life in all its stages.

SHAKUNTALA thought for a while and proposed a condition that her son would be accepted as the heir apparent and would succeed him as the emperor. RAJA in love agreed. The two lived together for some time. Then the RAJA went away promising to send an army to escort her to the palace, but he forgot his promise later. When RISHI KANVA returned he approved of her GANDHARVA marriage. A healthy son was born. At age 6, he was playing with wild animals, riding them and racing with them.

Disciples of RISHI KANVA escorted SHAKUNTALA and the child to the court of RAJA DUSHYANTA. He refused to recognize her. She was upset.

She said: ANTARYAMI DEVA, who controls you from inside, was a witness to their marriage. That Supreme Self knows your sins and virtues. You cannot cheat him even if you cheat me. Your own self will tell you that you have spoken a lie and your mind will condemn you. A husband is born as son in his wife. A son takes you to heaven and a grandson to immortality. A wife is an expert in keeping the house. She gives you children and takes your life as her own. She is half of her husband and his only true friend in the whole world. Man achieves righteousness, prosperity, and satisfaction of desire through his wife. These are the three major aims of life. She even takes him to the threshold of freedom, the fourth aim. Man can do great work through her help. She is like a father in DHARMA and a mother in sorrow and a friend in love. She is man's resting place even in wilderness. No helper is greater than a wife. No DHARMA is greater than truth, wisdom and commitment to truth. Do not break your promise. Your promise is the basis of all your commitments, as it makes the law and contracts and treatises. You cannot break it. You may or may not accept your son, but I am sure he is going to rule the world. I am grown up enough to take care of myself. But why are you insulting your wife and your son?

RAJA DUSHAYANTA was sitting in the company of his ministers, guru and advisors. They saw the resemblance between the king and his son and felt that the lady was speaking the truth. They advised him to speak and accept the truth, which he did.

He named his son BHARATA. India is named after him, BHARATAVARSHA. He grew up to be a great warrior and conquered many lands. He started a dynasty of BHARATA kings that produced great kings and scholars.

A descendant of RAJA BHARATA was RAJA SHANTANU. He was so pious that when he touched old and sick people they became youthful and normal. He wanted to marry a girl named GANGA, pure like the river. She agreed to marry him on the condition that he would not take away her freedom to do whatever she wanted to do. She did not know that becoming wife and mother is not loss of freedom, but a changed expression of freedom. She did not know that both husband and wife change and become father and mother when their baby is born and they blossom when their child blossoms. Thoughtlessly the RAJA in love agreed to her condition.

They had some good time together and a baby came along. The lady wrapped up the baby in a cloth and offered it to River GANGA. She wanted to remain pure and young forever without the troubles of bringing up a child. The RAJA was stunned, deprived of an heir. Seven children were drowned in the river in this way. The lady kept growing old, but refusing to learn. When the eighth baby was born, the king could keep his promise no more. He stopped the lady from doing what she wanted to do. So he broke his promise of not interfering in her freedom. She offered the baby to her husband and drowned herself in GANGA, the river of purity.

The king brought up his son as a single parent with great devotion and skill. He taught him all the games and skills, arts and sciences known at that time. The boy grew up to be a handsome young prince, an expert in warfare. He was called DEVAVRATA.

Then the king thought it was time to love again. He found a beautiful fisher woman called SATYAVATI. She already had had a son from RISHI PRASHAR. Her son was called VYAS. Later on he became MAHARSHI VEDVYAS, who compiled the VEDAS and the epic MAHABHARATA. She agreed to marry the king on the condition that her own son from him would be the next king. The king refused and returned to his palace in disappointment.

As the days passed, he lost interest in life. One day his son learnt about the cause of his father's trouble. He stood up in the court. In the presence of the GURU and ministers he declared that he renounced his claim to the throne and that he would never marry so that no child may be born to him to lay a claim to the throne. Everyone was shocked in admiration of him and his stunning vow. So they called him BHISHMA, the awesome.

King SHANTANU married SATYAVATI. Two children were born to them. The father and their eldest son died fighting in a battle. The mother got worried about how her line would continue. So she asked BHISHMA to arrange the marriage of her second son VICHITRAVIRYA.

BHISHAMA went to KASHI and kidnapped three daughters of the king, AMBIKA, AMBLIKA, and AMBA. AMBIKA and AMBLIKA agreed to marry the young boy, while the third refused, as she was in love with RAJA SAIVA. BHISHMA took her to this king, who refused to marry her, as another man had abducted her. She accused BHISHMA of ruining her life and wanted him to marry her. He refused because of his oath never to marry. AMBA took to penance and worship of SHIVA. Later she was reborn as woman who some time later became man and was called SHIKHANDI. He was responsible for the death of BHISHMA on the battlefield of KURUKSHETRA.

VICHITRAVIRYA died before he could produce a child. So SATYAVATI asked her eldest son VYAS, born to her before her wedlock, to solve their difficulty by producing children on his sisters in law.

AMBIKA closed her eyes when she met the ugly looking VYAS. She gave birth to a son, named DHRITRASHTRA, who was born blind, though strong. AMBLIKA went pale when she met VYAS. She gave birth to a son, named PANDU, who was born weak and pale, though he became a warrior. Their maidservant who had come along with them was bright and playful when she met VYAS. She gave birth to a son, named VIDHURA, who was born wise and later became an expert on diplomacy and political affairs, an advisor to RAJA DHRITRASHTRA.

DHRITRASHTRA married an AFGHAN princess, GANDHARI, and produced many children called KAURAVAS. PANDU married KUNTI, the sister of KRISHNA'S father. He also married MADRI, as second wife on payment of wealth. PANDU extended the boundaries of his empire but could not father a child.

When KUNTI was growing up she acquired a secret magic by which she could invite any divine power she wanted and have a child from him. To experiment with her power, she invited SURYA DEVA and produced a son. To avoid social embarrassment, she set it afloat on a river. The baby was picked up by DHRITRASHTRA'S charioteer and was named KARNA. He was brought up in the company of KAURAVA princes.

When KUNTI found that her husband was unable to give her a child, she used her secret magic three times and invited YAMA RAJA, VAYU DEVA, and INDRA DEVA. She gave birth to YUDHISHTRA, BHIMA, and ARJUNA. She gave her secret to MADRI, who had twins NAKULA and SAHADEVA, from ASHVANI KUMARS, the medical doctors.

Once upon a time, the children of DHRITRASHTRA and PANDU were playing at ball in a forest near HASTINAPUR, when it fell into a dry well. They tried their best to bring it out but could not. They saw a BRAHMAN nearby and requested him for help.

He was DRONA. He took a reed, sharpened it and shot it like an arrow. It stuck to the ball. Then he took a second reed, sharpened it and shot it like an arrow. It stuck to the tail end of the first reed. He continued this way till he could catch hold of the reed. Then he carefully pulled the reeds and the ball out. The children clapped their hands in admiration and asked him what they could do for him. He asked them to tell their grandfather BHISHAMA that he was DRONA, son of GURU BHARDWAJA.

BHARDWAJA was a well-known guru who had an ASHRAM near River GANGA, where he trained princes in the skills of martial arts. BHISHAMPITAMA was pleased and invited him to the court and requested him to be the teacher of the princes. He set up a GURUKUL, which came to be called GURU DRONACHARYA'S GRAM, now called GURGAON, near DELHI.

DRONA had been brought up along with numerous princes in his father's academy. He married and set up an independent house. A son was born. He was named ASHVATHAMA. When DRONA had to provide for his son's needs, he suddenly became aware of his own poverty. He decided to grow rich with the help of his childhood friends who were princes. One of them was DRAUPADA, who was now the RAJA of the kingdom of PANCHALA. DRONA approached him. The king laughed. How can there be friendship between a king and a beggar, he asked. Friendship is between equals, he said. DRONA felt humiliated and decided to take revenge. He thought he could destroy DRAUPADA with the help of other princes. That is why he had come to the forest where KURU princes were playing. He was now happy that he had an ASHRAM for teaching military sciences to princes. He worked hard.

A student named EKALAVYA the son of the chief of boats men came to him for admission to his school. DRONA looked at his face and saw his intensity and felt a fear that he might outdo his favorite student ARJUNA. So he refused admission to him on the ground that a low caste boy cannot study along with princes, as he was running an exclusive school for princes. It was a refusal based on the difference in status, and the teacher alone decided to admit or not to admit a student.

EKALAVYA was a determined student. He went home and set up an image of DRONACHARYA in his admiration of him. He would carefully observe the princes doing martial exercises from a distance and practice those very skills himself day and night. Close observation and constant practice and dedication took him to great heights.

Once, a dog was barking. EKALAVYA shot seven arrows at great speed into his mouth. When the princes saw the dog they felt admiration for EKALAVYA and asked him who his guru was. He said he had learnt his skills from guru DRONACHARYA. The princes were happy at finding an expert student and took him to their guru.

Now this guru was not a straight man. He had carried his own humiliation for many years, and had fear and anger, hatred, revenge and duplicity in his heart. He asked the new student to give him his fee, which was an unreasonable request because the guru had not put in any effort to teach this student, who had learnt and acquired his skills entirely on his own. When EKALAVYA agreed to pay out of his innocence and simplicity, the teacher asked for his right thumb. It was an immoral request to make, because this guru was depriving a student he had not taught of whatever skills the boy had acquired through self-help. The brave student at once cut off his right thumb and offered it to his guru. It was a wrong thing to do, as he lost his archery skills forever.

DRONA decided to test his students. He placed a dummy bird on top of a tree and asked his students to aim at his head. When they were on the ready, he asked each one of them what they saw. Each one except ARJUNA replied that they saw the teacher, many trees, the bird and their brothers. Only ARJUNA said that he saw nothing but the head of the bird he was going to shoot. He was asked to shoot and he brought the head down. ARJUNA had become the best archer in the country.

Once, DURYODHANA felt so jealous of BHIMA that he mixed some herbs in his food. BHIMA went off into deep sleep after eating the food and DURYODHANA threw him into a lake. BHIMA came back alive with the strength of a thousand elephants.

After their studies were completed, DRONA requested DHRITHRASHTRA that a tournament be organized in which his students could display their skills. This was done. They displayed their skills of wrestling, using swords and maces, shooting arrows, their accuracy and speed, maneuvering chariots while fighting, and riding horses and elephants. ARJUNA turned out to be the best of all. When this was about to be announced, a brilliant young man entered the field and challenged ARJUNA.

The princely titles of ARJUNA were announced and they looked around for somebody to announce this young man's titles, because the rules of the tournaments required that only princes fight with princes. Silence was unbearable. At that time an old man entered the field. Everyone recognized him as ADIRATHA, the retired charioteer of DHRITHRASHTRA. The young man bent down and touched his feet in respect. The old man said that he had found this young man as a baby floating in a basket in the river with this necklace, which he displayed, and that he named him KARNA and brought him up as his son along with the princes. KUNTI recognized the necklace and her son and fainted. The judges refused to allow a commoner to challenge a prince in this friendly tournament. DURYODHANA at once saw his opportunity. He got up and announced that he appointed KARNA the RAJA of ANGA in northeast India. KUNTI felt happy at this, but the judges were not moved.

After the studies were over GURU DRONACHARYA wanted his students to pay him GURU DAKSHINA, the fee due to the guru. They were to capture RAJA DRAUPADA alive and bring him bound to the guru. The princes fought a battle with DRAUPADA and his forces. ARJUNA managed to capture DRAUPADA alive and bring him bound hand and foot to DRONACHARYA, who humiliated the king by taking away half his kingdom north of River GANGA, and returned the second half to DRAUPADA as a gift and charity from GURU DRONACHARYA to his prisoner of war. In this way DRONA satisfied his desire for revenge and soothed the feelings of humiliation inflicted on him by RAJA DRAUPADA, who saw through the play of strong emotions in this game of life. He did penance and produced a son and a daughter. His daughter DRAUPADI later married ARJUNA and brought his strength to RAJA DRUPADA'S side. His son learnt warfare from DRONACHARYA and later used his skills to kill his guru in the war.

According to the customary law, no blind man could become a king. So the younger brother PANDU inherited the kingdom. DHRITRASHTRA got only a maintenance allowance. This sowed the seeds of jealousy and hatred in the elder brother, and his son DURYODHANA kept trying his best to harm PANDAVAS.

PANDU died in a battle soon after. His wife MADRI died on his funeral pyre. The eldest son YUDHISHTRA succeeded to the throne. His cousin DURYODANA was wily and wicked. He was greatly upset. He invited PANDVA brothers to a religious festival at VARANASI, where they were housed in a specially built palace made of combustible materials. After they were comfortably settled, the palace was set to fire that spread all around and lasted for fifteen days. But their virtuous uncle VIDURA, the younger brother of DHRITRASHTRA, had already informed them of the wicked design. So they had employed miners to build a tunnel through which they escaped secretly. DURYODANA and his brothers were happy at the destruction of their cousins.

PANDAVA brothers wore the disguise of BRAHMANS and wandered about in wild forests in search of food. They met a GANDHARVA, who taught ARJUNA the skills of seeing distant objects when they were invisible to the normal eye.

They entered the kingdom of PANCHALA. Its RAJA DRAUPADA had organized the marriage ceremony of his daughter DRAUPADI. The invited princes were required to shoot an arrow through a revolving wheel into the eye of a fish placed above it by looking at its reflection in a tub of water placed on the ground below. No prince succeeded in this contest. So the test was thrown open to all castes.

ARJUNA in the guise of a BRAHMAN got up and shot the arrow into the eye of the fish. The princess garlanded him. They took her home to their hut and said loudly to their mother inside that they had brought beautiful alms. Without waiting to see what it was, the mother shouted back to say that they should share it equally among the five brothers. In those days a mother's word was the law, which could not be disobeyed. So the five brothers married DRAUPADI. Polyandry was a custom in some parts of India.

DRAUPADI'S brother was unhappy at what had happened to his sister. So he had followed the beggars secretly to their hut. He overheard the brothers introducing themselves to DRAUPADI as PANDAVA princes. He invited them to the palace. From there they went to DHRITRASHTRA along with their forces to claim their kingdom. He gave them half of the kingdom, partly out of fear and partly out of his sense of justice. He thought that equal division of inheritance between cousins would be a reasonable solution of their conflict. PANDAVAS were happy but DURYODHANA did not like it. He thought that if you have the power, why be just and give anything to anybody?

PANDVAS extended their kingdom through conquest. They built for themselves a beautiful city, calling it INDRAPRASTHA, now DELHI. They performed an imperial ritual sacrifice called RAJASUYA YAJNA.

MAHARSHI NARADA visited them and decided to instruct them.

He said: We should always spend our wealth ethically without wasting it just as we earn it ethically. We should think of wealth early in the morning and plan to spend little and earn the maximum. We should always control wealth with ethics and pleasure. Our earning and spending should be good and pleasant.

A king should be heroic and communicative, just in making policies keeping in view the strengths and weaknesses of his own as well as of his enemies. He should do his duty of protecting and pleasing his people effectively and be result-oriented.

A king should not tell lies, act unjustly, show anger, be shortsighted, act lazy, delay decisions or accept advice from fools.

He should meet experts regularly, keep secrets, and deal with enemies one by one.

He should improve agriculture, mines, trade, forts, bridges, elephants, and treasury and establish people in uninhabited areas.

He should send his spies to his enemy kings and their crucial officers.

He should take care of the leaders of his defense, and experts in different forms of fighting and weapons, and see that they do not revolt against him. He should look after their families after their death.

He should honor learned and virtuous teachers and see that they teach all that they know, including the arts of fighting.

He should honor medical doctors and grow medicinal herbs and meet all their needs.

RAJASUYA YAJNA required all princes of India to pay their tribute to PANDAVAS, which they did except RAJA JARASANDH of MAGHAD, who refused to pay his tribute and prepared for war.

KRISHNA negotiated with him and it was decided that he would play a wrestling match with BHIMA instead of the two armies fighting, which would result in numerous deaths.

BHIMA killed JARASANDH after wrestling with him for thirteen days. All the princes held captive by JARASANDH were released.

DHARMA required that after conquest a relative of the defeated king be made the new king so that the pride of the people is not hurt. But JARASANDH had occupied the lands and taken the wealth of the kingdoms he had defeated, which was a form of theft. The released kings paid tributes to PANDAVA brothers as a form of thanksgiving.

DURYODANA was invited to the ceremony. When he saw the scene, he was struck with jealousy. He invited RAJA YUDHISHTRA to a game of dice, which the king accepted. In those days gambling was considered to be a royal game. It strengthened virtues like aptitude for taking risks and understanding the opponent and his movements from his appearance. Acquiring great wealth and winning in wars, military or commercial, is always risky, a form of gambling. Wealth and victory depend on chance, gambling or destiny. However all actions including war and gambling had to be done within the limits of righteousness.

DURYODANA never cared about righteousness. He wanted to impose his own will on others, whatever the means. So he asked his crafty uncle RAJA SHAKUNI to play loaded dice on his behalf. He played a false dice and won many games. RAJA YUDHISHTRA kept losing everything he put on stake. Finally he lost even his brothers, himself and their wife DRAUPADI.

DURYODHANA and his brothers started humiliating DRAUPADI. They went to the extent of trying to remove her clothes in public. She asked crucial questions from the elders: Was the dice checked? Was it false and loaded or fair? Did YUDHISHTRA lose himself before putting her on stake? Did he have a right to put her on stake after he had lost himself? The elders remained silent at the injustice being done to her in this game of politics. Their silence was their participation in the act of injustice. If you see injustice and do not act against it, you are yourself committing injustice. Therefore all the elders including BHISHAMA PITAMA turned out to be weak and immoral at a crucial moment. KRISHNA at once intervened and saved her from public shame.

The blind king exiled the PANDAVA princes, their wife and mother to twelve years of stay in a forest, followed by one year to be spent incognito. They lived in different forests and had varied experiences of life. Many sages came to meet them and they narrated numerous stories.

When they were passing through the forest in disguise, RAKSHAS HINDINMA, who lived for his own pleasures, tried to capture them for his food. BHIMA killed him and married his sister HINDIMBI. A son was born to them. They named him GHAṬOTKACCHA. He grew up to be a powerful man who later fought in the MAHABHARAT war and compelled KARNA to use his BRAHMA ASTRA, the missile that never missed its target, on him rather than ARJUNA. It was an act of supreme self-sacrifice for another person, which was highly admired.

They moved farther on and started living in a village called EKA CHAKRA PURA. A RAKSHAS named BAKASURA harassed the people here. He demanded a cartload of food along with a human being every day. BHIMA went to the forest to meet him and killed him.

ARJUNA made a powerful chariot and his GANDHIV bow with a store of arrows. He caught a wild boar and SHIVA rewarded him with PASHUPATA weapons.

He took him to INDRALOKA, where ARJUNA stayed for five years. He learnt music and dance from a heavenly woman who wanted to marry him. He refused her and she cursed that ARJUNA would change his sex and become a woman for a year. ARJUNA became a woman and worked as the music and dance teacher of a princess, when PANDAVAS had to live for a year without being recognized.

RISHI MARKANDEYA narrated to them the story of SAVITRI.

RAJA ASHVAPATI was a master of horses. He had a daughter, princess SAVITRI. When she grew up, her father asked her to choose a husband for herself. She traveled in the company of old and wise courtiers to distant regions in chariots escorted by guards. No prince could attract her. At last she came to a holy hermitage.

RAJA DYUMAT SEN had been defeated in a war. He was deprived of his kingdom and eyesight. He had retired to a forest and built this hermitage. His son SATYAVANA looked after him. SAVITRI fell in love with this dutiful son.

She came back to her father and disclosed to him her feelings. He consulted his guru RISHI NARAD, who said that SATYAVANA would die in twelve months. The king was greatly upset. He tried to dissuade his daughter. But love is blind. She said that a young girl chooses her husband only once in a lifetime. The two were married.

SATYAVANA would go to the forest and pick up fruits and roots and bring them home. The princess would cook the food and the family would eat. On the fateful day after twelve months, the wife accompanied her husband to the forest. He said that he was feeling hot and heavy. She asked him to lie down and place his head in her lap, which he did. Soon he died. The messenger of death came to pick up his soul, but could not go near the body as SAVITRI was enveloped in the intense heat and fire of purity and chastity. He went back to YAMA RAJA, DEVA of death. He came to witness the scene and take away the ATMA.

YAMA said: Daughter, every mortal has to die. So let your husband go.

SAVITRI said: A woman follows the man she loves, come hell or heaven.

YAMA: Women do not follow their husbands beyond death.

SAVITRI: But women do not give up their love.

YAMA: A few do give up their love and a few do not. But take a boon from me. Give up the soul and let it fly away. Do not stick to it, as it gives pain to the departing soul.

SAVITRI: If you are pleased, give back his eyesight and kingdom to my father-in-law.

YAMA agreed to do so and started moving away. But he felt the pull of SAVITRI'S soul tagging along.

YAMA: You are still sticking to this dead man.

SAVITRI: It is not in my power. My soul is stuck to my husband's. It cannot leave him.

YAMA was pleased to see that her love was so deep as to unite at the very root of life, where death no longer exists and does not frighten. She had risen above it.

YAMA gave SATYAVANA back to SAVITRI. Their love is eternal.

BHIMA went across the Mountain GANDHAMADANA to the land of YAKSHAS and fought with them to get the flowers that DRAUPADI wanted. Such was the labor and sacrifice he was willing to make in love of his wife.

One day DURYODHANA wanted to humiliate PANDVAS. He along with SHAKUNI and KARNA went to the forest on the pretext of checking their wealth of cows, but really to see PANDAVAS living in poverty.

On the way they were waylaid by GANDHARVAS, who bound DURYODHANA and his wives in ropes and tried to carry them away.

PANDAVAS came to know of it. YUDHISHTRA asked BHIMA and ARJUNA to help their cousin. But they refused.

YUDHISHTRA said: Divine blessings, royal sovereignty, and a son to carry on the family line are sources of happiness. But helping the enemy gives greater happiness, as we learn to rise above our petty hatreds.

So BHIMA and ARJUNA fought and defeated GANDHARVAS. They brought DURYODHANA and his wives bound hand to foot to their elder brother. He set them free and blessed them. DURYODHANA who had come to humiliate went home humiliated.

Some DANAVAS helped DURYODHANA get over his feelings of humiliation and focus them on revenge. They told him that demonic feelings and attitudes that had entered KARNA would enter BHISHMA and DRONA also and they would just start obeying him in his schemes for destroying his cousins.

KARNA conquered many lands and increased the wealth of DURYODHANA, who kept thinking of how to harm PANDVAS. An opportunity came when DURVASA RISHI visited him. He was known for his hot temper. DURYODHANA showed him great hospitality and requested that the RISHI should visit PANDVAS. He felt that they would not be able to look after DURVASA and his followers. When DURVASA reached PANDVAS, KRISHNA also came there and provided hospitality. The RISHI blessed them and went away. So the clever stratagem of DURYODHANA did not work.

KARNA was the son of SURYA DEVA. He was born with a mail of gold and a pair of earrings, which made him invincible. He used to pray to the sun every day in the morning. If anyone asked him for a gift in charity, he never refused.

INDRA DEVA the father of ARJUNA came to him in the disguise of a BRAHMAN while he was praying. As he started giving charity, INDRA asked him for his mail of gold and earrings.

KARNA knew that only INDRA would ask him for such a gift to protect ARJUNA, but he could not go against his habit of giving in charity. He gave him his mail and earrings and requested that INDRA give him only one arrow that would not miss its aim, as that would be enough, which INDRA did.

After this exchange of gifts KARNA ceased to be invincible.

One day the PANDAVAS got thirsty while roaming around in the wilderness. They could not find water anywhere. YUDHISHTRA sent the youngest brother in search of water. He found a lake. As he was about to drink, he heard a voice asking him not to drink water till he proved himself qualified to drink it. He ignored the warning as absurd and drank the water as much as he liked and fell down unconscious. One by one the brothers suffered the same fate, till YUDHISHTRA came to water.

He heard the voice: Do not consume water till you show yourself qualified to drink it. You must justify your consumption with your wisdom.

YUDHISHTRA looked upwards and saw that it was YAKSHA, the spirit present in trees and plants with their eyes shining out of their sparkling leaves. The spirit was as vast as the lake, as radiant as fire, and as huge as a mountain. YUDHISHTRA agreed to the test to show that he was qualified to consume water.

YAKSHA asked him many questions in reply to which YUDHISHTRA said:

BRAHMA is the final invisible reality that supports the universe. It gives light even to the sun. DEVAS move around the sun. They are the forces of nature. The sun is truth and existence. Righteousness rises like the sun and it sets too. We see men die every day, but do not believe that we too shall die.

To know DEVAS and their reflection VEDAS, contemplating the forces of nature every day with devotion, is to be divine for a BRAHMIN. To know weapons and warfare, to be the best fighter in all situations is to be divine for a KASHTRIYA. Daily penance in pursuit of reality is the best for BRAHMANS. The ritual of conventional action for public welfare is the best for KASHTRIYAS. To find faults in others is the worst for BRAHMANS. Not to protect the weak is the worst for KASHATRIYAS. All die, but to think of death and express this thought in one's actions of daily life is to be human for a BRAHMAN. To fear his own dominating nature and its aggressive flow in actions on others is to be human for a KASHTRIYA.

The secret of DHARMA is not known through words, discussion, disagreement, belief or scriptures. It is buried deep in the dark caves of the heart and mind. It is rooted in the final reality and is discovered through action following great minds.

Breathing is a ritual act of sacrifice and the focused mind is its MANTRA. A song of praise accompanies ritual action, but it should not destroy the sense of wonder.

A fellow traveler is the friend of those who travel abroad and wife is the friend of those who stay at home and doctor is the friend of those who are ill and charity is the best friend of those who are about to die. Fire is the guest of all beings, as it stays inside them. The immortal being which is present in our daily actions is SANATANA DHARMA.

DHARMA lives in being skillful in doing one's duty. Fame lives in charity. Heaven lives in truth. Joy lives in good conduct. Expertise is worthy of thanks. Knowledge of a subject is the best wealth. Health is the best profit. Contentment is the best happiness. Compassion is the best DHARMA. Devotion to nature brings fruits every day. Controlling the mind raises it above suffering. Giving up pride makes one dear to all.

Giving up anger makes one free of sorrow. Giving up sex makes it meaningful. Giving up greed makes one happy. Give tax to the king out of fear of punishment. Give salary to the servant to nourish him for more work. Give prizes to actors and dancers for fame. Give charity to BRAHMANS to strengthen knowledge and spread DHARMA. The world is covered with ignorance. The world does not reveal its reality because of the delusion created by our senses and mind.

YUDHISHTRA gave many more answers to questions put to him. Finally YAKSHA, the spirit present in water birds said: I am DHARMA, the DEVA of justice in the form of a bird. You have a sense of wonder even in the commonness of life. You are wise and you follow SANATANA DHARMA, the eternal truth. You are qualified to consume water to your heart's content. Your brothers have regained awareness through your wisdom.

One day, RAJA JAYADRATHA of SINDH, son in law of DHRITRASHTRA, saw DRAUPADI alone, as PANDVAS had gone out hunting. He kidnapped her in his chariot, but PANDVAS saw him. They gave him a hot chase, captured him alive and brought him to YUDHISHTRA, who punished him with compassion, not death, but a severe warning, as his wife was the only daughter of DHRITRASHTRA and he did not want to punish the father of an only daughter by sentencing her husband to death.

After twelve years had passed in adversity in the forest, PANDAVAS in disguise went to the kingdom of RAJA VIRATA.

YUDHISHTRA became a BRAHMAN advisor to the king. BHIMA became a cook in the royal kitchen. ARJUNA had changed into a woman. He became a music and dance teacher to princess UTTARA. NAKULA became the keeper of king's horses. SAHDEVA had charge of cows. DRAUPADI and KUNTI were appointed servants to the queen. They spent a year in disguise and had numerous experiences.

One day RAJA VIRATA'S brother in law wanted to seduce DRAUPADI. He asked his sister the queen to send her maid to him. She did not like it but obeyed her brother. DRAUPADI sensed what was coming. She informed BHIMA, who went in her place and killed the great brother in law along with his numerous brothers.

DURYODHAN tried his best to find them out, but he could not. His spies reported that PANDAVAS were hiding in the kingdom of VIRAT. So he sent the king of TRIGARTA to capture all the cows in the VIRAT kingdom, as he wanted to see who would come to recover them. This was done. But five unknown soldiers defeated the army and freed the cows. DURYODHANA felt sure that they were PANDAVAS. He ordered his own army to march against VIRAT. A fierce battle took place in which KAURAVA army was made unconscious, and the turbans of all the soldiers except BHISHMA and DRONA were removed and sent to princess UTTARA to make her dolls.

When KAURAVA army regained consciousness, they felt ashamed, as their turbans of respectability had disappeared. DURYODHANA claimed that he had discovered PANDAVAS, but on calculation it was found that the year stipulated for disguise had already passed.

YUDHISHTRA sent a messenger to DHRITRASHTRA and asked for return of his kingdom, as promised. The king refused. That was unjust and dishonest. KRISHNA tried to settle the dispute and reduced their demand to only five villages for five brothers. But DURYODHANA refused to return even an inch of land.

DRAUPADI had told KRISHNA that she wanted revenge for the humiliation inflicted on her when KAURAVA brothers tried to molest her in the royal court and the moral goodness of YUDHISHTRA did not succeed at all.

KRISHNA reminded DURYODHANA that he had poisoned BHIMA and tried to burn the brothers and molest DRAUPADI in court. Such things cannot be forgiven, nor can the right to inheritance be given up. So justice demands a war. KRISHNA warned them of the consequences of war. He informed KUNTI DEVI that war was unavoidable.

KRISHNA knew that KARNA had an invincible arrow that must hit its target. He tried to persuade KARNA to join the PANDVAS because he was their elder brother even though his mother in fear of public scorn had offered him to River GANGA.

KARNA felt sad. He had floated up to the land of CHAMPAS, where the royal charioteer ADIRATHA was leading a retired life. He had picked him up and brought him to HASTINAPUR and educated him with princes. His wife RADHA had given him a mother's love. He had married into the caste of charioteers and had children. He felt overwhelming love and gratitude for his foster parents and wife and children and relatives and caste. How could he declare himself a prince, a brother of PANDVAS, and reject and insult their upbringing, love and care and self-sacrifice? He felt sad that his natural mother had felt compelled to reject him and leave him to die, because she did not want to be called an unwed mother. Why should society be so domineering that it compels a mother to commit an inhuman act? He accepted the truth told him by KRISHNA, but refused to let it altar the course of his life set for him by his natural mother. He said to KRISHNA that he had dreamt of YUDHISHTRA and his brothers dressed in all white sitting in the king's court. So victory was going to be theirs. He was not fighting a war, but they all were sacrificing themselves to celebrate one blind man's ambition.

Next day after KARNA had offered his worship to SURYA DEVA, he turned around to see his old mother waiting for him. She had thought that if KARNA could join his brothers, DURYODHANA would be weakened.

KARNA controlled himself to say that he was the son of ADIRATHA, the charioteer, and what could he do for the noble lady.

The aged mother trembled and said: that is not true. You are my son and of SURYA DEVA. Disclose yourself to your brothers and do not fight against them.

Just then KARNA heard the voice of his father in his heart, saying: Obey your mother, son!

But KARNA could not give up what he thought was right. He said: when it was your duty to look after me, you left me to die. How can you ask for obedience? But I will fight only ARJUNA. So your other sons will be safe. Either ARJUNA or I will die. So your five sons will still live. The old mother embraced her son and thanked him.

On seeing the war preparations, DHRITRASHTRA lost heart. He invited his brother VIDHUR to teach him what to do.

VIDHUR said: The king should know his resources and capability and not annoy the powerful and the wise. YUDHISHTRA is wise, capable and friendly. He knows political economy. He is sharp and intelligent, ahead of all your sons. Why deprive him of his share? Why change him into an enemy? Why create an avoidable war? Give him his due share or his minimum demand and live happy.

We cannot be protected if we are guided by the folly, jealousy and hatred of the weak. We should not look down upon another as weak, but do our duty as right, just as our ancestors did. We should share our wealth with the needy and so increase our enjoyment of life. Nor should we stretch our actions beyond our capability. We should have friends around us who guide us to peace and honor. We must control our senses, greed, injustice and partiality towards sons.

That king is honored who gives up lust and anger and gives wealth to those who are qualified to receive it. He should know different subjects and do his duty quickly, and punish the criminal within limits.

He should remain alert towards enemies. He should first engage in careful thought and be clear about his aims and objectives, profit and loss and the situation. He should not act improperly. He should take only what can be taken and digested and is beneficial. If his pleasure does not benefit and his anger has no effect, he is not fit to be a king. Even if a kingdom is received through ancestors, we can destroy it through injustice and immorality. We should acquire power through good actions and retain it through good actions.

As was the custom in those days, both the sides in conflict sent invitations to all the kings in India, explaining their side of the story and asking them for help in the war. It was considered dishonorable to refuse such an invitation and remain neutral. There is no such thing as neutrality in human affairs. A neutral foreign policy means deception and opportunism, an inability to decide and stand by principles.

Both KAURAVAS and PANDVAS asked for KRISHNA'S help. He offered them a choice. They could choose between his army and him. DURYODHANA chose the army for military strength. ARJUNA chose him for divine wisdom.

RAJA RUKMI came to PANDAVAS and said that he wanted to help them as their protector and destroy KAURAVA army on their behalf. His offer of help was refused. Then he went to KAURAVAS and said that he wanted to help them as their protector and destroy PANDAVA army on their behalf. His offer of help was refused.

DURYODHANA sent SHAKUNI'S son ULUKA to PANDAVAS to provoke them. He said that YUDHISHTRA'S goodness was only pretence and BHIMA was an expert only in cooking and ARJUNA was impotent and time had come to expose their wickedness and hypocrisy. He spoke falsehood all around.

In those days armies followed the rules of fighting that they had agreed upon. They agreed on some fifty kilometers of land proper for use as the battlefield. Different armies put up their camps on it. The armies consisted of elephants, chariots, horses and foot soldiers. Each wing had to follow a discipline and kill their enemy in the same discipline. They had to fight as the sun rose and stop fighting as the sun set. They took the war as a game in which they were to display their skills and courage.

All the kings of India assembled on the wide plains of KURUKSHETRA that included mountains, forests and streams. They established their camps and arranged for the supply of weapons, food and water, medical attention and wood for cremation. They made plans for attack and defense. Different units were given different names, clothes, and flags. People from all VARNAS came to participate in the war.

Both the sides believed they were right. Their leaders met to agree on the rules of moral goodness that must control war to reduce its barbarity. They agreed to meet each other as friends after the day's fight to attend to the wounded and the dead. They agreed not to cheat or deceive and to alert the enemy before the attack. No one was to use weapons while debating an issue. Charioteers were to fight with charioteers, elephant riders with elephant riders, and horse riders with horse riders and foot soldiers with foot soldiers without crossing these limits. They were to fight only those who wanted to fight according to their strength and spirit. If one left fighting he was not to be attacked. They were not to attack a soldier who was visibly frightened or unaware. They were not to attack a soldier who was already fighting with another or who had lost his weapons, shield or mail. They were not to attack servants who carried luggage, brought weapons or water, or played on conches or martial music. Such were the rules they agreed to impose upon themselves. The leaders felt happy at having agreed on such rules, though they broke many of them while fighting.

ARJUNA prayed to DURGA DEVI for success in the war. But he had doubts about war as an instrument of justice. One can win a war without being right. One creates suffering through war. On seeing his relatives as enemies on the battlefield, he lost his urge to fight. He had a conversation with his charioteer SRI KRISHNA on the morning of the day the war began. Later, it became a scripture for Hindus. It is called BHAGVADGITA.

VEDAS say: Satisfy your desires for health, strength and long life, for birth of a son and continuity of the family, for prosperity and power, for victory in battle and enterprise, for peace at home and abroad, for knowledge of natural powers and wisdom in dealing with them, for production of goods and services for exchange through occupations and forms of earning livelihood. Satisfy all these desires through actions of sacrifice done with intense fervor and self-discipline, as a form of charity and giving something valuable to others, creating and projecting relationships and bonds, duties and obligations around you that will ensure your safety, protection and satisfaction.

BHAGVADGITA says: Express your nature in action. It is a divinely given function or duty and you have no choice, though you can choose to ignore your nature and pay a price for it, die before your death. You are born with a disposition to act, feel and think in a certain way. Be aware of it through reflecting on it or meditation on your experience of living while directing your tendencies to action towards the best of your custom or tradition and high ideals. Act out your nature as appropriate to your age and time, whether you are a child and learning, grown up, married and earning a livelihood, supporting other members of society, retired and withdrawing from society and contemplating your life, or old, wise and experienced, guiding others to their benefit and welfare and enjoying it. If you do not act out your nature, you lose your true color, committing a form of suicide. Do this duty of self-expression of your nature while fully absorbed in the skills of doing it, forgetful of your limited desires, expectations and personal benefits. It will show your love for the divine, who will take care of your welfare and meet your genuine needs. Do this duty of self-expression with awareness and reflection, directing it to noble ideals like what brings people together, their interest and welfare, reconciliation, peace and harmony, as all beings are organically related, making one Cosmic Being, a happy family. In this way your actions have a cause, a source, a mother, as well as a purpose, a reason, a meaning, direction and justification.

KRISHNA is called an incarnation of VISHNU, of that which sustains life. As a son, he was full of mischief, separated from his mother by the tyranny of a king. Villagers who nourish humanity with the milk nourished him as a child. He was a great lover playing with older women as a child. Later he married many women and had many children. As a young man he defeated kings. He became a king and nourished his people. He was a wise man whose conversation with his cousin on the battlefield became a scripture for Hindus for millennia. They feel reverence for him and worship him as divine.

KAURAVAS appointed BHISHMA as the chief of their forces. He accepted the appointment on two conditions that while he would destroy the enemy, he would not harm any of the five PANDVA brothers and that KARNA would not be allowed to fight against PANDVA brothers, as he is their brother. So a chief who did not want to destroy the main enemy completely led the large army of KAURAVAS.

PANDVAS appointed DHRISHTHADYUMNA as their chief. They divided their armies into smaller units and created different formations on different occasions with names like crow, eagle, thunderbolt, elephant, crocodile, circle, crescent, and so on. They used over a hundred different weapons, poisons, wild animals, and combustible materials, and numerous strategies, tactics, and formations.

YUDHISHTRA asked ARJUNA to create a field formation of his force that is proper for an unequal army since KAURAVA army was very large and PANDAVA army was much smaller. A large army could spread out over a large area and attack from many sides of their choice, while the smaller army had to be concentrated in its attack and save its resources. ARJUNA prepared a thunderbolt formation with the pointed front led by BHIMA defended by a few warriors on both the sides with the aim of piercing through the weak spot of the enemy in their spread out line. A gradually widening line of warriors fighting on all the sides, protecting the rear as well, followed the pointed front.

The formations were changed according to changing situations, and this change was communicated through martial music for which different types of drums made of hollow woods tightly covered with animal hides were beaten and different sound sequences and signals were produced. Big drums were mounted on elephants while soldiers carried smaller drums. Commanders of forces carried their own conches and flags.

BHIMA attacked KAURAVAS and destroyed the army of brave KALINGAS under RAJA HANUMANTHA.

BHISHMA devastated the PANDVA army and fought fiercely with his young grandson ABHIMANYU. KRISHNA got so angry at this unequal fight that he jumped out of his chariot to kill BHISHMPITAMA but ARJUNA reminded him of the ethics of war and his promise to act only as his charioteer and not to fight. This persistent moral attitude of Indians towards the war led to their many defeats later.

DHRSHTHADYUMNA used a poisonous weapon that made the enemies unconscious, and DRONA used another to bring them back to consciousness.

BHIMA swooned while fighting BHAGADATTA, who was killed by GATOTKACCHA.

DURYODHANA swooned while fighting BHIMA and BHISHMA gave him herbs to heal his wounds quickly.

BHISHMA destroyed numerous soldiers of PANCHALA, CHEDI, KASHI, and KARUSHA armies, injuring ARJUNA, but not killing him, revealing his two minds as he was under compulsion to defend injustice.

BHIMA killed many brothers of DURYODHANA, who ran away in fear. He turned back many of their elephants and they crushed their own soldiers under their feet, a feat that was repeated in many battles later.

DURYODHANA accused DRONACHARYA of not doing his best. DRONA replied that DURYODHANA was not aware of the enemy strength. War required an accurate estimate of the enemy strength and a response based on that estimate.

KARNA did not fight so long as BHISHMA acted as the chief of KAURAVA army. DURYODHANA asked BHISHMA to hand over the leadership of the army to KARNA, but BHISHMA refused and gave him facts and figures about the enemy killed to justify his leadership.

GATOTAKACCHA defeated DURYODHANA, who ran away from the battlefield in fear and so escaped death. BHISHMA was frightened of the magic of GATOTKACCH.

SHIKHANDI fought with ASHVATHAMA, but was defeated and he ran away.

YUDHISHTRA went to BHISHMPITAMA in the evening of the ninth day of war and asked for his blessings.

BHISHMA understood his intention and said: ARJUNA should shoot at me from behind SHIKHANDI, who should appear to be shooting. SHIKHANDI was born a woman who has become a man. I shall not raise my hand against her or him. Such people need compassion and protection.

This was done the next day. ARJUNA shot at BHISHMA from behind SHIKHANDI and BHISHMA did not hit back. He fell from his chariot wounded all over. But he did not give up his life.

Everyone stopped fighting, struck with admiration for grandfather BHISHMA, as he had sacrificed his life for an ideal. His body was pierced with arrows and his head was hanging down. He asked for a pillow. DURYODHANA offered him a soft cushion, which BHISHMA refused. ARJUNA shot an arrow that provided him headrest. He felt thirsty and asked for water. DURYODHANA offered him a flask of water, which he refused. ARJUNA shot an arrow and water came out from under the ground, which he accepted. KARNA asked for his blessings and BHISHMA told him to join his brothers. KARNA refused.

Grandfather BHISHMA lay on his deathbed of arrows. As the oldest of them all, he had the duty to advise them.

He said: The first duty of a king is to protect and please his people. While doing this duty he must respect nature and the learned people. He must work for righteousness, prosperity, and satisfaction of desires and for freedom. If a work suffers obstacles, he should not waste time in regret, but continue his effort. He must base his actions on truth and be virtuous and never give up patience.

If a king is soft, he is not respected. If he is harsh, he is feared. Therefore he should be neither soft nor harsh but combine harshness with softness as the situation demands.

A learned man is expected to be virtuous, but if he acts in a wicked manner, he should be punished. To destroy troublemakers is RAJ DHARMA. Always punish the criminals. If a learned man is to be punished, exile should be the preferred mode of punishment. Physical punishment should be avoided.

A king should think of what is good for the people and not what is good for him just as a village woman eats what is good for the child in her womb and not what pleases her taste.

Never be close to any servant. Punish them immediately if they are disobedient.

A king should be active, planning and preparing for conflict and war with other kings. He should have treatise with them if they are worthy of it, but be prepared for war always.

The state has seven limbs: the king, advisors, friends, treasury, the land with all its resources and people, forts and the defense services. If anyone works against any one of these, he must be punished.

If any one is to be paid, he should be paid on time.

The king should never share his secret thoughts with any one.

If an enemy is strong it is better to have a treatise with him. If he is your equal, continue the fight. If he is weak, capture his fort. If he is stronger and attacking, protect yourself in a fort. If his strength is middling, keep only a part of the defense in the fort and send out the remaining force to capture his supplies. Combine with a friendly king to attack a stronger king. Keep a close watch on neighboring kings and study their strengths and weaknesses. Study the limbs of their state.

Increase your treasury but always be just.

Look after those who cannot look after themselves and serve the aged.

DRONACHARYA was appointed chief of KAURVA army and KARNA joined it.

DURYODHANA asked DRONA to capture YUDHISHTRA alive so that he may play dice with him and send him back to the forest.

DRONA gave a warning to YUDHISHTRA and tried his best to capture him alive, but ARJUNA always came in the way. RAJA SUSHARMA challenged ARJUNA to take him away from YUDHISHTRA. ARJUNA used his weapons, moving so fast that his enemies saw him everywhere, destroying enemy arrows with his weapons.

DRONA killed PANCHALA warriors and VIRATA'S brother.

ARJUNA killed RAJA SUSHARMA and brothers of RAJA SHAKUNI of GANDHAR. SHAKUNI used magic, new weapons, and let loose wild animals that frightened PANDAVAS. ARJUNA used fiery weapons to get rid of them.

KARNA used a fiery weapon against ARJUNA who countered it.

DRISHTHADYUMNA killed RAJA CHANDERVARMA of KAMBHOJA.

DURYODHANA criticized DRONA for not capturing YUDHISHTRA. DRONA asked him to see the strength of the enemy before making childish accusations. He created a wheel formation of his army and ABHIMANYU entered it.

JAYADRATHA of SINDH prevented the entry of warriors from outside the circle. Single-handed ABHIMANYU defeated DUSHASANA and KARNA who ran away. Numerous warriors including DRONA attacked him. This was against the rules they had agreed on. The young boy was killed in this unjust fight.

ARJUNA vowed to kill JAYADRATHA, son in law of DRITRASHTRA. KAURAVAS prevented him from reaching his target. Suddenly they stopped fighting, thinking the sun had set. The sun came out brightly again from behind the thick and dark clouds. ARJUNA quickly killed JAYADRATHA, sending his head flying into the lap of his father meditating in a forest. The RISHI burst into pieces.

Then the armies started fighting without observing any rules, increasing their cruelty. ARJUNA cut off the hands of BHURISHRAVA, who complained of this injustice. Accusations and conflicts spread among the chiefs of the DURYODHANA camp.

YUDHISHTRA started fighting DRONA and KRISHNA warned him. He should fight against warriors, not a teacher.

The battles continued at night with blazing lamps and no holds were barred.

GHATOTKACCHA killed ASHVATHAMA. KARNA got so angry that he used his INDRA weapon against GATOTKACCHA. This weapon always hit its target and could be used only once. He had preserved it for ARJUNA, but in the blindness of his anger he forgot his plans. KRISHNA felt happy at this waste of a powerful weapon against an unworthy target.

DRISHTADYUMNA attacked DRONA, who realized that his end was near. He felt he should give up his weapons and stop being cruel. He asked YUDHISHTRA, who always spoke the truth, if his son ASHVATHAMA was alive. KṚISHNA told YUDHISHTRA to save life by telling a lie. YUDHISHTRA said that ASHVATHAMA is dead. He was an elephant. His second sentence was drowned in martial music. At once his chariot came down to the ground, though it had moved inches above it like a hovercraft, ethically elevated, because of his devotion to truth and wisdom.

DRONA came down from his chariot, sat down on the ground in a YOGIC ASANA and closed his eyes to meditate in the thick of battle. At that time, DRISHTHADYUMNA killed him. On seeing DRONA killed his army ran away.

Then KARNA was appointed chief of the KAURAVA army, but he had already exhausted his best weapon. His charioteer SHALYA was in two minds about the help he was giving to KAURAVA army. So he kept discouraging KARNA, glorifying the strength of PANDAVAS and belittling the force of KAURAVAS. KARNA abused him as a man from MADRA where women had immoral character, and SHALYA took out his sword to kill KARNA who had to defend himself inside his own chariot. DURYODHANA intervened to bring peace between them.

KARNA continued fighting without any hope of victory. He attacked YUDHISHTRA to capture him alive and to take him as a prisoner of war for the pleasure of DURYODHANA. He destroyed the chariot of YUDHISHTRA who was badly injured but escaped into the chariot of SAHADEVA who brought him back into the base camp for medical treatment. KARNA attacked ARJUNA in the same way and the battle of two giants started. In the midst of it ARJUNA heard that the end of YUDHISHTRA had come. So he stopped fighting and asked KRISHNA to take him to the medical camp. When YUDHISHTRA saw him coming he asked him if he had killed KARNA. On learning that he had stopped fighting to enquire about his health, YUDHISHTRA lost his temper and abused ARJUNA for giving up doing his duty for the sake of a courtesy. How could he be so weak and his bow so untrustworthy? Then the unthinkable happened right on the battlefield. ARJUNA started abusing his eldest brother, using foul language, calling him incompetent in playing dice and gambling away his family and bringing pain and suffering to them, and incapable in war, unable to bring it to a successful conclusion. He took out his sword and tried to kill his eldest brother he loved so deeply and held in reverence. KRISHNA pacified them saying that non-violence is always better than finding faults, even if they are truthful. ARJUNA regretted that so much anger and evil was in him. KRISHNA asked him to learn to appreciate himself and remember his good actions.

ARJUNA went back to continue fighting with KARNA, and the two fought like bulls, like elephants, like suns and stars and meteors. Arrows flew and weapons hit but they managed to ward off death. Then KARNA'S chariot got stuck in the mud. He got down for pulling up the wheels, asking ARJUNA to follow the rules of war and not to attack him while he was out of the chariot. KRISHNA asked him where the rules of peace were when they tried to remove the clothes of DRAUPADI in their royal court. Can you be moral here and immoral there? ARJUNA let fly an arrow that cut off KARNA'S head, bringing it down to the ground.

Then drums were beaten and PANDAVA army shook their weapons up in the air and raised shouts of victory while KAURVA army raised their lamentations and mourned at the death of their hero.

Then they made SHALYA the chief commander of what was left of their forces. He continued fighting lifelessly the next day and many warriors killed each other and were carried away by heavenly women crying at their loss. Some were wounded and were carried away for medical attention.

The plains became bloody and remained barren for centuries. DURYODHANA was left all alone. YUDHISHTRA came to console him and found him relaxing in water. He said that he had no weapons left to fight with.

YUDHISHTRA offered him a choice of weapons and promised him that if he could kill any one of the PANDVA brothers he would get back his kingdom.

KRISHNA said that YUDHISHTRA was foolish as he was taking risk without any reason. But because of this promise all of them agreed to a dual between BHIMA and DURYODHANA.

BHIMA was stronger but DURYODHANA was better trained with better skills. ARJUNA asked KRISHNA if BHIMA would win. KRISHNA replied that if BHIMA fought fairly he would not win, but if he fought unfairly he would win. Moral goodness harms worldly success.

BHIMA and DURYODHANA fought for a long time trying all the skills they had learnt from their teachers. Finally BHIMA hit

DURYODHANA below the belt with his mace and DURYODHANA fell flat with a shriek that took his soul away. The earth trembled and the trees shook and the winds blew wildly.

Did PANDAVAS win? What was proved on the battlefield? Who won? Who lost?

GANDHARI mourned. DRISHTHARASHTRA performed the funeral rites for the dead. YUDHISHTRA went to pay his respects to him. The embrace of YUDHISHTRA aroused his pent up anger, jealousy, hatred and enmity. BHIMA moved forward to embrace him, but KRISHNA stopped him. He placed a statue before him. The blind anger crushed the statue in his embrace. He felt relief and expressed his regret at having killed BHIMA. As he learnt the truth, he felt foolish.

RAJA YUDHISHTRA remained a king for thirty-six years after the war. But he had lost his large family. Then he learnt that KRISHNA had died. ARJUNA went to DWARKA to find the truth and came back to confirm the news. KRISHNA and YADVAS were dead. They all were overcome with sorrow and decided that it was time to die. In those days, when people grew old and tired, they decided to quit life. They had the right to do so. They would retire to the HIMALAYAS and keep going on and on till they fell down dead.

They made the grandson of ARJUNA, PARIKSHAT the next RAJA. They gave him the necessary instructions and advisors, and started on their final journey to the HIMALAYAS. One by one they fell. They would stop and cry for the dead one, but keep going onwards. Only YUDHISHTRA and his faithful dog were left alive when they reached MOUNT MERU, the gate to heaven.

A voice said: DHARMRAJA YUDHISHTRA can enter heaven alive with his body, but his dog cannot.

RAJA YUDHISHTRA sat down on the ground refusing to move without his faithful dog. How could he leave behind anyone who was devoted to him?

There was a big laughter, and a voice said: Who is man and who is dog? Sameness is all.

Both of them entered heaven. It turned out that faithfulness and devotion present in the dog was DHARMA.

Chapter VIII

Bhagvad Gita

Karma Yoga

Chapter One: Arjuna's Yoga of Suffering and Despair

ARJUNA SAID: We are at war, in a state of conflict. I do not know what to do, as I see that my opponents are related to me, not strangers, even though they have committed crimes. I belong to them they belong to me, and so how can I kill them?

When everyone is related to everyone else, like the limbs of an organic being, how can we kill? Is our just cause higher than our unbreakable relationships?

Violence is a sin. What good is there in destruction?

My opponents see no evil in the destruction of families and communities, no sin in deception and treachery. So they want to fight. But we see evil in destruction and suffering of families and their traditions. How can we sustain society and keep tradition alive, if we destroy families and their traditions?

When families and communities are destroyed, ancient traditions and customs perish, their ancestors and ideals are degraded, women are raped, lawlessness, exploitation and corruption follows, social order is disturbed and torn apart. Imagine the effects of war. The effect is hell for the defeated and hell for the victors. Those who defeat and create hell for others live in hell themselves, because we create what we are. The victors are degraded and debased by violence, killing and destruction, by telling lies to others and themselves, by deception and treachery, though they may not know it.

Only lack of understanding of others leads to our killing them. It would be better not to seek victory and empire.

I would rather beg than seek power based on violence. For the sake of our power and pleasure, why should we fight and produce pain, suffering and sin? Why should we base our power on violence?

Chapter Two: Sankhya Yoga

KRISHNA SAID: Do not be a coward full of fear while facing conflict. Do not be faint hearted, ignoble and despondent. Arise and fight. Do your duty, as fighting is necessary when other means of resolving conflict fail.

ARJUNA SAID: They are my elders, my teachers and my relatives. How can I kill them who have nourished me? The people I have to fight against are related to me. How can I fight?

What is the point of conflict and war? Why should our power and pleasures be soaked in blood? Which is better: we kill them or they kill us? If we kill them, how will we be good, better than them? How will our life be worthwhile?

I feel compassion and do not know my duty. Teach me what is right and free me of sin and sorrow. I do not know what to do in this hour of crisis and conflict.

KRISHNA SAID: The wise do not grieve for the dead or for the living. So why grieve for them? Why grieve for any one? There never was a time when I did not exist or you did not exist or they did not exist. Nor shall there be time in the future when we all shall cease to be. We are truly our eternal selves. How can we kill the eternal?

Just as the individual passes through childhood, youth and old age, but remains essentially the same, so our true self passes into another body. Are we not the same as adults that we were as children though our physical appearance has changed? An enlightened person, who has experience of the eternal self in his body, is not deluded by changes of form, by birth, decay or death, and so he does not grieve.

When the senses come in contact with their objects, feelings of heat and cold, pleasure and pain arise. They do not last long. Endure them. Such endurance is training for permanence. Otherwise, how are you worthy of the immortal self?

The unreal cannot become real. The real can never cease to be real. The invisible that pervades you and the universe is real and cannot be destroyed. Nothing can cause its destruction because it is eternal. It is incomprehensible, wonderful! Only the bodies that this eternal self takes on come to an end. You do not come to an end. Therefore, fight without fear, as only the body and its mind comes to an end, and you are not your body and its sensuous mind. You are the eternal self that pervades the body and mind and the universe. To think that it kills or is killed is ignorance of the true self. It neither kills, nor is killed. It is never born. It never dies. After taking on a body, it does not cease to be. Unborn, eternal, abiding, and primeval, it is not killed when the body is killed. Therefore, whom will you kill? How will you kill? Weapons do not cut it, nor fire burns it. Water does not wet it, nor wind dries it. It is stable, immovable, unchanging, invisible, and inconceivable. When you know it thus and directly experience its existence, you cannot grieve. This embodied being casts off worn out bodies and enters into new ones, like we change clothes. This is so of all embodied beings. Therefore you cannot grieve for anyone. The wise do not grieve. They observe.

If you think that you are only your body with its mind, that you are born and you die, even then it is not right of you to grieve, because death is certain for the born and birth is certain for the dead. There is only a cycle of energy. It is divine power transforming itself. It is fire burning. Therefore, you should not grieve for what must happen. There is no choice.

What is there to grieve for, when your beginning and end are unknown and only your middle is known?

Some people think of the true self in wonder; some speak and hear of it in wonder; but even after hearing of it, they do not know it.

If you think only of your duty, you cannot waver. The duty of a warrior is to fight. For him, there is no greater good than a righteous war. He is happy when a war comes on its own, as it opens the gate to honor and heaven.

If you do not fight this righteous war, you will be turning away from your duty and honor. You will be incurring sin. Then, people will speak ill of you for all times to come. Dishonor is worse than death for those accustomed to honor. They will think you have fled from battle in fear. They will make fun of you. Your enemies will slander you, speaking words that should not be uttered. What could be more painful than that?

If you are killed, you will go to heaven. If you are victorious, you will enjoy the earth. In either case you will benefit. Therefore, get up and fight.

If you have the same attitude to victory and defeat, gain and loss, pleasure and pain, or if you are even-minded, you do not incur any sin, undergo any suffering. This is the true self. This experience will make you a yogi of steady mind, established in wisdom, undisturbed, the same in all circumstances. Experience this reality and be free of the effects of your actions. When this YOGA is practiced, its effect is never lost. It protects one from the great fear of death and evil does not come.

If one is firm in the practice of YOGA, the mind becomes concentrated and one pointed, focused entirely on whatever is being done, absorbed in doing the sequence of actions at hand. To be single minded is YOGA. Otherwise, the mind branches off in many directions that are endless. One gets many minds. Unwise people have unending desires and many minds.

Some say that there are only flowery words and rituals in the VEDAS. People follow them for attaining heavenly pleasures and powers. These people are unable to develop the resolute will of a single, concentrated mind.

VEDAS concern knowledge of nature and its three constituents. These three are qualities like truth and reality, action and energy, limitations and inertia. You must rise above nature. Free yourself of its constituents and discrete pairs of opposites, like pleasure and pain, which emerge from contact of the senses with nature.

If you do not have your body and its senses, where are pleasure and pain, and all that you sense? They are creations of your senses. They do not exist in nature. You can rise above them. Abide in pure reality, the essential self that pervades your body and mind and the universe, and all that you sense. Then you need only little to journey through the body in health. You do not need many things and protect accumulations.

What is the use of scriptures for a person who knows reality? What is the use of scriptures for a person who does not know reality? If you know reality, what you say becomes a scripture. Be your own scripture, self-enlightened. If you do not know reality, your practical action is needed to acquire this knowledge. Therefore learn YOGA, the practical action to experience this reality, beyond the senses. Be identified with it.

You have the right only to work, not to its fruit. Fruits depend on many things other than your present action, like the past actions done by you and others, the available methods and materials, your knowledge and skills and expectations of all concerned. Fruits of your action are not entirely in your power. Therefore expectation of rewards brings misery.

View success and failure with an even mind, keeping the mind undisturbed in all conditions of life. Evenness of mind is YOGA. Action done with evenness of mind is superior to action done with expectation of results. A man with an even mind discards good and evil here and now. He concentrates on acquiring the skills of doing actions alone. Skillful action is YOGA. Then you are so absorbed in doing action skillfully to the best of your ability that you forget yourself and the consequences of your action. Only the action remains.

You should not renounce action because inaction is impossible. Do not stop working. Do your duty skillfully without expectation of any reward. Concentration on the skills of action creates a mind that is beyond suffering. It forgets the demands of the body and its mind. This mind becomes free of the bondage to nature, as you rise above nature. That is a divine experience.

When you know the true self, you pass beyond the delusion created by the body and its senses and mind. You feel disgust at what you hear and what you have heard from others that is unrelated to experience. When you understand all this clearly, with a single mind, you are enlightened with a vision of the true self.

ARJUNA SAID: What indicates that a man is enlightened in the sense that he knows his true self?

KRISHṄA SAID: An enlightened man is free of desire, fear and anger, the three gates of hell. He is satisfied with himself, in himself. He is not disturbed in pain, nor has he any longing for pleasures. He has no love for any side. He does not judge. When he finds good or evil, he neither rejoices nor hates. He is able to withdraw his senses from their objects. If his senses overpower him sometimes, he strives to recover his even mind. Even his relish for sensuous objects disappears when he develops a clearer vision of his self. While controlling his senses, he contemplates the self

Contemplation of the sensuous objects creates attachment to them. It produces desire for them. Desire creates delusion and its frustration creates anger. These produce loss of memory, destroying discrimination, which ends in a fall from spiritual growth.

But he who is free of love and hate, he loses suffering. He attains wisdom and grace. He is self-disciplined and self-controlled. He does the duty that emerges from his nature efficiently like an expert doing his duty for which he is created. His nature is the cause of his actions, as he expresses it. He has no choice. His deep devotion to the ideal he chooses is the purpose that shapes his nature. That is his self-discipline and spiritual growth towards the idol he has chosen as it emerges from his nature.

There is no peace, happiness and wisdom for him who has no integrity in his mind, speech and actions and who does not contemplate his true self. When the mind follows and the senses experience their objects, the understanding becomes rudderless, without any direction. One mind becomes many minds. But when the mind is self-directed and restrained and the senses controlled, the mind becomes one and wisdom becomes firm.

One who is disciplined is awake to what is ignorance for all beings, awake to YOGA. He is asleep to what is wakefulness and knowledge for all beings, like worldly objects.

He whose desires have ended attains peace, as he is entirely absorbed in cultivating his divinely given nature towards his chosen DEVA. He has no longing, no sense of I and mine. This is the

BRAHMA state of mind. There is no delusion in it. Then one attains and experiences immortality.

Chapter Three: Karma Yoga

ARJUNA SAID: If wisdom is better than action, why do you advise me to act?

KRISHNA SAID: There is the path of knowledge for those who follow reason. There is the path of action for those who act to reach the truth. Your practice, your actions that make your path in life, depend on who you are, what your nature and training and circumstances are.

No one experiences freedom from action by not doing work. No one succeeds by renouncing work. No one can rest even for a moment without doing work. Nature forces one to act, even when one does not want to act.

He who dwells on sensuous pleasures even after controlling his organs of action is a hypocrite. He lives in delusion. He who is detached, who does his duty while keeping his senses subdued in his mind, he is excellent. If you renounce action, you cannot even sustain your body. Therefore, do your duty, your obligatory actions emerging from your nature. Fighting this war is your obligatory action, as you were born and brought up to be a warrior.

Action is superior to non-action and more in keeping with nature. This world is bound in a network of actions when action is not done as YAJNA. Do action as a sacrifice of your nature to the subtle forces that constitute the universe. Do action as an offering of your devotion to the universe and in it to the only One, without a second. Do all your actions for the Supreme Being. When you act with detachment, then your action is an offering of your limited nature to the universal That One. Then you are free of action as you do actions that must be done. You have no choice. Do all your actions as an expression of your nature, as acts of charity. Do not act for mere sale and purchase, for your own benefit and the loss of others.

In the beginning, the lord of beings did YAJNA. He sacrificed his being to become the universe, including man. He said: By this you shall prosper. This universe is the cow that shall satisfy your needs. By this, you shall support DEVAS, the powers that constitute the universe. And these powers shall support you. Thus nourishing one another, making a wheel, you may obtain the highest good. These powers shall satisfy your needs. But if you do not offer them your actions, you are a thief, breaking the cycle of energy. He who eats what is left after he has paid his debt to his creators, he is a good man. But he who cooks only for himself, he is sinful.

Action produces the duty of discharging your debts to your creators. They have made you and your actions possible. They give you rain and food, earth and body and mind.

Your action is produced by your body and mind, which is produced by the imperishable. The all-pervading being is constantly sacrificing itself to project this changing world. He who does not follow the wheel, this cycle of energy set in motion, lives in sin. Satisfying his senses, he lives a meaningless life, in vain. But he who dedicates himself to the highest self makes himself sacred through sacrifice of his limited body and mind, heart and will, action and ego. He rejoices in his dedication to the highest self. He has nothing more to do that attaches him to his narrow world. He has nothing to gain by work done or not done, no aim to achieve and depend on. He has found freedom in the universal self, his own essential nature. Therefore, without attachment to your narrow world, do the work that ought to be done. Do it skillfully with undivided attention and so attain the highest.

Take an example from history. It is through royal work and wise action that RAJA JANAKA attained perfection. Combine the divinely given duty emerging from your nature with the spiritual wisdom of a high ideal. Do your duty for what brings people together, binds and benefits them, without any selfish motive for personal benefit, and so have a purpose, a direction, and guidance for starving the evil in you and nourishing the good in you.

People do what a great man does. They follow the standard he sets. So take care of what you do. Be an example, a model for them.

There is no work that I have to do in the three worlds. There is nothing that I have to achieve. Yet I am constantly active. If I do not act, men will follow me and destroy themselves. In that case I would be causing chaos. Do not create disorder. Search for order and sustain it and so nourish the world of divine powers, men and animals, plants and mother earth.

The ignorant is attached to his work. The learned does his duty without attachment or expectation of personal benefits. In this way you reduce suffering and grief and work for the welfare of the world. The learned should not confuse the ignorant. He should act with devotion and detachment to inspire others to work in the same way. He knows that constituents of nature work on other constituents of nature in what is called action. Therefore, he is not attached.

Nature works constantly but the ignorant thinks that it is he who is doing the work. He is attached to his work. Nature deludes the ignorant. He who knows the whole truth should not upset the ignorant man who does not know the whole truth.

Focus your mind on ATMA. It is the self that pervades you and the universe. Do all your actions for it. Be free of selfishness and desire and fight skillfully without excitement. Skillful action is YOGA. Be absorbed only in doing your duty efficiently.

They who receive this teaching with trust and practice it constantly become free of desire and action. Otherwise they remain ignorant and lost. Even the learned man acts according to his nature, as all beings do. Your nature is the divine mother of your actions and duty. You have no choice. What can repression of the senses do, since each sense loves or hates its own objects? No one should be guided by the senses. They are the enemies. Instead, one should guide them with the divine wealth of moral values and noble purpose.

The duty that emerges from our own nature even if it is not done well is better than the duty that emerges from some other nature, though it is done well. Death while doing our own duty is better than doing the duty of another nature, which is our death anyway, since it is rejection of our own true nature.

ARJUNA SAID: What compels man to commit sin against his own will and not act according to his own true nature?

KRISHNA SAID: It is desire and its frustration, anger, born of energy, which impels one to sin. Know it to be an enemy. This world is enveloped by desire, which cannot be satisfied. Its instruments are the senses, the mind, and the intellect. Desire empowers the embodied self as well as hides it. Desire controls the intellect, which controls the mind, which controls the senses, which act in the world. Control the energy of your desire, working through its instruments. Take the help of this KARMA YOGA so that you may know your true self.

Chapter Four: Gyana Yoga

KRISHNA SAID: I first taught this immortal KARMA YOGA to the sun. He taught it to man. He taught it to the solar race that saw that life depends on the sun. It was then handed down through a succession of royal sages and their disciples who combined wisdom with power. After a lapse of time, I am now declaring it to you, as you are my devotee and friend full of love for me.

ARJUNA SAID: You were born later than the sun. How could you teach him?

KRISHNA SAID: I have been born many times and so have you. I know all my previous births, but you don't know yours. I am the unchanging, governing presence in all beings. In that sense, I am never born. Yet my free will masters nature when I resolve to take birth and form.

Whenever DHARMA declines and unrighteousness flourishes, I take birth. I take birth from age to age to protect the good, to destroy the wicked, and to establish DHARMA.

He who experiences my divine nature is not born again. He is identified with the immortal, seeing birth and death as a change of forms. He comes to me after the death of his body and mind.

Many attain my state through freedom from desire, fear and anger. They are absorbed with fervor and knowledge in meditation on my teaching. They do their duties that emerge from their nature, leading it to high ideals. Whatever the way they adopt, in the same way I meet them. They experience me in many ways.

They who do rituals desire the results of their rituals. They get them. Success comes quickly in the world of men, as actions produce consequences. The world of such men has four colors, if their actions emerge from their natures. These are colors of the mind, the arms, the belly, and the feet, acting in harmony with each other for the welfare of all and not for their separate welfare, as it will destroy them.

Though I am their creator, I am unchanging and not the agent of their actions. Action does not attach me to actions, as I do not desire its results.

If a person acts without expectation of results, he is not attached to those results. Our ancestors acted in this way in search of freedom. You too act in the same way. Follow your tradition, your ancestors. Learn to do action that brings freedom from evil.

What is action? What is non-action? Action is a mystery. There is something in action that ought to be learnt, something that changes form and something that is not action at all.

He is a wise man who sees non-action in action. He does action as duty skillfully with full attention. He is detached and does not expect personal benefits. He sees action in non-action, removing ignorance that hides his self. He stays in detachment, without desire and expectations. He carries out all actions that he ought to do without any false identity with the body, mind and ego and without dependence on anyone. Therefore he does not act in a sense, even though he engages in action all the time. Free of desire, with intellect and mind controlled, he gives up his feelings of possession. He does work with his body and mind skillfully, aware of the action alone. Thus he is engaged in sacrifice of himself to the divine order and presence in the universe, not subject to evil. He has found freedom from evil. He is content with what chance may bring. He rises above opposites like pleasure and pain. He is free of ill will. He is even minded in success and failure. So he is not bound to results of action, though he engages in action as sacrifice all the time.

One who is not attached to the body and its mind and objective world, knowing that he is ATMA, and whose action is only sacrifice of his nature into action leading to his chosen great ideal, his action becomes non-action. Whatever he offers in whatever action through whatever means for whatever objective in whatever manner, he is aware of BRAHMA, the organic being, the cosmic order that becomes the universe, remaining detached and present in it. He reaches that being, that order of reality.

Some YOGIS offer sacrifices to the limited forces that constitute the universe, through their worship of this or that power.

Some offer sacrifice to the formless BRAHMA by doing actions as their offering to him.

Doing NAMASHKAR to the formless being present in the person you meet is a sacrifice of your ego, your sense of your self-importance.

Some sacrifice their senses in the fire of restraint. Others sacrifice material objects along with the functioning of their senses towards those objects into the fire that burns upwards. Some may give up an object and their attachment to it for some time. Some offer their breathing, their life, into the fire of restraint. They regulate it in their mind. They search for the truth of their self. They fix their gaze between their eyebrows, commanding all their energies to see a vision of their self clearly. Many do not know what their self is.

Some practice austerities and YOGA through self-control and firm resolve. Some study scriptures and their self to acquire knowledge of their true self. Some restrict their diet and equalize their breathing. They sacrifice the inward breath into the outward breath, or the outward into the inward breath. They see only this cycle of breathing and nothing else, losing consciousness of time and space and their anxieties. Some reduce their breath slowly to the minimum or stop it altogether. They all know the meaning of sacrifice and its different forms and techniques. Subsisting on what remains after their sacrifice, they work to reach the eternal presence and peace.

Even this world is not for him who does no sacrifice, as he does not know how to live. Then what to say about the other worlds that are present here?

Thus are many forms of sacrifice laid down for reaching the innermost reality of the universe. This reality is the same as the innermost reality of the individual. Experiencing this reality, you shall be free.

The sacrifice of your nature into action with self-awareness is higher than the sacrifice of material objects. Actions and objects are composed of knowledge. You learn to experience this with the help of the wise, who have experienced this knowledge. Serve them through following them and questioning them. Ask for elucidation and simpler techniques that can be followed in the situation in which you live. Practicing what they say is what worship means. This constitutes the path, your actions in life.

When you learn this, you will see all beings without exception first in your own ATMA and then in ATMA of the universe, which is BRAHMA. You will cxpand your limited individual self into the unlimited, universal self. With this knowledge you will overcome your sins even if you have committed them. This is the fire of knowledge that burns up all actions.

Nothing purifies as much as knowledge. You will find this knowledge on your own through experience in due time when you become perfect in KARMA YOGA, as it leads to knowledge.

One who has humility and faith and who intently masters the senses attains this knowledge and supreme peace. If one is without faith and full of doubts, one does not get this knowledge and happiness in this world or the next. Actions do not bind him or attach him to the world, who has renounced them in this way. His doubts are resolved through this knowledge. He has a steady mind. Therefore destroy the doubt in your heart, based on ignorance of your true self. Practice this YOGA and fight. Do your duty.

Chapter V: Karma Sanyasa Yoga

ARJUNA SAID: You praise action and also its renunciation. Which path is better, leading to the ultimate good?

KRISHNA SAID: Both action and its renunciation lead to excellence. Action is better than renunciation.

One who neither hates nor desires, and is beyond the pairs of opposites like pleasure and pain, is the one who has renounced action. He is free of attachment to the body and mind and the objects of its senses of perception and organs of action.

The ignorant speak of the pursuit of knowledge as different from doing action, but they who know do not speak in this way. He who is firmly established in either path attains the results of both.

The followers of YOGA do actions to experience the unity that underlies all this diversity that they experience. They reach that unity, which is also reached by the followers of SANKHYA who reason, calculate and think of reality and removal of suffering.

He is wise who experiences the result of both. But the renunciation of action is difficult without the help of YOGA, as it is through absorbing action that we reach non-action.

One who practices meditation with the silence of mind as through YOGA techniques sees his limited individual self first. Then he reaches the self of all beings soon, seeing himself in others and others in himself. He finds that the two are the same. Individual experience is not particularly individual alone. This is experience of their identity.

He who follows YOGA by restraining his senses, controlling his mind, becoming pure in the sense of being detached from the non-self, and seeing his own individual self as the self of all beings, even when he is engaged in action, he is free of his limited individuality. He who knows this truth of freedom knows that he does not act at all, even though he does all actions, as they work out through him. It is only the senses that are acting on their objects, not he.

A YOGI does all actions with his body and mind, intellect and the senses. He does not renounce, denounce or repress them. Only he sees them emerging from the final reality, not his own limited will. So he cannot have any attachment to them. In this way he becomes pure, detached from the non-self. He sees only tendencies inherent in his body and mind doing their work as he tries to direct them in his devotion to a noble purpose. He expects no personal benefits from his actions, and so he attains lasting peace. He mentally resigns all his actions as belonging to the body and mind. He becomes self-controlled, living in happiness. He neither himself acts nor causes the body to act. He only sees the body and mind acting on their own, as he remains devoted to his chosen deity. He does not act, or unite actions with their results in the world of embodied selves. He only sees actions already united independently of him as cause and effect, ends and means, as expected and unexpected, intended and unintended consequences.

This knowledge of relationships of actions is covered by ignorance, which deludes all creatures. When this ignorance is removed through knowledge of the individual self, it enlightens like the sun that removes darkness.

They whose intellects pursue the self, whose minds think about it, who undergo discipline for it, and who hold it as their highest object to be experienced, their impurities, attachments to the non-self are removed and they are reborn into their second birth. They deal in the same way with one who is learned or humble, a cow, an elephant, a dog or a dog-eater. They conquer the world when they conquer their minds, experiencing the sameness of all.

When the self is not colored by its individual urges and demands, by its nature, it is seen to be the same in all beings. Then one abides in BRAHMA, the final expanding and creative order. When one lives in this state untouched by the consciousness of the body and mind, one does not rejoice at the pleasurable or grieve at the painful. He finds happiness in the self and so lives in bliss that does not lead to sorrow.

Pleasures that come from contact of the senses with their objects lead to sorrow as they begin and end. The wise do not rejoice in them.

He who can withstand the impulse of desire and anger is a YOGI. His joy, his light is within, his self. Being free of the pairs of opposites, like pleasure and pain, mine and yours, he is devoted to the welfare of all beings without expectations of personal benefits. He dedicates his actions to the supreme lord present in the world. Becoming a friend of every being, he attains peace.

Chapter Six: Dhyana Yoga

KRISHNA SAID: A YOGI does actions that ought to be done without seeking any personal benefits. He is not the one who lives in a forest, isolated from society, burning no sacred fires, doing no rituals and actions that lead to results.

Renunciation happens when identification of the self with the body and mind ceases, when actions are done skillfully without love or hatred or expectations of personal benefits.

One reaches the height of YOGA through actions. Then one has freedom from the body, the senses and the mind, freedom from rituals and actions that lead to results while he continues to do them. One sees the self and peace.

Rise higher through your mind. Do not sink lower than what you are in the present. Your mind is the friend of your self. Your mind is the enemy of your self.

Your mind is your friend when it expresses your nature as you direct it in your devotion to noble ideals. Otherwise your mind is your enemy. If your mind expresses your nature and you are devoted to the great ideal of bringing people together, working for their welfare, it is at peace and your higher self is well secured in heat and cold, in pleasure and pain, in honor and dishonor.

If a YOGI is content, well established in his knowledge of his self and its difference from nature, if his senses are controlled and rightly directed, if he is not tempted by the non-self, so that he loses the desire for possessing gold and earth, he is integrated.

He regards all – friends, foes and neutrals, the good, the evil and the indifferent, relatives and the unrelated– as his own self.

He retires to a place, where he is alone. He is in control of his thoughts and mind, desires and the sense of possession. He is alone in his mind even while living in society. He is established in himself, in a clean spot, on a firm seat, neither too high nor too low, covered with cloth on an animal skin spread on sacred grass.

He practices YOGA, visualizing his limited individual self and the unlimited universal self. He holds his trunk, neck and head straight, motionless and steady. He gazes at any object, like the tip of his nose, where the subtle channels of his energy pass out into the vast world, and inter-change between the visible and the invisible happens, and he stops seeing any directions, space or time, stops remembering the past or visualizing the future. He is serene and fearless, firm and focused on the path, the sequence of actions that lead to his experiencing the eternal presence. So he attains peace.

YOGA is not for him who eats too much or too little, sleeps too much or too little.

A YOGI is joined to his vision of the self, while sleeping, waking, working, eating food or playing. His mind is subdued by this vision of his self, at peace, free of evil and not yearning for objects of desires. He sees his self, outside the range of the senses, as the source of joy. He never leaves his vision even in sorrow, as there is nothing beyond it.

He is delivered from suffering and his tendencies to action. His mind is free, never depressed. When the mind wanders, he subdues it only with his vision of the self.

He is identified with the universal self. He sees sameness everywhere. Do you think your suffering is yours alone? Many others have gone through it. He sees his self in all beings and all beings in his self. He sees the universal in the individual and the individual in the universal self. He is fixed in oneness. In whatever way he lives, he worships the universal self that pervades all beings. For him, the true self of the individual is universal and an individual's pleasure or pain is the universal pleasure or pain. This YOGA of sameness of all is the highest.

ARJUNA SAID: Since the mind is fickle, impetuous, powerful and stubborn, its restraint is difficult. Therefore this YOGA of sameness cannot be steady.

KRISHNA SAID: The mind is fickle and hard to subdue. But through practice and renunciation, it is brought under control. Without controlling the mind one cannot be a YOGI. Therefore practice the right means to restrain it.

ARJUNA SAID: If a person striving hard in good faith on the path of YOGA does not achieve perfection, what happens in that case?

KRISHNA SAID: Neither in this world nor in the next is there destruction for him. No one who does what is good ever comes to an evil end.

He who has fallen away from YOGA is born again in the house of the pure and the prosperous after having lived long in the world of those who do good actions.

Or he is born in a family of wise YOGIS, though that is rare. There he regains the disposition of mind he had in his earlier birth, from where he begins his further practice for spiritual evolution. He is carried forward even against his will. Though he is a seeker, he transcends nature.

The YOGI strives through many lives. Cleansed of all imperfections, he reaches the supreme state. He is higher than those who practice rituals and austerities and acquire learning. Therefore become a YOGI, worshipping what pervades the universe as your own innermost self.

Chapter Seven: Gyana Vigyana Yoga

KRISHNA SAID: Practice YOGA with your mind fixed on me as your support. I shall tell you how to do it. Learn this knowledge along with the method of experiencing it. After this there is nothing more to be known here.

Very few strive for perfection. Of these, very few know me. Of these, very few experience my reality.

Earth, water, fire, air, space, mind, intellect, and ego – these constitute my lower nature. My higher nature is the principle of life that sustains the universe. These two natures are the source of birth of all creatures. Therefore I am the birth and death of the universe. There is nothing higher than me. All that you experience is strung on me like gems on a thread.

I am the taste of waters, the light in the sun and the moon.

I am the sacred vibration AUM that initiates expression of the universe in all the VEDAS.

I am the manhood of men, the smell of earth and the brilliance of fire.

I am the life of all beings, their primeval seed.

I am the austerity of ascetics, the intelligence of the discerning, the brilliance of the brilliant.

I am the strength of the strong, without desire or passion.

I am the desire not forbidden by DHARMA.

The constituents of nature arise from me alone. I am not fully in them. They are fully in me.

The world is deluded by the elements that constitute nature. I am the one beyond the elements and energy of nature.

I am the one that does not change.

Nature is my power and hard to overcome. But those who take refuge in me pass beyond it. The evildoers, the demons, the foolish, the lowest of men, those who are deluded by nature, they do not take refuge in me.

Four types of doers of good deeds worship me. They are the distressed, the seekers of wealth and of knowledge and those who have known me.

I am dear to the man of knowledge and he is dear to me because he is devoted to the only One. After many lives the man of knowledge finds refuge in me when he experiences that all is expression of the same supreme self.

Men devoted to the world are controlled by their nature and its numerous desires and so they follow various disciplines. In this way they worship different DEVAS. Whatever the form of devotion a worshipper adopts with faith, I come to him in that very form and grant him the object of his sincere desire for which he struggles.

Men of limited understanding gain limited fruits and go to the DEVAS they worship. My devotees come to me.

Not knowing my unchanging nature, the ignorant think of me as the one who is born. They are deluded. I know all beings, past, present and future. But they do not know me.

The delusion of oppositions springs from desire and hate. It begins right from birth. But those whose sins have ended through good deeds are freed of this delusion. They worship me steadfastly. Striving for deliverance from old age, suffering and death, they seek to know the self of all as well as the nature of action that leads to birth. They seek to know the lower nature that is material and objective, and the higher nature that is inner and divine, as well as the only one master above both who receives all their sacrifice and devotion. Their mind is fixed on me at the time of their departure.

Chapter Eight: Yoga of Imperishable Brahma

ARJUNA SAID: What is the meaning of BRAHMA, ADI ATMA, KARMA, ADI BHUTA, ADI DEVA, and ADI YAJNA? And how is it ADI YAJNA? And how are you to be known at the time of death by the self-controlled, the self-directed?

KRISHNA SAID: BRAHMA is the eternal presence in the changing universe. It is its creative order that does not perish. It is therefore supreme.

ADI ATMA is the self of every being, his nature that remains the same in the flow of his actions.

KARMA is the flowing energy that appears as related actions of material beings.

ADI BHUTA is material existence, the beings that change.

ADI DEVA is the cosmic being, alive and conscious, that relates everything to everything else.

I am the ADI YAJNA, the initial sacrifice, the One that is ever present here in the body and projects the other that the body experiences.

While leaving the body, he who remembers me comes to me. One enters the form one remembers while leaving the body, the form towards which one had been moving in feelings, thoughts and actions throughout one's life. Therefore remember me at all times and fight. If your mind and understanding is fixed on me, you will come to me.

Through constant practice in focusing consciousness on the highest self and not allowing your attention to go anywhere else, you come to the highest self.

Meditate on the ancient, ever present eternal source of all existence. It is the One that keeps the universe in order. It is subtler than the subtle. It the One that gives all that is. It is beyond thought.

It is the One that gives light to the sun. It is the One that is without the darkness of ignorance and delusion. If you meditate on it at the time of death, you are full of devotion to the supreme self. Fix your consciousness between your eyebrows on the wheel of energy in the front of your brain. Visualize that One and be absorbed in him to reach the Supreme Being.

I shall tell you what the VEDAS say and what the detached and the diligent seekers experience. For this they remain undistracted by the senses. Control the senses and hold the mind within the heart. Fix breathing within the head, keeping steady concentration. Utter the sacred sound AUM, the vibration of existence. Thinking of me, abandon the body to enter the highest state. Integrated with me all the time, reach the highest perfection and do not return to the world of sorrow.

All the worlds from the biggest self of the universe downwards to the smallest self of the individual are subject to birth, death and rebirth, the cycle of change. But on reaching me there is no rebirth.

The day and night of BRAHMA is a thousand ages each. When his day begins, the manifest universe comes out of the non-manifest self. When his night begins, the manifest universe goes back into the non-manifest self. This cycle of birth and death of the universe keeps repeating. But outside the motion of this cycle of birth, death and rebirth of the universe, there is an eternal non-manifest, beyond birth and death. It is not born. It does not perish. Reaching it, the self does not return. That One is the Supreme Being in whom all reside and who pervades all.

Know the time departing in which the YOGIS do not return, and in which they return. When there is light and knowledge, like the fire, the day, the bright fortnight, the northern course of the sun, they reach the eternal non-manifest and do not return. When there is darkness and ignorance, like smoke, night, the dark fortnight, the southern course of the sun, they reach the absence of light and return. A YOGI who knows these two paths of light and darkness, of knowledge and ignorance, which are eternal, is never deluded. He transcends the fruits of merit prescribed for the study of scriptures, for doing rituals, practicing austerities and giving charity.

Chapter Nine: Yoga of Royal Knowledge and Mystery

KRISHNA SAID: Since you do not doubt, I shall tell you of this mysterious knowledge. It will enable you to experience freedom from evil. This royal mystery purifies as it is directly experienced in accordance with DHARMA. It is pleasant, as it is based on love, and it never dies. Men without faith in what I say never attain me and remain in the world of suffering and death.

I stay non-manifest in the universe. All depend on me but I do not depend on any one. I cause all existence and uphold it. Nothing supports me. As the air is in space, so is existence in me. All beings enter my nature at the end of a cycle of time. I send them forth at the beginning of each cycle of time. Regulating my nature, I send forth all this diversity of beings again and again. They are helpless under the power of nature that gives them birth and death under my control. The world is cyclical. These actions do not bind me, as I remain detached from them, unconcerned.

Fools disregard me in the human form. I am present in all forms. They do not know my nature as the supreme lord of all beings. They are deluded like demons and monsters. They have vain hopes, knowledge and actions.

The wise are associated with my divine nature constantly, without wavering, as the unchanging source of all being. They aspire for eternal communion with me with a steadfast resolve. They worship me, appreciate my presence in all beings, and sing praises and bow to me with devotion.

Some worship me through the knowledge that all realities are one and the same. They experience the sameness of all. Others worship me as separate forces that they call DEVAS, different powers that they try to attain. Still others worship me in various forms, even though I become all these forms. Many are the ways of worship.

You can meditate on me as the best of any form in nature or culture.

I am the flower of every seed, the full realization of every potentiality.

I am the ritual action, the sacrifice.

I am the food offered to ancestors and tradition and to higher nature and ideals.

I am the herb that cures and gives life and warmth.

I am the cycle of energy that repeats.

I am the act of offering and what is offered and the fire in which it is offered.

I am the father and mother of the universe and its grandfather who nourishes it.

I am the subject that knows and the object that is known.

I am the sacred vibration of existence and the holy speech.

I am the path of ritual actions and the goal they reach.

I am the upholder, the master, the witness, the abode, the refuge and the friend.

I am the beginning and the end and the resting place, the imperishable seed of all.

I am the heat and the rain, immortality and death and what exists or does not exist, the seen and the unseen.

They who worship according to VEDIC rituals and drink the fermented juice of SOMA to forget and purify themselves of sin, they worship me with actions of restraint and sacrifice, seeking the way to heaven. They rise to the heavenly world of pleasure and power. Because of their right actions, they enjoy divine pleasures. After exhausting the rewards of their good deeds, they return to the world of death. They seek the satisfaction of their desires through actions that become rituals. They follow the cycle of birth and death, pleasure and pain.

There are others who worship me alone, meditating on me constantly. I take care of their prosperity, security and welfare, as they consume the minimum only to keep their body and mind in good health and efficiency.

Even they who worship other powers with faith worship me alone, though not as prescribed, because I am the recipient of all offerings. But they do not know my true nature and they fall back into the world of death.

They who worship DEVAS go to the DEVA they worship. They who worship their ancestors and tradition go to the ancestors and tradition they worship. They who worship the elements of nature go to the elements of nature they worship. They who worship me, as the best, the highest support and the presence in all, come to me.

Whatever is offered to me with love and devotion, be it a leaf, a flower, a fruit, or some water, that I accept with love.

Whatsoever you do, whatsoever you eat, whatsoever you offer and give away, whatsoever austerity you practice, do it as an offering to me present in all beings. Thus equipped in mind with renunciation of your personal benefit, the fruit of your action, you will be free of the bonds that produce auspicious and inauspicious results. Thus free, you will come to me and be like me. I am the same to all creation. No one is specially hated. No one is specially loved.

They who worship me with devotion, they are in me, as I am in their mind. If even the most sinful man worships me with undivided devotion, he is holy, as his resolve is holy. Soon he becomes righteous as his ignorance leaves him and he obtains everlasting peace. My devotee never perishes.

By taking refuge in me, in my teaching, those who are evil and sinful, and those who have a low status, be they housekeeping women and agriculturists and traders and servants of society, attain the highest state. This path is even easier for those who are devoted to reality, and those who are royal and learned because they are pure and devoted.

Having obtained this transient, joyless world, worship me. Focus your mind on what I say as the supreme goal.

Chapter Ten: Yoga of Divine Manifestation

KRISHNA SAID: Even the powers that constitute the universe and they who see visions of reality do not know me, as I am their source. You cannot know your source.

I am unborn, without a beginning, the ruler of the universe. Know me as such to be free of sin. From me arise intelligence, knowledge, truth, non-delusion and cheerfulness. From me arise restraint, self-control, austerity, non-violence and forgiveness. From me arise pleasure and pain, exaltation and depression, fear and fearlessness, equality and benevolence, fame and infamy that flow in beings. The ancients were born of me, out of my mind, with their thoughts fixed on me. From them were born all creatures in this world. This is the YOGA of manifestation, expression and evolution of the world. Hold it firmly in your mind.

I am the source of all. Everything comes from me. Therefore the wise love and adore my presence in all beings. Their minds are fixed on me. They talk of me and enlighten each other. They experience me everywhere and rejoice. To them so concentrated in love and worship, I give a mental disposition that reaches me. I destroy their darkness and give them the light of knowledge out of compassion.

ARJUNA SAID: You are the light of knowledge, the Supreme Being that sanctifies and becomes everything. You are the primal lord, divine person, eternal, unborn, all-pervading. You have proclaimed what the divine RISHIS saw. What you say is true and I believe it.

Neither the virtuous nor the demons know all your manifestations, all expressions of your divine being. You are the supreme person, the creator, the cosmic being, the ruler, the regulator of the universe, and creator of forces that make the universe. You are the mother of all powers. You only know yourself by yourself, since all emerge from you.

Tell me about your divine manifestations, how you rest pervading all the worlds. How can your devotee know you by constantly meditating on you? In what ways can one meditate on you?

KRISHNA SAID: My manifestations are endless. But I shall tell you of the prominent ones. Focus your attention on any one of my forms for meditation.

I am the self in the heart, the center of all beings. All beings are the same. See their sameness. I am their beginning, middle and end.

I am VISHNU, the power that sustains the universe between its birth and its dissolution.

Among the bodies of light that you can see, I am the radiant sun that gives life.

Among the constellations, I am the moon that nourishes herbs, the sap of life.

I am the fire that burns upwards among the gross elements of nature, the moon, the sun, and the stars.

Among all the mountains, I am Mount MERU, the center around which all the heavenly bodies move, and the Mount HIMALAYA high on earth.

I am wind among those that move. Among the howling winds, I am the fastest wind that blows and the winds that howl in the open wilderness and make men cry. I am the one that destroys.

I am the snake of infinity with heads of gross elements.

I am the imperishable time, facing in all directions.

Among the reservoirs of water, I am the ocean. I am the pure GANGA among rivers.

Among all the forces of nature, I am the power of the senses and what is just beyond them. Among the sense organs, I am the mind.

Among all that is known, I am the devotional form of music, the musical hymn that combines sublime feelings in praise of the divine presence in all beings.

Among the sciences, I am the science of the individual and the universal self.

Among those who argue, I am fair reasoning.

I am the lord of divine musicians and physicians.

Among all the priests, I am the guru who guides families into actions that lead them to the joy of living.

Among the great RISHIS, I am BRIGHU, the astronomer and astrologer, the scientist who predicted the future.

Among the heavenly RISHIS, I am the traveling NARADA, changing quarrels into blessings everywhere, creating new harmonies of music.

I am RISHI KAPILA among the perfect, silently seeing the divine evolving into the universe of many forms.

Among the generals, I am the commander in chief, who directs all the forces.

I am RAMA among those who bear weapons and use force as warriors.

I am thunderbolt among weapons that effectively destroy.

I am death that snatches all away, the origin that gives birth to all.

I am the lord of wealth among its devotees, and among those who do not follow the rules of law and discipline.

I am the lord of wealth among those who live in water that gives life.

Among the living beings, I am consciousness.

I am the best of horses, the best of elephants, the monarch of men.

I am lion among the beasts.

Among the cows, I am the earth that satisfies all needs.

I am crocodile among the fish.

Among the trees, I am PEEPAL that gives life even at night.

I am the season of flowers among seasons.

Among the months, I am November and December when the cold stimulates.

I am the desire that leads to progeny. I am the one who carries life.

I am the power that churns the universe around its axis to produce immortality.

I am AUM, the initial sound of the vibration of existence in speech.

I am the initial letter A of the language that expresses all knowledge. I am the link that joins compound words.

I am GAYATRI among the meters, meditating and praying for enlightenment.

Among the rituals of sacrifice, I am JAPA the repeated meditation on the divine name and form.

I am the first among the ancestors.

I am death among those who subdue and reckon.

I am the one who loves the divine among those who do not.

Among women, I am fame, prosperity, speech, memory, intelligence, endurance and forgiveness.

I am gambling among the fraudulent, magnanimity among the magnanimous, and brilliance of the brilliant.

I am the victory and the effort.

I am the best of my community and I am you, the best of your community.

I am the best of those who have silenced their minds.

I am the poet with intuition that brings the dead back to life among those who see.

I am the principle of punishment and the policy that leads to victory.

Of secrets, I am silence.

I am the wisdom of the wise, the seed and the source of all beings.

Nothing that moves or does not move exists without me.

I express myself in many ways, in many forms. My manifestations are endless.

Wherever there is wonderful power, splendor or energy, know that that comes from me.

I sustain the whole universe with a fragment of my power.

To know me, be the best of your nature.

Chapter Eleven: Yoga of Seeing the Universal Form

ARJUNA SAID: You have told me the most profound mystery of the highest self and its expression. My ignorance is removed. You are the origin and dissolution of all beings. You are the unchanging greatness. You are as you have described yourself. O Sovereign! If you think of me as worthy, reveal to me your cosmic form.

KRISHNA SAID: See my forms, hundreds of thousands of them, manifold, divine, varied in color and shape. I am fully present everywhere. Learn to see me for your growth. See the forces and elements of nature. See the winds that cry and howl. See physicians traveling on horses to provide aid to the needy. See marvels never seen before. See as you desire. The whole universe with its motion and non-motion is centered in me.

But you cannot see it with the eyes that you have. I give you divine eyes that see reality. See my supreme power.

ARJUNA SAID: I see in your body all DEVAS, diverse beings, forces and powers. I see BRAHMA, the ruler, sitting on the lotus flower, unattached. I see many sages full of wisdom and divine serpents full of poison. I see arms, bellies, mouths and eyes and endless forms all around.

You are everywhere. I see you as a mass of light, brilliance immeasurable, shining everywhere. You have diadem, mace and discus of your present form. You are like the burning fire, a thousand suns.

You are the imperishable, the supreme goal to be experienced. You are the basis of this universe, unchanging. You are the guardian of the eternal law. You are the supreme presence in the universe, ever lasting.

I see you without beginning, middle or end. Your power is infinite. The sun and the moon are your eyes. Your mouth is emitting fire. Your radiance warms the universe. You pervade the space between the heaven and earth in all directions. The whole universe fears your terrible form of wonder, O MAHA ATMA! Into you enter hosts of DEVAS, the forces of nature. Some in fear praise you with joined hands. RISHIS and seekers who achieved perfection welcome you with praises full of meaning. Forces and elements of nature and winds that howl and cry and the ancestors and the divine musicians and physicians and the wealthy and the wicked—all gaze on you in amazement.

Seeing your great form with numerous mouths and eyes and arms and thighs and feet and stomachs and terrible teeth like fangs, the world trembles and I quake. I tremble in fear, finding no support, no peace, sinking in the void, seeing you going beyond the sky, shining, multicolored, with wide-open mouths and eyes of vast splendor. I see the enemy warriors and many of our side too hastening into your frightening mouth, crushed to powder between your teeth. As rivers flow into the ocean, these great heroes are entering your flaming mouth. Tell me O terrible form! Who are you? I desire to know. Be gracious. I do not know you.

KRISHNA SAID: I am Time that destroys the world. As I manifest myself, I begin to destroy the world. Even without you these warriors will not survive. They are doomed. You are only an instrument. Therefore arise and win glory. Conquer your enemies and enjoy a prosperous kingdom.

ARJUNA SAID: Appreciating your presence, the world is moved to joy and love. The wicked flee in fear. Those who are perfect bow down to you, losing their ego.

You are great as you are the creator of order of the universe.

You are the individual self, imperishable, the resting place of the universe, of what exists and does not appear to exist and has to come into existence and what is beyond these two. You are the primeval force, the ancient being, the knower and what is known. You are the supreme rest with infinite forms.

You are the air and fire, water and death and the moon. You are the lord of creatures, the great grandsire who nourishes and takes care of children. I bow to you a thousand times, again and again from all sides. You are infinite power, heroic action, measureless. You are all, pervading all beings.

Unaware of your majesty from negligence or love, I may have been rude and disrespectful to you, while resting or working and playing, alone or in company. I beg you to forgive me.

You are incomprehensible. You are the father of the world, of what moves or does not move, animals and plants. You are the teacher of the world, the one most worthy of reverence. There is none equal to you or greater than you. Therefore I bow to you, prostrating the body, imploring your mercy, adorable lord, forgive me, like a friend, a father, a husband. Seeing what was never seen before, I am delighted and full of awe. Abode of the universe! Be gracious! I want to see you as earlier.

KRISHNA SAID: I have shown you this cosmic, infinite, primeval form of radiance by my grace. Not through the study of scriptures, nor through doing sacrifices and rituals, nor through giving gifts and charities, nor through doing austerities can anyone see what you have seen. This form is difficult to see even for the forces of nature. Only through one-pointed single-minded devotion to me can this form be seen by my grace. He who works for me, accepting what I say as the supreme goal, he who is devoted to me without attachment or enmity to anyone, he can have this experience.

See my form you are used to seeing. End your distress and confusion on seeing my terrible form.

Chapter Twelve: Bhakti Yoga

ARJUNA SAID: Who has greater knowledge of YOGA_ the devotee who worships you as the best self of all beings, or the devotee who meditates on what is abstract, the imperishable and non-manifest?

KRISHNA SAID: Those who worship me, joined to me in love and faith, focusing their minds on me, the best fruition of their highest nature, are the highest among the YOGIS. But they who meditate on the imperishable, the indefinable, the non-manifest, the omnipresent, unthinkable, immovable, constant, and what is common to all beings, having subdued all their senses, even-minded, engaged in the welfare of all beings, working in the best interest of all, they too come to me only. But their difficulty is greater, because the way of the abstract, the non-manifest is hard for embodied beings.

Those who dedicate all actions to me, present in all, as their supreme goal, focused on me with exclusive devotion, they make me their savior in life. You live in me alone. When your mind is focused on me, your intellect enters me.

If even now you are unable to focus on me, practice repeating my name, while meditating on my form. If you cannot practice keeping my name and form in your mind, while meditating on its significance, then devote yourself to my service and work for me present in all.

If you cannot do even this, leave the fruits of your actions to me, present in all.

Knowledge of the self of the individual and of the universe is better than keeping its name and form in the mind. Easier than this knowledge is meditation on the self. Easier than this meditation is renunciation of any expectations of the fruits of your actions. From such renunciation comes peace.

He who never hates any being, who is friendly and compassionate to all, who is free of the feelings of I and mine, who looks upon all pain and pleasure as the same, who is enduring, contented, meditating, self-restrained, firm in his convictions, dedicated to me, he is dear to me.

He who does not frighten any one, who is not frightened by any one, who is free of joy and impatience, fear and repulsion, he is dear to me.

He who is free of desires and agony, who is pure, expert, indifferent to events, having renounced all purposeless initiative, he is my devotee, dear to me.

He who neither rejoices, nor hates, nor grieves, nor desires, nor judges good and evil, who is full of devotion to me, he is my devotee, dear to me.

He who is the same to friend and foe, honor and dishonor, heat and cold, pleasure and pain, who is free of attachments, who regards praise and blame alike, who is silent, content with any lot, who is unattached to any home, who is firm of mind in this path, devoted to me, he is dear to me.

All these devotees who acquire these virtues with full faith, regarding me as supreme, are dear to me.

Chapter Thirteen: Yoga of Discriminating the Field and its Knower

KRISHNA SAID: This body is a field of forces in a larger field of forces. The one that knows the field within all fields is ATMA, the self of the individual. I am the knower of all fields. The knowledge of the field and its knower is true knowledge.

Learn about this field of forces, its modifications, its purposes, its organic living self and being and its powers. RISHIS have talked of these fields in various ways in different songs. It is discussed in BRAHMA SUTRAS as an abstract summary.

The field and its variations are the elements of nature, the differentiating ego, intellect, the non-manifest nature, ten capacities for action and perception, one mind, and five objects of the senses, and binary oppositions like heat and cold, desire and hatred, pleasure and pain, and their combinations that constitute the basis of consciousness.

Knowledge of the self comes from moral qualities like devotion to the final reality alone, contemplation on the self and reflection on how to experience its truth, without attachment to anything else, firmness in this path, understanding birth, death, old age, disease and sorrow, even-mindedness towards the desirable and undesirable events, self-restraint, absence of desire for sense objects, non-attachment and not clinging to son, wife, home, wealth and the like, resorting to lonely places and being alone in the mind and dislike for crowds, practice of non-violence, patience, sincerity, modesty and absence of pretension, absence of egotism, service to the guru, purity of mind and purity of living. The opposite of these moral qualities leads to ignorance.

Know BRAHMA, the ultimate reality of the universe, without beginning, neither existing, nor not existing. On knowing this, one experiences the immortal self.

Everywhere are its hands and feet, eyes, ears, mouths and heads, and the actions they do. It encompasses all things. It appears to have all the senses and organs and their functions at every point. In truth it is devoid of them.

It is not attached to anything, but it sustains all.

It has no constituents, yet it experiences all constituents.

It is inside and outside all beings, the moving and the unmoving, the far and the near, all this at once.

It is hard to know because it is too subtle to be perceptible to the senses.

It is indivisible, yet it appears as if divided among beings.

It devours all, yet causes their generation.

It is beyond ignorance, the light of all lights. It is knowledge present in the heart of all, because of which they are what they are.

On knowing this field of knowledge and its knower, you know me.

Know that both nature and self are without beginning.

Know that all modifications and attributes are born of nature. It causes the body and the sense organs to act.

The self seated in nature experiences the qualities born of nature. Its attachment to these qualities is the cause of its birth in good and evil wombs.

The self in the body is called the seer, approver, supporter, and the one who experiences, the great lord, the supreme self.

He who understands the self and nature with qualities in this way is not born again. Birth ceases to exist for him. Birth becomes a transformation for him. All effects are transformations of causes.

Some understand the self through meditation. Others understand it through thought. calculating the forms it assumes. Still others know it through actions done skillfully with detachment and an even mind without expecting any fruits for themselves.

Some others do not understand it in these ways, but hear of it from others and worship a symbol or an image of it according to their capacity for understanding with devotion. In these ways they pass beyond the fear of death and suffering.

Whatever is born, whether it moves or not, animal or plant, is born through the combination of the field and the knower of the field. He who sees the supreme ruler dwelling alike in all beings sees truly.

On seeing the supreme ruler abiding alike in all places, he does not cause injury to anyone. Through this non-violence, he reaches the highest goal of spiritual evolution.

He who sees that nature alone acts universally and that the self does not act he sees truly. He who sees that numerous forms of independent existence of all beings center only on one and expand from that one attains to the supreme self. This supreme self, dwelling in the body, is unchanging and without beginning. It does not act. It is not acted on. It is without qualities.

As space is subtle, unaffected by what happens in it, so is the self in the body present everywhere but unaffected. As the one sun illumines the whole world, so the one self illumines the whole body. Those who discriminate between the self and nature and the means of deliverance from nature attain the supreme.

Chapter Fourteen: Yoga of Discriminating Three Constituents of Nature

KRISHNA SAID: Another way of knowing can take one beyond the appearance of birth and death to the reality hidden underneath them.

My womb is the BRAHMA, in which I place the germ for the birth of all beings. Whatever forms are produced in any womb, nature is the great womb and I am the father.

Existence and truth, energy and action, limitations and ignorance are the three constituents of nature that bind the unchanging self to it.

Existence and truth is pure truth. It gives light and the state of being well. It binds by attachment to happiness and knowledge.

Energy and action is the energy seen as action. It causes attraction, craving and attachment. It binds the self to action, change and transformation.

Limitations and ignorance delude the self with appearances and bind it to error. It causes negligence, indolence and sleep.

Truth leads by dominating action and ignorance. Action leads by dominating truth and ignorance. Ignorance leads by dominating action and truth.

When truth prevails, the light of knowledge shines through all the doors of the body. When action prevails, greed, activity, initiative, unrest, conflict and craving arise. When ignorance prevails, non-illumination, inactivity, negligence, and delusion arise.

If truth prevails at the time of death, the self goes to the pure world of the highest. If action prevails at the time of death, the self is born among those attached to work. If ignorance prevails at the time of death, one is born among the deluded.

The fruit of a good deed is pure truth, of action is pain, and of limitations is ignorance.

From truth arises knowledge, from action greed, and from limitations arise negligence, delusion, and ignorance.

Truth raises one upwards. Action keeps one in the middle, and limitations downwards.

When one sees no agent of action, but only these qualities at work, one transcends them. Then one attains my state. Then one sees no birth, death, age or pain. One attains immortality.

ARJUNA SAID: What shows that a man has gone beyond these three constituents of nature? And how has he done it?

KRISHNA SAID: He does not hate truth, action or delusion, while these prevail. Nor does he long for them, when they cease. He is undisturbed by them, unconcerned.

He lives in the self, alike in pleasure and pain. He sees all things like praise and blame of himself as of equal value. He remains the same towards what is hated or loved, in honor and dishonor, the same to friend and foe. He does not react even though he is intelligent. Such a man can be said to have gone across these three constituents of nature.

Serving me with devotion, he is fit for the state of BRAHMA. He sees the ground, the basis of eternal DHARMA, of perfect bliss. He sees the immortal and immutable.

Chapter Fifteen: Yoga of the Supreme Self

KRISHNA SAID: There is an unchanging PEEPAL tree known as the world with its roots in truth in the worlds above and branches in beings below. Its leaves are scriptures that lead to the knowledge of truth.

He who knows the tree, living through its diversity of experience, its transformations, knows the scriptures through awareness.

Constituents of nature nourish its branches. Their shoots are sense objects. Its secondary roots come downwards, resulting in actions that bind in the world of men.

One should seek the goal from where one does not return. Otherwise it is not a goal at all, but a means, right or wrong.

One should seek refuge with the self, the source and the cause of all action.

Be without delusion about your self. Be aware of it. Be devoted to it. Be without desires or attachment. Be free of dualities like pleasure and pain.

They who have no delusion go to my unchanging state. The sun does not illumine it, nor does the moon, nor the fire.

The unchanging is embodied in the changing world of life. It attracts the senses, of which the mind is the sixth sense. It abides in nature. Whatever the body it takes or leaves, it goes on its way taking along impressions of the senses. Presiding over the eye, the ear, the sense of touch, the tongue, the nose, and the mind, it experiences the objects of senses. It is joined to the constituents of nature, when it leaves the body or stays in it and has experiences. It is seen through the eyes of knowledge, not delusion. The YOGIS strive to see it established in them. The unintelligent and unrefined minds do not see it.

The brilliance in the sun, the moon, and the fire is my brilliance.

My strength upholds all beings on the earth.

I am the juice that nourishes all herbs.

I am the fire in all beings that live, digesting food, united with breath.

I am present in the hearts and minds of all.

From me come memory and knowledge, and their absence.

I alone am known through all scriptures, giving the fruits of their actions. I am their knower.

There are the many forms that change and perish. There is one being that does not change or perish. The supreme self is other than these two, as it witnesses them and so rises above them.

It is known through the scriptures. It is the immutable ruler. It enters and supports the world of matter, life and consciousness. I am that supreme person. He who knows me thus worships me in everyway.

One who knows this mysterious doctrine becomes wise and fulfils his duty that flowers from his nature.

Chapter Sixteen: Yoga of Discriminating Good From Evil

KRISHNA SAID: One who is born to a divine destiny acquires and expresses virtues like steadfastness in seeking wisdom and practicing YOGA, study of scriptures and study of one's own self, doing necessary rituals to internalize the essence of scriptures, giving alms as a means of enlarging one's sympathy, fervor and intensity of self-discipline, purity of heart, mind and body, truthfulness, fearlessness and straightforwardness, energetic and radiant character, detachment and peace, compassion, forgiveness, nonviolence and self-restraint, patience, modesty and gentleness, absence of anger, faultfinding, enmity, malice, greed, restlessness and conceit.

These divine qualities lead to freedom from bondage to nature and the world. Cultivate them.

Demons express vices like pretension, arrogance, anger, ignorance, absence of purity and proper conduct. They do not know spiritual action, renunciation, truth, right conduct or cleanliness. They believe that the universe is without any underlying truth, any foundation, any governing presence or cosmic being. What exists for them is lust and beings born of sexual intercourse.

With such beliefs, these lost individuals and feeble minds do violence and cruel deeds, amass great wealth and power, creating avoidable inequality, believing that they are good.

They destroy the world and kill others for the sake their own feelings of insecurity.

They turn to insatiable desires, acquire unjust wealth, live in delusion and follow impious vows. They act with ostentation, pride and arrogance. They have unlimited cares and worries till death. Enjoyment of desires is their highest aim.

They are full of hopes and anger. They think, " Today I have gained this, tomorrow I will gain that. Today I have destroyed this, and tomorrow I will destroy that. I am the lord, the enjoyer, successful, strong and happy. I am wealthy and high class by birth. Who is equal to me? I shall even do rituals, give charity and rejoice."

Thus they are deluded by ignorance. They are addicted to sensual pleasures. They fall in hell. Glorifying themselves, without humility, intoxicated with wealth and pride, they do ceremonies ostentatiously for form only but without the genuine spirit of sacrifice. They do not know the sacred, the holy. Depending on their ego, power, pride, desire and anger, these malicious men hate the divine present in their own bodies and in those of others. Cruel, vile and inauspicious, they are born again and again in the wombs of demons. They sink to the lowest level.

Desire, anger and greed are the gates of hell, ruinous of self. Abandon these. They do not lead to perfection or pleasure or the supreme state.

Divine qualities lead to freedom. Demonic qualities lead to bondage.

These are two types of beings in the world. You should work for the good of the self to reach the highest state. Make scriptures your guide in deciding what to do and what not to do. Do your duty as it emerges from your nature, nourishing its goodness and starving its evil and in this way shaping it in the light of great ideals and idols.

Chapter Seventeen: Yoga of Discriminating Three Kinds of Faith

ARJUNA SAID: What is the basis of those who ignore scriptures but worship with faith? Is it truth, action, or ignorance?

KRISHNA SAID: Embodied beings have three types of faith, born of their nature. It depends on whether truth, energy or ignorance is predominant. Their food, rituals, fervor, and charity are different.

Man consists of faith. He is what his faith is. The faith works according to the internal actions of his mind.

Truthful men see reality and worship the powers and elements of nature, as they are devoted to them. Energetic men of action worship lawless disorderly powers, because actions go ahead of the laws that are used to control these monsters. They create disorder, which is then led to order. Ignorant men worship unseen ghosts and spirits as they experience them.

Those who practice extreme austerities, not enjoined by scriptures, are conceited and ostentatious. They are prompted by sensual desires and passions. They torture their own bodies. They torture me dwelling in their bodies. They are demons in their resolves.

Truthful men eat foods that promote longevity, truth, strength, health, pleasure and happiness. These foods are fresh, sweet, oily, substantial and agreeable. They eat what the body needs when they are hungry. Energetic men of action eat foods that are bitter, sour, very salty, very hot, very pungent, dry and burning. These foods produce activity, pain, sorrow and disease. Ignorant men eat tasteless foods that were prepared long back, foods that are decaying, nearing the end of their life, unclean, left over surplus.

Truthful men perform rituals without expectations of any personal gains, desiring no fruit, with their minds focused on their nature and its duty, their highest self, as worship, an offering to the divine present in all. Energetic men of action perform rituals and ceremonies for personal benefits and display, impressing others. Ignorant men perform rituals without faith or understanding, without charity or giving of food, without remembering or acting according to sacred formulas and the right rules of conduct.

Truthful men do penance of the body through devotion to the forces of nature and to the learned, the cultured and the enlightened ones and to their spiritual teachers and through purity, uprightness, non-violence and single-minded pursuit of BRAHMA. Their penance of speech consists in being truthful, pleasant, beneficial, without shocking, and in reciting scriptures. Their penance of the mind consists in being mentally silent, peaceful, self-controlled, skillful, pure and benevolent. They do penance of the body, speech and mind with devotion and faith without desiring any fruit. Energetic men of action do penance with ostentation for the sake of gaining honor, praise, and reverence from others. It is never constant and permanent. Ignorant men do penance with delusion through self-torture or in order to injure another.

Charity of the truthful is given to the deserving at the right time and place as a duty without expectation of any return. Charity of the men of action is given grudgingly as a consideration for something received or yet to be received. Ignorant charity is given to the unworthy recipient at the wrong time and place, with contempt and without due respect.

AUM TAT SAT is a MANTRA that refers to the truth that lives in the universe with its forces and laws. From it emerged the learned, their knowledge and actions for acquiring knowledge in ancient days. Knowledge requires sacrificial rituals and methods for its acquisition. It requires detachment, austere intensity and discipline in its pursuit. Knowledge is given as charity to the competent and deserving.

AUM expresses an attitude of welcome, an open-minded, trusting acceptance of reality and existence. TAT means the duty of self-expression, as all beings do, sacrificing one's divinely given nature into good actions through self-discipline, as an offering in faith and devotion to SAT, the supreme reality and truth that pervades all, like a seed bursting into a tree, a practical ideal.

If this duty is done without self-expression, faith and devotion, then it is insincere and false.

AUM TAT SAT is a prayer that must emerge from appropriate actions. Otherwise they are sounds without their accompanying life and actions that give them meaning and make them a prayer.

Chapter Eighteen: Yoga of Freedom and Renunciation

ARJUNA SAID: What is meant by SANYASA and TYAGA?

KRISHNA SAID: SANYASA means giving up actions motivated by personal desire. TYAGA means giving up expectations of fruits of all actions.

Some people say that all actions should be given up as evil, which is not right. The body cannot give up actions. Only their fruits can be given up by offering them to the divine presence in all beings.

If fruits of actions are given up, they do not pursue one after death. Otherwise the fruits come and they may be desirable, undesirable, or mixed.

Sacrifice, self-discipline, and charity are obligatory actions. One must do them. They purify the self. They are to be done without expectation of any personal benefits. To abandon them through delusion is ignorant renunciation. To abandon them as painful actions that involve suffering is renunciation of men of action. To abandon attachment to them and to their fruits while continuing to do them is truthful renunciation. Truthful men do not hate disagreeable actions. They do not cling to agreeable actions. They do their duty without any doubt.

All actions have five causes. The first is the gross body with its mind, including its own nature, capability and capacity. The second is the subtle ego that includes past experience and its present effects, impressions and ideas with which the ego is identified. The third is different instruments and methods that are available and used. The fourth is the strength of effort applied, whether it is mild or intense, intermittent or constant. The final cause is divine intervention, which some call destiny and some call chance or luck.

Destiny alone is not entirely responsible for what happens, nor is one's free will the only cause that produces action, as there are other causes too. Therefore he who sees only himself as the cause of action is uncultivated and without understanding. He does not see at all. He who is free of the notion that he is the doer of the action does not do the action at all, though he kills all these men. He is not affected by his actions.

Knowledge, the known and the knower, incite action. The instrument, the act and the agent constitute action. Truthful knowledge shows one undivided existence present in all the divided and varied beings. Knowledge of men of action shows all beings as distinct and separate individuals. Knowledge of ignorant men is irrational, untrue, insignificant, and shows a single act as if it were the whole act.

If an obligatory act is done without attachment, without desire or aversion, and without seeking any personal fruit, it is truthful. If an action is done with great effort to gratify desire, prompted by ego, it is of the men of action. If an action is done through delusion, without regard to consequences, loss, injury, and one's own nature and capacity, it is ignorant.

The doer of action is truthful, if he is free of attachment, not making much of himself, endowed with steadfastness and zeal and unaffected by success or failure. He is active, if he is passionate, seeking personal fruits of his action, greedy, harmful, impure and moved by delight and grief. He is ignorant, if he is unqualified, unrefined, stubborn, depraved, dishonest, indolent, despondent and dilatory.

The understanding is truthful, if it knows clearly how to act in the world as well as how to withdraw from the world, what ought to be done and what ought not to be done, that knows what to fear and what not to fear, and what attaches one to the world and what does not attach one to the world but makes it free. The understanding is active, if it confuses moral and immoral commands, and does not know which is which, as it is so attached to the world. It is ignorant, if it reverses every value so that fair is foul and foul is fair.

Perseverance is truthful if the mind, vitality and the organs are focused through YOGA. It is active if one desires fruits, longing for them with attachment, holding fast to duty, desire and wealth.

It is ignorant if one does not give up sleep, fear, grief, depression, and passion.

Pleasures end in pain and are acquired through practice or habit. They are truthful if they come from a peaceful mind focused on the self. They look like poison at first, but later become elixirs. They are active if they come from contact of the senses with their objects. They look like elixirs but end as poisons. They are ignorant if they begin and end in delusion, sleep, sloth and error.

There is no creature anywhere who is free of these constituents of nature.

BRAHMINS, KSHATRIYAS, VAISHYAS, and SHUDHRAS constitute the four colors of society. Their duties are divided according to the qualities born of their nature and freely expressed and directed in their actions.

An individual must understand his own nature, be aware of it, before he can do his duty of expressing himself in good actions freely. Otherwise he is expressing another's nature, another's duty, fashions, newspapers, rulers or neighbors.

BRAHMINS are those whose inherent nature produces duties like control of the senses and mind, austerity, purity, forbearance, righteousness, knowledge, spiritual experience, and faith.

KSHATRYAS are those whose inherent nature produces duties like heroic action, brilliance in spirit, firm resolve, never running away from battle, generosity, being like a ruler or an officer.

VAISHYAS are those whose inherent nature produces duties like thinking and using resources, making profit, loss and wealth, taking risks through agriculture, cattle, trade and commerce, making and exchanging things for sale and purchase.

SHUDHRAS are those whose inherent nature produces actions like laboring and doing service to others in return for a living.

Within each color of society are numerous occupations. They all are related to one another as limbs of an organic being, working for collective benefit.

One attains perfection through doing one's own duty with devotion. It is a form of worship of the One who creates all natures and their functions. That One is present in everyone in all the colors of society. Therefore expressing one's nature in action, directing it to the best it is capable of, is a way of being devoted to and worshipping the One who created that nature.

Doing the duty that emerges from one's own nature, though it is not done so well, is better than doing a duty that does not emerge from one's own nature, though that is done well. There is merit and no sin in working out one's own nature, whereas not doing a duty that emerges from one's nature is killing it, a form of suicide. Never abandon your duty even if it is imperfect, because all work is imperfect even when it looks perfect.

If one is self-controlled, free of all desires and attachments, one transcends work. Then renunciation happens on its own, even while one is doing all one's duties. Then the understanding becomes pure, as the mind is subdued through firm resolve. Love and hate is put aside. Objects of the senses are given up. Body, mind and speech are restrained. Little food is consumed. One becomes alone, dispassionate and meditative. Egoism, power, pride, desire, wrath and the sense of possession are given up. One becomes worthy and qualified to know the universal self. Then there is no grief or craving. Then all beings are seen as the same, whatever their status in society. Then he knows and enters me and becomes like me.

Therefore focus your thoughts on me and do your work. Go across the sea of your difficulties in this way and find peace. Do your duty impelled by your nature. Otherwise your nature will compel you in many ways.

ISHWAR lives in the heart, the center of all beings, as they go round and round by his power, mounted on the wheel. Seek refuge in him alone with your entire being. Give up other paths and find supreme peace. Reflect on it and do what you will.

This instruction is given to you because you are my devotee. You are sincere and austere. You want to open up and listen without being condemnatory. Teach it to others. Give it as charity, not for returns or personal benefits.

Wherever KRISHNA guides ARJUNA, and wisdom guides action, there is good fortune, victory and wealth within the limits of sound morality.

Chapter IX

Celebrating Life

MAHARSHI VEDVYAS said to MAHARSHI NARAD: Sir, I have edited the VEDA and divided it into four parts. I have entrusted each part to a different set of disciples for their care and exposition. I have expounded the aims of life, like living righteously, earning wealth and power and satisfying physical and mental desires within the right limits, and finding meaning in freedom from attachment to it all. I have foreseen all human history as the play of time and expressed it in an epic called MAHABHARTA. It is open to all castes whatever the quality of their mind or qualifications. Yet I feel unhappy, unsatisfied. I do not know the cause of my anguish, my nameless sorrow. Please enlighten me.

MAHARSHI NARAD said: You have missed the joy of living at its source, love for the supreme. What is the point of any action, any philosophy, any rituals, any duties or any aim of life, if action is not done with a song in the heart, as a dedication to the reality present in all beings at their very center, free of fear and anxiety? Without this joy and dedication in the heart, knowledge is dull and action is repetitive and meaningless.

MAHARSHI VEDVYAS felt blessed. He touched the feet of NARAD in reverence and sat down to celebrate life. He composed the story of SRI KRISHNA.

The highest duty of man is to realize his true self. His highest self is divine. Therefore his highest duty is devotion to the divine and its personal experience.

This duty is cultivated without desire for personal benefits. It yields to no obstacles. It fills one with peace and energy. Then one rises above the life of the body and its senses and their narrow mind in pursuit of the chosen ideal.

This devotion to the divine is a way of realizing one's true nature. One moves from identifying oneself with his mortal body associated with food, safety and sex, to identifying oneself with the immortal self, vision and experience of his highest potential.

If rituals and social duties do not generate this devotion to one's highest self, they should be discarded.

One aim of life is to search for sensual pleasures. We can be devoted to food, sex, security and comforts of life. We can have so much of food and sex and comforts that we may fall ill, or find life meaningless and repetitive. One can never feel secure in this mortal body, which can die any moment. But we desire to continue living endlessly.

Another aim of life is to earn wealth and power. We can aim to have a hundred cows, or a thousand, or hundreds of thousands of cows or money. No series of such numbers has any end. One more can always be added to the maximum. Therefore the desire for increase in wealth and power cannot be satisfied.

An aspect of this aim of life is to dominate people, force or manipulate them to do the work that we want them to do. We can rule our family, our neighbors, our colleagues, our village or town or country or all countries in the world, and even discover more earths to rule. We can challenge the stars and dominate the worlds, but not dominate or control our own urges and instincts. Are these truly the highest ideals of life? Is this the best that man is capable of doing? What is the best we can do?

Life to be meaningful is to be lived in search of the supreme truth. The supreme truth is the truth that underlies all other truths. It is variously named, like BRAHMA, the creative order of nature, or PARAM ATMA, the supreme self, or SHAKTI, the power that underlies all other powers in nature, or BHAGVAN, the one with blessed, holy and auspicious qualities. The truth of truths has many names.

Devotion to the supreme self comes through many ways.

One begins by visiting temples, meeting authentic holy people, listening to scriptures, thinking about the divine power, reflecting on one's experience of life, repeating sacred formulas, learning to concentrate the mind on various objects, to praise the divine presence in all beings and to appreciate them, observing the tendencies of one's own body and its animal mind, rising above desires and anger, greed and sex, and acquiring moral values like truth, non-violence, detachment, love and helpfulness and expressing these values in one's feelings, urges and actions.

One starts emptying the mind of the impressions of actions in this or earlier lives. One starts developing spontaneous spiritual intuition of the truth that underlies all truths.

Many Hindus worship the supreme truth as KRISHNA. They try to be like him and acquire his qualities, like being so absorbed in doing actions emerging from one's nature and directing them towards the noble ideals that they forget themselves and do not feel elated or humiliated, and try to identify themselves with the best of everything. They try to develop the best they are capable of doing and becoming, trying to be even-minded, skillful, keeping the same silent creative consciousness in all circumstances.

If we focus our mind on KRISHNA with devotion, understanding his names and actions, we will be librated from sin, the bondage to desire. We will do our duty with detachment without expectations of personal benefits. We will withdraw our senses from their objects and keep them still for some time every day. We will experience unity.

KRISHNA is powerful and attractive. He exists as spirit, after beings dissolve into their spirit. Man is what his spirit is. All beings are what their spirit is. The spirit becomes all beings. All powers of nature sleep in him. He reveals them in their forms. He is the source and the goal of sages and their wisdom. They empty their minds of everything else through their devotion to him.

KRISHNA lives in nature, in plants, in animals and men. He flowers in the best of men in all walks of life. He remains detached from everything. Everything is a play for him. He takes birth when the rulers become wicked, filled with dark unmentionable passions.

He protects people from the might and anger of royal houses. He is the wealth of those who are poor. His presence brings prosperity. When we feel his presence in danger we become fearless. He is neither a friend nor an enemy. Even the death he brings is auspicious, a blessing.

The world is a chain of cause and effect, desire and ignorance, birth and death. He frees us from its compulsions with his play. He feels compassion at the ferocity that human beings express towards each other and towards nature around them.

Once upon a time, RAJA UGRASEN ruled MATHURA. His wife PAVANAREKHA was violently assaulted by a RAKSHAS. She gave birth to a son who was cruel from early childhood. He overthrew his father, the king of MATHURA, and became RAJA KANS. He was without DHARMA. He started collecting high taxes and revenue from village chiefs every year. He used to kill those who did not pay or whom he disliked. People were full of pain at his greed and cruelty. He imprisoned his own father who had tried to make him into a good man. He offered his sister DEVAKI in marriage to RAJA VASUDEVA though the groom was already married to ROHNI. But then he heard a voice that DEVAKI'S son would kill him. He started killing every child born to DEVAKI. The seventh child came along. He was an incarnation of the serpent of infinity, the resting place of VISHNU, the lord of life. VISHNU passed him on to ROHINI, who took the child to their friend NANDA, who was the chief of cowherds. He was named BALARAMA.

Then KRISHNA was born to DEVAKI and VASUDEVA. At the hour of KRISHNA'S birth in the prison, the guards fell asleep. The prison gates opened. VASU DEVA took the baby out of the prison and went across the river YAMUNA. It was a dark night in the rainy season and the river was in flood. The waters touched the child's feet and receded. His birth was a miracle. Is not birth a miracle?

They went to the village of cowherds to the house of their chief. The village was GOKULA, meaning the family of the earth born. They all lived close to mother earth, plants and animals. They who follow KRISHNA live close to mother earth, plants and animals.

KRISHNA was brought up here. He had dark color and sharp features. His birth is celebrated on the night of JANAM ASHTHAMI.

We should celebrate KRISHNA'S birthday. First we should clean up and decorate our house, take a bath and empty our mind of all mundane concerns and sit quietly. We should do PRANAYAM for some time, focusing our mind on the breathing alone. This will help us empty our mind and make it stable and peaceful.

Then we should remember our ancestors, their life-giving moral values and actions and remember the powers of nature that shape us. We can begin with the powers that we can sense, like the earth, water, air, fire, space, sun, plants, vegetables, fruits, changing seasons, our mind, intelligence, ego, and so on. Then we should think of the powers that we cannot sense like that from which the seen powers of nature come and into which they go back and what stays in these powers when they are around. We should visualize these powers and make formless, abstract designs, idols and symbols of them.

We should pray for the well being of all children in the world and pray for the blessings of SRI KRISHNA and resolve to understand what he says. We should gift a cow, the source of nourishment to the learned people, who do not have any other source of income and make a donation to the cause of learning and education. We should feed children in the neighborhood and give them gifts.

Rituals become pure through charity. The mind becomes pure through knowledge of the self. We should sing songs in praise of the divine and listen to devotional music and learn to appreciate all beings as the same divine lives in them. How can we praise the divine if we cannot praise and see the good in those around us? We should resolve to do our duties skillfully with detachment for the welfare of others, for what brings people together.

KRISHNA grew up a free child. He faced death many times when the king sent demons to kill him. He destroyed them all. Self-defense is obligatory.

PUTANA was sent to him as a wet nurse. She offered him her breasts smeared with poison. He tasted bitterness and bled her to death in self-protection.

The ceremony of taking the baby out of the house was performed. The child was fed and bathed to the sound of songs of praise and folk music. He was placed on a cart full of pots of milk, sweets and curds. He was being taken out of the house with joy and boisterous laughter. The child kicked the pots with such force that they tumbled down. He was strong. We should build up our physical strength.

Once baby KRISHNA was lying in the open. A demon in the form of a powerful whirlwind came. He lifted the baby up and carried it away. The hot and dry village was in the grip of strong and dusty winds and darkness. KRISHNA became heavier and the demon got lighter and could not carry him further. He strangled the demon to death. People were so terrified of the king that they thought he controlled nature. Kings think so highly of themselves and create such impressions of their grandeur, greatness and goodness that the people think they can order whirlwinds to destroy them.

Once women complained against KRISHNA to his mother. They said he releases the calves before the milking time. The calves suck away all the milk. When asked not to do so, he says that the milk is for the calves. Why should human beings take away the milk meant for calves? He asks difficult questions. If they do not milk the cows and sell it in the nearby towns, how shall they earn their livelihood? Do calves have a right to all the milk of their mothers? He enters their houses with all his friends and disturbs the peace. The boys drink all the milk and eat all the sweets and curds and butter. He says the children have a right to eat and drink what they like. As a result the order in society is disturbed and people are running into losses. Are children not to be checked and controlled?

Hearing such complaints every day, KRISHNA'S mother got fed up. She tied him up to a mortar to punish him. KRISHNA opened his mouth to explain. The mother saw her whole world in the mouth of her child. Wonderful is a mother's love for her child. She said one should learn to be critical of practices taken for granted.

One day KRISHNA along with his friends took their packets of food and went out to graze the cattle on grass near a lake and to water the calves. A huge crane swooped down at KRISHNA to bite him. It found KRISHNA to be a ball of fire so quick he was, though he looked like a child. He tore apart the beak of the bird in self-defense. He taught his friends to be out-going and overcome difficulties.

Once KRISHNA went on a picnic into woodlands along with boys of his village. They carried their food and playthings with them. They played copying forms of plants and imagining their feelings. Who would stand still for a long time in the manner of this or that plant? They played copying the sounds of birds and animals and imagining their feelings. Who would produce a larger number of sounds of the same bird or animal? Who would look like this or that animal and imagine his feelings? Who would produce one sound along with another to produce laughter? They created their own games and toys for their entertainment and growth. Some of these games gave birth to different forms of YOGIC postures. KRISHNA built up a magical world with his games and his flute and musical compositions. He taught his friends to create their own games and play and entertainment, as they can become useful to others later.

A python lay on their way. He was released there to destroy them. He opened his mouth to eat them all and so take the very life of villagers. The boys entered the mouth, as they do not know the difference between play and reality. But KRISHNA knew that play merges into reality and reality merges into play and there are no fixed boundaries of the two. He enlarged his body and the python burst. The play was bigger than reality.

Then they went to the nearby river. Its water was clear and the banks were full of sand. They had their lunch on plates of fresh leaves. They played and watched the birds and listened to the music of waters. The cows grazed far away. Suddenly they disappeared. KRISHNA went in search of them, but could not find them. He came back to tell his friends. His friends had disappeared.

BRAHMA had played a trick on him. KRISHNA stood still and started playing on his flute. Music has magical powers. Suddenly he became all his friends and their playthings. He was one but he became many. They all went home and their mothers were thrilled to meet them. After a moment BRAHMA looked to see how KRISHNA had dealt with the difficult situation. But a lot of time had already passed on the earth. Time in the universe is not the same as the time on earth. KRISHNA had played with his friends as he played with his own self. This is what reality is. When we play with others, we are playing with our own impressions of them, playing with ourselves. BRAHMA was thrilled to see the nature of reality, so much beyond reason, as it includes reason.

One day KRISHNA was playing with his friends. He saw that some BRAHMANS were doing the ritual of YAJNA in an open field nearby. Rituals require free distribution of food to all and help us experience the same spirit present in all. So KRISHNA sent his friends to them to ask for food. The BRAHMANS ignored them. The boys asked for food from their wives. The wives gave them food and brought it to KRISHNA too. They thanked the boys for giving them a chance to serve them. KRISHNA praised women, as they were more loving than men. He asked them to teach love and charity to their husbands. YAJNA does not lie in the action of the ritual. It lies in its effect on the mind, cultivating a generous and compassionate heart.

One day they went far away into a grove of date palms. They shook the trees and dates fell down. They wanted to eat the dates. Some demons came rushing at them and asserted their ownership and right to the dates. Their chief was an ass. He tried to kick KRISHNA with his legs. KRISHNA caught hold of the legs and whirled him away. The ass fell far away and the trees were uprooted. Their fruits littered the ground. The cowherds and villagers ate to their fill. Who has the right to the fruits of nature? Those who need the fruit have the right to take it, he said. Those who use their power to assert their right to take it even when they do not need it do not have this right. Might is not right, only right is right, but one must have strength to destroy the brutes and asses who assert that might is right.

The water of River YAMUNA became poisonous and polluted. Even the birds and animals would not drink it. Those who drank it perished. Plants started dying and the breeze smelled foul. KRISHNA was born to destroy evil. He climbed up a tree and jumped right into the water, where the problem lay. The poisons rushed up in all directions. The source of poisons was snakes. Their head was KALIYA. He rose up in anger to give a fight. Everyone was frightened, but not KRISHNA. He was a master of all arts. He danced on the head of the snake. Other snakes appealed to him for mercy. But how can there be mercy for him who spreads poison and terror and kills others? KRISHNA told them that there is place for everything, including snakes. But they must go into wilderness and not live near human habitations. The poisons in rivers must go to their proper place. They should not be where they do not belong.

One day KRISHNA and his friends were making merry in a forest. They danced and sang and clapped their hands and KRISHNA played on the flute. There was a demon wearing lots of gold ornaments and still wanting more gold. He was always drunk and had red eyes. His body was powerful but used for wicked purposes. He decided to kidnap one of the boys for gold. So he joined them in the game as a friend and looked for his chance. KRISHNA saw through his plan. From the outward appearance he could know the inward reality. We should learn to see the motives of actions. The boys split the group into two and started playing KABBADI. As a part of the game the loser had to carry the winner on his shoulders up to a fixed distance. The demon lost in the innocent game. He had to carry BALRAMA, but he ran away fast beyond the fixed goal. BALRAMA was frightened at first. Then he remembered that the divine power lives in him and fear has no existence. He faced reality and started hitting the wicked man's head with his forceful fists. He knocked him dead. Awareness of one's divinity destroys fear and danger.

One day the cattle entered a forest full of MUNJA grass. This grass used to be cut and twisted into long threads to knit cots. The grass was dry and dusty. The herd entered it with such force that it caught fire. KRISHNA acted at once and guided them out to safety. He was always alert to dangers and reacted quickly and helpfully.

As winter started, the village girls went to the nearby river early at dawn. They celebrated the arrival of winter with the worship of DEVI. They had their ritual bath and made an idol of DEVI with sand, a beautiful work of art. They decorated it with flowers and fragrance. They prayed for marriage with KRISHNA. They vowed to carry on this worship of DEVI every day for a month.

One day, KRISHNA with his friends came there. They gathered up clothes of all the girls and climbed up a tree. He shouted to them to come out of the river and request him to give their clothes back to them.

The girls had to struggle with many emotions. How could they come out of the river naked? How could anyone be without clothes? They were afraid. Would they be beautiful without the clothes on their bodies? Is being naked the only way of meeting the beloved, be it man or god? They disliked doing what they were not in the habit of doing. They felt proud. How could this stranger dare to demand nudity? They felt the pride of their noble birth. Nobility lay in moral values like self-reliance, usefulness and contentment. Their sense of socially proper conduct was hurt. But they came out of the river nevertheless with the bravery of their innocence. They faced KRISHNA and got their clothes back.

One day KRISHNA and his friends were tending cattle and went far away. KRISHNA saw a grove of trees. The trees excited his sense of wonder. He sang a song in praise of their beauty. Trees live and die for others. They give us their fruits and roots, their leaves and flowers, bark and timber. Plants give medicines and health, cool air and life. They are alive like us. We should be alive like them. Plants of yesterday become us today. We of today shall become them tomorrow.

The people of GOKULA engaged in rearing cows and selling milk. They worshipped INDRA every year to thank him for the rains for their fodder and for protecting them from the theft of cows. INDRA was known as a great warrior who protected his people and their wealth. Wealth was counted by the number of cows one had, as it is done in some parts of India even today.

KRISHNA did not like worshipping INDRA for rains. How could any DEVA be responsible for their prosperity, he asked. Every thing that happens is an action. Only actions exist. One action results in other actions. One is born and one dies and these are actions that happen. Pleasures and pains, prosperity and adversity are actions. One gets them as a result of one's actions. We are born with certain tendencies to actions. These result from actions done in earlier lives. Our duty is to express our urges through actions, and experience the resulting actions. When they are bad, we suffer and learn not to repeat them. When they are good, we enjoy and repeat them. So we learn to improve, ignoring the one and cultivating the other. We alter them to reach our aims. When we produce milk and rear cows, we should do this work with skill and devotion. Good fortune will come as a result of our action. We ourselves bring about our fortune or misfortune. How does a DEVA come into this picture? How can he reward and punish? How can he give results of actions? Results of actions are contained in those very actions. No DEVA is needed for this. Rains come and fodder grows as results of actions of nature. Praying or not praying to a DEVA has no effect. Where is the need to pray to INDRA?

So he asked the people of GOKULA not to waste their time in praying to INDRA. Instead of this, they should worship the cows that give them wealth. They should feed them greener grass. They should take care of the cows so that they give more milk. They should worship the mountain where they live. The place where we live has a spirit in it. We create that spirit and that spirit creates us, constitutes us. This makes a cycle. We must worship and be devoted to the spirit of the place where we live and not make it like every other place. We must become more aware of the local flavor and nurture it.

KRISHNA himself became the spirit of the mountain and lifted it up, changing the way we see nature. People worshipped him. INDRA got angry. He sent down heavy rains. It rained heavily non-stop for seven days and seven nights. The whole place was flooded. KRISHNA protected his followers with his little finger.

INDRA realized that genuine worship and prayers could not be enforced on others. Prayers must come from within, springing from our nature and how it expresses in actions and aspirations. They express our nature and actions and aspiration for the best in it. One cannot ask people to worship and pray in this way or that way. So he cooled down and the rains stopped. He came down and worshipped KRISHNA. He called him GOVINDA, which means the INDRA of cows on earth, the source of nourishment and wealth. The heavenly cow that gives all that is needed came down and bathed KRISHNA with her milk. INDRA bathed him with the pure water of GANGA. In this way, the divinity of KRISHNA was announced.

Once the whole village of cowherds was upset at the absence of security. They felt harassed at the way the king was treating them, demanding high taxes. They all met to decide on what to do. As was the custom in those days, they decided to quit the land of GOKUL. If the ruled quit, the ruler ceased to exist. So they migrated to a forest called VRINDAVANN, the forest of the heart, where KRISHNA plays. Many people harassed by the king used to withdraw their support to him and go into the forest.

KRISHNA started the group dance known as RASLILA. All the men and women of the village put on their best clothes, as everyone must enjoy life whatever the conditions in which he lives. If we wait for the right conditions to come before we can enjoy life, then we wait forever, because the right conditions never come. They formed a circle linking their hands. Each one felt that he or she was holding divine hands. They danced to the rhythm of drumbeats. Bells around their ankles and waists danced and made their music. Beats became faster as they clapped their hands and felt strong emotions.

Later on they played water games. They entered a pond of clear water and thrashed water right and left and laughed and threw jets of water at each other. They bathed each other and enjoyed the feel of water and the feel of each other. Then they rested on fragrant grass nearby, enjoying each other's company.

KRISHNA played on his flute that absorbed their minds completely. Some people thought that they enjoyed each other without restraints, but his devotees think, KRISHNA always remained fully self-controlled. In any case, one picks up many things from older people, be it language, culture or sexual pleasures. Sex was never thought of as sinful. It was a momentary experience of ecstasy, a foretaste of the experience of oneness of all.

Once KRISHNA and his brother BALRAMA were playing with women in a forest. It was moonlit evening. An officer of the king passed by on a chariot. He carried away some of the women by force. This was undesirable. They shrieked and shouted for help. Both the brothers pursued the rascal and caught up with him. They punished him with death and rescued the women.

RAJA KANS invited chiefs of villages to come to MATHURA. They were to come to pay their tribute and revenue and participate in DHANUR YAJNA. In this ritual ceremony, there were wrestling matches and fights against elephants. Animals and men ran races. Many village sports were played. The villagers displayed their strength and skills before the RAJA every year. The best among them were chosen for reward and recruitment into the royal service.

RAJA KANS sent AKRUR, a distinguished YADAV, to bring KRISHNA and BALRAMA to this contest. He felt jealous of their fame and wanted to get rid of them.

AKRUR was well received. NANDA family offered him welcome, sweets and gifts. They asked him a difficult question. What should a tribe do if their RAJA is cruel? How can a king be wicked, demanding heavy taxes and tributes and his people live well? How can a tribe fare well under a king who kills his own people? If a king does not please his people by working for their welfare, how can he be called a RAJA? Why should he receive honor and tribute?

AKRUR invited them to MATHURA. They accompanied him in carts full of milk and curds, sweets and honey. The village women cried at their departure, unsure whether they would ever meet again. They felt jealous of the city women and their fine ways of dressing and talking. The only way for them now to meet KRISHNA would be through memory and meditation.

On the way they rested on the banks of YAMUNA. AKRUR bathed in the river, reciting GAYATRI MANTRA. As he dipped into the water, he saw KRISHNA lying on the serpent of time with many powers attending on him. When he got out of water he saw KRISHNA playing with BALRAMA on a cart. He was amazed.

He said: You are NARAYANA, the ultimate cause, and PURUSHA, the cosmic organic being. You became BRAHMA, the creative order of nature, its forces and elements. You became intelligence, ego and mind. You became the body, its senses and their objects. Everything leads to you. Everywhere is an opening to you. Every point is a door of entry to you, if one knows how to enter.

You became the fish and the horse, the tortoise and the boar. You became man-lion and the dwarf and the man with the battle-axe. He was the leader of BHRIGUS. He killed all warriors on earth for the sake of peace in order to stop fighting. You became RAMA and now you are KRISHNA. You will become BUDDHA and KALKI, who will destroy the barbarians. You are VASUDEVA, the self of all selves. You are the support of ego, controller of the mind and the senses.

Soon they entered MATHURA, surrounded by a large moat, high wooden gates and walls. They rested in a public garden at the outskirts. AKRUR went ahead and informed the king.

BALRAMA and KRISHNA went sight seeing in the city. They saw wide roads and mansions with gardens, and rest houses, assembly halls for conferences of tradesmen and granaries made of copper and brass. They saw smaller houses and wooden sheds for workmen. They saw streets and shopping centers. They saw courtyards with garlands of flowers and auspicious banana leaves at their entry gates. They saw a big difference between city, village and forest life.

KRISHNA saw a washer man carrying fine clothes for the king. He requested him to give the village boys some fine clothes, since the king had so many. The man refused and asked how dare a coarse man from the jungle ask for fine clothes. KRISHNA twisted his arms and distributed the clothes to the village boys with him. The message of his distributing fine clothes to villagers reached the king.

KRISHNA saw a hunch back woman carrying sandal paste for the king. He asked the young beauty to give some fragrant paste to village boys, which she gave with smiles and a pleasant face. KRISHNA looked at her with love and her back felt straight. The message of his helping the handicapped too reached the king.

BRAHMANS sprinkled rose water on KRISHNA and received him. Traders offered him flowers and welcomed him. Women kept on looking at him in love and admiration.

KRISHNA went to the hall where a bow like INDRA'S rainbow was being worshipped. He walked in boldly in spite of the resistance offered to him. He picked up the bow and with one twang he broke it. In the scuffle that followed he killed the guard. The people rejoiced that their savior had come.

Next day KRISHNA and his brother BALRAMA went to the wrestling arena. RAJA KANS had placed his elephant at the gate. Its driver had instructions to kill KRISHNA. As soon as the driver saw KRISHNA, the elephant ran towards him and lifted up KRISHNA in its trunk. He stuck a powerful fist on its eye and slipped down from the trunk. He quickly moved to its behinds and caught hold of its tail, pulling it backwards. The elephant kept turning towards its behinds, trying to get at him, but it could not. KRISHNA remained at the tail end clubbing its vital organs with great force. He knew the weakness of the enemy and hit him there. Then he jumped on to its back and pushed the driver down. KRISHNA gained control of the elephant. The crowd rejoiced at his victory. RAJA KANS felt humiliated.

Then BALRAMA and KRISHNA grappled with two wrestlers. Holding their hands, pushing and pulling, whirling their arms and throwing each other on the ground, they tried to gain victory. The women had a greater sense of justice. They protested at the unequal fight between two adolescent boys and two mature mountain-like wrestlers, and that too soon after one of the boys had tamed the royal elephant. But RAJA KANS turned a deaf ear. The fight continued till the boys gained victory. The other wrestlers fled in fear.

RAJA KANS was furious. He ordered that the boys be imprisoned, their friends be killed and their wealth confiscated. He ordered that his own father UGRASEN who had sided with VASUDEVA be killed. While he was giving such deathly orders to others, KRISHNA jumped on to the high stage with the speed of lightning. He caught hold of the RAJA from the tuft of long hair on his head, which was the symbol of his intelligence, and whirled him round and round and threw him down far away. He fell down from the height broken and dead.

RAJA KANS had two wives, daughters of the RAJA of MAGHDA. They started beating their breast and mourning.

You were a great king full of strength and power, our lion! You struck terror in the hearts of your enemies. You snatched the kingdom from your father and imprisoned him. You were so ruthless! You imprisoned your sister and her husband in fear of death, but death came. You were so careful, but death knows the way. You increased the revenue collected from villages till the people cried and deserted their places. Your need for your comfort and security was great. You increased the taxes and the people started cheating and you confiscated their wealth. You thought so much of yourself, but it did not help. What is the limit of comfort and security, O king? Why should a king take so much? Is there a limit to what you can tax, to what you can take? You gave good reasons. But were they true? Were they real? Was your spending for your self or for your people? We mourn for you, our lion! We think of the past and prepare for the future.

KRISHNA said: RAJA KANS was my uncle, the brother of my mother. But his actions were evil and so he had to be killed. It is not enough to be powerful. One must combine power with goodness and wisdom. Wisdom lies in doing what is good to others and not in doing what is good to one's own petty self and pretending that we are doing what is good for others. We cannot be good and take away our father's kingdom because he is old. We have to be a pillar of strength to him.

Now MAHARAJA UGRASEN shall regain his throne and rule according to DHARMA.

It was decided to educate KRISHNA and his brother BALRAMA. GARG ACHARYA was the guru of YADAVS. He performed the ceremony of the sacred thread, admitting them to formal education. He taught them GAYATRI MANTRA, a prayer for change from ignorance to knowledge and from being identified with the mortal body and its limited senses and mind to being identified with the immortal self that is present in all beings.

Then the boys were handed over to GURU SANDIPANI. He gave them a two-month full day crash course on the essentials of VEDAS and rituals, UPANISHADS and philosophy, grammar and pronunciation, prosody and music, logic and laws, administration, war and weapons.

On completion of this course, they made an offering called GURUDAKSHINA to their guru. His son had been utterly lost to liquor and drugs. KRISHNA brought him back from sensuality to rationality and self-control. The guru was satisfied with this payment.

KRISHNA sent a messenger to inform his foster parents and friends about his welfare. They were thrilled to learn that KRISHNA never forgot those who were devoted to him.

His messenger said: The world of dream is as real as the world of wakefulness. The world of sleep is as real as the worlds of wakefulness and dream. In their depth, these three worlds are expressions of one and the same power. Be devoted to that depth which remains the same in sleep, dream and wakefulness. There you meet KRISHNA, the depth and the height of your being.

The hunch back woman KRISHNA had praised invited him to her house. He visited her and satisfied her pent up desires.

KRISHNA sent AKRUR to HASTINAPUR to find out if RAJA DHRITARASHTRA was treating his younger brother's sons properly. Their mother KUNTI was the sister of KRISHNA'S father VASUDEVA.

DHRITRASHTRA was born blind, and so he could not become the king. His younger brother PANDU inherited the kingdom, leaving the elder brother full of jealousy and anger, helplessness and hatred. His sons felt jealous of their cousins and tried to harm them. However the younger brother died young. The elder brother, though blind, gained the throne.

AKRUR said to DHRITRASHTRA: You have come to the throne on your brother's death. Govern the land according to DHARMA. Treat alike your sons and your brother's sons. Otherwise you will have ill fame in this world and hell in the next. We are born alone and we die alone. We do not take any of our possessions along with us. Therefore we should be just and treat all alike. If we gain wealth through wrong ways, we become unrighteous. Then we lose our claim to the divine present in us. Our life becomes base, empty and meaningless. Justice is better than evil.

The two widows of RAJA KANS went to their father and narrated their story to him. He was RAJA JARASANDH of MAGADH. He gathered a large army and marched to MATHURA. KRISHNA and BALRAMA destroyed his army, but the king was sent back to his kingdom dishonored. JARASANDH came seventeen times and every time he was defeated. When one of these wars happened, KRISHNA was withdrawing to an island off the coast of GUJRAT. It was full of sand and stone, but well protected and difficult to reach. KRISHNA built a well-planned city from scratch in it. It had highways, wide roads and side streets with trees and flowers. It had tall buildings and houses with wooden balconies for moon bathing. People were fond of bathing and relaxing in the moonlight in the hot summers. This was DWARAKA, the capital to which the people of MATHURA had withdrawn.

RUKMANI was the daughter of RAJA BHISHMAK of VIDHARBA. She sent a message to KRISHNA that she loved him and wanted to marry him.

Her brother wanted her to marry his friend SISUPAL, the RAJA of CHEDIS, now BUNDELKHAND. The RAJA of MAGHDH was also interested in her.

She said that if KRISHNA was willing he could kidnap her and defeat those who would oppose him and marry her as permitted by law.

After receiving her invitation, KRISHNA went to VIDHARBA. He kidnapped her when she had gone to DEVI temple. RAJAS assembled for the marriage opposed him but he defeated them. He took her to DWARKA, where the two married according to VEDIC rites.

A devotee of SURYA DEVA acquired a jewel as bright as the sun. Some courtiers suggested to KRISHNA that he should own it.

KRISHNA requested the devotee to offer it to their king. The devotee refused but his brother took it with him when he went hunting. A lion killed him and his horse. Later a bear took away the jewel and passed it on to his son. Meanwhile it was rumored that KRISHNA had stolen the jewel. He was upset. So he started tracing the footsteps of the horse and reached the dead bodies. Later he traced the steps of the bear and reached the jewel in a cave. He had to fight the bear for many days, before he caught the jewel and returned it to its owner and narrated the story of how the jewel was recovered. The devotee asked to be forgiven. He offered his daughter SATYABHAMA in marriage to KRISHNA.

KRISHNA tamed seven bulls in a bullfight without using any nose rings. He was offered the prize of a beautiful girl, named SATYA. He married her. She desired to have a branch of the KALPATRU tree from heavens as it fulfilled all desires. To fulfill his wife's desire, KRISHNA went to heavens and fought with DEVRAJA INDRA. He brought back a branch of the wish-fulfilling tree. It was planted in the courtyard. It became a tree and kept satisfying his wife's unending desires.

KRISHNA married BHADRA, born in KEKAYA in PUNJAB and offered to him by her brothers. He married LAKSHAMANA, daughter of the RAJA of MADRA, between Rivers RAVI and CHENAB, in a SWAYAMVARA and carried her away against the wishes of other suitors present there.

NARAKASUR was a son of mother earth. He was the RAJA of PRAGJYOTISHPUR ASSAM, in North East India. His city had layers of fortifications. There were barriers of mountains and weapons, heavy rains and water, forest fires and strong winds. He was so powerful that he became lawless and started terrorizing his own people. He took away the umbrella and sovereignty of INDRA and occupied his throne. He took away the ornaments of ADITI, the mother of INDRA. So KRISHNA attacked him with a powerful army and weapons. RAKSHUS MURA gave a brilliant reply with howling winds and powerful tridents. But KRISHNA knew all the tactics of war. He challenged him with a mace and killed him with a discus. Mother Earth made KRISHNA an offering of gold and praised him as supreme. He married all the women held captive by NARAKASUR. He captured all his army and wealth.

KRISHNA lived in DWARAKA as a householder. In his state, plants flowered and birds warbled and peacocks danced. The lakes were crystal clear full of lotuses and the land was full of crops and the cows full of milk. Roads were clean free of robbers and protected from the hot sun with trees. Streets were full of active merchants and manufacture. Houses flourished with gold and diamonds and people were prosperous. They had goodwill towards all beings and suppressed evildoers.

KRISHNA passed his time in jovial talk, or playing games with his wives or friends, or playing with children, or bathing or swimming in a pool. Sometimes he would do rituals, recite GAYATRI, make offerings to AGNI, or feed holy men and give them cows in charity. Sometimes he practiced the use of sword and shield with his friends, or rode horses, elephants and chariots. He would go far away on horses with his friends hunting wild animals. Sometimes he listened to bards reciting stories or heard music. Sometimes he saw dances and dramas. Sometimes he meditated on nature and the meaning and purpose of life. Sometimes he discussed politics and public affairs with his ministers or friends. He had wells and water tanks dug up and gardens and rest houses built in various places. He would collect secret information about what was going on in his state. He was always busy doing useful things. He slept only for a short time.

KRISHNA created new ways of worship that came to be called BHAGVAT DHARMA. He said that we should fight wars only to uphold justice and preserve order and not for getting more land or gold. DHARMA sustains life. Therefore we should not kill unjustly or loot people or acquire selfish gains.

He did not think highly of the worship of nature and the aims of satisfying natural human wants like food and sex, security and feelings of self-importance, but gave it a value as lower divine nature.

He taught people to rise above this lower nature to a higher nature like doing one's duty that emerges from one's divinely given nature, cultivating its goodness in a detached way while working for bringing people together in their interest. We should be single-minded and devoted to the best in us, which is divine, and personally experience it through an attitude of acceptance of all without injury to anyone, especially man and nature, without torturing our own body or the bodies of others, as the body is a divine animal that carries divine power. We all ride through life sitting on this animal.

We should lead active lives devoted to knowledge and wisdom, especially of the UPANISHADS and DARSHANS and keep our search for wealth and pleasures within restraints of moral goodness. He explained numerous ways of YOGA for experiencing union with the divine, like an absorbing proficiency in skills of doing one's duty of self-expression leading to realization of great ideals and the consequent loss of our selfish and petty ego in this vast and wonderful universe.

Once RAJA JARASANDH went on a tour of conquest and imprisoned many kings. They appealed to KRISHNA to help them.

He also received a message from his cousin YUDHISHTRA to visit HASTINAPUR and help him in doing RAJSUYA YAJNA for establishing his political power.

KRISHNA consulted with his ministers and friend UDDHAVA who advised him to defeat JARASANDH and help the imprisoned kings. KRISHNA informed the messenger that he would help the kings and destroy JARASANDH.

He ordered a royal march towards INDRAPRASTHA. He passed through the regions of ANARTA, SAUVIRA, MARU, and KURUKSHETRA, and crossed rivers like DRISHADVATI, SARASVATI and the lands of MATSYA in MADHYA PRADESH, and PANCHALA north of River GANGA and reached INDRAPRASTHA.

PANDAVA brothers and spiritual leaders received him. KRISHNA showed all due respect and love to his relatives and the leaders of the tribes of KURUS, SRINJAYAS, KEKAYAS and chiefs of various groups.

An ASURA architect MAYA had built a beautiful temple for ARJUNA, in which KRISHNA and his family were housed. KRISHNA said to YUDHISHTRA: RAJSUYA YAJNA is performed after subjugating neighboring kings, and uniting many kingdoms into a big one under one umbrella and keeping their pride unhurt. This you must do first. So a war was declared. SAHADEVA led SRINJAYAS to the south. NAKULA led MATSYAS to the west. ARJUNA led KEKAYAS to the north. BHIMA led MADRAKAS to the east. They conquered many kings and brought back tributes to YUDHISHTRA.

KRISHNA devised a strategy to destroy JARASANDH. Disguised as BRAHMANS, BHIMA, ARJUNA, and KRISHNA went to JARASANDH. They asked for a favor when the king was distributing gifts to his guests. After the king had promised to grant them favor, they declared that they were BHIMA, ARJUNA, and KRISHNA, and the favor they asked for was a dual fight with one of them. JARASANDH laughed at their cleverness. He refused to fight a dual with KRISHNA because he said KRISHNA was a coward who had run away from the battlefield and had withdrawn his capital from MATHURA to a low-lying island called DWARAKA in fear of him. He rejected ARJUNA on the ground that he was a junior, of slender built and no match for him.

He agreed to fight with BHIMA as his equal. He gave a mace to BHIMA and took one himself. They went out of the city and selected a proper arena and started exchanging blows. They made skillful movements. Sparks flew and maces broke and they grappled and rained blows on each other. But they were not tired. They fought like this every day for many days. Then KRISHNA gestured to BHIMA to split JARASANDH into two. BHIMA pulled apart the legs of JARASANDH and tore him into two parts. People mourned at the death of their king.

KRISHNA appointed JARASANDH'S son SAHADEVA as the ruler of MAGDHA. He did not have the ignoble desire to annex the kingdom of the defeated king. He liberated numerous kings from the prison house. They bowed to him and became his devoted followers. KRISHNA said: Wealth and power are good, but they end. Therefore look inwards and rule according to DHARMA. Use wealth and power for the benefit of all beings in their interest. The kings were sent back to their countries.

Then YUDHISHTRA performed the RAJSUYA YAJNA. A large field was ploughed up as the arena for the ritual. This form of worship did not have fixed temples in those days. When the divine power is present everywhere how can it be restricted to a small place called the temple? Every place is a door of entry into the divine, if one changed the way of seeing and cultivated the resulting attitude towards it. Many kings and priests and common people and women were invited to participate. They lit up the sacrificial fire and made offerings to it. They expounded and displayed different forms of YOGA. They worshipped KRISHNA as the ideal guest of honor, a great warrior who was wise, loving others and having full control of his senses.

RAJA SISUPAL of CHEDIS, now BUNDELKHAND, felt jealous at this fulsome praise of KRISHNA. He was a reincarnation of RAVANA, who was a reincarnation of HIRANYAKASHIPU, who hated VISHNU because VISHNU had exiled him out of heavens for his immoral behavior. He was asked to choose between three evil births or seven good births and he chose three evil births, as that would mean shorter duration away from heaven.

RAJA SHISHUPAL got up to say that there were many other warriors greater than KRISHNA. Why should this rustic cowherd be honored?

He does not have any VARNA. Is he a KASHTRIYA or a SHUDRA by birth and actions? We do not know. Are his parents KASHATRIYAS, DEVAKI and VASUDEVA? Or are his parents SHUDRAS, cowherds YASHODA and NANDA?

Does he live by the force of his arms, receiving tribute from others? Or does he live by selling milk and paying tribute to a king?

He is not affiliated to any ASHRAM. Is he a student living in celibacy devoted to truth? Or is he a householder, married to one wife and supporting society? Or is he a pleasure loving light-hearted man about town trying to find satisfaction with any woman whatsoever who comes his way?

He is not a member of any family. Is his family the family of his birth or of adoption? Is his family one family or two families, or all the families of his village or the world? Is he aware of the difference between one family and another?

Is he a virtuous man or a libertine? How can he be honored? He ran away from his motherland in fear of my friend RAJA JARASANDH. He has left the land of RISHIS and his ancestors, his motherland. He has gone away to live in a low-lying island surrounded by the sea. It is difficult to reach and full of sand and stones. It is devoid of holy men devoted to truth. How can such a deserter of motherland be honored?

RAJA SISUPAL continued his condemnation of KRISHNA, who kept smiling, but PANDVA brothers and the leaders of MATSYA, KEKAYA, and SRINJAYA tribes got ready with arms to reply to this attack from the RAJA of CHEDIS.

When KRISHNA saw the battle imminent, he used his right seeing discus called SUDARSHAN and cut off RAJA SISUPAL'S head, and said: One can criticize a hundred times but not a hundred and one times. Reasonable criticism has a limit beyond which it ceases to be reasonable and should not be tolerated.

The ceremonies restarted. All relatives performed their allotted duties. KRISHNA washed the feet of learned visitors. DURYODHANA acted as the treasurer, as he was fond of wealth. BHIMA controlled the kitchen. He was an expert on PAKSHASTRA, the science of cooking. SAHADEVA was in charge of reception. NAKULA collected the stores. After the rituals and distribution of charity, they had a ceremonial bath in the River GANGA. Then they made merry.

On seeing the grandeur of the ceremony and the palace of PANDVA brothers, DURYODHANA felt jealous. He showered abuses at the guards and servants to show off his importance. He did not know how to deal with lowly people with due respect. The palace architecture had some optical illusions built into it. He saw water on dry floor and held up the ends of his clothes. Everyone laughed. Elsewhere he mistook watery surface to be a dry floor and fell into water. DRAUPADI laughed at his ignorance of the latest fashions in architecture. She lived to regret this laughter later. DURYODHANA was deeply wounded. He decided to take revenge. This desire for revenge led to the war of MAHABHARATA that destroyed all of them.

He invited the PANDVA brothers to a game of dice. The invitation was accepted. His experienced uncle played with a loaded dice. The PANDVA brothers lost the game, including themselves and their wife DRAUPADI. She was humiliated as KAURAVAS tried to molest her, but KRISHNA saved her. PANDVAS were exiled from their kingdom for fourteen years. When they returned after the exile, the kingdom was not returned to them.

KRISHNA went to HASTINAPUR many times to bring about peace between cousins bent upon destroying each other in a war, but DURYODHANA'S hatred for PANDVAS could not be overcome. He refused to give even an inch of land to them out of half of the kingdom that came to them in inheritance, though they had reduced their demand and asked for only five villages for five brothers. So the war could not be prevented. The only way to prevent the war was to be just in the distribution of wealth. But people who feel they are very powerful do not like to be just.

DURYODHANA came to DWARKA to ask for KRISHNA'S help. ARJUNA also asked for his help. There was a tie between them. KRISHNA did not believe in neutrality. A neutral foreign policy is a policy of incompetence, immoral and unprincipled. So he offered them a choice between himself and his army. DURYODHANA chose his army, as he believed in physical strength, and ARJUNA chose him, as he believed in wisdom and divine power.

SALVA was a friend of SISUPAL. He vowed to destroy all YADAVAS. He acquired a large aerial vehicle that could go anywhere and not be destroyed. It moved fast and could be seen anywhere and everywhere. He flew towards DWARAKA and his army surrounded the town. He threw down rains of stones and boulders, lightning and fire. His army destroyed the outer woodlands and gardens of the city. He destroyed some of the towers of its high buildings. KRISHNA was not in town. He had gone to reconcile the cousins at HASTINAPUR. His sons and army generals put up a good defense. They shot a hundred arrows at the same time, carrying fire and poison and decimated the invaders. Finally they managed to kill SALVA.

KRISHNA'S brother BALRAMA went on an all India pilgrimage tour. He bathed in rivers KAUSIKI, GOMATI, GANDAKI, and VIPASA. He went to the holy lake, the source of river SARAYU. He walked along this river visiting shrines and learned people. He spent nights in village inns on the way. At PRAYAG, he had a holy bath and sacrificed to the divine power in nature. He spent some time at the ASHRAM of RISHI PULAHA. At GAYA, he sacrificed to ancestors, custom and tradition. He went to MAHENDRA Mountain, the range of hills on the eastern GHATS from ORRISA to MADHURAI, and worshipped PARSHURAM. who had tried to reach peace and non-violence through killing warriors. He traveled to SAPTAGODAVARI and to VENA, Lake PAMPA, and BHIMARATHI. He worshipped at the temple of SKANDA and proceeded to SRISAILA, the abode of MAHADEV SHIVA. He worshipped at TIRUPATI, the holy shrine of DRAVIDA country. He went to KAMAKOSHNI, KANCHIPURAM, the holy river KAVERI and SRIRANGAM, and RISHABHA Mountain and southern MADHURA and reached RAMA'S SETU. He traveled on to rivers KRITAMALA, and TAMRAPARNI, and to MALAYA Mountain full of fragrance of SANDAL trees, south of River KAVERI, later on the kingdoms of PANDYA and CHOLA kings, where he worshipped AGASTYA RISHI who had spread SANATANA DHARMA across the seas. He went to the southern sea and worshipped at the shrine of DURGA, known as KANYAKUMARI. He went to ANANTPURAM, now called TRIVANDRUM, where MAHAVISHNU manifested as PADAMANABHA. He bathed in the lake PANCHAPSARAS. He traveled through KERALA, TRIGARTHA and reached GOKARNA and worshipped PARAMESHVAR SHIVA. Then he worshipped at DURGA of the ISLAND, called MUKAMBIKA, now MUMBAI. He went on to bathe in the holy rivers of TAPTI, and reached DANDAKA.

He heard from travelers that numerous warriors had died at the battle of KURUKSHETRA. He reached there to find himself in the thick of war. He tried to stop a fight between BHIMA and DURYODHANA. He praised both of them, saying that BHIMA is stronger but DURYODHANA is better trained. He said the two were fighting because of what they thought of each other in their minds. But if they changed their thoughts, the war would stop. But his wisdom fell on deaf ears. BALRAMA returned to DWARAKA.

UTTARA, ARJUNA'S daughter in law, appeared before KRISHNA and said that wherever she went a missile pursued her. It looked to her like a mass of molten iron. She was willing to die but wanted to protect the child inside her.

KRISHNA knew that it was BRAHMA missile that would not miss its target except when the force of VISHNU intervenes. He protected the pregnant mother as she brings forth a baby at the risk of her own life and women must always be protected. Later the child that was born became RAJA PARIKSHAT. He continued the PANDU line.

At the end of the war, PANDUS and KRISHNA performed the ceremony of last rites for all those who had died in the war.

When GANDARI, the mother of DURYODHANA, met KRISHNA, she felt smothered under a wave of hatred, as she thought that he was the source of all her troubles. She cursed him saying that all his tribe would destroy each other and he would die a miserable death. This happened thirty-six years later.

KRISHNA had a childhood friend, who was called SUDAMA. He was a learned BRAHMAN but very poor. He and his family starved on most days. His wife prodded him to request the RAJA to support him and his learning. After a great deal of hesitation, SUDAMA took a handful of husky rice as a gift for his childhood friend KRISHNA and visited DWARKA. The gatekeeper would not let him into the palace. SUDAMA sat down there waiting for the time when KRISHNA would come out. When he did he was thrilled to find SUDAMA there. The two embraced each other and SUDAMA offered him his poor gift, which the king received with great courtesy. The two chatted with each other for a long time about their Guru and of the glorious time they had together in the GURUKUL.

SUDAMA spent a night in the palace he had never imagined before but he could not ask for help. He left the palace, feeling happy at the good fortune of his friend. When he returned home he found that his hut had changed into a big house with all the comforts that the divine grace provides.

An eclipse of the sun occurred. RISHIS had the power to predict it. So many YADHAVA princes had assembled at the river SYAMANTAPANCHAKA before the eclipse. They had come well dressed in their chariots along with their wives and armies. They fasted, prayed and had their ritual bath with their minds focused on the powers of nature and the source of the power of nature that lies just beyond the senses. They gave gifts in charity to holy and learned people. Then they feasted and had good time with their relatives and friends. They met the rulers of MATSYA, USINARA, KOSALA, VIDHARBHA, KAURAVA, SRINJAYA, KAMBHOJA, KEKAYA, MADRA, ANARTA, and KERALA. They met old friends NANDAS, GOPAS and GOPIS. Their hearts and faces bloomed. Many of them wept tears of joy.

KUNTI DEVI said to KRISHNA: how come you forgot us in our adversity?

VASU DEVA said: Dear aunt, RAJA KANS persecuted us. Then we left our land and went far away to a distant island. Now the divine has restored to us our glory.

BALRAMA and KRISHNA touched the feet of their foster parents. They remembered the sorrow of separation. Their mothers ROHINI and DEVKI embraced YASHODA, saying that the help that she had given them in adversity could not be compensated for even with the wealth of RAJA INDRA. She had looked after two children separated from their parents as if they were her own children. What could be greater than the action of looking after children especially when they are not your own? She did not distinguish between her children and the children of others and helped them grow without fear or danger.

KRISHNA met each one of the GOPIS privately in their minds and had long conversations, as they were deeply devoted to him. He said that the divine brings people together for a short time and then separates them. That is nature. Devotion to that which is behind nature liberates one from it. The body creates the difference between inside and outside. But for the spirit there is no such difference. What you see and want lives in the body, not in your self. Both your self and matter live in me, the cause of all causes. They are my expressions.

DRAUPADI asked KRISHNA'S wives how he came to marry them.

RUKMANI said: JARASANDH wanted to enforce his decision that I marry SISUPAL, RAJA of CHEDIS. I wanted to marry KRISHNA and eloped with him. He defeated all the princes assembled there.

SATYABHAMA said: My father accused KRISHNA of killing his younger brother and taking his jewel. This was a false accusation. KRISHNA searched for my uncle and found him out dead in a forest and brought back the jewel from a cave. In return my father gifted me to him, as I wanted to marry him.

JAMBAVATI said that her father fought with KRISHNA for a jewel called SYAMANTAKA for twenty-seven days. On finding KRISHNA'S divinity, he gifted the jewel and me to him.

KALINDI said that she did penance to marry him and he married her.

MITRAVINDA said that he came to her SVYAMVAR ceremony and she married him.

SATYA said that in her SVYAMVAR, he was able to tame seven untamed bulls, which others could not do. So she was gifted to him.

BHADRA said that she loved KRISHNA and requested her father to offer her to him. KRISHNA accepted the offer.

LAKSHMANA said that in her SVYAMVAR, KRISHNA shot an arrow at a fish on seeing her reflection in water and fought with the assembled princes and took her away.

Many other wives came to KRISHNA through the death of NARAKASUR, as they were his kidnapped women.

Many ill omens started appearing. KRISHNA'S friend UDDAVA felt frightened and asked for advice. KRISHNA told him that his death was near and YADAVAS will use their wealth, strength and courage in fighting with each other and this beautiful city will go under the sea in seven days after his death. When I die, the KALI age will begin. He gave advice to him.

Learn to recognize my one and only one presence in all this multiplicity, all these numerous beings and things and abandon possessive attachment for them. Control your mind and senses and see the spirit everywhere and feel benevolent.

Learn how to live by observing elements of nature like air, water, fire, sun, moon, space and time, and so on. Observe their ways and characteristics. Learn from them. Learn from your own body and its mind and their silent promptings. Whatever teaches you is your guru.

Man is essentially his spirit and this has to be experienced, not just heard. Experience it through reflection on your life and meditation. Man has the capacity to find out truth of things. He has intelligence and the power to observe and discriminate. He can be his own teacher. Rise above your instincts and evil tendencies.

I have created many types of bodies, but man's body is the best. I am present in every body. Find it out. Are you your instrument of finding the truth, like your senses, mind, or intelligence, or are these instruments lifeless and there is a spirit operating through them?

BHAGAVATA DHARMA requires that you accept your divine nature given to you at birth and develop from there towards great ideals. These are given to you by the traditions of your family, region and culture, and by MAHARSHIS, MAHADEVA and incarnations of MAHAVISHNU. In this process, nourish your goodness and starve your wickedness. Unless you begin from where you are, you cannot begin at all.

You are born with certain tendencies to action and in a certain occupation and mode of living of your parents. Begin your spiritual journey from there. There is nowhere else from where you can begin. Do not follow others, neighbors, fashions or crowds. Be aware of your nature. This is easier said than done. It requires watching yourself, remembering your experience and reflecting on your actions and their private motives and public purposes and the gap between the two and the difference between what is and what ought to be. It requires study of VEDAS and DARSHANS with understanding and devotion to DHARMA and great ideals, and realization of your highest potential because the divine lives in the best of everything.

You are first a child and you grow up with time and nurture, education and culture and you marry and have children and earn your livelihood and support society. Be aware of your actions. Be absorbed in doing your duty that emerges from your nature skillfully for bringing people together, reconciling them, doing your best in resolving conflicts peacefully but fighting to the finish when necessary.

You have certain customs and traditions given to you by your family and community and region. Live accordingly, expressing them in the best way possible, but reflecting on them and eliminating their flaws, trying to improve upon them by following the highest values and ideals present in them and suited to your nature and the situation. Be the best of your tradition, howsoever small it might be. There is nothing small and nothing big, nothing without value and nothing entirely valuable. Learn to laugh and celebrate. This will make your living into a divine game.

Bound by his senses, man tries to acquire pleasures, wealth and power. These are desirable ends within limits and beyond those limits they become undesirable. Man works for his narrow objectives alone. Naturally he lands up in suffering. He should rise above his senses, above his limited objectives through detachment to them and be free. His work, his duty should become his divine play. But instead his divine play becomes his depressing work.

This context reveals your true color, which is your VARNA. Its hues and expression change with time, according to your ASHRAM, whether you are a child, an adult, retiring or finally retired. Your family or extended network of relationships kept alive by love and nourished by duties and obligations influence your color too, which reveals the importance of your KUL and RASHTRA DHARMA.

Do your duty sincerely and rise up into freedom. That freedom from the senses and the body and its narrow mind and society and from the evil of your nature and your context is MOKSHA, the final aim of life. Experience that freedom and be your spirit riding on your animal body through time.

When you do your actions and intensely desire their consequences, you are bound in the chain of action and its consequences. You lose your freedom. You become a cog in the wheel, a thing. Rise above it through working for the general benefit and so offering the results of your actions to the divine who is present in all, including nature. If you do an action and expect its results for your personal benefit, you may not get them, as the result of actions depends on many other forces. Honor those forces.

KRISHNA said that holy men sanctify sacred rivers and places of pilgrimage by living near them. They embody all VEDA, which is always alive in the self and hearts and minds of all beings, including nature. They bring auspicious and virtuous tendencies into action and intensify them through sacrifice, austerity and charity, study and contentment, having me in their mind and heart, their center. One should adore them to worship me. Meeting holy people purifies the mind more quickly. Devotion to nature, speech and mind does not purify, as it does not remove sinful tendencies. Effort and grace are necessary. Self-centered motives create a consciousness of one's difference from others. Rise above it to see what unites you with others. Contact with the enlightened ones gives this help.

When KRISHNA'S end came near, DEVAS came to inform him.

RISHI NARAD said: One should perform all the duties and actions as religious rituals of sacrifice, dedicating their results to VISHNU who sustains life with full faith and sincerity. One can overcome desire for wealth through using it for social benefit and desire for sex through devotion to the family and community, seeing all people as related through blood. One should pay one's debts to nature, ancestors and RISHIS and study the VEDA and oneself and learn to see everything as an expression of the divine. One should continue the family life based on good traditions and high moral values but remain detached from everything.

BRAHMA along with many other DEVAS sang the praises of KRISHNA. They said: Sir, you came down to earth for a purpose that has now been achieved.

KRISHNA said: The YADAVA people are so full of wealth, power, courage, pride and aggression that they would dominate the world. Such aggression needs to be restrained. I shall come to your world of truth after their destruction.

YADHAVAS took common meals in a ceremony and drank honey wine. It brought out to the surface their hidden mutual hatreds and aroused their killing instincts. They started talking loudly, finding faults, abusing and quarrelling. They fought with swords and maces, spears and javelins, bows and arrows. They destroyed each other. KRISHNA and BALARAMA killed many of them.

BALARAMA bathed in River SARASVATI and sat down under a PEEPAL tree as yogi. ANANT NAG, the serpent of infinity, came out of his mouth. Many snakes came to meet him. He disappeared in the sea of dissolved elements, known as KSHEER SAGAR.

KRISHNA bathed in River SARASVATI and sat under a PEEPAL tree and started meditating. When he was meditating, a hunter whose name was JARA, old age, pierced his foot, which had a print of lotus flower, meaning detachment, on the sole. On seeing the divine power, the hunter was frightened and he apologized. KRISHNA asked him not to fear, because he had only done his duty. When you do your duty, you have no choice and no fear.

He asked his charioteer to inform DWARKA of the mutual destruction of YADHVAS, and to take women and children for safety to INDRAPRASTHA for the protection of ARJUNA. He said that no one should grieve, as the whole universe is ours, and every one should follow his way. All alone, he left his body to enter the infinite.

MAHABHARTA war was fought on the question of inheritance. Two sets of relatives united by blood had an equal share in their common inheritance. PANDUS were denied their share of wealth and subjected to difficulties and humiliations. KRISHNA tried to resolve their conflict on just distribution of wealth peacefully in many different ways. But KAURAVAS were powerful and thought that division of wealth should be based on the use of force, which is a common practice today. They insisted on fight, as they felt sure of victory. So the war was fought with devastating effects on both the sides. KRISNA took part in it, because there is no such thing as moral neutrality in human affairs. On the battlefield, he gave a profound discourse on how to live. It is BHAGVATGITA, a scripture of Hindus that they try to live by.

KRISHNA worked as a charioteer for ARJUNA, who was his cousin, a son of his father's sister. He gave him the right advice at the right time during the war. Violence is a play that is necessary sometimes and unnecessary at other times, depending on the context and who you are dealing with. He knew that killing is of the body and its mind. But the self, alive in the body and its mind, is never killed. Non-violence however is always necessary for accepting the spiritual reality of one's own and of others and finding that the two are always the same.

KRISHNA replaced the worship of INDRA and the forces of nature. Since we are produced by nature, we should live in close touch with it. This would give us health of the body and its mind. But nature is not independent. It depends on an invisible force. We should be devoted to that power, which is present in us too. We should become aware of it. What is supreme is not nature, but the power that lives in nature and remains different from it. We should offer water and flowers, leaves and fruits, the flow of our nature and its best produce, our noble actions with our devotion and dedication to this higher power, by whatever names we call it.

We should not sacrifice human or animal life for our narrow satisfaction. Instead we should support and sustain life.

We may create an idol, an image or an abstract design or model to visualize that formless, invisible power and its presence, because the human mind requires some form or the other for clearer understanding and devotion. Whatever image we create can represent that power for us. But that image is not that power. The directions that guide us are scriptures, but they are not that power either.

Temples, our personal attachment to one incarnation of the divine or the other, opening up rituals of worship to all castes and occupations, song and dance became important ways of contacting that power.

KRISHNA talked of incarnation of the divine who gives a new direction to society when it decays. He talked of rebirth of man to experience the consequences of his actions for the sake of his spiritual evolution, because otherwise there would be chaos.

KRISHNA laughs, sings and dances, accepting life as it comes, both peace and war. Life for him is a play, a game, because the self is eternal and the body has to die.

Chapter X

Patanjali's Systematic Yoga

Yoga is a practical method that disciplines the mind and gives the experience of unity, the experience of oneness of all beings, all higher powers, human beings, animals, plants, and matter. This is the One Supreme Being that yoga enables one to experience. However the seeker has to be qualified to receive this knowledge. If he is morally qualified, as he expresses his nature in actions and directs them to high ideals, he is introduced to the discipline of Yoga.

Yoga is discipline and control of variations in the mind. Mind is an internal organ with the will to know. It consists of enlightening truth, energetic action, and deluding inertia, the three constituents of nature. These constituents of nature are variously mixed to produce varied minds. The mind may wander, distracted or forgetful. But it can become concentrated, focused, one pointed, disciplined and obedient.

The mind sleeps, dreams, and wakes up, which are its three main expressions. That which unites these three is deeper than the deepest sleep and more aware than the fullest wakefulness. The two ends of this underlying reality are never reached.

Once upon a time, a column of fire appeared. VISHNU, who sustains life, tried to reach its one end, and BRAHMA, who creates and orders reality, tried to reach the other end. They could not find its ends. It came to be known as SHIVA'S LINGA, a symbol of the supreme and only power.

Its knowledge removes suffering and makes the impressions of actions ineffective. Its grace leads to restraint and absorption of the mind. Its knowledge is gained through rational curiosity and examination, meditation, and the joy of being one's self.

Whatever one does leaves an impression behind in consciousness. Actions are born and they die. Their impressions stay on in consciousness. This is a form of continuity, the root of varied actions. One may not be able to recall them, but they are never lost and are continued from one birth to the next. Sometimes they emerge in dreams, though they may be distorted. These impressions include impressions of all experiences in this life and earlier lives, when we may have lived as plants or animals. They exist as urges and potential tendencies to action that can take birth to work out their consequences.

The mind is one, but it takes on many forms. It searches for truth, which is its essence. But its search is mostly miscarried because of its impurity, resulting in error. Impurity consists of identifying one's self with the non-self, like one's urges, actions, desires and their effects and consequences, inertia, limitations, sleep and ignorance. This impurity is eliminated through actions of self-discipline. Then the mind becomes pure and qualified to receive the truth. That truth is awareness without any specific object.

When control of variations in the mind is firmly established, the self, who sees and experiences, exists in its own form. At that time there are no objects, no objective world. There is only consciousness, unaffected by the will to know.

When control of variations in the mind is not firmly established, the self who is the seer is identified with the non-self, with the seen, with objects of experience, with impressions of events in the consciousness.

Broadly speaking, these variations in the mind are five. Some of these are painful and some are without pain. Some create suffering and some enable us to go across life without suffering. These five variations are truth and proven knowledge, falsehood and erroneous knowledge, verbal delusion and imagination or truth-neutral knowledge, sleep or void, emptiness and memory or the impressions, retained or recalled.

Right knowledge proven to be true is based on direct perception, inference from direct perception, and evidence checked against experience, as proofs. False knowledge is not so established in the real nature of the object or idea. Verbal delusion is imagination flowing from words and expressions corresponding to no reality in existence. Sleep is a change that has the feeling of void or absence, when the mind does not seem to have any content. Memory is retaining impressions of experiences in this life and in earlier lives and bringing some of them back into consciousness when they are recalled. Each of these variations can be further elaborated in details in many ways.

These variations in the mind are controlled through practice with devotion and detachment. Continuous effort to restrain these changes is practice. Practice is effective only when done with love and devotion constantly over a time and results in detachment. One gives up craving for objects, seen or unseen, and the will to control them. Detachment comes spontaneously when one is focused on a high objective and aspiration. Knowledge of the Supreme Being through transcending nature with its variations results in extreme detachment.

At first, one begins with reflection on one's given nature and freely chosen high aims and ideals. One becomes conscious of impressions and happenings in the mind, as one begins observing them. This observation of impressions and thoughts in the mind enables one to rise above them.

One engages in helpful reasoning that directs consciousness towards noble ideals. One starts discriminating between the eternal and the non- eternal, between the pure self and the impure non-self. One starts rising above suffering towards joy that does not end in pain. Then one has the feeling of being one with oneself, integrated.

As one ceases mental activity through restraint and control, one becomes conscious of impressions that are normally dormant and have not as yet been manifested in actions. One gradually merges into forces that constitute one, of realities that are separate from their physical expression. Material nature dissolves away as one becomes conscious of higher forces and feels bodiless, without any material nature.

Later on, deep consciousness happens through trust and confidence in your self and the higher forces. One starts experiencing an unknown, unexpected energy. Energy does not come from food alone. Energy is in and around you. It can come directly through concentration and trust. Have you experienced boundless energy after a period of full absorption in doing an action that expresses your nature directed towards a noble ideal?

Memory of experiences in this life and earlier lives becomes clearer as one reflects on experiences and visualizes them fully while concentrated on the self.

Success in this evolution of the mind varies according as the means, like practice and devotion, are mild, medium or intense. It is speedy for the energetic.

Divine power is the special being in the body and mind. It is untouched by suffering and actions. Actions are enacted desires and their consequences. It has no desires or consequences, painful or otherwise. This is divine awareness, the seed of all knowledge. It is the true guru of all, including the ancients. It is not limited by time or space. Its symbol is AUM.

While meditating one tries to listen to distant almost inaudible sounds. When this ability is developed further, one learns to listen to the sound of creative vibrations of reality and repeat it with feeling while meditating on what it signifies.

From all this effort comes absence of obstacles to an understanding of the self. The obstacles on the way to awareness are disease, mental laziness, doubt, indifference and lethargy, craving for sense enjoyments, false perception and relapse. Suffering, despair, nervousness, irregular breathing, and distraction are their symptoms. To remove these obstacles, practice focusing awareness on only one object or aspect of truth at a time for as long as you can. This will help you silence your mind.

Cultivate friendliness, compassion, celebration and indifference to happiness and suffering, vice and virtue. Focus on these virtues one by one for a long time, and try to internalize them in your feelings and attitudes, urges and actions. This will remove negative attitudes and bring grace to awareness of impressions of this and earlier lives in the subtle body.

Remove negative reason by throwing your breath out completely, keeping it out for some time, restraining and slowing it, and focusing your mind on it. You can change your mind through your body. You can change your body through your mind. Focus your mind on the positive helpful opposites of what is negative in you.

The seeker engages in withdrawing the senses from their objects, as attention to them strengthens them. One looks inwards at the mind and its contents, which are impressions of actions, feelings, urges, motives, intentions, tendencies, images, hopes, desires and fears, etc. The mind becomes an object separate from the seeker. This helps him to clean up his mind.

Deprive your senses of their food or objects for some time every day. They remain deprived during sleep any way, which refreshes them. Deprivation enables them to become sensitive enough to receive extra-ordinary sense perceptions. Keep your mind steady by training it to remain focused on any one object to the exclusion of everything else.

The seeker learns to focus his mind on six psychic centers that are like coiled up creepers of electricity in his subtle body, one at a time, for some time every day for a few months. These are in the pelvic floor, where the spinal cord ends, at the navel, at the base of the heart, at the pit of the throat, between the eyebrows, and at the top of the head.

The seeker learns to focus his mind on numerous mental forms of the divine power, names with their significance, one at a time for a long time in such a way that only that one name and form and nothing else, not even the fact of meditating, remains in the awareness at that time. He learns to internalize them. This is JAPA, remembering the name and form of the divine power with their significance. Later on, by divine grace, the seeker may acquire the state of mind that remains conscious without any object, without any name and form of the divine power.

Learn to meditate on the effulgent light that lies beyond sorrow. Meditate on one who has given up attachment to sense objects. Meditate on knowledge that comes in sleep or dream. Meditate on the centers of your energy. Recall vividly and with feeling the details of your wakefulness, dream, and sleep. Meditate on anything good and auspicious that keeps your awareness steady.

There are many ways of meditating. One has to choose the one that suits him. Thus meditating, the mind of the yogi passes from the individual to the universal, from the smallest to the largest self, from the narrow limits of the animal self to the boundless divine self.

The yogi who has controlled variations in his mind understands the self, the connecting mind, and the external objects as one. That is the experience of unity. The knower is one with the known and the instrument of knowing.

The consciousness that raises questions alternates between knowledge derived from word-meanings, true knowledge and knowledge based on perception and reasoning.

The consciousness that does not raise questions happens when memory is purified, or devoid of subjectivity, expressing only true knowledge of the meditated object. These two concentrations, with and without reasoning, also explain more subtle objects. These states of consciousness of subtle nature go as far back as the unborn, before consciousness takes birth as object or nature. These meditations are with impressions of experiences that can take birth.

When one is fixed in consciousness that does not raise questions, enlightenment comes as grace, without effort. Knowledge in that state is of absolute truth, whereas knowledge gained from inference and testimony is of common objects. This knowledge of absolute truth is of a higher order, able to reach where inference from direct perception and testimony of proven truth cannot go. It reaches all other forms of knowledge. Then effects of actions are controlled. Now the consciousness is deepest and highest, without an object.

YOGA requires practice of techniques that burn up impurities in the body and mind so that life flows freely and one lives simply and spontaneously. Numerous techniques have been grouped into eight limbs of YOGA.

The YOGI observes his own mind and its variations in order to understand his self. He studies YOGA scriptures with clear understanding. He learns to be receptive to vibrations of reality normally outside the range of the senses. He places himself under the direction of divine consciousness, untouched by suffering, actions and their fruits. Yoga enables one to rise above suffering to reach the divine consciousness that constitutes DHARMA.

Suffering is produced by ignorance of reality, assertion of one's ego, attachment and aversion to the objects of senses, and clinging to life.

Ignorance of reality is the field that produces afflictions, whether the suffering is dormant, weakened, overpowering, or expanding. Ignorance of reality means mistaking the non-eternal, the impure, the painful, the non-self for the eternal, the pure, the pleasant, and the self respectively. It means not seeing reality. The YOGI acts to know reality.

Assertion of ego is the identification of the self with the instruments of experiencing. This means identifying your self with your body and its senses and mind, which in fact is only an instrument through which your self experiences objects. Your body and mind change the object that you see. They see what they are capable of seeing. They cannot see what they are not capable of seeing. The instrument includes intellect, the faculty that determines the truth. The mind is the coordinative and constructive function of the senses of perception and organs of action that are of the body. It is receptive to higher forces. The self is the seer, the one who experiences as the body and mind present their objects.

Attachment or aversion to objects of the senses happens as the senses constitute those objects and linger on their pleasure or pain. Clinging to life, even in the wise, results from its own taste, because of its earlier experience of death.

Resolving suffering into its source eliminates its subtle forms. Its gross forms are rejected through meditation. The root of suffering is in the past impressions of experiences in this or earlier lives. Every feeling, thought, or action, done or felt, happy or unhappy, is stored in memory as impressions. They are the roots of suffering as they express themselves in life. The root being there, the fruit comes in the form of their expression like birth in a particular species, the length and quality of life, and the nature of experience in it. They bear fruit as pleasure or pain, caused by virtue or vice. Remembering them does not eliminate them, but reliving them vividly in the mind does.

To the discriminating, everything brings pain. Pain may come as a consequence of pleasure. It may come as anticipation of the loss of happiness. It may come as fresh craving arising from impressions of happiness. It may come as an opposition between the three constituents of nature, truth and light, energy and action, limitation and ignorance. Misery is avoided by avoiding the identification between the seer and the seen.

The universe has the nature of light, energy, and limitation. It is composed of elements of nature, and instruments of perception, action and thought. The purpose of the universe is experience of the self and emancipation of the self from its limitations. These constituents of nature pass through stages, the specialized and the unspecialized, the differentiated and the undifferentiated.

The seer is consciousness. Though pure, it sees through the intellect. The experience is for the self. Though nature is destroyed for him whose goal has been gained, yet it is not destroyed because it is needed for others. The self and nature unite so that the self may understand the power of both. This union is caused by ignorance. When ignorance disappears, the union disappears. That is freedom of the seer.

The means of destroying ignorance is unbroken practice of discrimination of that which does not change from that which changes. This discrimination passes through seven stages, each to be completed before the next can begin for the self to experience.

First be conscious of suffering in all its various concrete details in life. Then be fully conscious of the cause of suffering. Trace suffering to its source. All suffering begins in that which is not the self. Do not identify yourself with suffering and its cause. Be directly conscious of the disappearance of suffering. Thus be free of the external phenomena.

Be conscious of the body and its mind working out their paths in their own flow. Be conscious of your freedom requiring no one and no thing for peace and happiness. Be firmly established in this consciousness.

Through sustained practice in different parts of yoga, impurities are destroyed. Then the light of wisdom emerges through discrimination. These different parts are inter-related like the limbs of an organism. Isolating one from the others may not produce the best of results.

YOGA is rooted in the actions of living, not in words. One has to act rightly and practice with devotion in order to understand it.

The first limb of YOGA is YAMA. It is a form of self-discipline for social action and spiritual evolution. It requires internalizing and practicing five moral values in active social life.

The first moral value is AHINSA or non-violence. Be non-violent in speech, thought, and action. Feel love for what exists, including your self. When you feel love you cannot kill or hurt. When non-violence is firmly established, enmities cease.

The second moral value is SATYA or truth. Be truthful and honest in speech, thought, and action. Always find the truth, what the reality is in a situation. Be always on the side of truth, even if it is against you. When truth is firmly established even in intentions and dreams, what is said or dreamt comes true.

The third moral value is ASTEY. Take only what you earn, what is morally and legally yours. Do not take what belongs to others. When this moral value is firmly established and spontaneous, wealth comes to you on its own.

The fourth moral value is BRAHMCHARYA or celibacy. Follow the path to divine consciousness, expanding the narrow limited individual consciousness into universal consciousness. Do it with such a single focused mind that your mind does not go astray towards the other path of natural urges like food, sex, desire, anger, money, power, domination, and so on. This makes all your senses chaste. When this moral value is firmly established, unknown cosmic energy comes into you.

The fifth moral value is APARIGRAHA. Take only what is needed to sustain the body and mind, to keep it alive, healthy, and efficient. You have a right to satisfy your needs in order to sustain your body and mind. Know your needs. You have no right to pursue desires unrelated to your needs. Ignore them. Be free of greed. Rather give to others. Do not grasp at anything, including your convictions. Be open to what others say. When non-acquisitiveness is established, knowledge of actions and their results in this and past lives comes to you.

For the followers of yoga, these moral values are absolute vows of discipline, not to be violated by conditions of time, place, purpose, caste or social rules. Do not try to find exceptions and so excuse yourself.

The second limb of YOGA is NIYAMA, a set of five rules of regular observance for personal evolution.

The first rule is SAUCH or purity. The seeker has to be clean externally and internally in his body and mind. Keep your body clean and pure through bathing, right food and yoga exercises. Keep your mind straight, happy and positive. Negative and hurtful thoughts result in suffering and ignorance. They obstruct yoga, whether they are committed, caused, or approved through greed, anger, or ignorance, whether they are slight, middling, or great. Eliminate negative thoughts by focusing the mind on the contrary positive uplifting thoughts. When internal and external cleanliness is established, one feels disinclined towards the body and interaction with others.

The second rule is SANTOSHA or contentment. The seeker is required to be content with what he is and what he has. Do your duty well, but do not be competing with yourself or others. From contentment comes happiness. Contentment means accepting yourself and others. It means beginning to live, instead of living in the hope of living better one day.

The third rule is TAPAS, intense effort or self-discipline. It burns out what is limited and impure in him. The limited is that which is not universal. The impure is that which is not the self. One learns to accept opposite experiences like heat and cold, pleasure and pain, success and failure, remaining active or non-reactive, silent and austere, while focused on the aim of spiritual evolution. When one becomes pure, one becomes cheerful, single-minded. One has control of the body and mind. Then one is qualified to experience the self. Through such actions come super-normal powers of the body and its senses.

The fourth rule is SVADHYAYA, the study of scriptures with a clear understanding and observation of the mind, its feelings, urges, intentions, motives, images, etc. Study of the self and scriptures brings the experience of one's own personal deity and a vision that controls or guides one's own nature and its flow. Find out your own ISHTHA DEVA through your own effort, even if you think you are not devoted to any. Find out your own flow of life, the cycle of your own feelings, urges, attitudes, motives, intentions, secrets, images, longings, and desires. Find out your own images that goad you. Find out what controls and guides you. That is your DEVA. Project it into a vision, a form, an image, an idol or a geometric shape. Gradually learn to hear the subtle vibrations of reality. Many people do not know their own DEVA. They copy others.

The fifth rule is ISHWAR PRANIDHANA, surrender of one's actions to the divine being that does not act or suffer. It is present in all beings, in us and in the universe in all its beauty and variety. Struggle to be mentally close to the divine and devote your life to it.

The third limb of YOGA is ASANA or postures of the body. They must suit the seeker. He must find them comfortable. He should be able to stay in them for a long time. There are 84 classical positions, which are well known. In summary, these body-postures help a yogi to relax, to activate his vital organs and structures, to concentrate his mind so that he learns to live focused in the present time and space, to make energy flow freely in the body and mind and so rid the body of disease and the mind of thought, to remove suffering, to gain freedom from what is not the self and so to make him pure and to adjust his body and mind to his self and to have a clear, spontaneous vision of his self. One or more of these effects are achieved gradually, if practice is done regularly with devotion. By meditating on the limitless and removing the limits of all forms of thoughts and feelings, the body-posture becomes firm and pleasant. When this happens, the pairs of opposites, ups and downs of life, do not disturb.

This training should be received from an experienced yoga teacher, who will know what postures are meant for the beginning, intermediate, and advanced seekers, and for differently constituted bodies and minds with their different illnesses and mental obstructions. YOGA is related to AYURVEDA, the knowledge of living, of the body and mind, of beneficial and harmful herbs.

The fourth limb of YOGA is PRANAYAMA, or regulating breathing and life. Observe your breathing. Do you breathe through your left or right nostril, or both? Place two fingers under the two nostrils and breathe normally to find out. Do you breathe in the same manner throughout the day and night, or do you change? Is your breathing deep or shallow? Do you normally breathe with your chest or stomach, fully or partly? Do you breathe out as much as you breathe in every time you breathe? Do you take in as much air as you are capable of taking in? Regulate your breathing consciously by prolonging, slowing, expanding, and observing the cycle of breathing, which includes inhalation, retention, exhalation, and keeping the breath out. Do this first from one nostril, and then from the other, then from both, a few times in the morning and evening. Continue till your normal breathing becomes slow and deep from the stomach, and life force rises into the brain and energy expands and radiates from the body and mind.

Breathing is the bridge between your body and life. Life is constantly present in wakefulness, dream, and deep sleep. It is reached by going beyond these. Then the mind becomes fit for focusing on external objects, or different parts of the body, or mental visualizations.

The fifth limb of YOGA is PRATIHARA, withdrawing sense organs from their objects. Focus them on the form of the mind stuff. When you look outwards you see the objective reality. When you look inwards you see the subjective reality. Continue till you learn to see both the realities as one. Thence arises the supreme control of the sense organs.

The sixth limb of YOGA is DHARNA, concentrating the mind on only one chosen object. Only that object remains in consciousness and nothing else remains in it. That object may be outside you, like an image, an idol or a design. That object may be inside you, like the top of your head, or the space just behind your eyebrows.

Then the object disappears and only its consciousness remains. Receiving a constant flow of sensation from that object without any consciousness of the object is meditation. This is DHYANA, the seventh limb of YOGA

Then the consciousness of the subject also disappears and only consciousness remains. This is SAMADHI, the eighth limb of YOGA, more commonly understood today as awareness.

When the last three concentrations are practiced together on one object, one merging into the next, it is focused consciousness. Focusing consciousness in this way gives direct knowledge. Consciousness should be focused in stages.

The last three limbs of yoga are more internal than the earlier five that preceded these.

Even then, these three limbs are external when compared to divine consciousness in which impressions left behind by actions and feelings of this and past lives have been eliminated.

When impressions arising in the mind from hidden tendencies disappear, one attains control of changes in the mind. Then the mind flows in peace.

Consciousness is one-pointed when the impression that is subsiding and the impression that is rising are the same. Time and memory vanish. What is past and what is present is the same.

That which is constant is acted upon by transformations, past, present, or yet to be manifested. The distinctness of succession is the reason for the distinctness of results.

By focusing consciousness on changes in form comes knowledge of the past and the future. By focusing consciousness on distinctions between words, meanings, and external objects comes the knowledge of living beings.

Be conscious that verbal reality is separate from existential reality. Word, meaning, and knowledge are separate from reality. They are impressions to be eliminated.

By bringing into consciousness the hidden impressions of past actions comes knowledge of past lives. Whatever happens is recorded in the mind and can be recovered. If all actions done are regularly remembered clearly, childhood memories can come back into vision. If one persists in clearer visualizations of the past, one can make a jump into past lives.

Actions bring results sooner or later. By directing consciousness beyond the senses while in meditation, he knows the subtle, the hidden and the distant.

When the bondage of consciousness with the body is loosened, the yogi can separate from the body. He can have out of body experiences. The experience of ATMA going out of the body and coming back into the body destroys ignorance of the self.

By consciousness focused on the organs, comes mastery of them. From this comes the power to know through intuition without using the senses.

By giving up all these powers comes destruction of the seed of evil, leading to independence. When the essence of objective reality and subjective reality become the same, it is freedom.

Super-normal powers are attained through birth, drugs, incantations, actions done to purify oneself, and divine consciousness. These powers are obstacles to further progress in experiencing states of consciousness. They are powers in the worldly state.

Minds are created from egoism. Though created minds act differently, the one initial mind is the controller of them all. Of these, the mind born of meditation is free of tendencies left behind by impressions of actions done in this and earlier lives.

Actions are neither good nor bad for yogis. They are merely actions and reactions. Bad actions are actions too.

For others, actions are good, bad and mixed. These actions leave impressions that manifest when suitable conditions arise. These impressions and memories continue appearing in numerous forms even though separated by different species, space and time. These impressions and memories have existed from the beginning since the desire to live is eternal. Impressions and desires are held together as cause and effect. When the cause ceases, the effect ceases.

The past and the future exist in reality. The manner of their existence is different. They manifest qualities, gross or subtle. The reality of nature comes from continuity of change in its constituents. The same constituents continue in different forms.

The same object is different for different minds due to variations in consciousness.

An object exists independently of its perception by a mind because it exists even when there is no consciousness to perceive it. An object is known or unknown according as the mind does or does not perceive it. The mind may also not be capable of perceiving an object, as it may not have developed an appropriate instrument of perception.

The mind is not self-luminous as it is a knowable object. The mind cannot comprehend the seer and the seen at the same time. If we assume another mind that knows this mind, there will be no end to such assumptions, which will confuse memory because each mind will have its own memory.

When the mind is silent, the seer knows its own intelligence. Consciousness knows the seer and the seen and understands everything. The mind varies according to impressions in memories of this and earlier lives. It acts for the divine power because it acts in combination with it. He who sees this distinction does not see the mind as the self. Through this discrimination, the mind moves towards that which exists alone, the one without a second.

SAMADHI comes to him who is ever free of desires in deep meditation. Then comes freedom from suffering and action. Then the veil of impurities is removed, infinite knowledge is attained and the finite mind appears small.

Then everything is present. Successive transformations of constituents of nature cease. Time stops. The power of consciousness is established in its own form. This is absolute freedom.

Awareness

ATMA is the self of the individual. It is awareness. His self is not his body and its mind. It is not his money, or property, or power, or status. It is not his family relationships, his caste, religion, society or the world. It is consciousness, pure, just itself, alone, not an object or anything else.

Time past, present or future and space inside and outside the limits of forms are just awareness in the present point of existence in which there is no time and no space. It enables the mind and its senses to function. What they do becomes an object of consciousness. In the absence of what they do, as in deep sleep, awareness exists without time or space. It witnesses their action and non-action. It is the self of every phenomenon. Every phenomenon has a being, a self. Awareness is the self of the individual, the self of the universe.

Ignorance of the self is knowledge of what is other than the self. It binds us to that other than the self. Awareness is not an object that is seen. It sees the object. Self-consciousness makes awareness into an object and so it ceases to be awareness.

Knowledge of words and ideas, books and scriptures, prophets and gurus, all knowledge that comes to us from others is consciousness of objects. It binds us to them. But we are awareness. We are not what we are conscious of.

Man is his awareness alone. Knowledge is of the other. All relationship with the other is false. There can be no knowledge of the self. The self is not an object of knowledge, as it is the knower. There can however be an experience of the self.

Nature and action is the body of awareness. Man's actions and tendencies to action are developed over many lives. They combine with the elements and actions of nature to create his life, his body and its mind, their products and relationships and his universe. Whatever man becomes is the result of his actions and tendencies to action. Therefore he alone is responsible for his actions, not God, not Fate, not others. He can however give up his tendencies to action. Similarly nature has constituents and tendencies to action that develop over time and create a body of visible beings and their invisible forces.

Knowledge is seated in its mother, the seed. Knowledge is of the other, the great elements of nature, their principles and actions. It lives in sounds of the language we receive and reproduce. It lives in the vibrations of existence in motion that we are and that our universe is. Yogis can hear and reproduce this knowledge. It lives in its mother, the source of existence.

Rising above nature is awareness. Nature is existence that is born and that dies. When we rise above nature in a spiritual effort we experience the supreme awareness that projects, maintains and dissolves the universe.

When we focus our attention on cyclical centers of energy in the subtle body inside us, the world disappears for us and we become conscious only of energy. Then there is only a flow of energy. These centers are located near the anus, the genitals, the navel, the heart, and the throat, behind the eyebrows and on top of the brain. We learn to focus our attention regularly with devotion, and so to activate them fully, beginning with the vision and going down to the base and coming up to the top of the brain till we experience an unusual flow of energy in us.

On witnessing variations in consciousness during wakefulness, dream and deep sleep, the experience of the fourth state of awareness that remains the same in these three states is produced. This fourth state of awareness is different from the other three. It witnesses whatever happens in wakefulness, in dream, and in deep sleep. It is ever the same witness. It is the same witness when the body is a child, a mature adult, or an old person. It witnesses ideas, emotions, actions, as they come and go. It witnesses the past in memory, the future in hope, alternative possibilities in imagination. It is inside and outside limits of forms in space. Present, past and future time is one for it.

Cultivate this fourth state of awareness, whatever the condition you happen to be in. Then you do not act or suffer, you only witness. Learn to witness your suffering. Then your suffering disappears. Then you become the temple of SHIVA.

Wakeful consciousness provides knowledge of the physical objective world through the senses and their receptive, organizing and constructive mind.

Dreaming consciousness provides imagination or thought constructions when the senses do not come in contact with the physical objective reality.

Deep sleep is absence of discrimination and distinctions in consciousness, a delusion because awareness never sleeps.

Master Yogi experiences what happens in wakefulness, in dream and in deep sleep as objects different from the self and the self as different from these objects.

Yoga begins with a sense of wonder at who we are. When we do not know who we are, how can we know who others are and what objects are?

An authentic experience of wonder is different from a linguistic expression of it. It makes us dumb and helpless. In a sense, it abolishes us including our language. We feel something mysterious, greater than us, as we live intensely in the moment. We become thankful for being alive, for our experience.

Yoga begins at the cycle of energy between the genitals and the anus. It rises like an electric lightning creeper to the cycle of energy between the eyebrows, the power of supra normal vision and the command center. From ejection to subtle vision and regulation is the spread of divine energy full of wonder. Everything is wonderful. Be full of wonder at the flame that you are, forgetting the body and its mind.

The power of SHIVA is his will, his knowledge-in-action that manifests itself as the universe unfolds. It withdraws itself as the universe rolls back. Identification with the ultimate awareness produces super-normal power spontaneously.

What is seen, or sensed and experienced, inside and outside, during wakefulness, dream and deep sleep, is the body of the self. Master Yogi experiences the objective, subjective and vital reality as his body even when he has a universal awareness of non-differentiation. Consciousness focused on the center of the body reveals the self.

A yogi develops his will power and his awareness merges into reality. He finds everything to be a form of awareness, wonderful.

Then differences between objective and subjective realities, full and void, disappear. That is the disappearance of Maya. All is awareness then.

Established in the self, a yogi has power. He is not controlled by his inherited tendencies to action. Constant awareness of objectless consciousness frees him of the limited individual consciousness.

Intuition is the opposite of reason. It leads to experience of the self. Reasoning leads to analysis, differentiation of consciousness and its objects into distinct and separate units and their relationships. Its opposite is synthesis or intuition that leads to undifferentiated, objectless awareness, emptiness or void.

SAMADHI is awareness of both the knower and the known. It is the joy of existence. You are alive. That alone is full of joy, enough cause for celebration. It is the joy of being ever the same, without conflicts and opposite pulls. It is not the satisfaction of a need, not a joy that ends in sorrow. You are the center of the universe.

On being united with the power of universal awareness, any form can be created. This union gives super-normal powers of different kinds. Elements of nature can be joined or separated across space and time.

When everything becomes awareness, super-normal powers happen naturally. Union with the Divine Power is the source of all forms and cycles of energy. Focus your attention on them. Stay there and meditate on that which is different from what happens during wakefulness, dream and deep sleep.

Feel the joy of being. Drop the consciousness of being your body and its mind. Experience the self. Then renunciation of that which is other than the self happens.

Your awareness is your repetitive energy. It becomes your body and mind, character and life. Reflect on your ideas, images, feelings, emotions, urges, motives, and actions. Find out what you repeat, what your mantras are. When you see your mantras, the seeing is a vision. The seeing is outside what is seen, a higher reality.

The effort to visualize your mantras, to observe the cycles of repetitions in your body and mind, in your ideas, dreams and images, feelings and emotions, urges and tendencies, to witness all that you reveal and all that you hide, all that you are, is to separate your seeing from what you see. This effort is the spiritual method to experience the divine, to get outside your mind.

One who lives outside the cycles of mental repetitions is perfect. His effort to rise above and so discard the repetitive mind is the method. Whatever you see is seen through the repetitive mind. Once you go outside it, you get energy of the self.

The mystery of mantra is the essence of identity. The identity of the individual and universal awareness, the sameness of the self of the individual and the self of the universe, is the mystery of mantras. Mantras are not what you repeat with your vocal organs or in your mind. They are what you learn to hear and see repeating in your mind, if you witness your mind and learn to hear and see what it repeats. To hear and see mantras as separate from you is to rise above your body and its mind and be one with the self.

The mind expands at the center of mantras as they disappear like a dream under observation. As the cycles of repetitions in the body and mind are closely observed, they disappear and the mind expands beyond its normal limits. Then one moves spontaneously into the state of universal awareness.

Guru is the means of reaching the mystery of mantras. He has escaped his mental repetitions, representations and constructions. Therefore he can help us escape our own mental prison and the tricks that the mind plays. He works within the present circumstances, which keep changing over time and place.

Body and mind are sacrificed and offered to higher powers. You sacrifice your body and mind when you give it its due only to sustain it but no more. You recognize its tendency to take more than what is its due. The rest you give to your self in the form of focused observation and knowledge of power in phenomena. In this way you learn to separate from these powers. Focused attention is the effort to live in the present time and place.

Knowledge is the food of the self. Knowledge is of power in phenomena. Observing phenomena intensely takes us beyond them to the self. When knowledge of phenomenal powers is assimilated, the phenomena become dreams and memories and their power is the reality.

Memory is a dead dream, imagination a future dream. The present is the truth. When we do not live in the present with full awareness, we go astray into dreams, like the past and the future, habits and visions.

Awareness is total knowledge, all phenomena, or knowledge-in-action, enacted knowledge. The knower and the known are the same.

Everything you do, feel or think is done by powers of nature in you, since they constitute you. Intelligence is constituted by truth and existence, mind by energy and action, ego or the "I do" principle by limitation and delusion. Not understanding the constituents of nature is ignorance. The presence of these constituents creates delusion and hides the power behind them. Beyond these constitutive principles is awareness.

Since awareness is your self, the ultimate reality, do not fight it. Understand it. Do not feel separate from it. Focus your consciousness on nature, its constituents and their source. Then your evil tendencies start disappearing.

You create evil with ego, I-am-the-doer. Since evil does not exist except as your creation, it disappears as your ego disappears. Ego is the same in sinners as in the virtuous. It separates man from higher forces and narrows him down to his limitations. There is only one sin, to think you are separate from the ultimate reality, the seed of all that is or can be, even though you are only a manifestation of it. There is only one virtue, to think of yourselves as an expression of reality and therefore identical with it.

Knowledge manifests in action and therefore binds us to what it creates, which is intelligence, mind, ego, the senses and the constituents of nature. This creates Maya, the delusion that shows the inability to distinguish the eternal from the non-eternal and the elements of nature.

Death of the body and mind is its dissolution into its constitutive principles. Nothing is destroyed. Nothing can be destroyed. Everything is only transformed. The flow of life through its channel is stopped and the mind is detached from its elements.

Super-normal powers are displayed due to attachment. Desires produce attachment with their objects that hides reality; otherwise there is no need for miracles. When desires end, miracles end. Super-normal powers become normal powers when we advance in spiritual evolution. Spontaneous knowledge comes through conquest of Maya. It is inherent in body and mind. It emerges on its own when the mind is detached from its elements. Detachment means freedom from dependence on the other, reliance on the self. It makes one the center of the universe, otherwise the mind moves from one desire to another, creating many minds.

Existence is the center. Life or death, joy or sorrow, success or failure, all these forms of dependence on the other become meaningless. Such a yogi wakes up to the effulgence of creation. The whole universe, including matter, is an expression of the power of awareness. As is awareness, so is the universe.

The self is the dancer. In a dance, the dancer and the dance, the doing and the being are one and the same. This is the dance of SHIVA. You are not different from your actions, past, present and future. Your inner self is your outer vision. Your actions in wakefulness, dream, and deep sleep emerge from your being. As you are, so you see and so are your actions.

If you are suffering, it is because you have chosen to suffer. You are responsible for what happens to you. To change yourself is in your hands. You create your own dance. You are free. Your experience depends on how you see life. Nothing enters your life except as you allow it, love it or hate it.

Inner self is the stage, where it dances inside you. Whatever happens outside you happens inside you. The dance is inside you.

Not the world but your awareness is the stage. Whatever you see outside is a projection of your inner dance. You see in life what you put into it. You put your intelligence, your ego, your mind and your senses into your living. The outside is blank. What is inside is seen outside. As you start becoming aware of the self inside you, you start changing your outside.

Many changes happen by themselves, without your effort. You are not hungry. Your body is hungry. As you stop identifying yourself with your thoughts, they will stop being your master. If you oppose your ideas, you are still controlled by them. Do not support or oppose them. See them. Change your inner life by becoming a witness.

As you become free of your body and mind, you start seeing the inner self as outside you. Inside and outside become one, as do energy and substance. Nothing changes. It is the same in all conditions.

The senses are spectators of the dance. The dancing being inside, constant observing too is to be done inside. Through spiritual intelligence, witnessing the dance, the self is experienced. See the truth that you are the self, that your outside is your own projection. Then transformations will happen. Then experience the flow of freedom. You abandon sorrow and joy, both being of the body and its mind. That is peace and bliss.

On being empty, you experience that you are the cause of whatever happens to you. You are the actor of your play. This realization helps you to change your dance. In the beginning, you are not the master of your mind and experience, of your thoughts and feelings, actions and reactions. Your mind is the master of your self.

Spontaneous knowledge and freedom means that the self is the master of the body and mind. Being free, not bound to the body and its mind, the self can stay outside the body and mind, while staying inside as well. Then your individual self becomes one and the same with the universal self.

Focused awareness is the seed. It has the potential of experiencing the self, if we nurture it. Be established in the self through awareness focused on the body and mind, banishing all other objects from your awareness. Mind looks outside. Awareness looks inside. Mind joins you to the other. Awareness joins you to the self and results in loss of ego. Then you are in no mind, alone.

The self creates all forms. As immortal knowledge arises, birth and death cease, and you see continuity. That knowledge is your nature, your flow. It is you, though you may not know it. You may even try to suppress it, forget or hide it. You can however discover it.

What exists cannot be destroyed, cannot be created. What does not exist cannot be created. There is no birth or death for what exists.

DEVI MAHESHWARI is the consort of MAHA ISHWAR SHIVA. She is his power, manifested in a variety of limited forms, called DEVIS.

One form is KALI DEVI. She is Time with its terrible form of destruction, holding human heads severed from their bodies, holding death and transformations.

Another form is TARA DEVI. She is the creative vibration of speech, of self-expression and manifestation. She creates the universe of language. Limited forms project and nurture limited beings and realities. In the universe of speech, that which is expressed is always limited or bounded and formed.

In wakefulness, dream and sleep, the fourth state of awareness is poured like oil. If we had no awareness whatsoever in deep sleep, we would have no memory of it. Who remembers the comfortable sleep and the dream? The one who remembers is the Seer. He is different from sleep and the dream. That One is the Fourth, flowing inside you. You are that seer, before any action you do, before you become a part of the world. Enter the Fourth, absorbed in the pure consciousness. Your awareness is pure, objectless. Objects and needs are of the body and its mind.

Anger and attachment gradually disappear as you learn to observe their appearance, growth and disappearance. Success and failure, joy and sorrow will come to the body and mind, but will not upset you, as your tendencies to action disappear. Then you will do the right action spontaneously by being right and the work outside will continue as play.

The vital principle of life connects you to the pure cosmic awareness, where everything is the same undifferentiated awareness. The same light is burning in everything. This is experienced after passing through intermediate stages. Normal awareness of numerous objects and constructions of thought is followed by super-normal powers of different kinds at first outside and then within one's control during the intermediate stages.

As the awareness of the self joins objects, cosmic awareness reappears. What is perceived by the senses, what the mind thinks of as pleasure or pain, good or bad, what the intellect certifies as true or false, what is imagined even if non- existent - all these are objects in awareness. When objectless awareness is felt in the apprehension of all these objects, one emerges into cosmic awareness. One becomes like SHIVA. Then one sees all forms, all boundaries and limitations as transformations of the divine powers.

Whatever a yogi says, when he is in a state of cosmic awareness, is a scripture. There is no final scripture in any language. All scriptures are only partial glimpses of truth.

What the yogi gives in charity is knowledge of the self. It is freedom from body and its mind, from society, from the other and from the need to react to the other. He, who is so established in yoga and this charity, is the means of this knowledge. He becomes the means through which wisdom flows, nourishing limited forms like plants, animals, humans attached to their bodies and minds, and humans awakening from this ignorance.

The power of supreme awareness unfolds as the universe is maintained and dissolved. The universe is the dance of SHIVA, his unfolding power, an expansion of awareness. His power unfolds as the universe is projected, maintained, dissolved, veiled and revealed. Dissolution and death too is a process of unfolding.

The knower is constant even as the universe unfolds. Awareness does not change, even though its objects change. To experience change, one has to be the same. Otherwise, who would know the change?

Joy and sorrow are variations in external objects of awareness. They are external to the knowing witness. They are born out of contact of the senses with their objects. Freed of them, one is alone. When there is no identification with any object, one experiences alone-ness, which is the true self.

Action lives in attachment. One engaged in good and bad actions is attached to the body and its mind, desires and society. Therefore he is attached to joy and sorrow. He does not know the One that is alone, without a second. On knowing that one, variations in creation disappear. Some of these variations are birth and death, joy and sorrow, success and failure.

The witnessing source of wakefulness, dream and sleep, gives vitality. One who is identified with this source ends desire. He may continue to live, detached. Then the gross body and its mind are like a cover of the self.

Even the mind is gross because it is a coordinating and constructive action of the senses, the organs of the body. It becomes separated from the self, like a covering, as one transcends the body.

The power of life is manifested when the knower and the known, the subject and the object become One, Alone, without a Second, without separation. This power is present in all channels of life in the subtle body of the individual and the universe. This power is non-dimensional, without space or time. Be aware of the source of this power. Meditate on it.

Chapter XI

Experience of Generations

Hinduism is a word used for SANATANA DHARMA, the ancient tradition of experiencing eternal spiritual truths that underlie living and dying in the world.

An individual is born to a family, father and mother. But the family is not restricted to them alone. They had their parents, grandparents, uncles, aunts, their children and grandchildren, a large network of relationships created by marriage and mixing of blood and experience. There is no end to the network of these relationships between all beings. All beings are related to each other, constituting one family, though they may not remember their relationships. They constitute a cosmic organic living and conscious being.

Many of these relationships are forgotten with time. But because they are forgotten they do not cease to exist. The individual brings with himself something from all of them, including animals, plants and minerals, something from his past lives, including the most primitive. He is never entirely blank. Numerous impressions and effects of past experiences are written on his mind. He has in him many tendencies and predispositions to action and feeling and many potentialities, which may or may not be realized. Some of these he shares with some others. Some of these are unique to him. These may be ignored and rejected or twisted and deformed, but it is more truthful and closer to reality to be aware of them and to try to cultivate the best of them in the direction of great and noble ideals. Therefore the basic constituent of society is family, remembered more or less, with its culture and impressions of past experiences and moral values, its numerous inherited and more or less distinct little traditions.

The term joint family may be taken to mean that there are many families that have been joined together and what is joined can also be disjointed. The idea of a nuclear family is already implicit in the idea of a joint family. But there is no nuclear family in reality, though selective memory and law can impose limitations for protection of narrow personal interests. The family is a vast network of relationships that include all beings, human, animal, plant and mineral, and its limits are like the horizon, seen but non-existent, depending on how far one feels, sees and remembers.

SANATANA DHARMA says that the whole world is one family and that there is an unlimited network of relationships through marriage and mixing of blood and strong emotions spread out in space and time. Some of these relationships are recognized, remembered and cherished. Others are ignored, forgotten, or condemned, but they exist. How wide or narrow this memory of family relationships is depends on one's culture and values. It is an indication of one's spiritual growth. The more one has grown up, the larger would be the family. Ancient oral and self-expressive culture tended to have a long memory. A culture based on utilitarian morality that calculates even the cost of education, hospitality and tangible returns of charity tends to have a short memory, even less than a nuclear family, like the one parent family. That which pays is remembered and cherished and that which does not pay is ignored and forgotten, be it love or divine experience. But rejection and forgetfulness of these relationships does not mean their non-existence.

A large number of people living together, sharing their experiences and remembering their relationships over generations made a KUL or family. Through their actions that they valued as good or bad, they created their own little traditions, their own values, which they cherished and remembered and passed on to their future generations. They had their notions of right and wrong and their skills of living and earning a livelihood and devotion to what they thought was ideal and true. They revered and admired some ancestors and rejected or forgot some others. They reflected on their noble actions. This created family ideals, customs and traditions.

These relationships of numerous families through marriage and emotions, descending from a common ancestor, like a man with many sons setting up a new village bringing forest land under cultivation, be it geographical, political, industrial or commercial empire of today, and passing it on to his children and grandchildren and their children having long memories is JATI, a grouping of relationships by marriage and emotions. Its members had rights and duties, which emerge from the family, not so much from the individual, as it is the larger family that creates the individual.

Family rights do not seem to exist today. They need to be clearly formulated and defended. Family now is a social contract, a breakable promise. But the blood that has mixed cannot be unmixed, whatever the man-made law might say. The unbreakable relationships created through marriage are now being made to flow on money and usefulness.

Homosexual marriage is non-procreative, a demand for family respectability without family duties and rights, especially of procreation and passing on the inherited mixing of bloods and family traditions to the next generation.

There were other emotional ways of forming JATI as well, like a dedicated disciple admiring his guru or RISHI or family priest so much that he adopted his name and became a part of that JATI. Some people working together to produce the same service or commodity felt that they were a close-knit brotherhood

Families tended to earn their livelihood by working in more or less the same occupation, as they passed on their occupational skills, as a form of inheritance of property. Many of these JATIS achieved high levels of skills in their occupations, which can still be seen at some places in some services and which became a source of considerable wealth. Execution of these skills with devotion became such a mind-absorbing and self-forgetting activity that SRI KRISHNA called it a form of YOGA.

Education in ancient ASHRAMS was mostly a rich man's affair, like royal princes and princely traders.

VISHNUGUPT CHANAKYA was a teacher at TAKSHSHILA University near RAWALPINDI, now in PAKISTAN. He came to

NALANDA University in BIHAR to present his thesis on ARTHASHASTRA for the consideration of his peers, which was a custom in those days, as had been done earlier by PANINI for his ASHTHADHYAYI. VISHNUGUPT CHANAKYA'S thesis was highly praised and he was offered the post of President, DANASHALA or the House of Charity, in which capacity he could give charity up to ten million gold coins to any worthy cause he thought right, but the presiding officer, the RAJA of MAGHDHA, did not like his ugly physical appearance and so he was rejected. He decided to take revenge. He noticed royal leadership qualities in an eight-years-old village boy who was playing rural games with his friends in a field. He met the boy's family. On obtaining their permission he took the boy with him to TAKSHSHILA, where he had him admitted to a school of martial arts run only for princes. He showed that a SHUDRA with inborn leadership qualities could be a king if rightly educated. There were one hundred and three princes from all over India learning martial skills in that school and this boy became one of them. He studied there for eight years, after which he did a practical exercise in politics and martial arts by interviewing ALEXANDER. That arrogant king did not like being interviewed boldly and ordered that the boy be killed. But the boy escaped. Later this boy became famous as CHANDRAGUPT MAURYA, who expelled the foreign invaders from the country and ruled an empire larger than British India.

GURU DRONACHARYA describes himself as the son of RISHI BHARDWAJA who had an ASHRAM on the banks of river GANGA, in which he taught martial arts to royal princes. It was therefore that BHISHAM PITAMA employed him as the teacher of KURU princes and DRONA claimed friendship with RAJA DRAUPAD as his class fellow, which the latter refused to recognize, as DRONA, the son of a RISHI, looked like a beggar even though he had studied with the princes during his childhood because he was the son of a teacher.

Common man's children received practical skills in crafts at home, as a form of inherited property to earn their livelihood, and went to the neighborhood school in the house of the local priest to learn to read and write the local language and do simple arithmetic.

It was a practical system of education that suited the needs of the local environment and pockets of the student. No one, not even those who are called DALITS today like cobblers or barbers, was denied education.

This system persisted in spite of the destruction of temples and associated social institutions in the dark ages as late as the nineteenth century, when the British conducted fact-finding surveys of the areas they had conquered, as summarized in DHARAMPAL'S book, THE BEAUTIFUL TREE: INDIGENOUS INDIAN EDUCATION IN EIGHTEENTH CENTURY. It includes selections from W. ADAM'S "Report on the state of education in BENGAL", 1835, which says that he found low castes like CHANDALS, MOCHIS, DOMS, KAHARS and KURMIS among the students, and like CHANDALS, GOALAS, TELIS, RAJPUTS, and KASHATRYAS among the teachers. DHARAMPAL also quotes G.W. LEITNER'S report on indigenous education in PUNJAB, which says that indigenous education sanctioned by SHASTRAS conferred dignity on the commonest every day duties. People themselves, not the officials, discharge not only municipal but also revenue and judicial functions and know how to read and write the local language and are proficient in doing simple calculations. In my childhood, students learnt multiplication tables not only with whole numbers but also with fractions like quarter, half, and three fourths.

Common man was educated in the house of the local priest in reading and writing the local language and in doing simple calculations, sufficient for their place and times. He was also educated through informal, adult instruction given by wandering SADHUS who went from village to village giving discourses on DHARMA that included folk wisdom, practical spirituality and tips for living, medicine and morality, as they still do now. Many ascetics go on foot across the country giving discourses on spirituality and useful practical wisdom and suggestions, narrating ancient stories. VISHVAMITRA traveled on foot from the HIMALAYAS in the north to River GODAWARI in the south to do homage to RISHI AGASTYA who had spread Hindu thought and culture to South East Asia, and then to lake PUSHKAR in the west to do his UPASANA of BRAHMA DEVA and then to the east and north, and then to AYODHYA to meet RAMA and to MITHILA in BIHAR to meet RAJA JANAKA. SHANKARACHARYAS travel across the country meeting people, listening and lecturing to them. GURU NANAK DEV spent twenty-six years of his life going from one place to another, meeting people, discussing with them and singing praises of the divine presence in all beings on the way. Highest wisdom along with practical tips on health and living and facing crises in life was distributed free in an easy to understand listener-friendly idiom in this way. This too is informal education, though today we do not give it this name, as we believe in examination and certification for employment, promotion and making more and more money, thereby creating inequality and ignoring education in the skills of living.

The individual is born with a certain nature, which expresses itself in certain qualities, like truthfulness, energetic action and limitations of actions and in rituals, which all together make his color. Everyone is born with tendencies to action. Some of these may be biological instincts, or less material mental attitudes, like the urge to see the truth and live by it, or to dominate others, control and manipulate them, and in the process even to deceive or tell lies, or to profit from all kinds of situations. One is born with a body that has juices inside it. Some of them will shape mental attitudes. It makes no sense to say that man is born with a blank mind on which anything can be written. The truth is that man is born with a body that has ten senses, five of perception and five of action, which work within upper and lower limits, even when those limits are greatly enlarged, raised or lowered. These senses create a mind that shapes the information it receives. Of course more things can be written on some minds than on some other minds, as there is a great diversity of human bodies, the natures and capacities of their senses and minds. These differences are related to the body, which emerges from matter and goes back into it, and which is a powerful influence on the mind, though not the only influence.

The first duty of the individual is to express his nature, his inherited tendencies to feel and think and act in a certain way. These tendencies may be more or less good or bad. It is the duty of the parents, relatives, neighborhood and the teacher to encourage and nourish the good tendencies and discourage and starve the bad tendencies and to help the indifferent ones along the lines they think desirable according to their family spirit and the local neighborhood spirit too. Different regions of India have been under the influence of different scriptures and historical actions, which included their ideals, dreams and images and modes of living, and which were not mere words. The families and regions differ in their experience of life, in their sense of what is more or less right and important. The material, traditional and cultural differences will nurture children differently. These geographical cultural variations are gradually being eliminated in the name of standardization to suit factory production, the same behavior and scripture, the same foods, articles, entertainment and house designs, imposed on all the diverse peoples of the world.

One may not do his duty of expressing his nature freely however, as when a person follows others rather than his own nature. He may never learn to reflect and meditate on his own experience of living or try to know himself. When we follow fashions or heroes from films or sports or politics or commerce, we may refuse to express ourselves. In a sense we die and our nature ceases to live. This is a form of rejecting ourselves, our nature given to us by unknown powers, leading to illness, evil and suffering. And then we are surprised to find that life is empty and meaningless. In fact we never tried to find our meaning for ourselves, as no one else can find it for us, just as no one else can eat food for us. We have to do it ourselves and try to be aware of our nature, both its goodness and evil, and see the games it plays and dedicate it to noble ideals of our choice. The second related duty of the individual is to create his own meaning and direction of growth, his own path in life. This requires that he reflect on his experience of life and be more and more aware of his own nature, without self-deception, and express it in the light of great ideals that he himself chooses according to his nature and direction of its self-expression.

The word meditation has many meanings or stages in actual practice, not just one, even though nowadays we hear mostly about the highest form of meditation in the very beginning. Just as we understand yoga only through doing yoga, not through hearing or reading about it, similarly we should understand meditation only through doing it.

In the initial stages of practice, meditation only means remembering our experience of life, reliving it in detail, visualizing it, reflecting on it, becoming more and more aware of our actions and dreams and their patterns and their invisible sources, motives and intentions, and finding out why we act as we do and what effects it has on ourselves and others, demeaning or ennobling, and what it reveals about our nature, especially our secrets and hidden dreams and urges. It is a form of our study of our self. It is not a matter of giving yes and no responses to questionnaires prepared by others. It requires freely exploring the dark secrets of our heart and mind, including making mistakes, as part of the learning process, and revising them later on finding what we are and what we pretend to be, how our ideas come into us and how they go out, how we influence others and how they influence us, and how this vast, glorious and personally indifferent universe provides us with our own small, private and often petty and limited pleasures, conflicts and suffering that we create, how we see and sense life and how we direct it and make our own path, our own career, with our own decisions and judgments. It requires making our heart pure and empty. It requires contemplation on what happens to us and through us, and whether these happenings are independent of us, and whether we control them, and the color of life we produce. The more we reflect on our experience of life, the more capable of such reflection we become, and we become more aware and capable of expressing our flow of nature, which is the cause, the source and mother of our actions in our initial state. We begin our spiritual journey from there, because there is nowhere else to begin it from except from where and what we are. We may pretend in ignorance that we are where our father or mother or neighbor is, or where our hero or guru is, or where our newspaper or scripture is, and then we do not begin our spiritual journey at all, though we can kill others for our religion, never reflecting on what is meant by the word "our". We stay where we are throughout our life, the same dreams and the same urges, the same reactions repeating endlessly, meaninglessly. But where do we go? We must have a purpose, a direction of our action too in addition to our cause. It is the purpose, the ideal to which we sacrifice and dedicate our life that gives it heat and light and fire and self-transformation, as we offer what is most precious in us to the divine powers that give meaning to it.

Purposes are of many kinds. Many people spend a whole lifetime searching for pleasures and prosperity and their numerous variations. This search for pleasure and prosperity is necessary, but has to be within the limits of righteousness, moral goodness and law to satisfy our needs in a manner that leads to experience of freedom from them rather than slavery to them. It should lead us to experience of unity and peace beyond thought and mind rather than thoughts, conflicts and wars, exploitation of resources and destruction of environment. Therefore the aim has to be far-sighted, larger than our personal satisfactions, which is what ennobles us, morally elevates us.

One enabling condition of this aim is minimum necessary consumption for efficient maintenance of the body and mind, not maximum unnecessary consumption that makes relationships adversarial, competitive and destructive and degrades the human body and mind in avoidable illness and suffering, merely feeds them to the machinery of making profits. This would give us the freedom to grow spiritually.

Pleasures are products of the senses of perception and action and mind. They result from our interaction with the world. Therefore we create our pleasures. Otherwise in reality without us there are no pleasures and no pains.

There are pleasures of good health, food, clothes, ornaments and perfumes. There are pleasures of sexual activity, family, children, houses, lands, cows, milk and nourishment, wealth, horses, elephants, chariots and cars. There are pleasures of conversation, speech, song, music, dance, and drama.

Pleasure is the path of INDRA DEVA, SOMA DEVA, and KAMA DEVA. In ancient India, as now, people were dedicated to the path of INDRA, the lord of the senses, liquor and love, close to nature, in open fields and gardens, fresh air and flowers where they invited and entertained their guests in stead of meeting them in their limited houses created by our boundaries.

They celebrated the festival called INDRA MAHOTSAVA for 28 days when the rains came down after a hot and dusty summer and released beautiful fragrance of the earth along with crops and prosperity. They drank liquor, got intoxicated, munched roasted barley, ate meat and bread, talked and wept or laughed and were closely bonded. Even today Yoga exercises that copy animals and plants and bow to the sun with the body and mind, becoming a part of the cycle of nature, breathing in abundant life, are to be done in open fields and gardens, close to nature, not inside air-conditioned rooms. They bathed in moonlight during hot summers, and celebrated full moon and new moon, and the change of month and told the time, looking at the sun or the stars. They celebrated the rituals of sacrifice to internal and external fires through renunciation of personal benefits and dedication to public causes and distributed free food and laughter.

They celebrated the festival called VASANT UTSAVA, the pleasures of spring, birth and innocence in nature, the sheer playfulness of being alive and healthy. Do we feel today the happiness of just being alive and healthy?

Remnants of this form of worship and dedication of the self to nature can still be seen in some other festivals like LOHRI and HOLI and the public ritual bathing in a flowing river as in KUMBH MELA or in tanks near temples.

It was realized through experience that pleasures end, leading to a memory of their loss, which results in suffering. An excess of pleasures may cause ill health and hoarding, high prices and deprivation of others. Pleasures however are not to be rejected just because they are abused, making us ill, pompous or dominating, but must be experienced within the limits of righteousness.

Pleasure is a principle of action that has its own laws and their expression, knowledge and techniques. MAHARSHI VATSYANA composed KAMA SUTRAS to describe the pleasures of sex and love and food and beautiful clothes and fragrances and gestures that express secret feelings and the general way of living of the man of pleasure. There are numerous texts on music and dance and drama and architecture and drawings, like SAMA VEDA, full of song and music and the supporting GANDHARVA VEDA and

NATYA SHASTRA, music, dance and drama. As SRI RAMA said to his younger brother while refusing to return to AYODHYA that pleasure and prosperity are necessary, but they have their time and place, and SRI KRISHNA said that of all forms of knowledge, SAM VEDA, or singing hymns in appreciation and praise of the divine presence in all beings, keeping it in mind, internalizing it, and so being devoted to it was the best form of knowledge.

To say that man was born in sin is to insult one's parents. Man is born in a moment of ecstasy that blanks out all else in an experience of oneness, even though momentary. Nor is wealth a devil, because without wealth, the stomach is empty and we cannot worship or realize our supreme self on an empty stomach. A minimum of material satisfaction that satisfies our genuine physical and mental needs without enslaving us is a necessary requirement for spiritual growth.

Some pleasures are difficult to obtain without a measure of prosperity, which is objective, measured in terms of land and cows and horses, or money and cars in modern terms, as well as subjective, experienced in terms of feelings of being happy and helpful, well and satisfied.

Prosperity too is a principle of action, of engagement with the world that has its own laws, knowledge and techniques. MAHARSHI KAUTALYA composed ARTHA SHASTRA to describe its nature. It happens to have survived the ravages of time and destruction of wars inflicted on India, but there were earlier speculations on prosperity too, as is implicit in the text, which cannot be the first and only one.

Since other people too are searching for pleasure and prosperity, and wanting more and more of them, it often results in struggle and conflict, even war. Therefore it is necessary to guide these preliminary aims of man. This guidance is received from high ideals like working for what unites people or public welfare, or selfless action without personal expectations of rewards, or remaining the same in all circumstances of joy or sorrow, or welfare of all beings including animals and plants. There were many other ideals to choose from according to one's nature. We must work for DHARMA, maintain and sustain people and their life and society, bring them together, reconciling conflicts, and work for the common public good. Search for pleasure and prosperity that brings people together is better than that which takes them apart, creating conflicts. Therefore peace is better than war. But this preference does not mean renunciation of war, as SRI KRISHNA asks ARJUNA to fight for what is right and just, because some people's search for their own pleasure and prosperity, not limited by righteousness, may harm our life and force us to accept injustice, evil and even death, and then we must fight. But as a general rule our actions should sustain people in peace and prosperity.

Bringing people together, sustaining them and their general welfare and the welfare of all beings including animals and plants, requires action without searching for personal profits and acquisitions, focusing the mind on the practical skills of doing our duty with such dedication and absorption that we forget the limited personal benefit of making a living out of it and leave it to the divine powers to provide for the satisfaction of genuine material needs. Maintenance satisfaction always comes to those who are engaged in public welfare, even when they forget their own interest. But these needs have to be genuine, emerging from doing one's duty of expressing one's nature in action with dedication to the high and noble ideals of sustaining people and nourishing them, not exploiting them or taking away their wealth or belittling them or manipulating them to do and be what one wants them to do or be.

If one aims at maximizing one's needs and profits, then conflict and war is the only way to obtain the limited resources for oneself and denying them to others, and for selling our produce at our own prices. Yesterday in BENGAL, the hands of craftsmen had to be amputated to eliminate competition to the growing industry in the United Kingdom, and starving people had to be shot dead in large numbers because they were trying to block the loading of wheat on ships that were to carry it away to satisfy the needs of the British empire, declared to be sovereign and so above the law and moral goodness by the right of force or for reasons of state, a preferred phrase today, which often hides actions that seek personal comforts and security and murderous competition of the governing class of people in the name of serving the common people. Do we really have to compete when we aspire to serve the people? Ruthless competition in serving the people is a deceptive basis of democracy.

To maximize human needs and to manipulate people to satisfy them in the interest of maximum profits for a small percentage of rich people while talking of human rights and morality in a rationally brilliant manner while hiding the barbarity of sucking others to extinction is not a highly desirable and noble ideal to follow.

In reality there is no such thing as maximum profit or maximum satisfaction, because one can always add one more to it and it ceases to be maximum. Maximum profit is eternal dissatisfaction. Therefore maximizing needs and satisfactions is an unreal, unrealizable, self-deceptive and destructive ideal.

SANATANA tradition has produced idols and ideals like INDRA, SHIVA, SHAKTI, VISHNU, RAMA, KRISHNA, MAHAVIRA, BUDDHA, and influential RISHIS, ACHARYAS, GURUS and numerous people who put their ideas into practice and keep the tradition alive and promote it, sitting mentally close to the ideals, externalizing them through inner fires, an intensity of effort and actions.

INDRA is the natural mind, life of the senses, satisfying natural urges and desires, beyond good and evil, searching for pleasures and prosperity, worshipping nature and its resources, the sun changing into the fire in the evening, and the fire changing into the sun in the morning, calling it a cycle of divine powers, finding heat and light that enter all beings in various ways, like day and night and through seasons, fruits and vegetables, giving us life and removing our darkness, ignorance and sin that do not really exist, except in darkness and ignorance, that are only absence of light and enlightenment, created by our seeing and experiencing, worshipping nature like rain and water and the harvest and prosperity they bring to a dry and dusty land, satisfying bodily needs, giving fun and laughter, and intoxication, the necessary conditions of bodily satisfactions for spiritual growth, because unless we have how can we give, though of course we can give even if we have only a little, worshipping nature like the mother earth and its produce on which we flourish and which flourish in us too, worshipping nature like the air and water and space outside and inside us, especially the space in the mind that is like the sky free of clouds, consciousness without objects.

INDRA says: Cultivate your senses of perception and action and their mind, as that is all you have, and cultivate nature, as that is all that is given to you. Have a teacher to help you in this cultivation.

INDRA is an ideal fighter, a great savior, one with his horse and thunderbolt, his vehicle and AK47 rifle in today's idiom, protecting and defending his people and their cows and wealth, destroying their enemies and looting their wealth for distribution among his followers as political leaders do.

INDRA destroys avoidable interferences with the flow of nature like building dams on flowing waters, injuring nature without wisdom, creating artificial prosperity that cannot be sustained, because DHARMA of water to flow downwards clearly must be protected and nature allowed to flow as it wills, as its laws ordain, while enjoying the pleasures of all the senses that it gives, including food and clothes and ornaments and fragrances and sex and family and music and dance and drama, getting into sexual escapades, including undesirable behavior and getting punished for it through the law of actions and their necessary consequences, even to the extent of having the female genitals imprinted all over his body, or getting AIDS in today's idiom, and gracefully accepting the punishment instead of complaining, because punishment of evil is a law too, and suffering is as short lived as pleasures, and then again reverting to his earlier way of living for the senses after the punishment, one changing into the other, as the nature of pleasure is to change into its opposite.

INDRA is a divine hero and what is moral or immoral in one tribe may not be so in another, even though morality like standardization today is becoming more uniform and diversity of behavior is becoming extinct like some greatly endangered animal species.

INDRA mind is an eternal truth, born every time a child is born anywhere in the world, though sexual escapades now happen in a cowardly manner mostly in imagination and dreams within the confines of marriage, like imagining a hero or heroine of films or sports or even the neighbor next door, while uniting sexually with the socially respectable married partner, and punishment takes the form of AIDS or divorce, and other things remain the same like a thirty-six or a mere ten course meals or ten roomed house with ten bathrooms, and dances that present in public the strokes of a sexual intercourse without removing all the clothes though hardly any are left on the body and calling it freedom of expression of the artists in entertainment, a new name for slavery to the juices in their small bodies or their acting, pretension and hypocrisy.

INDRA mind is creative because moral conventions cannot be violated without questioning intellectual and cultural conventions that support them. Search for pleasure and prosperity, war and destruction are highly creative actions, creating new forms of enjoying and destroying and what is called good things of life and their unintended effects and their supporting institutions and laws.

As the senses start withdrawing from the world, losing their life and vigor, they are re-awakened into a deeper, richer and less physical engagement with the world through reflection. So INDRA mind gets visions of RAMA and KRISHNA and even of SHIVA, the ideal YOGI, self-controlled through meditation, but first one must have an active mind that has to be controlled.

INDRA produced a great civilization, one town of which was called HARIYUPPA, the golden tree of life where men on the opposite pole, who had experienced the bitterness of pleasures, who wanted to sacrifice and dedicate their life, mind and senses to a higher and deeper life, to go just beyond nature, were tied into the crotch of a tree, its trunk and two uplifted branches later abstractly symbolized as SHIVA'S TRISHUL. After the ritual ceremonies of carrying fire clockwise around him with recitation of MANTRAS were over, a ritual still continuing in the form of circumambulation around the temple, they were adopted into the families of great RISHIS, like VISHVAMITRA adopted SUNAHSEPHA, dedicated for life to a higher culture beyond the senses, like today men who want to be dedicated to SANYASA for life are first ritually drowned in the River GANGA of purity for a second after the ritual ceremonies, meaning death to the past and living a new life, adopting new names as permanent reminders of ideals that they try to live by. That human sacrifice of life, the senses and their mind was a renewal and dedication to DHARMA, which was understood as the nature of everything, including water and air and fire and space and time and society and the individual and relationships and what constitutes and sustains them and finally destroys them, because that which gives birth also gives death. They produced mathematics like SULBA SUTRAS, and music, like a thousand versions of SAM VEDA, planned towns and architecture of multi-storied houses, sometimes prefabricated, with a planned drainage system and street lighting, experimented with herbs and medicine and skills of living and the arts of warfare. MAHABHARTA mentions a hundred different army formations and a hundred weapons of different kinds. A Greek historian mentions 500 towns between Rivers JHELUM and BEAS. INDRA was creative, abundant and full.

Men devoted to INDRA feel reverence for nature, like rains falling on dry and dusty lands, yielding harvests and prosperity and pleasures, satisfying desires. They feel awe, forgetting themselves on experiencing the beauty and majesty of high mountains, dense forests, clean flowing rivers, vibrating seas and vast stretches of sand, open cloudless skies and a sense of divine presence there. They are like fire and sun, full of heat and light, giving knowledge, life and wisdom to all, not to a chosen few. They are like the moon with their changing minds, reflective and contemplative. They are like water, flowing and nourishing with feelings of well being, expressing their own flowing nature. They are like air, felt in effects, giving life to all, carrying sounds, language and self-expression. We should learn from them how to live and breathe. They are like the earth supporting all, and productive. They are like space, empty, unattached, vast, unrestricted, universal. We should learn to see spaces between objects, not the objects alone, and learn the skills of seeing, emptying the mind of all objects, uniting people.

Devotees of INDRA remain close to nature, staying in open countryside and by rivers and streams and seas, and in mountains, forests and deserts. They satisfy their desires, learn to fight and ride, use effective weapons, cultivate strength and intelligence, live long and learn the use of herbs and health, of weapons for defense and music for relaxation. They eat and drink, enjoy and celebrate. They follow their senses wherever the senses may lead them, even if they lead them into difficulties, which difficulties must then be experienced gracefully and overcome with strength and intelligence. Such men are creators and fighters, dangerous to established conventions. But they are as necessary as the conventions they destabilize. And destroying their idols does not destroy them. They will create new idols and new forms.

This attitude to life is grounded in the philosophy of MAHARSHI BRHASPATI, who rejects all mumbo jumbo of religion, basing life on sense impressions and their continuity, doubting everything else, aiming at comfortable living and the good things of life. Obviously we are only the body and its mind and nothing more. When we die, we die, and that is the end. Obviously there is nature that we can see and nothing more. So make money while the sun shines for you. And have more food and more clothes and more security and more sex and more children and sing a song of more and more. When a person marries, builds up a house, brings up children, and when he supports the family, as well as the elderly people who give up the world, and young students who engage in study to prepare for future, and various institutions that constitute society, providing free food and medicine to the needy in sacred groves and rituals, he can hardly have time for anything other than pleasure and prosperity. These are the only two aims of life worthy of cultivation even though most of the great conflicts and wars have centered on them alone, especially when the hunger is unlimited and uncontrolled, even when the wars are fought for justice and other noble ideals to hide the search for pleasure and wealth. After all war is a pleasurable experience, excruciating almost, bringing us to the full of our manliness, strength and ingenuity, leading to honor and heavenly pleasures, as well as to death, destruction and devastation.

At the root of these aims is the common man's level of spirituality, focused on the stomach, the anus and the genitals, the basic wheels of energy. They are thought to be the highest ideals that man is capable of achieving. The more we have the larger and better we are. That is the highest and the noblest ideal to which man can aspire, say the powers of state and politics.

Over generations men leave behind impressions of their actions that produce customs and traditions. Normally, one does not question customs, but grows up in them, internalizes them and follows them. SRI RAMA, the best man of tradition, was one such man, who acquired the high status of MAHATMA, as VALMIKI says, and came to be known as incarnation of VISHNU DEVA, who sustains life, enabling others to live happily through the rough and tumble of life for centuries.

Reverence for custom and tradition over time came to be called PITRI PUJA, or worship of ancestors, which was absurdly reduced to the ritual of SHRADA ceremony alone, which came to mean feeding BRAHMANS, altogether forgetting the mental content of UPASANA that went into the remembrance of ancestors and their good actions based on high moral values. We cannot give food to another man and declare that we have remembered our ancestors. Remembering ancestors is a personal effort to witness in our mind the past that shaped us and the ancestors who created it. Remembering the past in the mind and living it out in feelings, thoughts and actions is the only tradition possible. It cannot be reduced to history. Objective history is empty of life. The ritual of feeding BRAHMANS, without fixed regular incomes, was to thank them for keeping the ancient tradition alive in an oral culture, which was a marvelous feat, inviting admiration of at least some people. We did certain things with awareness that our ancestors had done those things as they lived by certain moral values that we struggle to follow. We receive guidance from family precedents in the conflicts of life and so keep the family traditions alive.

SRI RAMA began his day with going to DEVA MANDAR and doing UPASANA of his ancestors, ideals, customs and tradition. They included among others MAHARSHI MANU who had composed MANAVA DHARMA SHASTRA, laying down the law of man. His law governs numerous Hindus even today without compulsions of any state or coercive authority and the loss of political power for a thousand years, even though many millennia have passed. Another ancestor was RAJA HARISH CHANDER, who gave up all that he had in charity. MAHARAJA ASHOKA and MAHARAJA HARSHA later on in historical times practiced giving all in charity after every few years, as a way of redistributing personal wealth, though the official public treasury had already been passed into the hands of a minister of treasury from the king for wise public expenditure. Another ancestor was RAJA BHAGIRATH, who brought River GANGA to the plains from heavenly mountains. Distribution of water to dry lands from wherever it is available in abundance in ancient India required great skills and practical observation and calculations and invites admiration even today at some places.

SRI RAMA had ancestors worthy of dedicating oneself to. But everyone has ancestors worthy of dedicating oneself to. Every action, howsoever limited, can be done badly or admirably, and if it is done admirably it is great and worthy of remembrance and learning from. Every action is a mixture of good and bad things and the skills of seeing require that we learn to see and do the good and the auspicious and promote it, while ignoring the bad and starving it of our attention. Everyone has ancestors who did things worthy of remembering and being guided by, even if their field of effect was personal and not public. Even small actions can be worthy of remembrance if they reveal high moral values. From the divine way of looking, the greatest action is small enough and the smallest action is great enough. So remembering good things from our past, our ancestors, customs and tradition, and finding guidance from them for our future and dedicating a little time every day to this remembrance of things past and even re-living them clearly is the subjective part of the objective external ritual of ancestor worship, or PITRI UPASANA that goes with their PUJA. SRI RAMA did this everyday in the morning. He was a hero who internalized high customary values so profoundly that they were spontaneously reflected in all his actions and ideas.

SRI RAMA created a kingdom in which he made everyone happy. And this action of making others happy became the definition of RAJA, the one who makes everyone happy, working for their interest and welfare.

Two doubts about SRI RAMA however lurk in the modern mind. One is his exiling his pregnant wife, seen as an action against women. The other is his beheading a SHUDRA who wanted to be a king, seen as an action against lower castes.

SRI RAMA had a network of spies or intelligence officers in today's idiom through whom public opinion was ascertained. As his father had told him, public speech is never to be trusted because it is motivated to create impressions that hide the truth and are beneficial to the speaker. The spies were tried and trustworthy people who found out the truth in a situation and informed the king. The issue on hand was the continuity of the royal succession. After RAMA, who? That was the question. There was a persistent doubt in the public mind. The child that SITA was carrying could have been the child of RAJA RAVANA. If yes, the line of royal succession would pass from the ancient and admired SURYAVANSHI dynasty of MAHARSHI MANU and his son IKSHVAKU to the RAKSHAS dynasty that belonged to an entirely different culture, moral values and tradition. This was not acceptable to the people. But his ministers were finding it difficult to communicate the truth to the king. To protect the sanctity of the royal line of succession in the eyes of the people and so to please them, SRI RAMA did an act of self-sacrifice giving suffering to himself, his wife and the unborn child and exiled his pregnant wife to the ASHRAM and protection of MAHARSHI VALMIKI, who was a SHUDRA, but who engaged in noble actions and composed the epic RAMAYANA, admiring the high-principled hero and looking after the queen as his own daughter and bringing up her twin sons as royal princes with appropriate culture and training who ruled the country later and set up new towns.

SRI RAMA killed a SHUDRA who was hanging upside down from a tree, doing penance in order to be a king. He thought that neither by nature nor by its nurture and culture through training in penance was he preparing himself in the arts and skills of royal warfare and public administration of a large kingdom. The aspiration did not fit his nature and culture. RAMA judged him unfit and beheaded him. This penalty appears cruel today and arouses strong and adverse emotional reactions, but what does rejection in an interview for employment amount to for a poor, unemployed young man without self-confidence or independent financial means, offering himself as a commodity for sale, rewriting and revising his bio data and misshaping himself constantly in order to suit the anticipated expectations of this or that prospective employer who has the money to pay so that he may be selected and be able to fill his and his family's stomach everyday? Do you think this system is not beheading him every day? Selection procedures are not entirely reliable. They are lax and faulty in a soft and insecure state where much depends on friendships and considerations irrelevant to the actual skills that would be required for the duty of doing the job. The examinations and interviews do not necessarily fit the job requirements and the grading system cannot be but untrustworthy especially in humanities and the arts of living and doing actions. The divinely given nature and its training to suit one's aspirations do not always match. And justice was speedier in old days.

SRI RAMA is known for his self-sacrifice for public good. Today promises are broken without a guilty conscience, be they in commercial contracts or treatises between states. Sometimes promises are made intentionally ambiguously to have an escape route in case a need to violate them arises. But this was not always so. Even as late as the twentieth century in rural India, debts of grandfathers were paid by grandsons along with interest without there being any thing in writing only because a promise had been made by the grandfather. The promise given by SRI RAMA'S father was without any specified content, merely an expression of gratitude to his wife for saving him in a crisis in battle. But RAMA with his wife and brother sacrificed fourteen years of their life and royal comforts only to honor his father's empty promise, a thank you. While in the forest he knew how to live off the lie of the land and he raised an army of allies without the backing of any political power, except his hands, intelligence and speech. SRI RAMA had numerous qualities and values that people admired, as they drew nourishment from them. They started worshipping him.

Many Hindus worship SRI RAMA and do his UPASANA, as they try to be the best persons of the tradition they follow. Some of them remember their ancestors, follow their customs and reflect on their history. They try to preserve the past, modifying and interpreting it to suit the present conditions. They think of their RISHIS and AVTARS and try to apply their teachings to their practical life. Many of them read the RAMAYANA in a local rendering and enact some of its scenes in ceremonies associated with the festival of DUSSEHRA and DEEPAVALI and try to understand its deeper meanings. They try to create their future in line with their past, building on it rather than suppressing it or breaking away from it.

Customs and traditions change with times unnoticeably. They tend to grow stale and unresponsive but still carried on. Therefore a mind is needed that questions custom and common practices in a tradition and finds new interpretations and introduces profound changes in fundamental ways of living, without rejecting the past entirely. This was SRI KRISHNA, with a flute on his lips and music and joy in his heart and deep thought in his mind, the creative mind that went beyond the ordinary mind to the self that is present in everyone everywhere. It is towards this experience of the same juice present in all beings that spiritual growth or evolution takes place. SRI KRISHNA made a profound criticism of the VEDAS without rejecting them at all in the best of Hindu tradition and presented many new ideas and interpretations.

SRI KRISHNA says that we all have our own DHARMA, which emerges from the flow of our nature and its qualities, whether truth, action or limitations predominate in us. This results in our action, an expression of our nature as our single-minded duty. But our nature has both goodness, which we must nourish with dedication, and evil, which we must discard. We must reflect on our nature and become more and more aware of it, observing our actions and feelings in our mind as a witness, seeing their nobility or depravity, cultivating the best in our nature, our highest self. Perfection in doing the duty that emerges from the best in our nature is a great ideal for an individual. It is our fundamental duty to give expression to our nature and transform it towards great ideals. If we do not do this, we reject our nature and suffer the consequences of our folly.

Many ideals are proposed. One ideal is such proficiency in doing our duty that we are entirely absorbed in the skills of doing it, forgetting everything else, like our ego, renouncing everything else in a sense. Then our action becomes action done with detachment, without expectations of personal benefits, as an offering to the divine presence in all beings, including enemies, animals and plants. We should do such actions for the interest of all beings and for what brings people together, their welfare.

Man is ever engaged in satisfying his desires, but desires can never be satisfied. He is engaged in a pursuit that cannot end, as one desire leads to another, and they strengthen each other. Man himself creates his dissatisfaction through satisfaction of his desires. He experiences what he himself creates. Therefore the way out of this dissatisfaction is to satisfy only genuine needs to keep the body and mind in a healthy and efficient condition. Since this is a genuine need, its satisfaction is real and it puts a limit to our desires. This requirement limits the extent of desire. Beyond this limit there is no fulfillment.

Since the ideal of minimum consumption frightens everyone because one feels insecure about an uncertain future, SRI KRISHNA advises faith and trust in the divine who will always supply for one's genuine needs as a way to overcome this fear, because there is plenty in the world for everyone to consume. He sets up minimum consumption along with public action that brings people together and faith in the divine power that takes care of our welfare as an ideal to follow. He calls it action without acquisitiveness. This gives freedom from suffering which results from numerous desires and their dissatisfaction. It helps us rise above our ego and see actions and their consequences happening. Then one remains the same in all conditions of joy or sorrow, and realizes the ideal of wisdom, seeing all in the same way. Such whole-hearted devotion to a noble ideal leads to freedom from the possessive power of the lower centers of energy.

SRI KRISHNA says that we must preserve the little traditions of numerous families and communities and do our best to reconcile conflicts. But if all our efforts at reconciliation fail, we must be ready to do our duty and fight to defend our rights, for which we must acquire necessary physical strength and fighting skills, intelligence and wisdom. We live with the earth born, but live a noble life full of action and devotion.

Countless Hindus through the millennia have worshiped SRI KRISHNA and felt drawn and devoted to him and his teaching. It was said that when KRISHNA spoke philosophy flowed. He talked philosophy right on the battlefield, facing life and death as a play, a game, just as any enterprise, be it political or commercial, artistic or personal, like acquiring power or money, poems or food or sex, after the minimum level of genuine satisfaction and proficiency, becomes a play, a game, a fun. If living does not become light, a play, it is because we are not genuine, proficient and detached.

This way of living relates us to the cause and aim of our life, our nature and ideals, making it meaningful and joyful and a celebration. Then we have music on our lips, living in the present moment with a song in the heart. Then we play with friends, both boys and girls, and become like SRI KRISHNA.

If the same self lives in all this diversity of beings that we see, then this same self must be invisible to the senses, because we do not sense it. What we sense is diversity, not the sameness. Then how do we experience it? We do so through YOGA, says SHIVA. Without this experience of sameness or oneness of all beings, we cannot talk of the existence of one God, one reality everywhere.

We cannot say there is one God if we split mankind into those who follow us and those who do not follow us, and if we command our followers to kill or convert or over-tax or condemn, or enslave or rape or belittle those who do not follow us, and make false and condemnatory accusations against them, inciting our followers to violence, to a permanent condition of war and terror. If we still talk of one God, we are confused, living on borrowed knowledge even if from a holy book or its teacher and do not have any personal experience of oneness of divine unity.

SHIVA is lord of the whole world, both outside and inside us. He is known through many names. The subjective and the objective world have to be one for one reality to exist. What is outside goes inside us like the food or our impressions and experiences. What is inside comes outside like our nature shaping our experience.

We create the sensations we experience, like the sky, the horizon, color and taste, and the limits of our seeing. Divine will projects its reality into the world, from the invisible seed to the universe of visible forms outside.

An invisible reality lives in the visible reality that we experience. There is a body that we have. Inside it there is life that disappears on death. Inside life there is a mind that receives information, remembers, organizes and creates it more or less. Inside mind there is knowledge and intelligence that relate one thing with another, like cause and effect, actions and consequences, the path and its destination, and networks of relationships with all beings. Inside intelligence there is joy, a clear vision of sameness, without conflicts and oppositions. There are layers of reality that we are, that we deal with. Each layer has its own knowledge and laws.

The body is made up of food or matter and we can control it to some extent through our breathing and body postures. A still body tends to create a still mind that opens up the possibility of a deep insight. There is an invisible life that expresses itself through motions, the one that breathes air in and out, the one that takes food from the stomach to different parts of the body, the one that expels feces, wind, urine, and semen, the one that carries commands of the mind to various organs, and the one that moves ideas, feelings and urges. There are wheels of energy that control these motions of life. One could become aware of these wheels of energy. Inside life is mind, a function of what the ten senses do and the effects of their doing that it receives and remembers, fully or partly, and modifies and shapes. We learn to purify the mind and keep it on one track through repeating and visualizing MANTRAS. Inside the mind is intelligence, wisdom that sees the whole, like effect in the cause or center in the periphery. We experience it through reflection and concentration, through experiments and practical techniques and abstract models, designs and symbols. Inside intelligence there is joy and silence beyond the mind, which one reaches through meditation that includes numerous methods depending upon who is meditating at what level of experience and spiritual evolution with what objective. Then meditation stops and one enters the icy mountain of SHIVA alone, at peace, where nothing moves, not even air, full of joy. Such is the inward journey that begins after the outward journey through birth, education, culture, rituals and moral values.

SHIVA is a practical DEVA who asks the seeker of truth to experiment with spiritual techniques to find out the truth himself and not to believe or speak borrowed ideas even if they come from gurus, prophets and scriptures.

We have moved from the natural mind to the traditional mind to the creative mind to the technical mind, and each contains numerous forms, all within the tradition of SANATANA DHARMA, because these minds flow and merge into each other, forming clusters of features that make various ways and no one way excludes the other entirely and there is continuity, and opposites unite one above the other till we reach the final whole. There are many possibilities of spiritual evolution, many techniques and paths, like the steps we take in our life from birth to death. Some of these are the paths of DHARMA, KARMA, BHAKTI, GYANA, SANYASA in addition to KAMA and ARTHA. Pleasure and prosperity when rightly used also lead to the divine experience.

The path of DHARMA sustains life, helps in dealing with suffering inherent in living, and elevates it to a nobler, higher level of moral living and being.

VEDAS require seeing ourselves as forms of nature, just like other human beings, animals, plants and minerals, each layer of being with its own laws and sequences of actions. But nature itself is a form of the invisible formless power beyond it. It dissolves into its cause, the power from which it emerged, its mother and support, its source and refuge. We experience it in many ways, as in deep sleep that renews us every night, as in sexual orgasm, momentary satisfaction of desire, or in experience of awe and wonder at the mystery of nature, its vast immensity, its utter simplicity, when our ego and pride is abolished for a time, and we are dwarfs no more, only fields of actions and energy that keep ever widening. Who can say he digests the food he eats? But digestion keeps happening more or less. This abolition of ego, the I-do principle and merging into vastness is a powerful experience. There is the beyond, the final step, beyond language and comprehension, beyond the human mind, the awareness of no mind, of the severed head, its power and ability, for which the right expression is silence.

VEDAS invoke numerous powers present in the world for our senses, reflection and engagement, like VISHVADEVAS, numerous powers of the world, like the power of rains on a dry land, ISHWAR, these numerous powers seen as expressions of one almighty power inherent in the universe, VISHNU, the power of life, LAKSHMI, the power of wealth, INDRA, the power of the senses and the beyond, DURGA, the power of overcoming obstacles, SAVITRI, the power of maintaining the social order, SOMA, intoxication of well being, KAMA, pleasures of sex and love, satisfaction of desires, SURYA, light and heat, freedom from ignorance and sin, reflection, AGNI, fire, change and transformation, ARYAMA, tradition and ancestors, GANGA, the river of purity.

Numerous devotees over the centuries gone by have seen these powers as concrete figures, not as abstract ideas. They created a language of symbols, like INDRA in the rainbow or riding an elephant, sprinkling water through its trunk or with a thunderbolt, riding a horse, SHIVLING and SALIG RAM, columns of stones that give form to the formless, like the presence of absence, expressing a zero by writing a point without dimensions that is given dimensions, SHIVA dancing, or holding a TRISHUL, or sitting on a bull, or sitting with his family, DURGA riding a lion, killing a demon, SARASVATI on a swan, playing on a musical instrument, LAKSHMI standing on a lotus flower, symbol of detachment, SURYA riding a chariot driven by seven horses, GANAPATI on a mouse that nibbles away at things, cutting them into pieces, HANUMAN tearing apart his heart to reveal the presence of RAM and SITA, VISHNU riding on a bird that kills snakes full of poison, or reclining on the snake of infinity in the ocean of dissolved elements, with wealth in attendance and BRAHMA holding knowledge in his hand, sitting on a lotus flower, RAM with a bow and arrows standing alone, or with his family, SITA, RAM, LAKSHMAN and HANUMAN, or KRISHNA playing on a flute standing by a cow, or dancing with boys and girls or talking to ARJUNA in a chariot on the battlefield.

VEDAS say that one divine truth underlying all limited beings perceived through the senses is beyond any conception or name of it. They talk of it as the truth of existence, the law of actions that regulates activity of nature, including our body and mind that is always right, that emerges from universal consciousness rather than our sense-mind, the law of regularity and cycles of energy. They talk of the universal truth that is constantly expanding. They talk of the vast immensity around us. They talk of the manner and skills of seeing that create our universe.

They say that truth can be approached through many paths, scriptures, gurus and DEVAS.

There is the path of entry that requires birth and nurture and life ceremonies and engages the world in numerous ways. It requires the UPASANA of the chosen DEVA or the nature one is born with or inherited from the family and the local community. One has to face difficulties, drink poisons while churning life into good and evil and overcome them. One chooses and devotes oneself to an ideal like gathering food and matter, satisfying desires especially sex and procreation, having rains, harvest and prosperity, senses and the beyond, intoxication of liquor and self-pride, the fire that transforms one, and the law of actions and their consequences, and so on. All these were called DEVAS with different names.

VEDAS mention three moral values that we should practice in order to go deeper into life. They are YAJNA, TAPA and DANA, or rituals of sacrifice, offerings to the external and internal fires, renunciation and dedication, self-discipline, and charity.

YAJNA is the ritual of self-sacrifice, dedicating one's life to higher powers. The original sacrifice was of the divine power that sacrificed itself to numerous forms of existence. It was like seeing oneself as the other. Over time, many kinds of sacrifices were created. We should sacrifice ourselves for our ancestors and tradition, for other human beings, for the great people who created our culture, for developing other beings like animals, plants, nature, and those people who are evil and those people who are identified only with their bodies and minds. We should sacrifice something precious for rising above nature and time on which we travel, for rising above the level of spirituality that is fixed on the cycles of energies associated with the stomach, the anus and the genitals and so become sacred and holy and experience higher powers.

TAPA as penance and austerity is only a form of TAPA, which is more like self-discipline of the eleven senses of perception, and action, and their mind in the presence of extremes of heat and cold, joy and sorrow, remaining always the same in changing seasons, physical or emotional, and so rising above transformations of nature and its actions, and in this way to qualify ourselves to experience the divine, when other things fall away, and we become full and free.

DANA is charity first given to the creators of our culture and those who nourish it, ASHRAMAS of RISHIS, and GURUS, temples, and learned people for acquisition and transmission of learning, and then to the poor, the needy and the handicapped, sharing wealth with others, distributing it fairly, decreasing the harshness of natural inequality that emerges from diversity. The institution of renunciation, detachment and other similar moral values like work for public welfare helped in redistribution of wealth.

When RAJA DASHRAT dies and the kingdom is left without a king for a few days, the council of ministers discusses what happens in a kingless state. One interesting argument they give is that the king organizes public functions, works, and different forms of use and entertainment, which helps in redistribution of wealth from the rich to the poor.

One should distribute savings or excess of production over consumption to the deserving as an offering to the divine from where it came, which is charity. It is charity that completes the affluent. It is unwise to think of riches as the number of cows or the amount of money one has. A poor man with charity is rich. A rich man without charity is poor. And the deserving people are those who remove ignorance and suffering and resolve conflicts and make living valuable, meaningful and noble. Then civilization flourishes and flowers in peace that has no history.

VEDAS require our listening and opening up to reality, reading scriptures with understanding, remembering, reliving, thinking and reflecting on our experience of life, singing praises of the divine present in all beings, and so learning to appreciate them, seeing their goodness and highest potential, reconciling and harmonizing conflicts, creating peace, silence and aloneness. They talk of actions as affected by age, and the aims of living like satisfaction of desires, acquiring wealth and prosperity within the limits of moral goodness, and working for noble ideals like peace, fullness, compassion, and concentric selves made of matter, life, mind, intelligence, joy, and self-realization, experiencing oneness of reality, the individual self identified as the universal self, and tasting the same sap of life that flows in all beings, rising from immense diversity to the sameness of all beings.

VEDAS also talk of the path of withdrawal and exit, cultivating detachment, remaining the same in all circumstances, offering the fruits of ones actions to the divine presence in all beings and so to act with love and devotion and responsibility and be always ready to quit the world with a light heart. They talk of numerous methods and techniques of self-discipline.

UPANISHADS teach us to acquire the skills of seeing the same wonderful presence in all beings, even the most ordinary and the familiar, like ourselves, alive and conscious, knowledge in action, truth that controls and regulates, the play of coming together and going apart of higher forces, seeing the eternal self, and so be whole, full and wise, free of ignorance, sin and suffering, working for peace and welfare of all. They lay emphasis on actions leading to the self-realization that we all are essentially the same as the universe, uniting the inner and the outer life in search of oneness of all beings, changing our manner of seeing and being, qualifying ourselves to realize our highest self, which shows itself through its own grace, as it is beyond compulsion.

THE BHAGVADGITA talks of accepting and expressing the nature divinely given to us at birth and transforming it towards great ideals. This self-expression is our primary duty of accepting the divine presence. We should perform this duty skillfully with devotion, giving up all else, including the fruits that might come to us. We should pursue the aims of life through strict self-discipline, leaving it to the divine power that created the world to take care of our survival needs. In this way we remain the same in all circumstances, while working for the welfare and interest of all beings including animals and plants. Then life becomes a divine play, full of music and dance, as we become light hearted and celebrate life with strength and intelligence. We live with the earth born but work for noble ideals born of the higher mind. It asks us to acquire moral values like truth, fearlessness, purity of heart, straightforwardness, steadfast pursuit of the best in us, the study of scriptures and the self, control of the senses, sacrifice, self-discipline, charity, renunciation, compassion to all beings, forgiveness, fortitude, absence of excess of pride, anger, hatred and greed.

SHIVA promotes spiritual self-help as the highest moral value. Why borrow spiritual truths from others even if they are great scriptures, gurus and prophets? We should follow spiritual methods and techniques available in YOGAS and TANTRAS and test them on our body and mind, and know the truth directly, through self-discipline of various kinds, like meditating on the source and centers of energy in the body, changing our minds to change how we see the universe, stumbling into the divine super-normal powers through their grace, creating our own scripture and authority, being self-reliant, as our self is all that is there and it cannot be denied, and it is the same as the self in all other beings and the universe.

And so we start our evolution on the path of DHARMA that starts shaping our actions, not only in the general sense of social morality, but also in the sense of specific ritual actions purifying our minds resulting in spiritual growth. Some of these actions of high value are listed below.

YATRA or pilgrimage has taken numerous forms. MAHABHARTA talks of BALARAMA, the elder brother of SRI KRISHNA going on a YATRA in the VEDIC tradition to see the wonders of nature, like high mountains, dense forests, frightening caves, roaring waterfalls, clear rivers, cool and hot water springs, varied regions of the land, undulating deserts, foaming and vibrating seas. One should go on foot, if possible, or in a slow moving vehicle to give time to the mind to absorb the environment, along the sacred rivers and visit temples of divine beings and the residences of great and learned people and listen to their discourses and instruction, and discuss personal and social problems and raise doubts and receive clarifications and inspiration.

GURUS and SANYASIS even today crisscross the country often on foot, talking to people, as a form of non-formal education in wisdom. One should live near the wonders of nature for some time every year or visit them once in a while, alone without carrying the concerns of livelihood or the newspaper or the local gossip and the crowd along in the mind, and dedicate oneself to them, to this wonderful nature, actually experiencing wonder and making an offering of one's life, dedicating its mind and awareness to the vast grandeur and beauty of the world.

UPASANA means sitting mentally close to one's chosen DEVAS, expressions of the power of nature, like fire, earth, water, rains, air, sky, space, the sun, the moon, and stars, each of the ten senses doing their own duty efficiently under the uniting control of the mind, and the changing months and seasons and time of the year, and nature thundering and animal passions born and sacrificed. One can sit mentally close to images of great idols that reflect great ideals in all their details as they are practically worked out in life, to internalize them with firm vows and express them spontaneously. UPASANA means re-living experience, remembering the essence of scriptures, thinking of life, remaining focused and absorbed in it while doing one's daily actions. It means doing normal work with an elevated state of mind so that all work becomes light and acquires dignity and nobility. A closely related term is UPAVASA or living near often done through fasting or VRATA, making firm vows.

SAMA VEDA is concerned with UPASANA through music and songs of praise and internalization of great ideals and making firm vows to achieve them.

A possible modern version of this ancient mode of thought is given below. Since it is a summary of numerous lives and their ways of seeing and living, one would normally choose only one or two of these vows at a time and live practicing them for years.

Rishi Upasana

I visualize ancient RISHIS and their work and firmly resolve to

Discipline myself through sacrifice and yoga techniques

Light my inner fire to renounce what is not my self

Increase my inner fire, dedicated to my true self

Regulate my urges and desires towards noble ideals

Transform my lower nature into my higher nature

See higher forces acting through me, like powers of nature, history and society

Free myself from the confines of my limited individual consciousness

See the wheel of energy rolling on

Bear heat and cold, joy and sorrow, while remaining the same, unchanged

Remove past impressions on the mind through repetition of MANTRAS

Start life afresh everyday

Support life that animates all creation everywhere

Express my highest self in my actions

Increase my power, perfection and fulfillment

Be absorbed so deep in my highest self that I see visions of reality

Create culture, increasing wealth and men dedicated to noble resolves

Be like a star in the dark sky, the center of the universe

Be like motions of life in dead matter

Achieve secular aims through sacred means

Enrich social order through withdrawal of my personal selfishness

Engage in social and political life in this way as far as I can

Make the social and political order more moral

Uphold and protect DHARMA in dream and thought, speech and actions

Be a leader in chaos, doing my duty

Guide myself in peace and war for victory

Revive lost fortunes, sanctify and legitimize my life

Be one with all beings, an offering to the divine presence

Indra Upasana

I visualize INDRA, lord of my senses and the beyond, and firmly resolve to

Broaden and deepen my senses of perception, action and mind

Satisfy my natural desires

Enjoy nature, like the sun rising and setting and the airs still and howling

See waters clear and shining, spaces full and empty

Enjoy rains, harvest and prosperity, fun and laughter

Enjoy liquor and intoxication, foods without inhibitions

Enjoy clothes, ornaments, fragrances, sex, family, music, dance and drama

Keep my fires burning and transforming

Offer them to the earth, the sky and the invisible beyond

Visit the countryside, broad rivers, high mountains and forests, vast seas and sands

Feel admiration and reverence for nature, its wonderful diversity

Be a royal leader in my thoughts and actions

Be a fighter and savior, one with the horse and the thunderbolt

Defend my followers and their wealth

Overcome enemies with strength and intelligence

Enjoy freedom

Vishnu Upasana

I visualize the names of VISHNU and firmly resolve to

Express the best in my nature rather than hinder or suppress it

See my actions and their consequences as I relive them in my mind

Increase my awareness of what I do

Guide my actions with spiritual wisdom

Be an expert in the actions I choose to do

Acquire and use power to punish the wicked and help the good

Be open to reality and relate all beings to each other as one healthy family

Welcome others and identify myself with them

Protect and promote life rather than weaken or destroy it

Protect and promote the divine order present in nature and society

Rama Upasana

I visualize SRI RAMA and firmly resolve to

Follow the highest values and customs of my family, community and locality

Remember the powers of nature and the noble tradition of my ancestors

Build my future on the best in my past

Personify high moral values in my life and actions

Do all my duties in society without flinching

Keep my promises personal, commercial or political, whatever the self-sacrifice

Be self reliant, brave and strong in the face of difficulties

Fight for what is right

Be skillful in different subjects including warfare

Be in touch with the common people and honor their wishes

Make them happy, working for their interest and welfare

Krishna Upasana

I visualize images of SRI KRISHNA and firmly resolve to

Be aware of my nature and its constituents, truthful, active or limited

Be skillful in expressing my nature in actions effectively

Direct it towards noble ideals, nourishing its goodness and starving its evil

Cultivate strength and intelligence, knowledge of the self and oneness of all beings

Acquire virtues of peace, truth, renunciation, dedication, love and forgiveness

Do actions without expectations of personal benefits

Do actions as an offering to the divine presence in all

Direct my actions towards public interest, uniting people

Trust the divine power for my maintenance consumption

Feel compassion for all beings, especially the poor and the handicapped

Remain efficient without greed and fear, anger and enmity

Remain even-minded, the same in all situations of joy or sorrow

See all beings in the same way

Keep this light and joy in my heart and mind

Have song in my heart, music on my lips and dance with my friends

Live my life to the full as a play, a divine game

Accept the inherited tradition and enrich it with my creativity

Mahadeva Upasana

I visualize images of SHIVA and firmly resolve to

Follow high moral values and rules of self-development

Find spiritual truths through self-help techniques of YOGAS and TANTRAS

Have personal experience of the divine power

Not to depend on others, scriptures, gurus or prophets

Do breathing exercises, focusing my mind on breathing alone

Assume still but comfortable posture of the body without unnecessary movements

Feel reverence for animals and plants as one of them

Do all my duties in my family and society with love and devotion

Exercise detachment and self-restraint, remaining alone in my mind

Work for peace and bless others

▲

Practice sacred chants to empty my mind

Consume minimum foods that nourish life and cure ill health

Keep my body and mind in health and efficiency

Be aware of my energy, its centers and source

Create images of the source and centers of energy

Awaken them to release my super-normal powers

Create techniques to stretch my limits to bring out my divinity

Express my inner goodness in actions

Receive divine energy directly, feeling one whole

Shakti Upasana

I visualize images of divine power and firmly resolve to

See divine power in all beings doing their duty spontaneously

Devote myself to one or more powers like

MAHAVIDYA, the power of wisdom that leads to the highest self

MAHASARASVATI, the power of knowledge that regulates all beings

MAHALAKSHMI, the power of wealth, values and relationships

MAHESHVARI, the power inherent in the universe and me

MAHAKALI, the power of time that destroys to create

PARVATI, the power of the self that knows itself

BHAIRAVI, the power of force, of terror and war

DURGA, the power that overcomes enemies and obstacles

VAISHNAVI, the power that sustains life, fruits of actions

KAMESHVARI, also known as KAMAKHYA, the power of desire and creative will

BHUVANESHVARI, the power of space and earth, seed of all seeds

TARA, the power of creative speech and vision

TRIPURA SUNDARI, the power of matter, life and mind, waking, dream and sleep

CHINNAMASTYA, the power of no mind, intuition, direct seeing

PUJA is a ritual action that aims at externalizing and elevating inner states of mind. It has taken forms of numerous rituals and songs of praise and prayers that emerge spontaneously from one's nature as it struggles for self-expression towards the divine.

PUJA is accompanied by UPASANA, internalizing divine attributes and expressing them in one's feelings and actions. It is commonly done through recitation of MANTRAS during ritual life ceremonies associated with birth, growth and admission to education and culture, health, illness, marriage, retirement, decay and death or while celebrating festivals. Food, clothing, ornaments, flowers, water, fragrances, focused attention, and one's mind and actions are offered and dedicated to the divine power one is devoted to, while waving lights before it, appreciating its nature and relating oneself to it.

Some actions are done by choice to achieve this or that objective, like having children, achieving wealth and power, promotion and success in war or enterprise. MANTRAS are recited and appropriate actions and rituals are done to achieve specific desires and objectives.

Some rituals are duties done every day like worship in the morning and evening, meditating on birth and death, the cycles of energy.

Some rituals are done periodically, as on full moon or new moon days, the birthdays of GURUS, celebrating harvest, tasting the fruits of one's labor and sharing it with others, intensifying bonds of relationships but sticking neither to the dead nor to the living.

Some actions are duties during different stages of life, like a student who has to be devoted to study, or a householder who has to earn livelihood, raise a family and support other members of society in various ways, or a retired person who has to learn to disengage from society in a way that enriches it, which is a difficult process of wisdom and be fully detached before death, which is going to detach one from society any way whether we like it or not.

Some duties have to be done for the family, teachers, employers and the king.

Performance of duties purifies the mind, disciplines and concentrates it, enabling wisdom to descend as grace. This is the path of KARMA.

The path of BHAKTI is the path of love and devotion to the power present in all beings. It is expressed in love for nature and its source and for noble ideals, customs and traditions, and for persons who lived by those ideals, like living by truth, non-violence, cultivating peace and contentment, absence of desires, compassion and service to the deserving like students and their teachers, helpfulness and compassion towards the needy like the poor and the sick, nourishing them as a parent and caring for them as a lover.

Devotion to the Supreme Power requires internalizing its attributes and qualities. One strives towards oneness without selfishness, listening to spiritual discourses or reading scriptures. One learns to see divine glory and appreciate its presence in all. One remains mentally close to the divine, renouncing other things, doing its PUJA, externalizing the inner states of mind through the language of concrete symbols. One feels like a humble servant, a vehicle of the divine power present in all beings. One learns to remove suffering, sin and ignorance, starving passions that degrade one, like ego, anger and greed. One works to realize one's highest nature and potential, celebrating and praising the holy presence in all beings, doing one's normal duty for the sake of duty, for public welfare and not for the sake of narrow personal gains. It means doing one's normal work with a changed state of mind, living a full life with wealth and wisdom.

The path of knowledge requires opening up to reality, trusting and welcoming it, remembering experience and reflecting on it. One begins with memory that extends into the past more or less. We cannot recognize anything in the present without using the past. Nor can we listen or read, understand and speak without using the past traditions of language and experience. Therefore it is best to remember the past happenings of the day, even if they appear to be ordinary, and to make this remembrance clearer, fuller, detailed, including feelings, re-living the past, more recent first, more distant later, even stumbling into recollections of the earliest childhood and still earlier lives, even if in dreams at first. We should do this exercise as often as we can and think in various ways, distinguishing the rope from the snake, and wakefulness from the dream. Is wakefulness itself a form of dream? Is a dream a form of wakefulness? Can we think of answers on the strength of our personal experiences?

We should acquire a clearer understanding of our self. We should study our self with understanding, absorbed in meditation, learning to use methods like discrimination, analysis and synthesis, reconciliation, aphorism, enigmas, etymology, questions and answers.

We learn to see our mind reflecting environment, breaking it up like a crystal that reflects light, and splitting it into many colors, splitting nature into its constituents in the presence of a detached mind and clean consciousness.

We should see the lotus flower. How the rain falling on it slips away! Feel the air carrying smells. See the spider producing its thread with which it covers itself. See the reflection of one sun in many pots of water, or the same space inside and outside the pots. We lose our sense of self-importance while absorbed in the multitude of stars, while paying full attention to each one till we reach the one we are looking for. Imagine the seed bursting into a shoot, and see the widening cycles of energy. We learn to reject inadequate description of reality, not this, not this, eliminating all forms till we reach the formless truth in SAMADHI, awareness without objects. We learn to see actions and relationships, and vibrations of reality that we see as the universe.

We learn to open our eyes, increase our understanding and awareness, and learn to accept, appreciate and praise. We learn to separate reality from its illusion, the constant from the temporary, the present from the past appearing as a dream. We learn how our senses create their sensations and impose them on an invisible reality that we do not see. We learn to see the mirage we create in the desert, the horizon we create in the sky. Is the desert too a creation like the sky we create? We learn to see pleasures and sorrows like the colors we create in reality, which has no pleasures or sorrows or colors in it. We learn to distinguish gold from the ornament, which is made out of it, distinguish the substance from its form. We learn to see the waves as an expression of the ocean and ourselves as rooted in a seed beyond our boundaries and understanding that keeps increasing.

May we all be of one mind!

Bibliography

Adi Shankaracharya, *Bhagavad Gita Bhasya*, translated by Dr. A.G. Krishna Warrier, Sri Rramakrishna Math, Madras, 1983.

Adi Shankaracharya, *Brahma-Sutra Bhasya*, translated by Swami Gambhiranand, Advaita Ashrama, Calcutta, 1983.

Bal Gangadhar Tilak, *Srimad Bhagavadgita-Rahasya*, Tilak Brothers, Poona, 1908, 1986.

Bhagwan Singh, *The Vedic Harappans*, Aditya Prakashan, New Delhi, 1995.

Bhavani-Sahasra-Nama-Stutih, A Page from Rrudrayamala Tantra, English translation & commentary by Jankilal Kaul "Kamal" Sri Ramakrishna Ashrama , Srinagar (Kashmir) 1991, 1994.

David Frawley, *Hinduism, The Eternal Tradition, (Sanatana Dharma)* Voice of India, New Delhi, 1995, 2000.

Debiprasad Chattopadhyaya & Mrinal Kanti Gangopadhyaya, Ed. *Charvaka/Lokayata, An Anthology of Source Materials and some Recent Studies*, Indian Council of Philosohpical Research, New Delhi, 1990, 1994.

Dr. David Frawley, *Tantric Yoga and the Wisdom Goddesses*, Motilal Banarasidass, Delhi, 1996, 2002.

dr. Koenraad Elst, *Decolonizing the Hindu Mind, Ideological Development of Hindu Revivalism*, Rupa & Co., 2001.

Georg Feuerstein, Subhash Kaka & David Frawley, *In Search of the Cradle of Civilization*, Motilal Banarasidass, Delhi, 1995, 2005.

Gerald James Larson, *Classical Samkhya*, Motilal Banarasidass Publishers, Delhi, 1969, 2001.

Hiroshi Motoyama, *Theories of the Chakras, Bridge to Higher Consciousness*, New Age Books, New Delhi, 1981, 2003.

Jaideva Singh, *Shiva Sutras*, Motilal Banarasidass Publishers, Delhi, 1979, 1995.

Justice P. Kodandaramayya, *The Message of Mahabharata, The Nation's Magnum Opus*, Bharatiya Vidya Bhavan, Mumbai, 2004.

M.N. Roy, *Selected Works*, edited by Sibnarayan Ray, Oxford University Press, New Delhi, 1997, 2000.

Madhusudana Sarasvati, *Bhagavad-Gita with the annotation Gudhartha Dipika,* translated by Swami Gambhiranand, Advaita Ashrama, Calcutta, 1998.

Navaratna S. Rajaram & David Frawley, *Vedic Aryans and the Origins of Civilization*, Voice of India, New Delhi, 1995, 2001.

Osho, *Finger Pointing to the Moon, Adhyatma Upanishad*, The Rebel Publishing House, Cologne, Germany, 1994.

Osho, *Gita Darshan*, (*Hindi*) 8 Vols., Rebel Publishing House, Pune, 2000.

Osho, *Heart Beat of the Absolute, Ishavasya Upanishad*, The Rebel Publishing House, Cologne, Germany, 1980.

Osho, *Shiv Sutra, (Hindi),* The Rebel Publishing House, Pune, 2000.

Osho, *The Kaivalya Upanishad*, The Rebel Publishing House, Pune, 2000.

Osho, *The Message beyond Words, A Dialogue with the Lord of the Death, Discourses of the Kathopanishad*, The Rebel Publishing House, Pune, 1997.

Osho, *Vedanta Discounrses on Akshyupanishad*, The Rebel Publishing House, Pune, 1976.

Osho, *The Path of Yoga, Commentaries on the Yoga Sutras of Patanjali*, The Rebel Publishing House, Pune, 1976, 1998.

P.L. Bhargava, *Retrieval of History from Puranic Myths*, D.K. Printworld, New Delhi, 1984, 1998.

Pushkar Bhatnagar, *Dating the Era of Lord Rama*, Rupa & Co. 2004.

Param Pujya Ma, *Kathopanishad*, Arpana Publications, Karnal, 1995.

Patanjali's 'Yoga Sutras, with the commentary of Vyasa and the gloss of Vachaspati Mishra, translated by Rama Prasada, Munshiram Manoharlal Publishers, 1912, 1995.

Pujya Ma, *Srimad Bhagavad Gita*, Arpana Publications, Karnal, 1995.

Raimundo Panikkar, *The Vedic Experience Mantramanjari*, Motilal Banarasidass Publishers, Delhi, 1983, 2001.

Ram Swarup, *On Hinduism, Reviews and Reflections*, Voice of India, New Delhi, 2000.

Samkhya Karika of Ishvara Krishna, with The Tattva Kaumudi of Shri Vachaspati Mishra, translation and notes by Swami Virupapakshananda, Sri Ramakrishna Math, Madras, 1995.

Satya P. Agarwal, *The Social Role of the Gita, How and Why*, Motilal Banarasidass, Delhi, 1993, 1997.

Sita Ram Goel, *Hindu Temples, What Happened to Them*, Vol. II, Voice of India, New Delhi, 1991, 2000.

Sri Vishnu Sahasranama, With Commentary of Adi Shankaracharya trans.by Swami Tapasyananda, Sri Ramakrishna Math, Madras, 1986.

Shri Pundit Jaidev Sharma, *(Rig, Yajur, Sam, Atharv) Ved Sanhita*, 13 Vols. Arya Sahitya Mandal, Ajmer, 1929.

Shrinivas Tilak, *Understanding Karma*, International Studies for Cultural Studies, India & USA, 2006.

S.K. Ramachandra Rao, *Shiv-Kosha*, 2 Vols., Kalpatharu Research Academy, Bangalore, 1998.

Shrikand Talageri, *The Aryan Invasion, Theory and Indian Nationalism*, Voice of India, New Delhi, 1993, 2003.

Sri Aurobindo, *Essays on the Gita*, Sri Aurobindo Ashram, Pondicherry, 1920, 1993.

Sri Aurobindo, *The Bhagavad Gita*, Sri Aurobindo Ashram, Pondicherry, 1992, 2000.

Sri Aurobindo, *The Foundations of Indian Culture*, Sri Aurobindo Ashram, Pondicherry, 1959, 1998

Sri Aurobindo, *The Life Divine*, Sri Aurobindo Ashram, Pondicherry, 1939-40, 1997.

Sri Aurobindo, *The Secret of the Veda*, Sri Aurobindo Ashram, Pondicherry, 1956, 1996.

Sri Aurobindo, *The Upanishads*, Sri Aurobindo Ashram, Pondicherry, 1971, 1992.

Sri Aurobindo, *The Synthesis of Yoga*, Sri Aurobindo Ashram, Pondicherry, 1914-1921, 1992.

Sri Ramanuja Gita Bhasya translated by Svami Adidevananda, Sri Ramakrishna Math, Madras.

Swami Gambhirananda, *Eight Upanishads*, 2 Vols, Advaita Ashrama, Calcutta, 1986.

Swami Madhavananda, *Minor Upanishads*, Advaita Ashrama, Kolkata, 2002.

Swami Tyagisananda, *Narada Bhakti Sutras*, Sri Ramakrishna Math, Madras, 1991.

Ten Upanishads of Four Vedas, researched and edited by Ram K. Piparaiya, New Age Books, New Delhi, 2003.

The Rig Veda and the History of India, David Frawley, Aditya Prakashan, New Delhi, 2001.

The Samkhya Philosophy, Containing (1) Samkhya-Pravachanasutram, With the Vritti of Aniruddha and the Bhasya of Vijnanabhikshu and Extracts from the Vrittisara of Mahadeva Vedantin; (2) Tatvasamasa; (3) Samkhyakarika; (4) Panchashikhasutram, Nandalal Sinha, Munshiram Manoharlal, New Delhi, 1915, 2003.

The Supreme Yoga, Yoga Vasishtha, translated by Swami Venkatesananda, Motilal Banarasidass, Delhi, 2003, 2005.

The Siva Samhita, Translated by Rai Bahadur Srisa Chandra Vasu, Munshiram Manoharlal, New Delhi, 1914-15, 2002.

William Henry Robinson, *The Golden Legend of India*, Rupa & Co. New Delhi, 1898, 2003.